Urbanization and Locality

Fang Wang · Martin Prominski
Editors

Urbanization and Locality

Strengthening Identity and Sustainability by Site-Specific Planning and Design

Springer

Editors
Fang Wang
Peking University
Beijing
China

Martin Prominski
Leibniz University Hannover
Hannover
Germany

Funded by Sino-German Center (NSFC and DFG, No. GZ1156).

ISBN 978-3-662-48492-0 ISBN 978-3-662-48494-4 (eBook)
DOI 10.1007/978-3-662-48494-4

Library of Congress Control Number: 2015950881

Springer Heidelberg New York Dordrecht London

Printed on acid-free paper

Springer-Verlag GmbH Berlin Heidelberg is part of Springer Science+Business Media
(www.springer.com)

Preface

Urbanization, an irreversible trend in the economic and social development of humankind, can be regarded as an important index of prosperity and social progress in the country and region. Processes of urbanization yield many positive effects, but especially in phases of rapid urbanization, certain qualities are in danger of being neglected or overrun by the sheer forces of the processes. Locality, which refers to the specific natural and cultural characteristics of a place, is one such endangered quality. An increasing number of contemporary urbanization projects look the same; they do not address the local character of the site, which leads to urban areas with a low identity. Residents have a difficult time identifying with their environment in these new districts, a phenomenon that decreases the quality of living. In this book, researchers from Germany and China address the topics of urbanization and locality and then determine how identity and sustainability can be strengthened by site-specific design and planning. Pairing these two countries is relevant because both represent different stages in the urbanization process, leading to different problem definitions and solutions. Germany is a developed country where the urbanization rate has stabilized at a high level, whereas China is a developing country currently in a stage of rapid urbanization. Germany, as one of the world's most highly urbanized countries, already saw two periods of rapid urbanization (at the end of the nineteenth century and after World War II) and is currently implementing subtle strategies to achieve identity and sustainability in urban planning. A dialog with China might provide experiences in urban planning and design valuable for rebuilding a harmonious human–earth relationship in China. China is currently experiencing new-type, high-speed urbanization that has an impact not only on China but even beyond, in terms of the use of resources or as an example for countries that will enter the stage of rapid urbanization. Further, China's transition period of urbanization can provide different perspectives and ideas for German researchers, especially by reflecting on the large-scale planning and design strategies and their relevance for the rather small-scale urbanization processes in Germany.

In view of the above and in response to the contemporary necessity for people-oriented and sustainable development, this anthology addresses the following questions: How can the multiple contradictions in the human–earth relationship that arise in the process of urbanization be solved? How can one's own heritage be retained? How can cities and towns be developed by addressing their natural and cultural characteristics in a creative way? How can balance be struck between the specificity of a local situation and the uniformity of global urbanization trends? The authors of the articles are experts from China and Germany in such fields as planning, landscape architecture, geography, architecture, history, and public management. For the topic of urbanization and locality, their work will communicate problems and measures as well as develop new theories and practice strategies, thus presenting valuable knowledge for researchers, practitioners, and managers around the world engaged in urbanization.

China's urbanization process is in the context of scarce land resources and increasing conflicts between the people and the land. A high degree of spatial and temporal overlap as well as compression has caused the "China model" of urbanization, which reflects complexity, difficulty, and specificity. China has previously experienced initial expansive urbanization, leaving increasing contradictions in the human–earth relationship or the relation between urban and rural areas. First, land supply and demand are in ever-growing conflicts; second, urban sprawl brings directly or exacerbates "city diseases," such as environmental pollution, traffic congestion, population increase, energy dissipation, and other aspects; third, the decline of the countryside has led to the loss of land, rural hollowing, and other "rural diseases." In terms of easing the contradiction of land supply and demand, China needs to implement further optimized patterns of land development on a macroscopic scale and improve the quality of the national land comprehensive management strategy pattern. On the mesoscale, regional industrial structures and the intensive use of land resources should be regulated by defining urban growth boundaries and ecological red lines. On the microscopic scale, through developing underground spaces, more urban space is needed to ease the human–land relationship contradiction.

In response to "city diseases," smart land use is always a key point within new-type urbanization strategies. The conception of suitable strategies for land use that could alleviate the contradiction between the supply and the demand of land is a priority of new-type urbanization. In Chap. 3, Feng et al. apply a theoretical model analysis and measure land demand by reviewing the development stage and characteristics of China's urbanization; their work summarizes the problems and challenges in the course of urbanization and then discusses the connotation of new-type urbanization. On this basis, they propose countermeasures and practical references for land use. Han and Guo report that the development and construction of green roofs can ease tensions to urban construction land and can respond to ecological problems due to rapid urbanization. In Chap. 17, which raises the design requirements of green roofs implementation for program and architecture materials, Han et al. suggest layout principles, architectural design principles, and integrated design approaches. They propose zoning guidelines for green roofs implementation and offer recommendations and policies related to program implementation.

For rural districts, evoking respect for nature is an effective means to preserve and develop beautiful rural landscapes. At present, by driving such policies as "agriculture, rural areas, and farmers" and new urbanization, the advance of urbanization in mountainous villages is restricted not only by the development bottleneck of the industrial space and the settlement space in such locales but also by other problems due to the poor coordination between the two aforementioned zones. Further, ecological safety remains an inconvenient hidden danger. In Chap. 5, Long et al. seek to improve the status through space integration of industry and village. They further argue that control mechanisms and design systems of multiple regulatory integration and dynamic order should be established for urbanization in rural mountains.

In the process of urbanization, the architectural cultural heritage and traditional features of Chinese urban and rural areas, gradually formed through thousands of years, face a great threat from the strong influence of urban and foreign culture. The protection of natural and human resources has become a new challenge in new-type urbanization. In the dramatic process of urban transformation, stakeholders wonder how to preserve the context in urban and rural development and how to protect the characteristics and cultural deposits of urban and rural areas. These essential questions are discussed in this book. Site-specific planning and design are rooted in natural and human-made environments, addressed in the concepts of "geo-architecture and geo-planning" or landscape architecture. Akin to the two sides of a coin, this approach has two reciprocal aspects: The first aspect is related to the way in which natural and human environments impact designs and plans, and the second aspect involves how designing and planning respond to and alter natural and human environments. Designing and planning aim at altering space in material and immaterial ways. Urbanization is continuously inserting tangible elements and intangible values into physical space (even without design). To explain effectively the special dependencies between people and places, the concept of "locality" is used. This term refers to the features or characteristics found in specific places. In rapid urbanization, an area's locality is confronted with the challenges of variation and dissolution as well as the opportunity for transformation and development. Yuan et al. address these aspects in Chap. 18, which focuses on developing a novel methodology for site-specific urban design that integrates environmental performance simulation with ecological design strategies into a generative design process by using computational tools, thereby realizing sustainable urbanization with distinctive locality.

In planning at the urban and rural scales, priority should be placed on those elements that have a strategic meaning to culture, ecology, and society. As a design condition of urban and rural planning, these elements protect the local characteristics and historic context. Zhao et al. in Chap. 6 provide a summary and reflection of rural planning in Chengdu. In their work, a series of regulations or normative documents, formulated in the process of rural planning and management practices, guarantee the legality of rural planning and take full advantage of local resources and rural characters. They enhance the ecological and social resilience as well as reduce the clashes between people and place in future development projects. Shao in Chap. 20 points out that the multi-dimensional experience patterns of the rural landscape need to be understood to aid the decision making related to sustainable development in rural areas. In urban design, through collaborative planning and public participation, the urban local characteristics and historic context could be protected effectively, as Wang et al. demonstrate in Chap. 2. Through research on urban memory, an approach based on the environmental cognition and urban organic growth theory is put forward; this approach accepts the conditions of material space planning but is nonetheless capable of protecting traditional features and urban characteristics. The comparative study on locality helps form a correct understanding on the components and characteristic regulations of locality, which help avoid urban similarity and lack of locality and drive a comprehensive, healthy, and rapid urban development pattern.

On the level of the urban district, regarding urban memory as a core idea in historic district planning, a novel methodology for the protection and planning of historic cultural districts could be gained by excavating urban context, depositing and extracting memory fragments, joining and integrating urban memory, and then planning and establishing memory space. The preservation of historical streetscapes plays a crucial role in maintaining locality. Using a subjective-oriented approach, Zhao's Chap. 12 investigates the effects of urban regeneration in Beijing by looking at the case of the Qianmen-Dashilan area. The research identifies gaps between the preservation plan goals and the actual urban renewal outcomes. The differences between visitor and resident satisfaction suggest that the conservation of historical streetscapes in Beijing should strike a balance between satisfying the local residents' needs for improvement in their living situation and preserving the historical fabric in the old historical areas. Along with the rapid urbanization and the intervention of tourism, street preservation and tourism development form a pair of contradiction. Accordingly, recognition awareness or locality faces a challenge. Li and Xu introduce a theoretical discussion in Chap. 10 by studying the site's heritage value components and development status. They suggest, from the perspective of proactive utilization of cultural heritage preservation, an integrated cultural heritage street preservation and development model that encompasses several efforts ranging from the preservation of architectural nodes to spatial fabric preservation and material carriers to intangible heritage, and from safeguarding against the displacement of local residents to building of cultural recognition awareness.

Finally, on the scale of architectural objects, research on traditional dwellings after urban regeneration shows that the influence of urban regeneration on community residents' architectural heritage identity is contradictory. On the one hand, the recovery of traditional buildings reinforces the residents' identification with their local culture; on the other hand, the modern elements required by the young urban generation create the danger of identity loss. In exploring urbanization and locality, the use of interactive digital design could improve building performance and the utilization of local resources. A combination of traditional and modern culture could be used to develop resource-saving architectural structures as well as provide actual innovative architectural characteristics. Various types of vernacular dwellings can be found around China, and their spatial shaping corresponds to the natural environment as well as the cultural and architectural traditions of specific regions. Fan and Wang in Chap. 9 point out that the perpetuation of religious belief in settlement constitution is significant in protecting local culture within processes of new-type urbanization. Regarding the affront of the challenges of destruction to the locality of historical villages, Xie et al. analyze the vitality loss problem in Nan'anyang Village under urbanization in Chap. 11. They put forward an approach to conserve and improve the village; the approach is oriented toward sustainable tourism, based on landscape renovation, and guaranteed by community activation. Chu and Wei explore sustainable buildings in Chap. 15 and point out that effective design methods need to be realized in the context of rapid urbanization to achieve high sustainability goals. In the development of public buildings, such as medical architecture, the appropriate balance should be established between function and connotation of regionalism through coordination and integration, as Li summarizes in Chap. 8.

In Germany, the pressure for urbanization is on far a lower level than in China. Nonetheless, in recent years, cities have grown much more attractive, with most urban areas in Germany, e.g., Berlin, Cologne/Bonn, or Munich, expected to experience a population growth between 3 and 10 % until 2035 (BBSR Raumordnungsprognose, 2035). These new urban dwellers have a high demand for quality, and sustainability and identity play a big role in meeting these demands. In a recent survey by the German Institute of Urban Affairs (Difu) and Technical University of Berlin, local identity is found to be among the highest priorities for ensuring the quality of urban living. This demand is accompanied by a high consciousness of the necessity for sustainable urban design in the face of climate change. The contributions from German authors in the present anthology demonstrate how these two aspects of identity and sustainability can be achieved by strategies on different scales (region, settlement, house) or different aspects (building material, urban greenery, residents).

In terms of different scales, Schöbel offers strategies on a regional level to achieve locality and sustainability in Chap. 13. He transfers ideas from the urbanistic model of "critical reconstruction," which was developed in the 1980s for the inner city context of Berlin, to the regional scale of urban landscapes. With the example of the Munich region, he demonstrates that an analysis of a regional landscape from the perspective of critical reconstruction helps uncover hidden elements and structures that form the bases for a specific design of regional urbanization projects. In Chap. 19, Rode argues for a focus on multifunctionality when dealing with urbanization on a larger, regional scale. He analyzes suburban landscapes, in which the city spreads outward and different demands for land use collide: housing, food production, recreation, or nature conservation. The Kronsberg area at the urban fringe of Hannover serves as an example of how his proposed concept of an integrated multifunctional land use could work. The concept aims for a synergy between recreation, agriculture, and nature conservation through a unifying planning concept. Consequently, sustainable development is supported by ensuring social (e.g., recreation), economical (e.g., higher environmental quality to attract businesses or effective agriculture), and ecological functions (protection of biotic and abiotic resources). Further, locality can be strengthened especially by nature conservation measures, e.g., the protection of specific landscape elements or the development of new biotopes with local species.

On the urban settlement scale, three authors offer perspectives for locality and sustainability by proposing transferable design strategies. Carlow and Hong discuss methodological design principles formulated to accommodate urban growth in Chap. 21. These principles are 5-Minute City, Blue and Green Networks, and Preservation of Existing Structures, all of which can be adapted to meet the demands of sustainable development within the specific context of a project. By analyzing three projects from different continents, the authors show how the principles can be applied to establish a sound foundation for sustainable growth and adapted to local contexts. In Chap. 1, Prominski stresses that locality is not only an issue of conservation but also an issue of development. Even if a site for an urban settlement has very little to offer in terms of historic elements or specific character, locality can be created by design and planning. He discusses five case studies of newly developed urban settlements in Germany and China, and then concludes with three key strategies to establish new locality in future urban settlements.

The scale of a single house is addressed by Rudolph-Cleff in Chap. 4. The solar-active skin house is one of five projects she discusses, and this house and the four projects on the settlement scale she is mentioning express the necessity to work creatively with the local conditions to achieve resilience and sustainability. For localized planning strategies, the recognition of the microclimatic conditions, various uses, and different relations of a building site to the surrounding open spaces is especially important. These aspects are so diverse that any standard answer is impossible if their potentials are to be taken seriously. Such a scenario provides a great opportunity to work against the uniform scene of global standards and then find instead local answers that emphasize the special quality of a location without having to rely on historicizing images.

Three contributions in the present anthology focus on specific aspects to strengthen identity and locality in urbanization processes. Krieg, Schwinn, and Menges illustrate how far the decisions for a building material can reach. In Chap. 7, they describe the economic and ecological advantages of using the local material of beech wood. Beech is the most natural species in Central Europe's temperate seasonal climate and would normally make up two-thirds of the forests if not for the anthropogenic interventions in the past. In using new research on the qualities of beech wood as well as on design computation, the authors demonstrate how this traditional material can be used for modern construction demands. They conclude that the combination of a locally available resource, potential of strengthening the regional value-added chains, favorable CO_2 balance, and material's social acceptance is a promising foundation for the promotion toward using this local material in future urbanization processes. Welp et al. concentrate on the aspect of urban green spaces in Chap. 14. The establishment and maintenance of urban green spaces in both cases has depended on a specific institutional arrangement. The results have strengthened the sense of locality of the urban dwellers and their identification with particular urban spaces. The final aspect to address is probably the most challenging: the residents themselves. In newly planned urbanization projects, the residents are hardly included in design generation that leads to a higher locality, mostly because the residents are absent. Nonetheless, the locality of existing urban settlements can serve as learning references. Stollmann in Chap. 16 presents a way to work with the actual inhabitants of the Gropiusstadt, a mono-functional settlement with 36,000 people from the 1960s that followed modernist, universal design ideals. In founding the Academy of a New Gropiusstadt, he has raised the levels of satisfaction and identification of the residents toward their settlement. The academy has developed urban interventions as a co-production of designers and residents. Not every intervention has been successful, but the best cases have generated a new common ground rooted in the specific locality of the place.

In summary, the contributions to this anthology address the issues of urbanization and locality from diverse angles. Despite the diversity of the issues, methods, and strategies, which is natural for such a complex topic, one interesting, unifying connection becomes apparent, which runs through most of the contributions: the close relationship of locality and sustainability. Both are important goals in urbanization processes, but at first sight, the two issues seem to be separate and need different strategies to be achieved. However, in according due respect to local conditions, e.g., the microclimate (Yuan et al.; Rudolph-Cleff), historical elements (Wang et al.; Li and Xu; Fan and Wang; Ma and Zhao), landscape structure (Prominski; Carlow; Schöbel), food production (Rode; Shao), material resources (Han and Guo; Krieg et al.), and inhabitants (Stollmann; Welp et al.), the authors demonstrate that the results of site-specific design and planning have a higher sustainability compared with universal approaches. The research by Chinese and German scholars presented here provides instructive theories and practical examples to reach those important goals of identity and sustainability. We hope that this work motivates researchers worldwide to approach locality and urbanization with creativity.

Fang Wang
Martin Prominski

Acknowledgments

Many thanks for the great support by Sino-German Center, jointly established by National Natural Science Foundation of China (NSFC) and German Science Foundation (DFG), Grant No. GZ1156.

We also thank Ms. Xu Lu (master student in College of Urban and Environmental Sciences, Peking University), Ms. Chen Jie (master student in College of Architecture and Landscape Architecture, Peking University), Ms. Yu Fengyao (master student in College of Architecture and Landscape Architecture, Peking University), and Ms. Liu Xiaoyu (master student in College of Architecture and Landscape Architecture, Peking University) for their excellent support in the book production.

Contents

Part I New Trends: Bridges Between People and Place in Urbanization Processes

1 **The Dynamics of Locality: Inspirations for Designing Large-Scale Urbanisation Projects** . . . 3
Martin Prominski

2 **Measurement and Application of Urban Memory Related to Historic Areas in Beijing** . . . 27
Fang Wang, Wei Li, Yang Liu and Hongru Cai

3 **New Urbanization and Land Use in China** . . . 55
Changchun Feng, Zhuyun Xiao, Haojing Shen and Lei Zhang

4 **Urban Interplay** . . . 75
Annette Rudolph-Cleff

5 **Mountainous Rural Urbanization: Space Integration of Industry and Village** . . . 95
Hao Long, Jiayang Li, Feng Lu and Dongzhu Chu

6 **Rural Planning in the New Urbanization Process: The Case of Chengdu, China** . . . 111
Wei Zhao and Jiao Yang

Part II New Strategies: Locality Preservation and Development in Urbanization Processes

7 **Integrative Design Computation for Local Resource Effectiveness in Architecture** . . . 123
Oliver David Krieg, Tobias Schwinn and Achim Menges

8 New Characteristics of Medical Architecture Development in China's New-Type Urbanization 145
Hui Li

9 Study of Vernacular Dwellings and Settlement Renewal 167
Xiaopeng Fan and Zhennan Wang

10 Preservation and Tourism-Oriented Use of Cultural Heritage Streets: Case Study of Lhasa's Barkhor Street 179
Xia Li and Yongzhi Xu

11 Sustainable Tourism-Oriented Conservation and Improvement of Historical Villages in the Urbanization Process: A Case Study of Nan'anyang Village, Shanxi Province, China 187
Ye-Feng Xie, Lu Li, Yan-Dan Guo, Xu-Peng Sun and Yu-Jun Zhang

12 The Disappearing Historical Hutongs: Key Issues in Preserving Locality in Old Beijing 205
Pengjun Zhao

13 Restructuring the Urban Landscape: A "Critical Reconstruction" of Permanent Structures in Historic Cultural and Urban Landscapes 215
Sören Schöbel

Part III New Explorations: Site-Specific Planning and Design in the Context of Urbanization

14 Providing Urban Ecosystem Services for Human Well-Being: A Comparison of Exemplary Institutional Arrangements in China and Germany 229
Martin Welp, Natalie Ward, Siegmund Missall, Abdulla Abliz and Ümüt Halik

15 Research on IMGE^{SB} in Sustainable Building Design Process 249
Dongzhu Chu and Shuxiang Wei

16 Locality as Co-production of Common Ground: Urban Interventions by the Academy of a New Gropiusstadt 267
Jörg Stollmann

17 Ecological Plan: City Covered by Green Roofs 287
Linfei Han and Jianmin Guo

18 Urban Formation Based on Environmental Performance Simulation 301
Philip F. Yuan, Shuyi Huang and Chao Yan

19 Nature Conservation as Part of a Multifunctional Use of Suburban Landscapes 323
Michael W. Rode

20 Multi-dimensional Experience of the Rural Landscape in Chinese Organic Farms 345
Jun Shao

21 Generic Design Tools to Produce Site-Specific Solutions: Three Projects 359
Vanessa Miriam Carlow and Yeon Wha Hong

About the Editors

Fang Wang Ph.D. is Associate Professor at College of Architecture and Landscape Architecture, Peking University and a registered urban planner. After receiving a Ph.D. in Architectural Design and Theory from Tsinghua University, she completed her post-doctoral research in Geography, with a concentration in urban planning, at Peking University. From 2011 to 2012, Dr. Wang was a visiting scholar at Harvard University Graduate School of Design. Her research introduces geographical philosophy, methods, and techniques into the traditionally engineering-dominated fields of urban planning and architectural design. Her focus is also known as "geographical planning and design"—research on the influence of geography upon urban planning and design and, reflexively, urban planning and design responses to geography. She is interested in the following research, including preservation and renewal of cultural landscape and historical districts, planning and design of sightseeing district of geo-architecture. Dr. Wang has published over 70 articles and two books and has translated a total of eight books. She has piloted a China Natural Science Foundation project (NSFC, No. 51078003), two Sino-German Center projects (No. 1086-GZ, 1156-GZ) jointly subsidized by National Natural Science Foundation of China (NSFC) and German Science Foundation (DFG) and six other projects of provincial and ministry-level funding.

Martin Prominski Dr.-Ing. is full Professor for designing urban landscapes at Leibniz University of Hanover since 2009. He studied landscape planning at Technical University of Berlin and received a Master in Landscape Architecture from Harvard University, Graduate School of Design, with the support of a DAAD scholarship. He has a Ph.D. from TU Berlin, published in 2004 as "Landschaft Entwerfen." From 2003 to 2008, he was an assistant professor in "Theory of contemporary landscape architecture" at Leibniz University of Hanover. He co-founded the Journal of Landscape Architecture (JoLA) in 2006 and was an editor for it until 2010. He is a member of the Chamber of Architects, the German Academy for Urban Design and Land Use Planning or the STUDIO URBANE LANDSCHAFTEN, an interdisciplinary platform on research, practice, and teaching on urban landscapes. He has published three books and more than 45 articles in books and journals. He has piloted a German Research Foundation project (DFG, No. PR 920/2-1), a Sino-German funding project (Sino-German Symposium, No. GZ1086) jointly subsidized by National Natural Science Foundation of China (NSFC) and German Science Foundation (DFG), two projects for the German Federal Foundation for the Environment (DBU), a project for the Ministry of Science and Culture of Lower Saxony, and co-piloted two projects for the European Union.

Part I
New Trends: Bridges Between People and Place in Urbanization Processes

Chapter 1
The Dynamics of Locality: Inspirations for Designing Large-Scale Urbanisation Projects

Martin Prominski

1.1 Introduction

China's urban population will grow by 300 million between 2014 and 2050 according to the UN World Urbanization Prospects (United Nations 2014: 21). Will they inhabit cities where people enjoy living and working? What character will these new urban areas have? Will they be generic or will it be possible to create a specific, local character?

The respect for locality or the genius loci (i.e. character of a place) is an often-articulated motivation in urbanisation projects seeking to achieve a strong identity. Typically, the genius loci is seen as something to be preserved by retaining existing elements. However, Norberg-Schulz mentions in his book Genius Loci that implicit in protecting and preserving the genius loci is its continuous reification in changing historical contexts (Norberg Schulz 1980: 182). Thus, the realisation of the genius loci means taking a dynamic view and can include both preservation and development. The focus of this article will be on the latter aspect. It assumes that in most future urbanisation projects, e.g. in China, the proposed sites contain scant heritage that could be preserved and serve as an anchor for locality and identity. A preservation strategy to achieve locality is a common approach in Europe, where many contemporary urbanisation projects happen on transformation sites—post-industrial (e.g. Latz 1993), post-harbour (e.g. Braae and Diedrich 2012), post-military, etc.—and existing buildings, constructions, surfaces etc. could serve as a starting point for a new identity. If this is not the case, as in most future Chinese projects, locality needs to be created out of new elements. This article develops

M. Prominski (✉)
Department for Open Space Development, Leibniz University of Hannover, Hannover, Germany
e-mail: martin.prominski@freiraum.uni-hannover.de

F. Wang and M. Prominski (eds.), *Urbanization and Locality*,
DOI 10.1007/978-3-662-48494-4_1

strategies to achieve this. It starts with an introduction to locality as a concept, proceeds to five case studies, and concludes with a proposition of three strategies to achieve locality in new urbanisation projects.

1.2 What Is Locality?

Locality means the specific character of a place, and can be understood as a counterpart to universality, which refers to a place's global, generic character. It is a complex notion, one that has been addressed by many authors using different terms. Firstly, four seminal texts on the topic will be discussed, aiming to distil the main characteristics of locality in a concluding paragraph.

1.2.1 Genius Loci

The most frequently quoted reference on locality is probably Christian Norberg-Schulz's (1980) book Genius Loci . He stresses the importance of place for our existence—whatever happens, happens somewhere i.e. in a place. Place is not an abstract or quantifiable but a qualitative phenomenon. He criticises the way that modern architecture deals more with abstract functionality that can be applied in a generic way than with tangible meaning that is specific to a place. For Norberg-Schulz, "the existential purpose of building (architecture) is therefore to make a site become a place, that is, to uncover the meanings potentially present in the given environment." (ibid.: 18). In other words, the specific character of a site needs to be understood and developed. If this is achieved, people are able to really dwell there—a highly desirable goal for Norberg-Schulz, because it indicates a "total man-place relationship" (ibid.: 19). Two psychological needs are fulfilled in this ideal situation: orientation and identification. Following Kevin Lynch, he explains the importance of orientation for human dwelling: without orientation, "man feels 'lost'" (ibid.: 19). But identification with the environment is even more important. Identification means becoming friends with a particular environment and its properties (ibid.: 21).

Norberg-Schulz's phenomenological call for real things and the importance of character and orientation are useful advice for designers of urbanisation projects—but the issue of identification is more difficult if you have a site that offers little with which people can identify. How can you design for identification then? This issue exposes a problem with Norberg-Schulz's theory, which relies heavily on existing layers of history to which new construction has to relate. Although he stresses the importance of time and change in realising the genius loci by mentioning: "To respect the 'Genius loci' does not mean to copy old models. It means to determine the identity of the place and to interpret it in ever new ways." (ibid.: 182), most of his arguments have a preservationist perspective, which isn't much help in the face of rapid urbanisation. Another problem of his theory is the use of dualisms, like settlement versus landscape or natural spaces versus man-made spaces. Almost forty years after he wrote Genius Loci, these oppositions have become questionable in the light of contemporary debates on planetary urbanisation (Brenner and Schmid 2011) or the Anthropocene (Crutzen 2002).

To summarise: Norberg-Schulz offers a deep analysis from a Western point of view and raises awareness of the topic. However, he gives scant advice on designing for locality in contemporary and future urbanisation projects on previously unsettled territory.

1.2.2 Place

Like Norberg-Schulz's Genius Loci, Edward Relph's (1976) Place and Placelessness takes a phenomenological view, which means for him "to explore place as a phenomenon of the geography of the lived-world of our everyday experiences" (ibid.: 6).

Relph is concerned with the processes of modernity through which placelessness becomes the dominant force. This leads to a "weakening of distinct and diverse experiences and identities of places" (ibid.: 6). This is a serious problem for Relph, because from his phenomenological position, influenced by Heidegger, place is indispensable for human life: "To be human is to have and to know *your* place. […] It is a profound and complex aspect of man's experience of the world." (ibid.: 1). He starts his discussion of the dual poles with a list of major components of place by referring to Lukermann, who had already developed this in 1964. His basic ideas are that places are characterized by internal and external relations which in their sum always create a unique location; they are hybrids which integrate natural and cultural elements; they have a history, and at the same time they are continuously developing; they have meaning created by and for the people (ibid.: 3).

A major reason why these characteristics of uniqueness and meaning fade into placelessness is inauthenticity. It is "the prevalent mode of existence in industrialised and mass societies, and it is a commonplace to recognise that mass values and impersonal planning in all their social, economic, and physical form are major manifestations of such inauthenticity" (ibid.: 81f). Relph describes two features of an inauthentic attitude to places: kitsch and technique (what one would nowadays call technification) in planning. For our purposes the latter is more interesting. The technification of modern planning is typified by planners detached from the site and people who follow universal norms with the abstract goal of functionality and efficiency. Rationality takes precedence over emotion or individuality. By technification in planning, powerful processes are initiated like mass communication (e.g. motorways, airports, railways), mass culture (Disneyfication, museumisation, mass tourism, suburbia), big business (e.g. steel mills, quarries, oil refineries, waste disposal sites) or central authority (replacing local initiative) which all lead to placelessness (ibid.: 90–115). Relph summarizes: "Placelessness is particularly apparent in technique, the overriding concern with efficiency as an end in itself. In technique places can be treated as the interchangeable, replaceable locations of things, as indeed they are by multinational corporations, powerful central governments, and uninvolved planners. As an unselfconscious attitude placelessness is particularly associated with mass culture—the adoption of fashions and ideas about landscapes and places that are coined by a few 'experts' and disseminated to the people through the mass media. The products of these two attitudes are combined in uniform, sterile, other-directed, and kitschy places—places which have few significances and symbols, only more or less gaudy signs and things performing functions with greater or lesser efficiency. The overall result is the undermining of the importance of place for both individuals and cultures, and the casual replacement of the diverse and significant places of the world with anonymous spaces and exchangeable environments" (ibid.: 143).

To avert this placeless dystopia, Relph discusses strategies for designing significant places in his concluding chapter. This design standpoint is interesting for a dynamic understanding of locality because it addresses the future. He starts with a remarkable warning that the design of places needs more than a solely historical perspective: "The possibilities for maintaining and reviving man's sense of place do not lie in the preservation of old places—that would be museumisation; nor can they lie in a self-conscious return to the traditional ways of placemaking—that would require the regaining of a lost state of innocence. Instead, placelessness must be transcended" (ibid.: 145). Relph's proposals for placemaking include designing for diversity and difference as well as cultivating a responsiveness "to local structures of meaning and experience, to particular situations and to the variety of levels of meaning of place" (ibid.: 146). This is relatively terse, but precise. One difficult issue remains with regard to new urbanisation. For Relph, identity is a major component of places, and the most important aspect of identity is "the intensity of experience of a place" by people (ibid.: 141). This creates a dilemma, because any design is prospective and thus cannot be intensively experienced by people—you cannot experience a place that does not yet exist. Thus, from a designer's point of view identity is retrospective.

1.2.3 Non-places

Compared to Norberg-Schulz and Relph, Augé (2008) is less critical of places which have no character, genius loci or locality. He calls them 'non-places'. Augé assumes a more neutral position, trying to understand why they are so ubiquitous and looking for their qualities. His definition of place and non-place is quite simple: "If a space can be defined as relational, historical and concerned with identity, then a space which cannot be defined as relational, or historical, or concerned with identity will be a non-place" (ibid.: 63). Non-places are mainly transit spaces like airports, motorways, supermarkets, shopping malls, hotels, tourist resorts and hospitals. They represent a world "surrendered to solitary individuality, to the fleeting, the temporary and ephemeral" (ibid.: 63). Due to these characteristics, non-places create "neither singular identity nor relations; only solitude and similitude" (ibid.: 83). Surprisingly, Augé is hesitant about judging this disparagingly; for him it seems an inevitable process and consequence of supermodernity. In his introduction to the second English edition, sixteen years after the book first appeared, he again describes the ongoing acceleration of these processes dispassionately. For example the rise of the internet means that even the dwelling is losing its function as a place of social gathering and collective identity when each family member is sitting in front of a mobile device connected to global networks (ibid.: viii). One reason for his neutrality regarding the anonymity and solitude of non-places might be his assessment that places and non-places never exist in pure form: "Place and non-place are rather like opposed polarities: the first is never completely erased, the second never totally completed; they are like palimpsests on which the scrambled game of identity and relations is ceaselessly rewritten" (ibid.: 64). Thus, both types should be accepted as necessary parts in our age of supermodernity.

For urbanisation projects, following Augé's argument means non-places are inevitable, but each location always has aspects of place. In terms of design, Augé gives plenty of spatial descriptions of non-places, but the spatial issues of places are not addressed; he concentrates on the social aspects.

1.2.4 Site

After discussing an architectural theorist (Norberg-Schulz), a geographer (Relph) and an anthropologist (Augé), this literature review will be completed by turning to two designers: Carol Burns and Andrea Kahn, editors of the book Site Matters (2005). In their introduction they argue that an understanding of the site is mandatory for designers who change the environment (ibid.: viii). They differentiate three distinct areas in developing an understanding of the site: First, the 'area of control', which means the property lines; second, the 'area of influence' with "encompassing forces that act upon a plot without being confined to it"; and third the 'area of effect', which refers to the impact a design has on the site and beyond it (ibid.: xii). While the first area is obvious, the second and third suggest that a site is more than the plot itself—that it is always part of a larger picture to which it is connected in complex ways. These three areas also overlap in various fashions through the design process. There is, for example, a reciprocal relationship between elements of the area of control and the area of influence: "Geological and hydrological conditions, along with orientation, topography, and drainage, connect to larger systems that operate in various ways at multiple scales—the solar system, geomorphology, and the water cycle. Any place registers tangible certain aspects of many larger more spatially extensive patterns, orders, and systems" (ibid.: xii). While these are physical elements that should be reflected in any site-specific design, Burns and Kahn are aware that many more layers constitute a site, especially those of meaning and people. They conclude: "At once a real construct (of nature), a narrated construct (of discourse), and a collective construct (socially constituted), site presents a potent example of hybridity. Any attempt to meaningfully address its many registers of significance demands a constant crossing of knowledge categories. Site thinking must continually oscillate between material and conceptual, abstract and physical, discursive and experiential, and general and specific points of view" (ibid.: xxi).

Unlike the preceding three authors, Burns and Kahn do not discuss a distinction between place and non-place. For them, any place can become a site with a distinct identity—and to achieve this, it is important for designers to analyse the multiple relations within and beyond the site and to be open for change.

To sum up, the discussion of these four references leads to the following conclusions about locality:

Locality is important: It is simply an integral part of the human condition and will therefore always be an issue (Relph 1976: 1). Locality gives people the orientation and identification to create and reinforce emotional security. By integrating people in their surroundings, locality averts human alienation and environmental disruption (Norberg Schulz 1980: 23).

Locality is under pressure: All authors describe an exponential trend towards universality in the modern era. Non-places have their raison d'être and they have important functions; however, locality will persist. According to Augé, places and non-places will intertwine and stand in reciprocal relation to each other (Augé 2008: 86). 'Either/or' notions and approaches should be replaced by 'and'; even within a single urbanisation project, places and non-places could co-exist.

Locality is relational: Each location has internal and external relations. For the design of new urbanisation projects, both the elaboration of existing relations and the creation of new ones are indispensable strategies for creating orientation and meaning.

Locality is hybrid: Many factors must coalesce to achieve locality—natural ones like topography, water or plants, and cultural ones like sociality or symbols. This fact should deter designers from focusing exclusively on physical or spatial issues when working on urbanisation projects.

Locality is dynamic: Augé calls a place a palimpsest that is continuously overwritten (Augé 2008: 64). Thus locality includes the past, the present and projections into the future. This should be considered whenever the fascination with history gets too strong in debates on locality. Even sceptics of modern developments like Norberg-Schulz or Relph stress that locality cannot be achieved by preservation alone. In summary, locality is not only continuously renewed, but can also be made anew by designers.

1.3 Excursus: Is Locality an Outdated Concept?

All the above authors remark upon a massive growth of placelessness or non-places in this age of (super)modernity. Universality seems inevitable in the face of globalisation, while locality is losing ground. But is this actually a problem? Augé, for example, takes no sides on this. Do we really need locality? Or is locality an outdated concept? According to Rem Koolhaas' famous essay The Generic City (1995), the answer would be "Yes!" He opens his essay by asking: "What are the disadvantages of identity, and conversely, what are the advantages of blankness? What if this seemingly accidental - and usually regretted - homogenization were an intentional process, a conscious movement away from difference toward similarity? What if we are witnessing a global liberation movement: 'down with character!'" (p. 1248). For him, locality is an outdated concept and identity nothing more than a straightjacket. If identity is understood as sharing the past, there is not enough residual historical substance in areas with a fast growing population like Asia—"Identity is like a mousetrap in which more and more mice have to share the original bait." (p. 1248). The result is the 'generic city': placeless, relieved of the burden of identity. This urban type, which has grown enormously in recent decades, has many advantages: "It is nothing but a reflection of present need and present ability. It is the city without history. It is big enough for everybody. It is easy. It does not need maintenance. If it gets too small it just expands. If it gets old it just self-destructs and renews. It is equally exciting – or unexciting – everywhere" (p. 1250). So why bother with locality, place or genius loci? Well, even Koolhaas seems unconvinced by his brilliant rhetoric. Only a few years after Generic City he wrote another rhetorical tour de force: Junkspace (2002)—his term for non-places like shopping centres and airports, which have become a dominant space-category. For Koolhaas, this new space category is not "an aberration, but it is the essence, the main thing" (p. 175). Most parts of the essay are just descriptive; only very rarely are general characteristics or judgements of junkspace summarized. One negative assessment is given regarding the continuity achieved by escalators or seamless indoor spaces controlled by air-conditioning. Continuity "promotes dis-orientation by any means (mirror, polish, echo) … " (p. 175). This is congruent with Augé's assessment of non-places as transitional spaces and also echoes Norberg Schulz and Lynch's descriptions of the problems of orientation in non-places. This passage addressing 'disorientation' is one of the few sentences to include criticism of junkspace. Nevertheless, a cynical undertone is already set by the title, and the essay is a breathless rant, which can be regarded as a 7500-word diatribe on the dominant architectural products of our time.

Some years later, Koolhaas re-articulated this criticism of the generic city when he posited that China could have the chance to counter forces of the unifying market economy because the state had an unusual power, but "the situation results in highly debased forms of urban modernity and a consistent import of western precedents, which is not very useful." (Koolhaas 2007: 322). In turn, this means that Koolhaas argues for 'based' forms of urban modernity, i.e. forms rooted in the specific context, and the development of local precedents.

Thus, it can be concluded from this excursus that even Koolhaas, erstwhile protagonist of the generic city and (in)famous for his expletive "Fuck the context", has become discomfited by the non-places of urban modernity and has started a search for authenticity.

1.4 Locality in New Urbanisation Projects

The first part of this article summarised five different aspects of locality. It became apparent that locality is important, but under pressure, and that it is relational, hybrid and dynamic. In the following it will be asked what these issues mean for the specific case of designing new, large-scale urbanisation projects. It is a relevant topic because the rate of urbanisation will continue to grow rapidly—the World Urbanisation Prospect 2014 predicts that the worldwide urban population will grow from 3.8 to 6.3 billion people between 2014 and 2050 (United Nations 2014: 20). These 2.5 billion people moving into urban areas will either live in informal, unplanned settlements (important research is going on for this topic, e.g. Werthmann and Bridger 2015) or in planned districts. The latter will be our focus, and these planned districts will be built especially in countries such as China where the state has considerable power.

Locality is a difficult topic in new, large-scale urbanisation projects because most of them will be built close to existing cities on agricultural areas that have very little to offer in terms of history or character. In dealing with this problem one has little guidance from the authors discussed in the first part. Although they stress the dynamic character of places, their design recommendations rely heavily on existing, significant layers of natural and cultural history when they talk about placemaking. The case studies discussed by Norberg-Schulz, for example, are Prague, Khartoum and Rome, which have millennia of history and a specific topographical situation. But how do you design for locality if not much is there when you get the commission? The answer lies in strategies to create a strong locality by new elements. The following offers five case studies that exemplify this strategy. The criteria for choosing them were significant size and a dynamic, projective approach to create locality.

1.4.1 Case Study: Scharnhauser Park

Scharnhauser Park is a new district of Ostfildern, a town of 37,000 inhabitants near Stuttgart. The district itself has today 7600 inhabitants and 1500 workplaces. The site of 140 hectares takes its name from the horse-breeding stud and attached park founded by King Wilhelm I of Wuerttemberg in 1817. From 1951 till 1992 the area was occupied by the US Army's Nellingen Barracks, and immediately after the army left the city launched an urban design competition, won by the Janson + Wolfrum architecture and urban design office. Housing construction started in 1997, other important steps were the light rail connection with the city of Stuttgart in 2000 and the State of Baden-Wuerttemberg Garden Festival in 2002, which acted as catalyst for the creation of open spaces in the district. In 2006 the project received the prestigious German Urban Design Award.

The main characteristic of the design is its respect for the topography. The site is on a south-facing slope, and the new multi-family residential blocks on it all have the same height and a similar shape, thus accentuating the topography (Fig. 1.1). At the heart of the district, the monumental 'Landscape Staircase' opens up between the buildings and runs right down the hill for a distance of 1 km and a width of 40 m. It offers great views of the surrounding regional mountain range, the Swabian Alb. It is framed by rows of columnar oaks and well connected to the housing areas by bicycle and pedestrian paths on both sides (Figs. 1.2 and 1.3). The Landscape Staircase also functions as the central stormwater collector; between the steps are lawns with swales where stormwater from the adjacent housing blocks is collected, partly evaporates here or drains into underground gravel pockets and thence towards the nearby streams (Dreiseitl 2001: 80).

In summary, the project created a new hill with the landscape staircase as the backbone. In this central open space people are aesthetically connected to the larger landscape with its rich cultural and natural qualities—an intensive relationship only made possible by the new design.

Fig. 1.1 Urban development at Scharnhauser Park, articulating the hill with houses at the same height and orientation. The landscape staircase, framed by poplars, is the spine of the project (*Source* Dr. Bernd Gross; http://commons.wikimedia.org/wiki/File:Scharnhauser_Park.jpg)

Fig. 1.2 Scharnhauser Park during construction, showing the orientation of the landscape staircase towards the surrounding hills (*Source* SEG Ostfildern)

Fig. 1.3 Perspective from the top of the landscape staircase (*Source* SEG Ostfildern)

1.4.2 Case Study: Hannover Kronsberg

The Kronsberg district was part of the overall preparation processes in Hannover for the EXPO 2000 world exposition. Close to the EXPO exhibition grounds to the southeast of Hannover, it was intended to serve as a model for future sustainable urban development, while providing up to 6000 new dwellings for 15,000 people as a response to a report which predicted that Hannover would need 20,000 new apartments by the year 2000 (Rumming 2004).

From the very beginning an integrative approach was adopted to the issues of housing, open space and ecology. A first competition for the entire site was held in 1992, and the Arnaboldi Cavadini Hager group from Locarno and Zurich took first prize. Their basic ideas, a rectangular grid for the residential area at the foot of the Kronsberg, a long low hill extending for 6 km from north to south and 2 km wide, and re-afforestation of the hill crest, laid down the structure for subsequent, more detailed competitions (Rumming 2004: 24). In 1993, the Braunschweig office of Welp/Welp and Sawadda won the 'Urban development competition for Bemerode East' with a simple grid structure for 6000 dwellings on 160 ha (Rumming 2004: 26). A workshop with five landscape architecture offices for the open space design was held in 1994. The Kienast bureau's proposal was chosen: to structure the residential zone with five transversal park corridors leading up to extensive grazing land between the residential area and the new hilltop woodland planting. Additionally, two artificial hills were created on the ridge using excavated soil from the housing construction (Fig. 1.4). These ideas were all implemented and resulted in a stronger local identity. In place of monotonous agricultural land, the new woodland on the hill crest emphasises the topography (Fig. 1.5a, b); the additional 25 m to the treetops are significant because Kronsberg rises to 100 m above sea level and 'only' 30 m above the surrounding plain of the city (Fig. 1.6). The same is true of the two artificial hills. The northern one is 118.2 m above sea level and is the second-highest point in Hannover, topped only by the city's rubbish dump (Fig. 1.7). From the top one has an excellent view of the Hannover skyline. The park corridors also had an important influence on strengthening the local character. They link the existing urban fabric through the new urban development to the Kronsberg hill crest, which was previously cut off by agricultural use. In the new urban district, which currently covers an area of 3 km by 500 m with 3000 dwellings, the park corridors also collect the stormwater from nearby streets and roofs in open ditches (Dreiseitl 2001: 76–78). These stormwater corridors are visually attractive, and their prominence raises awareness and understanding of the local water regime (Fig. 1.8). In summary, the local identity could be strengthened by the new urbanisation and particularly by the open space system. The former dreary generic agricultural land was replaced by a more diverse structure that gave the urban landscape a stronger character, for example by re-afforestation of the hill crest. Furthermore it offers many ways in which people can connect with natural and cultural elements both within and beyond the district.

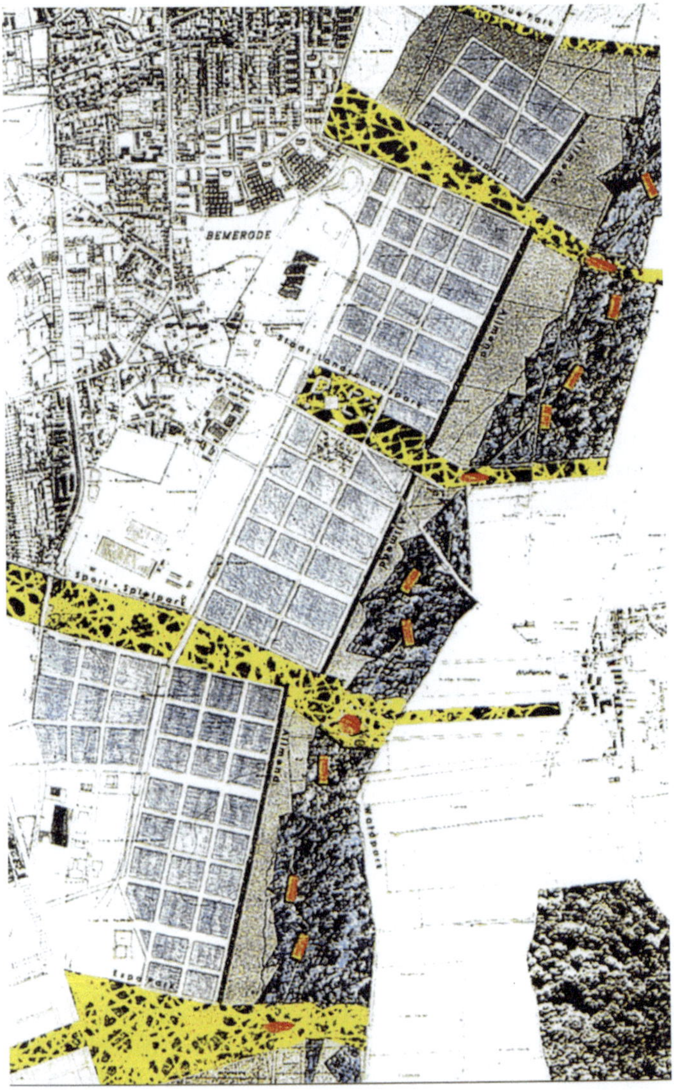

Fig. 1.4 The Kienast plan from 1994. The landscape framework included five transverse park corridors and woodland planting on the hill crest (*Source* Rumming 2004: 28)

1.4.3 Case Study: Munich Airport

Of the five case studies Munich Airport is the only project which is not an urban district with housing and its ancillary structures. It was chosen because airports are expressions of global regulation and orientation and are usually non-places in the

(a)

(b)

Fig. 1.5 **a**, **b** Before the urban development, the Kronsberg area was a stereotype agricultural landscape without structural elements (**a**, *top*), the urban development created a new structure including the forestration of the Kronsberg ridge (**b**, *bottom*) (*Source* Rumming 2004: 6)

Fig. 1.6 View from the artificial hill towards the new woodland planting (*Source* Prominski)

Fig. 1.7 Artificial hill created with excavated soil from the housing construction. In front is the new meadow where sheeps are used for maintenance (*Source* Axel Hindemith; http://creativecommons.org/licenses/by-sa/3.0/de/legalcode)

Fig. 1.8 Transversal open space corridor with integrated stormwater management (*Source* Prominski)

purest sense. Munich airport is an exception, one which shows how even the design of an airport can be orientated on the local character and enhance it.

The airport is located 30 km northeast of downtown Munich in the 'Erdinger Moos', a marshy area. The decision to build here was taken in 1969 but it was not until after lengthy legal clarifications that construction could begin in the mid 1980s, and the airport opened in 1992. Design quality was an important issue from the early stages; the process began with design round tables in 1979 that included the famous German designer Otl Aicher (responsible for the corporate identities of the 1972 Olympic Games in Munich and of Lufthansa), architects, landscape architects, engineers and representatives of the airport administration (Flughafen München 2015a: www). In 1982 the first six volumes of design guidelines appeared, and they have been continuously updated ever since. In them, the landscape plays a decisive role: "Structure and development of the Munich Airport are rooted in the landscape elements of the Erdinger Moos. The airport's buildings, open spaces and infrastructures are all designed in a horizontal, flat and linear way which integrates them into the Erdinger Moos and its surroundings" (Flughafen München 2015b: www; translation MP). One of Otl Aicher's first sketches depicts the flatness and linearity of the landscape very well (Fig. 1.9).

The clumps of trees and existing lines of trees and drainage channels were to be kept and whenever possible even extended on the airport site. Another result of this careful reading of the landscape was the depiction of a specific formal structure: The valley of the river Isar—the main regional landscape element—does not run exactly north-south but at an angle of 18°33′, which gives orientation to all the elements, such as streets, running north-south (Fig. 1.10a–c). The east-west landscape elements all run straight in the area of the Erdinger Moos, which creates an overall parallelogram structure (Fig. 1.11). The airport was designed to reinforce this formal characteristic. Essentially, Munich airport was firmly founded in the character of the local landscape with its flatness, the specific parallelogram structure or linear elements like rows of trees and drainage channels. The design guidelines ensure that all new construction is orientated on these characteristics, thus making them even stronger. From today's viewpoint this site-specific approach has been very successful; Munich is one of the few airports worldwide which is not an alien intrusion on the landscape but an important companion (Fig. 1.12).

Fig. 1.9 Sketch by Otl Aicher from the 1970s expressing the landscape character of the airport site before construction (*Source* Rathgeb 2006)

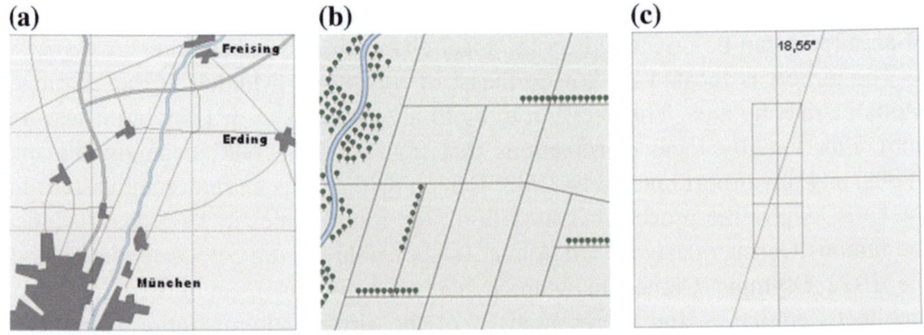

Fig. 1.10 a–c The direction of the river Isar in the larger landscape which determines an angle of 18, 55° (*Source* http://www.munich-airport.de/de/micro/gestaltung/1_landschaft/1_3_achsen/index.jsp ; accessed 18.03.2015)

Fig. 1.11 Alley planting which express the skewed angle (*Source* Werner Hennies http://www.munich-airport.de/de/micro/gestaltung/1_landschaft/1_5_pflanzstruktur/index.jsp; accessed 18.03.2015)

1.4.4 Case Study: Deep Ground/Longgang City Centre

'Deep Ground' was the winning entry by Groundlab in 2008 for the new Longgang City Centre and Longcheng Square for 350,000 new inhabitants in Shenzen. Groundlab is a London based practice with close links to the Architectural Associations Landscape Urbanism programme where both the founders, Eva Castro and Alfredo Ramirez, teach. A complex understanding of the landscape is the

Fig. 1.12 Harmonic integration of the airport in the landscape (*Source* Werner Hennies http://www.munich-airport.de/de/micro/gestaltung/1_landschaft/1_3_achsen/index.jsp; accessed 18.03.2015)

foundation of their work. They see "landscape as a model of connective, scalar and temporal operations through which the urban is conceived and engaged with: the urban is diagrammed as a landscape; a complex and processual ecology. With this model the urban can be connected to local, regional and global scales and understood in terms of its future orientation and performative potential. […] This implies considering the city as a part of a wider metabolic ensemble, where the metabolic and time-based processes of landscape and 'nature' become devices for human interaction and relationships. Thus the critical engagement with the environmental conditions becomes the crucial driver of a design process that is grounded on the experimentation of form as an operational/political device" (Castro and Ramirez 2012: 206).

Groundlab uses three strategies for the Longgang project. First, 'thickened ground' aims to achieve depth and spatial complexity by combining and overlaying different programmatic spaces. One example is the smooth transition of a square into a roof of a building to form one continuous public open space. Second, 'infrastructural landscape' means integrative consideration of blue, green and grey infrastructure. The Longgang River, previously detached from the urban fabric, becomes the central spine of a new open space system which combines a revitalized river with new green corridors along the banks. From the sides, several smaller green corridors and open rainwater drainage systems connect to this central spine to form a network that structures the whole new district (Fig. 1.13). The third strategy,

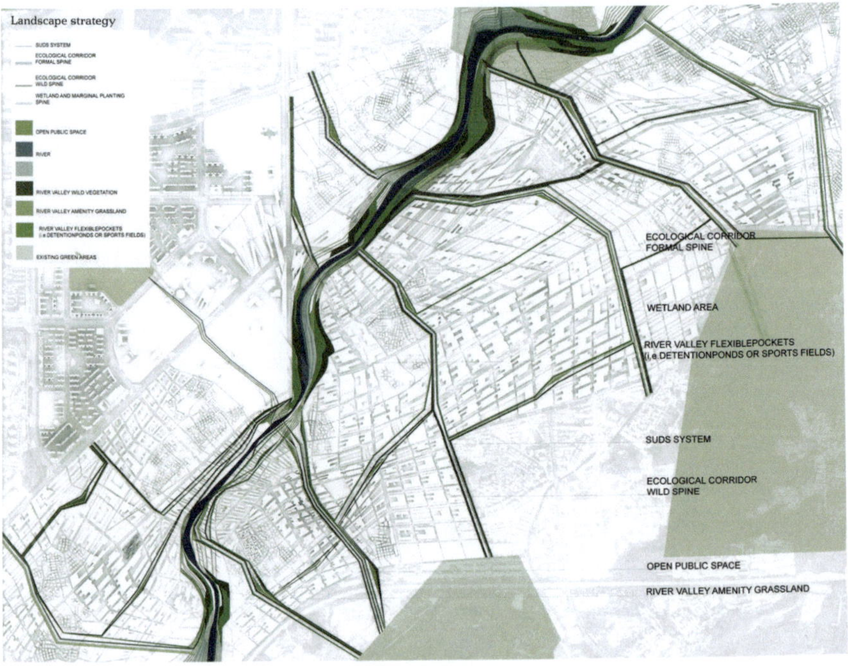

Fig. 1.13 Longgang, Landscape Strategy (*Source* Castro and Ramirez 2012: 217)

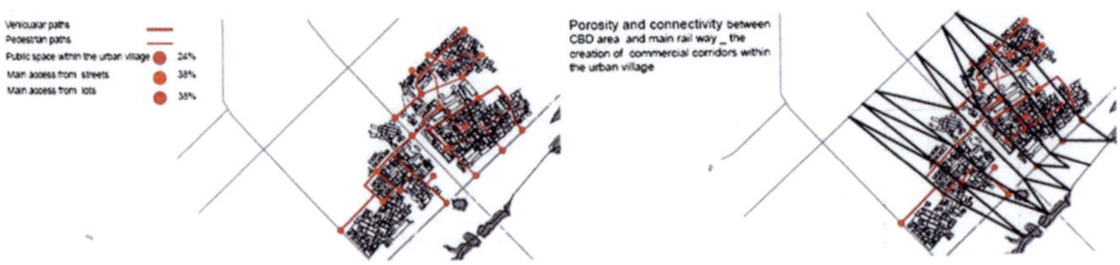

Fig. 1.14 Longgang, Urban village strategy "porosity and connectivity" with the creation of new commercial corridors (*Source* Castro and Ramirez 2012: 216)

'urban villages', aims to retain existing villages as the anchor points for the new city (Fig. 1.14). Groundlab sees many qualities in them: "They foster pedestrian-orientated urbanism, having a strong character based on the very local activities that exist, always within walking distance and generating a sort of inner ecology that establishes links among their inhabitants and creates a sense of identity among the community" (Castro and Ramirez 2012: 217). This positive assessment of the original communities is remarkable because the local authorities originally planned to demolish them.

This project offers several lessons for designing locality, especially in the strategies of 'infrastructural landscape' and 'urban villages'. Groundlab saw the existing urban villages not as passive preservation elements but as active catalysts that connect strongly with the new urban fabric. They carefully analysed the existing types and developed specific intervention strategies for them—some even as radical as proposing new commercial corridors running through the village. Thus, a transformation of the existing villages is considered but they will still keep many memories of the area to foster a sense of place and identity. The careful elaboration of the infrastructural landscape is probably the most important factor for connecting the future residents with the local elements of their district. Groundlab gives a logic to the terrain by using the valleys as the area for blue and green corridors. This is not only sustainable but also leads to a better understanding of the landscape characteristics and a relation to the 'real' local elements for the inhabitants, which in the end promotes identification by the people with their environment.

1.4.5 Case Study: Zhangjiawo

The harbour city of Tianjin, with almost 10 million people in its metropolitan region, is a good example of China's rapidly growing cities. Agriculture is being supplanted by industry and commerce at an exponential pace, and the new workers need dwellings. Zhangjiawo is a new district for these newcomers in the south-western part of Tianjin, and the design goal was a combination of high density and open space quality. The project was implemented in 2008 and its designers were from Germany: Theodor/Schaller and Schmitz as architects and Atelier Dreiseitl as landscape architects. The architecture is a mixture of two-storey patio houses derived from the traditional Chinese patio house typology, three-storey row houses, four-to-six-storey apartment blocks and individual villas. The material for all facades is brick, which creates visual unity across the district (Schaller and Theodor 2015: www; Fig. 1.15). In the open spaces, a water sensitive urban design concept is applied. All stormwater runs visibly through natural plant filters and is collected in central water bodies. This is common stormwater management practice world-wide, but Atelier Dreiseitl used existing canals, ditches and ponds in this district and made the design site-specific (Fig. 1.16a, b). Another strategy to use local elements was the integration of 200-year-old orchard trees from the former agricultural land into the settlement. Finally, the adjacent Feng Chang River was restored and integrated in the district. Previously, it had been fenced off and was nothing more than a polluted irrigation channel, but cleaning strategies and a new design for the banks have brought it into the open space system (Fig. 1.17). All these measures allow local people to establish their relations with the specific elements of the site; altogether, Atelier Dreiseitl's goals of high ecological and social value as well as a strong genius loci (Dreiseitl 2015: www) have been achieved.

Fig. 1.15 Sketch of Zhangjiawo by the architects (*Source* http://www.stefan-schmitz-architekten.de/de/details-22/id-142-zhangjiawo.html; accessed 18.03.2015)

Fig. 1.16 a, b Transforming existing canals and ponds for the contemporary stormwater management (*Source* Li Xin)

Fig. 1.17 Integration of the restored Feng Chang River into the open space system of Zhangjiawo (*Source* Li Xin)

1.5 Conclusion

This discussion of five case studies has shown that locality can be developed by new urbanisation projects on sites that previously had a more-or-less generic character. In the following, the key strategies to achieve locality are summarized in a way that makes them transferable to future urbanisation projects in China and beyond. Although they play a role in creating locality, two issues within these strategies cannot be covered in this article: the individual buildings (this is a completely different topic with a great deal of literature covered under 'regional architecture') and citizens' participation (an important but difficult topic in new urbanisation projects, because the future inhabitants are not yet there)—these are topics of other and further research.

1.5.1 Integrating the Larger Context

If a site offers little in terms of character, the larger context can be approached to create locality. At Scharnhauser Park the landscape staircase brings the regional mountain range aesthetically into the district by forcefully directing the awareness of the inhabitants towards it. This idea has parallels to the concept of 'borrowed scenery' (shakkei) from Japanese garden history, where views from the larger landscape are integrated into the garden—but at Scharnhauser Park it is more than scenery; it is an embedding of the residents in the larger environment.

The park corridors in the Kronsberg district are another example of integration. On the one hand, they connect the housing areas with the existing urban fabric to the west as well as the open landscape to the east, while on the other they reveal the topographical situation of the larger landscape. If people leave the dense housing blocks and come to the park corridors, they are suddenly able to see the Kronsberg crest on one side and the city below on the other side.

It would be very interesting to discuss this strategy in relation to Chinese feng shui theories, which also deal with setting a place in its larger context. This exceeds the scope of this article and in my view should be done by someone with a Chinese cultural background.

1.5.2 Transforming Existing Structures

If there are some existing structures on the site as a starting point for locality but they seem likely to disturb the future construction, consideration should be given to how these structures could be transformed. In Groundlab's Longgang proposal, it was decided to keep the existing villages but reshaped as part of the new gestalt, for example by proposing new commercial corridors through the old village that connect to the new urban fabric. At Zhangjiawo, old canals and basins were adapted and included as new elements of the stormwater management system, or orchard trees from former agricultural land are now the backbone of the new district parks.

By this strategy, existing structures are not preserved but transformed, with new functions and meanings.

1.5.3 Adopting and Adapting Natural and Cultural Elements

This strategy creates a new locality either by proposing new elements or by reifying or uncovering elements that had gone unrecognised. Careful reading of the existing situation is necessary with this strategy. The uniqueness of the 'landscape angle' and the resulting parallelogram structure in the landscape surrounding the new Munich Airport was a new discovery by the team of designers, and consistently applying this angle to all new landscape structures made it a strong element of the regional identity. Furthermore, by specifying linearity for new plantings and horizontality for all new buildings, the flat and straight-line character of the marshy area of 'Erdinger Moos' became even stronger through the airport's presence. At Kronsberg, a new element also changed a previously 'quiet' situation when the new woodland planting along the Kronsberg hill crest amplified the topographical identity of the site. The projective analysis in Groundlab's Longgang proposal turned the previously neglected river into a structural base for the new city of 350,000 people, further enhanced by connecting green corridors to it which were divined and located by careful territorial reading. As this approach fitted into the landscape, other green or blue infrastructural elements like a sustainable urban drainage system or ecological areas could easily be added. By this strategy, Groundlab was able to design a new identity by creating or highlighting elements that no one previously could have imagined or seen.

In summary, it can be seen that locality is not dependent on preservation strategies or thick layers of history. Locality is dynamic and can be created by the strategies mentioned above, even if at first sight there is almost no point of departure. With these three strategies, the two positive functions of locality that Norberg-Schulz mentions—orientation and identification—can be achieved even in new, large-scale urbanisation projects. If they are applied, chances are high that living in these new districts is not a matter of surviving despite the surroundings but of real habitation. How this value could be integrated into the strategies and checklists of real estate developers is an interesting and wide open question…

References

Augé M (2008) Non-sites. An introduction to supermodernity. Verso, London

Braae E, Diedrich L (2012) Site specificity in contemporary large-scale harbour transformation projects. J Landscape Archit 7(1):20–33

Brenner N, Schmid C (2011) Planetary urbanisation. In: Gandy M (ed) Urban constellations. Jovis, Berlin, pp 10–13

Burns C, Kahn A (eds) (2005) Site matters. Routledge, New York

Castro E, Ramirez A (2012) Multiplying the ground. In: Hensel M (ed) Design innovation for the built environment. Routledge, London, pp 205–220

Crutzen J (2002) Geology of mankind. Nature 415:23

Dreiseitl A (2015) Zhangjiawo New Town. www.dreiseitl.com/index.php?id=55&lang=en. Accessed 24 Feb 2015

Dreiseitl H et al (2001) Waterscapes. Basel, Birkhäuser (in German)

Flughafen München (Hg.) (2015a) Gestaltungsrichtlinien Retrospektive. www.munich-airport.de/de/micro/gestaltung/9_retro1/index.jsp. Accessed 24 Feb 2015

Flughafen München (Hg.) (2015b) Landschaft www.munich-airport.de/de/micro/gestaltung/1_landschaft/index.jsp. Accessed 24 Feb 2015

Koolhaas R (1995) The generic city. In: Koolhaas R, Mau B (eds) S, M, L, XL. 010 Publishers, Rotterdam, pp 1239–1264

Koolhaas R (2002) Junkspace, vol 100, pp 175–190

Koolhaas R (2007) In search of authenticity. In: Burdett R, Sudjil D (eds) The endless city. Phaidon, London, pp 320–323

Latz P (1993) Design by handling the existing. In: Knuijt M et al (eds) Modern park design—recent trends. Thoth, Amsterdam, pp 90–97

Norberg Schulz C (1980) Genius Loci: towards a phenomenology of architecture. Rizzoli, New York

Rathgeb M (2006) Otl Aicher. München, Phaidon
Relph E (1976) Place and placelessness. Pion Limited, London
Rumming K (ed) (2004) Hannover Kronsberg handbook. Landeshauptstadt Hannover, Hannover
Schaller C, Theodor H (2015) Tianjin Zhangjiawo New Town Residential Project. www.schallertheodor.de/content/p_china_zjw.htm pdf. Accessed 24 Feb 2015]
United Nations, Department of Economic and Social Affairs, Population Division (2014) World urbanization prospects: the 2014 revision. Highlights (ST/ESA/SER.A/352)
Werthmann C, Bridger J (2015) Metropolis nonformal. Applied Research and Design Publishing, Novato (forthcoming)

Author Biography

Dr. Martin Prominski is Professor for "Designing Urban Landscapes" at the Department for Open Space Development, Faculty of Architecture and Landscape Sciences, Leibniz University Hannover.

Chapter 2
Measurement and Application of Urban Memory Related to Historic Areas in Beijing

Fang Wang, Wei Li, Yang Liu and Hongru Cai

2.1 Introduction

China is approaching rapid urbanization, and simultaneously, globalization is dramatically changing the unique history and traditional style in traditional Chinese cities. The diminishment and reconstruction of historic sites in China comprise a common problem, leading to the "amnesia" phenomenon over the disappearance of unique characteristics and decay of the urban cultural context. China is currently in an active stage of global social and economic transformation. As its capital, Beijing not only suffers from problems of demolition, renovation, and regeneration brought by rapid urbanization but also faces the impact of globalization, which proves to be a huge threat to the city, whose history spans more than 3000 years. Amid tough situations during the process of rapid change, Beijing's development has brought to the fore the core issues of saving the context of urban development, protecting cultural heritage and urban characters, and dealing with new challenges of cultural preservation. All of these account for the necessity and urgency in the study of urban memory in Beijing.

Urban memory is the collective impression of the formation, change, and development of a city. In the case of Beijing, the preservation and continuation of urban memory are innovative means for protecting the ancient capital and carrying out urban regeneration. The study of the measurement and application of urban memory, based on historic areas in Beijing, aims to determine means to perpetuate

F. Wang (✉)
College of Architecture and Landscape Architecture, Peking University, Beijing, China
e-mail: wfphd@pku.edu.cn

W. Li · Y. Liu · H.R. Cai
College of Urban and Environmental Sciences, Peking University, Beijing, China

Y. Liu
Beijing Municipal Institute of City Planning and Design, Beijing, China

F. Wang and M. Prominski (eds.), *Urbanization and Locality*,
DOI 10.1007/978-3-662-48494-4_2

and preserve urban memory as well as provide unique development approaches in ancient cities, such as Beijing, especially in the context of rapid urbanization.

In its literature review, this research establishes a system of measurement based on theories on historical areas and urban memory, with historical sites in Beijing as examples. The article reaches the conclusion of "what to protect" and "how to protect," thereby offering comprehensive methods and theoretical guidance for the protection of historical areas and preservation of urban memory.

2.2 Literature Review

2.2.1 Memory, Place, and Urban Memory

Memory itself has a long evolution: as long as human consciousness. Memory is the mental capacity through which events are stored, preserved, and recalled in mind; it is in permanent evolution, open to the dialectic of remembering and forgetting (Nora 1989). The individual is the subject of memories, and individual memory processes are derived from social interaction. Maurice Halbwachs, the French sociologist, set the foundation for the research on the relationship between memory and society. In his 1925 landmark publication "Social Frameworks of Memory," Halbwachs emphasizes the influence of society on individual memory (Halbwachs [1925] 1992). He was the first to propose the idea that there is memory at the collective level and used the term "collective memory" to express the social contextualization of all individual memories. In a series of studies, Halbwachs argues that every memory is carried by a specific social group limited in space and time (Confino 1997). French historian Pierre Nora, the "true heir to Halbwachs" has documented all the "places of memory" in French society and noted the passing of memory into history as akin to losing a living relation to the past. Nora's multivolume project "Les Lieux de Mémoire" (Nora 1989) underpins further spatial takes on memory for its emphasis upon the realms and physical sites or places of modern, collective memory (Legg 2005). Along with the classic studies of Halbwachs and Nora, Olick and Robbins (1998) offer a similar argument and refer to distinct sets of mnemonic practices in various social sites, rather than to collective memory as a phenomenon. Bélanger (2002) understands collective memory as a social process, one that surpasses the understanding of memory simply as the accumulated recollections of actual historical events. Huyssen (1995: 7) mentions that humans search for and build places of memory that can provide a sense of "temporal anchoring" in a world of up-to-the-minute media saturation and information overload.

Meanwhile, thematic studies have paid attention to the relationship between collective memory and urban space. Memories are built as a city is built (Hebbert 2005), and cities serve as powerful symbols and repositories of memory (Ladd 2008). Halbwachs ([1925] 1992) set the roots for identifying the role that space plays in shaping collective memory; every collective memory unfolds within a spatial framework. Urban spaces as lived spaces shape collective imaginaries (Huyssen

2003), and the collective memory of a city participates in the actual transformation of space in the works of the collective (Rossi 1982). Le Goff (1992) identifies five distinct periods in the history of memory; he notes that city structures emerged in the second stage, following the emergence of mnemonic practices. As Casey (2004: 38) bluntly asserts, "public memory needs a place of enactment, a scene of instantiation"; public places as a component of public memory are designed to be long-lasting structures that assure continued remembrance. Hebbert (2005) focuses on streets and explains how a public space can be a locus of collective memory. Many studies on collective memory and urban space focus primarily on monumental landscapes, as monuments, memorials, and museums have proven to be fertile grounds for investigating places of memory (Till 2003; Jordan 2006; Henneberg and Clara 2004; Forest and Johnson 2002; Johnson 2002; Withers 1996). Stangl (2008) takes an alternative focus by considering the relationship between vernacular architecture and cultural memory. He argues that the vernacular and monumental are intertwined in urban space, sharing an ambiguous and fluid borderline. The distinction is significant in the analysis of how "some vernacular places become memorialized and some monumental places become vernacularized" (Stangl 2008: 251).

Recent research in different disciplines explores the political, cultural, spiritual, and socio-economic dynamics of what Crinson (2005) calls "urban memory." This term can be regarded as an expression of collective memory shaped within a particular space and time; thus, it expresses relations between the past and the present of a particular place (Ringas et al. 2011). As Srinivas (2001: xxv) suggests, urban memory provides a "means of accessing how various strata of society and different communities construct the metropolitan world". For Crinson and Tyrer, "modernism in architecture often seem[s] to erase memory from the city" (Crinson 2005: i); they chastise planners and developers for using memory "to aestheticize and co-opt the past into new forms of place-making" (Crinson 2005: 50). Maden and Temsiliyet (2009) follow Crinson's theory and propose that urban memory should be considered when making a planned design. Jorden (2006) focuses on the role of memory in Berlin's urban reconstruction and factors that influence forgetting and remembrance. Ekici (2007) views the complex relations between the urban manifestations of collective memory and contemporary architecture in Berlin. Jenks' article on Little Tokyo in Los Angeles addresses the issues of ethnic identity, urban space, and politics of collective memory (Rose-Redwood et al. 2008). Matten (2011) addresses the issues of national and cultural identity of China by applying Pierre Nora's approach "places of memory" (lieux de mémoire) to the Chinese context, and focuses on the most significant places of memory in modern and contemporary China. Blunt and Bonnerjee (2013) follows Srinivas' argument that different groups in a city create different landscapes of memory, highlighting the ways through which members of two minority communities living in London and Toronto remember Calcutta as home. Ringas and Christopoulou (2013) apply urban computing the three constituents of urban memory, namely, place, community, and infrastructure, in Corfu and Oulu, and present a survey of applications aimed to capture, preserve, and exploit urban memory as well as maintain and strengthen urban memory.

2.2.2 Elements of Urban Memory

The elements of urban memory differ according to different scholars. Rossi (1982) bases his view on the physical form of cities, looking for urban memory not in buildings but in the voids between them: Architecture, streets, squares, and monuments (large-scale architecture) are the important content embodying urban memory. Halbwachs ([1925] 1992) has called attention to the double nature of collective memory: first, the physical, pertaining to items in the material reality, such as statues, monuments, and places in space; and second, the symbolic, or objects of spiritual significance, including intangible resources shared by a group that adheres to and is superimposed upon the physical reality. Similar to Halbwachs, Nora's (1989) conception of lieux de mémoire (places of memory) highlights both material sites of memory, including burial places, cathedrals, battlefields, and prisons, as well as non-material sites of celebrations, spectacles, and rituals. Zhu (2005) adds the elements of subjective experience and time to urban memory, divided into corporal (participations in action), field and scenery (ambient and mental sensation of object characters), and symbolic elements (homonym, type, and landmark that emphasize the cultural experience of subjects). Alba (2012) takes Mexico City as a case study, using Halbwachs's notion of collective memory as theoretical framework, and summarizes the factors of urban memory: time [personal (life stages) and historical (city's past)], space (city, neighborhoods, areas or specific places), and groups (family and community context; education and job trajectory).

Other multi-disciplinary studies have explored the varied influence of urban memory. Kansteiner (2002) mentions three factors of collective memory: the intellectual and cultural traditions, memory makers, and memory consumers; his work gives a temporal dimension to collective memory. Bélanger (2002) and Mowla (2004) propose the idea that products of urban memory usually favor a small minority of elites; in other words, privileged groups are typically in a better position than others to propose their memory as the predominant urban memory. Postalcy et al. (2006) has considered the experiences of both inhabitants and observers as regards their effects on urban memory; he concludes that major changes in the physical or social environment can cause discontinuities and urban memory loss. After examining 200 sites in the greater Berlin area, Jordan (2006) reports that land use, land ownership, memorial entrepreneurs, and the broader public resonance are deterministic factors in the emergence of a memorable place. Lahiri (2011) adopts a multi-sensory approach to study trans-local urban memories, finding that the sensory factors influencing urban memory encompass visual, smell, sound, and taste. Based on traditional symbols suggested by Mowla (2004), Othman (2013) proposes that the influencing factors of memory toward place making can be divided into three components: individual or group, physical (demographic, socioeconomic status, location, and scale [spatial attributes]), and social factors (geographical perspectives, place experiences).

Based on the literature review, urban memory can be divided into three elements: subjective, objective, and time elements. Among them, the subjective elements serves as the producer of urban memory; the objective ones are the remembered memories of urban memory; and the time elements include the influential elements of urban memory.

2.2.3 *Historic Areas in Beijing*

Beijing is a city with a history of more than 3000 years. It has been China's capital for 850 years. The city features a well-preserved architecture system and square road network, and it was regarded as a "brilliant work of urban planning in ancient China" (Liang 1986: 51). American urban planner (Bacon 1974: 232) has described Beijing as "possibly the greatest single work of man on the face of the earth." Since its establishment under the Yuan Dynasty, the city has accumulated a wealth of cultural and historical resources.

Since the establishment of the People's Republic of China, research on historic areas in Beijing has undergone dramatic progress in theoretical innovation and practical attempt. In the 1950s, renowned architects Sicheng Liang and Zhanxiang Chen carried out a scientific planning of Beijing, claiming that "Beijing City is an entity with planning as a whole" (Liang 1986: 62), and proposed the protection of the old city. After Liang, his student Liangyong Wu continued to develop and improve the theory and practice of protecting historic areas in Beijing. Based on different theories of urban development and historic protection, combined with the situation in Beijing, Wu proposed the primary theory of "organic regeneration" in the planning and research of the Shichahai District, a historical and cultural scenic area in Beijing, which is also a conservation district of historic sites, in 1979. The theory was implemented in the successful renovation of old residences at Ju'er Hutong in 1987. Since then, many Chinese scholars have entered the field and produced varied results (Zhang 1996; Wang 1998; Fang 2000; Liu 2006). This issue has also attracted international scholars. Abramson (1998) studies the conflict between protection and development in old Beijing City from the perspective of cultural research, stressing the importance of cultural awareness. Broudehoux (2004) and Zhang (2008) analyze Beijing's urban conservation policies and suggest that such policies should be closely related to the promotion of urban growth. Abramson (2007) considers the practice of "protecting" designated historic structures by clearing the space around them. Further, he claims that the dependence on a totalizing bird's-eye view to define Beijing's overall characteristic form produces a city-wide preservation policy that is particularly ill equipped to accommodate change. Whitehand and Gu (2007) apply a type of morphological approach developed by M.R.G. Conzen to the protection of a historical area in Beijing; this endeavor emphasizes the historic–geographical environments in which historical sites, structures, and spaces exist. Heath and Tang (2010), Abramson (2001), Goldman (2003), and Stone (2008) study the development process of protection policies in Beijing, proposing appropriate strategies for protecting and regenerating Beijing's hutongs and old residences in the context of globalization.

2.3 Research Design and Data Collection

2.3.1 Study Sample

The historic areas in Beijing are the most important carriers of the city's memory, the protection of which has developed from single architectural pieces to architectural clusters, from the old city to the entire city domain. The current protection policies emphasize a comprehensive vision concerning the connection of the core and outskirts of the old city. The present research will expand the scope to the entire domain of Beijing, study its historic areas as a whole, and then reflect its collectiveness as carriers of urban memory. The selection of specific historical locations is determined via initial collection, secondary screening, and case sampling. After the screening, 367 historical locations are chosen, and their basic properties, including spatial characteristics (geographic location), temporal characteristics (age), degree of heritage protection, scale and scope, and functional features, are quantified to form a basic information database. Based on this, the research uses stratified proportional sampling combined with moderate Delphi method to select sampling cases from the database. The selection of samples covers all types of spatial, temporal, and functional characters seen in the selected historical cases. The selection also considers the reflection of experts. Finally, 19 historic sites within the domain of Beijing City are confirmed as study areas (Table 2.1). The following research will take these 19 areas as examples to study the urban memory of historic areas in Beijing.

2.3.2 Establishment of Measurement Scale

Based on the literature review of urban memory, combined with studies on historic areas in Beijing, analysis of Internet resources, and on-site interviews, the research proposes a set of scales of universal significance to measure urban memory. In this sense, urban memory comprises four level-one variables (subjective elements, mainly about the memorizer; objective elements, mainly about the memory carrier; time elements; and impact elements). Further, 10 level-two and 45 level-three variables are considered (Table 2.2).

2.3.3 Design of the Questionnaire and Investigation

According to the previous proposed measurement scale for urban memory, the questionnaire in this study contains the following: investigation and survey of the historic areas (16 factors); evaluation survey of historic areas (16 factors); time and memory investigations (5 factors), and personal information.

Table 2.1 Sampling of selected historic areas (*Source* ©Authors)

Time	Core area	Function	Expansion area	Function	Outer suburbs	Function
Yuan (1206–1368) Dynasty and Earlier	Nan Luoguxiang	Common residence	The summer palace Babacshan revolutionary cemetery	Royal palace Cultural-memorial site	The ming tombs	Royal tombs
Ming (1368–1644) and Qing (1644–1912) Dynasties	The palace museum	Royal palace			Cuandixia ancient buildings	Ancient towns and villages
	Bell and drum towers	Royal services				
	Shichahai	Common residence				
	Temple of heaven	Royal ritual site				
	Tian'an men	Cultural landmark				
	Dashilar commercials	Daily services				
	Mansion of the prince of Gong	Officials and nobles' mansions				
	City Wall in Ming Dynasty	Cultural heritage				
The Republic of China (1912–1949)	Former site of DuanQirui government	Administration and governance	Weiming Lake and Yan Yuan architectures	Education and research	Tanzhe temple	Cultural-religious site
Modern	Chen Duxiu's former residence	Former residence of celebrities				
	Cultural palace of the nationalities	Daily services	Modern architectures in 798 art zone	Industry and manufacturing		

Table 2.2 Measurement scale for urban memory based on historic areas in Beijing (*Source* ©Authors)

Level-one variables	Level-two variables	Level-three variables	Five-level evaluation/ Investigation survey				
Subjective	Retaining elements	Overall evaluation	1	2	3	4	5
		Protection value	1	2	3	4	5
		Urban-style promotion	1	2	3	4	5
		Hindrance to modernization	1	2	3	4	5
		Positive effects of demolition	1	2	3	4	5
	Characteristic elements	Urban culture inheritance	1	2	3	4	5
		Important part of Beijing	1	2	3	4	5
		Important city characters	1	2	3	4	5
		Deepen understanding of the city	1	2	3	4	5
		Better understanding of traditional culture	1	2	3	4	5
		Need for renewal	1	2	3	4	5
	Renewal elements	Overall impression after renewal	1	2	3	4	5
		Embodiment of original appearance after renewal	1	2	3	4	5
		Bearing original culture after renewal	1	2	3	4	5
		Continuation of original function after renewal	1	2	3	4	5
		Urban-style promotion after renewal	1	2	3	4	5
		Positive effects of urban development after renewal	1	2	3	4	5
Objective	Static elements	Location	1	2	3	4	5
		Surroundings	1	2	3	4	5
		Building form	1	2	3	4	5
		Traditional spatial pattern	1	2	3	4	5
		Representative buildings	1	2	3	4	5
		Cultural relic	1	2	3	4	5
		Protection level	1	2	3	4	5
	Evolution elements	Change of name	1	2	3	4	5
		Change of usage	1	2	3	4	5
		Renewal planning	1	2	3	4	5
		Change of style	1	2	3	4	5
	Temporal elements	Historical celebrities and events	1	2	3	4	5
		Backgrounds and anecdotes	1	2	3	4	5
		Historical function	1	2	3	4	5
		Former name	1	2	3	4	5
		Origin of name	1	2	3	4	5

(continued)

Table 2.2 (continued)

Level-one variables	Level-two variables	Level-three variables	Five-level evaluation/ Investigation survey
Time	Point of time	Festival activities	Investigation/Interview
		Renewal planning implementation	Investigation/Interview
		Significant events	Investigation/Interview
	Time section	Remarkable period	Investigation/Interview
		Declining period	Investigation/Interview
	Time axis	Building age	Investigation/Interview
		Dynasties survived	Investigation/Interview
Impact elements	Subjective properties	Residential time	Investigation/Interview
		Access to information	Investigation/Interview
		Degree of familiarity	Investigation/Interview
		Educational background	Investigation/Interview
		Per capita income	Investigation/Interview

The formal questionnaire survey was conducted from April 21 to May 9, 2011, including field research and Internet survey. A total of 419 questionnaires (including 103 online questionnaires) were handed out; 382 of the collected ones were valid, accounting for a 91.1 % validity ratio. By utilizing both field and online research, the survey reached a relative balance in the properties of memorizers studied. Field survey respondents were mainly the elderly in residential areas, with relatively low education and categorized under the long-term memory group; meanwhile, the online survey respondents were those able to use a computer, relatively of a younger age and with higher education, including a certain number of students. The two programs complemented each other in ensuring the diversity and balance of respondents' backgrounds in age, education, income, living experience, access to information, and other aspects.

After the questionnaires were recovered, a statistics process of the data was carried out using Excel 2007 and SPSS 16.0 for Windows. The data processing methods include descriptive statistics, modeling calculations, and correlation analysis (Pearson).

2.4 Measurement Methods for Urban Memory

This section mainly measures the urban memory of historic areas in Beijing from three dimensions: subjective, objective, and time elements.

2.4.1 Measurement of the Subjective Elements of Urban Memory

Using a Likert scale with five grades as measurement system, the research introduces subjective evaluation values (EVs) to measure the degree of subjective memory. The memory degrees for each individual surveyed can be obtained according to Formula 2.1 Integrated EVs on the issue can be reached by adding up all the EVs on the indicator from all memorizers (the total number in N). The EV value ranges from 0 to 1: a bigger value indicates a higher evaluation level. For convenience in analysis, the EV is primarily classified as follows: $0 \leq EV < 0.4$ is low, $0.4 \leq EV < 0.7$ is medium, and $0.7 \leq EV \leq 1$ is high (but these are not as stringent standards).

$$EV = \sum_{i=1}^{n} \frac{a_i - 1}{4n} \tag{2.1}$$

Formula 2.1: Subjective EV

In the formula, n is the number of samples of the research and a is the points given by the individuals in the sample (using 0–5 points).

2.4.2 Measurement of the Objective Elements of Urban Memory

Using a Likert scale with five grades as measurement system, the research introduces urban memory cognitive (UMC) to measure the degree of objective memory of the city. Memory degrees for each individual surveyed are obtained according to Formula 2.2. An integrated UMC on this issue is determined by adding up all the UMCs on the indicator from all memorizers (the total number in N). For convenience in analysis, the UMC is primarily classified as follows: $0 \leq UMC < 0.4$ is low, $0.4 \leq UMC < 0.7$ is medium, and $0.7 \leq UMC \leq 1$ is high (not stringent standards).

$$\begin{gathered} UMC = \sum_{i=1}^{n} \frac{b_i - 1}{4N} \\ Single\text{−Choice: } \mathrm{b_i} = \mathrm{a_i} \\ Mulitple\text{−Choice: } \mathrm{b_i} = \sum_{\mathrm{i}=1}^{\mathrm{k}} \frac{2\mathrm{a_i}}{\mathrm{iK}} + 3 \quad \mathrm{UMC} = 0\ (\mathrm{Null}) \end{gathered} \tag{2.2}$$

Formula 2.2: Objective UMC

In the above formula, n is the number of sampling, $n = 1, 2, 3, \ldots, N$; a is the points given by the individuals in the sample (using 0–5 points); and K is the number of multiple-choice items.

2.4.3 Measurement of the Time Elements of Urban Memory

Similar to the measurement of objective elements in urban memory, the UMC indicator is used to measure the time elements, as shown in Formula 2.3.

$$\mathrm{UMC} = \sum_{i=1}^{n} \frac{a_i - 1}{4n} \tag{2.3}$$

Formula 2.3: Time elements in UMC

In Formula 2.3, n is the number of samples, and a is the points given by the sample.

2.5 Applications of the Measurement of Urban Memory

This study is mainly focused on the empirical measurement of urban memory levels in Beijing historic sites. Using SPSS to analyze the urban memory level of 19 historic areas, this research identifies five main factors related to the urban memory of the historic areas under review. According to these main factors, a cluster analysis of the 19 historic areas is conducted, thereby classifying the historic areas in Beijing into five categories. This chapter summarizes the memory type of different historic areas, as well as the influencing factors of each type, as a reference to the protection measure of different types of historic areas.

2.5.1 Abstraction of Main Factors in Urban Memory

Urban memory data of the 19 historic areas (including UMC and EV) from the questionnaire and data processing are imported to SPSS 19.0. Using principal component analysis, a factor analysis is carried out for the urban memory level from 38 different elements of the 19 historic sites. The first round of KMO values is greater than 0.5, which indicates data fitness with factor analysis. Using principal component analysis, and by rotating the rotary component matrix for better results, the 38 different factors are reduced to five main factors. These five factors can succinctly explain 81.744 % of the historical memory of the city.

The above analysis gives the five principal factors as regards the urban memory level of historical sites in Beijing. According to the descriptive elements of urban memory in each of the factors, they are explained as follows.

Main Factor 1: Objective Dynamic Memory factor
This factor mainly includes urban memory elements related to object information in historic areas. Apart from static elements, such as location, vicinity, and

architecture style, the factor also includes dynamic information on the development and change of the historic areas, such as functional evolution, style changes, previously used name, and name replacement; therefore, factors of this type are used to describe residents' memory of the objective information of historic areas, which emphasize the memory formed in the process of development and changes. Thus, this factor is called Objective Dynamic Memory.

Main Factor 2: Integrated Characteristic Memory factor
This factor is from the comprehensive point of view as a descriptive factor of the urban memory of residents, mainly on their awareness in such aspects as the protection value of a historical area as a whole, cultural elements, important features, and importance as a cultural heritage of Beijing. This awareness is based on the cultural features and completeness of historic areas in Beijing. Thus, the term Integrated Characteristic Memory factor is used.

Main Factor 3: Continuous Time Memory factor
This factor includes elements on information on the urban memory level described in three dimensions: time axis, time period, and point of time. Specifically, these factors relate to the major events, prosperity, and decay of historical areas, as well as age of the area and dynasties survived. The survey not only investigates the formation of urban memory on a certain time point but also emphasizes the continuous memory formed throughout the development history of a historic area. Thus, the term Continuous Time Memory factor is used.

Main Factor 4: Lasting Retained Memory factor
This factor mainly focuses on citizens' attitude toward a historic area based on their perception regarding an area's positive effect on Beijing's development, including whether certain areas should be demolished.

Main Factor 5: Protection Renewal Memory factor
From the perspective of sustainable development of historic areas in future Beijing, this factor mainly includes the evaluation factor after the regeneration of a historic area, such as whether it reflects the original style, embraces the cultural context, continues the original function of the area, and offers a positive effect on the development of the area.

2.5.2 Classification of Historic Areas in Beijing Based on Urban Memory Measurement

According to the results of the principal factor analysis, the research uses Objective Dynamic Memory, Integrated Characteristic Memory, Continuous Time Memory, Lasting Retained Memory, and Protection Renewal Memory factors as the five main factors to describe the urban memory level in historic areas in Beijing. Subsequently, further study is conducted on the classification of urban memory features carried by historic areas. The method of classification is based on SPSS 19.0 classification software, taking the scores in five main factors of 19 historical areas as the fundamental matrix, with hierarchical clustering method, group average method, and cosine and Z-score transformation standardized method. The 19 historic areas are classified into five categories according to the vertical icicle diagram (Fig. 2.1) and cluster dendrogram (Fig. 2.2) drawn from the results of the analysis.

The average points of each historic area category is obtained based on the factor analysis scores for the five main factors of each historic area, as shown in Table 2.3.

Fig. 2.1 Factors in a cluster vertical icicle diagram (*Source* ©Authors)

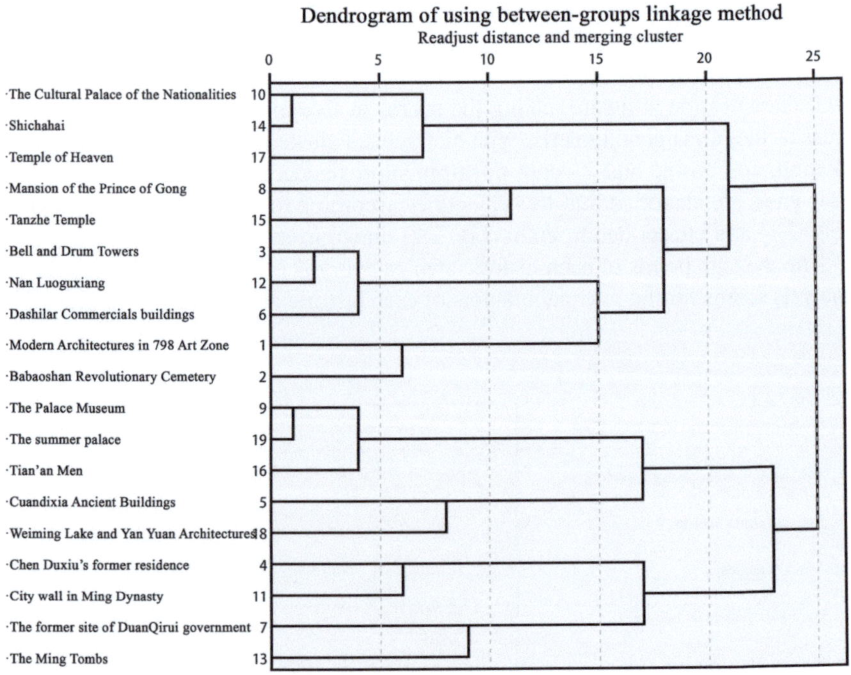

Fig. 2.2 Factors in a cluster analysis dendrogram (*Source* ©Authors)

After the scores of historic sites from five categories are obtained, the dataset needs to be standardized to determine the factor characteristics (as shown in Table 2.4). The values in the standardized factor scores average sheet are designated as high, medium, and low as follows: $1.5398 \geq X * ij > 0.8$ is high, $0.8000 \geq X * ij > -0.8000$ is medium, and $-0.8 \geq X * ij \geq -1.5807$ is low. This scale helps simplify the expression of the various factors on the features of diffident historic areas.

2.5.3 *Summary of the Classification of Historic Areas in Beijing*

Based on the factor-cluster analysis of historic areas in Beijing, the rules on the urban memory level in the five categories of historic areas can be concluded. Using Pearson's correlation analysis, the research analyzes the influence elements on these historic areas to provide bases for the protection and renewal of historic areas.

Table 2.3 Scores for the five main factors of historic areas in Beijing (*Source* ©Authors)

Categories	Historic areas	Objective dynamic	Integrated characteristic	Continuous time	Lasting retained	Protection renewal
I Objective dynamic memory factor	Cultural palace of the nationalities	0.65652	−0.69978	−1.07525	0.20385	−2.66136
	Shichahai	0.45636	−0.35992	−0.39522	0.18373	−0.68899
	Temple of heaven	0.90955	−0.00384	−0.95404	−0.98573	−0.72881
	Average	0.6741	−0.3545	−0.8082	−0.1994	−1.3597
II Integrated characteristic memory factor	Mansion of the prince of Gong	0.26732	0.27128	−0.36513	−0.03416	0.07211
	Tanzhe temple	−1.83616	2.10908	−1.9016	−0.05788	0.97729
	Average	−0.7844	1.1902	−1.1334	−0.0460	0.5247
III Continuous time memory factor	Modern architectures in 798 art zone	−0.41248	−1.61375	−0.57075	1.45087	0.83233
	Babaoshan revolutionary cemetery	0.02311	−0.84654	−1.26121	0.55782	−0.12869
	Bell and drum towers	0.18322	0.72553	−0.30763	1.04112	0.33276
	Dashilar commercials	1.05236	0.07331	−0.21331	1.27409	0.53903
	Nan Luoguxiang	0.17058	0.29341	0.12993	1.33914	0.57454
	Average	0.2034	−0.2736	−0.4446	1.1326	0.4300
IV Lasting retained memory factor	Cuandixia ancient buildings	−0.23667	−1.99886	−0.49957	−2.51267	1.63142
	The palace museum	0.79614	0.98499	0.9979	−0.20573	0.60173
	Tian'an men	0.01252	0.81538	0.87111	−0.26428	0.62984
	Weiming lake and Yan Yuan architectures	1.03552	−0.28259	0.24952	−0.68273	0.79813
	The summer palace	1.28949	0.5028	1.05316	−0.09888	0.33464
	Average	0.5794	0.0043	0.5344	−0.7529	0.7992
V Protection renewal memory factor	Chen Duxiu's former residence	−2.28931	−0.55756	0.92498	0.07517	−0.21109
	The former site of the DuanQirui government	−1.46605	0.46844	0.15302	−0.7967	−1.45855
	City wall in ming dynasty	−0.91721	−1.04065	2.25073	0.84532	−0.47503
	The ming tombs	0.30508	1.15924	0.91337	−1.33239	−0.9713
	Average	−1.0919	0.0074	1.0605	−0.3022	−0.7790

Table 2.4 Highest and lowest scores for the five main factors of historic areas in Beijing (standardized) (*Source* ©Authors)

Categories	Objective dynamic 1	Integrated characteristic 2	Continuous time 3	Lasting retained 4	Protection renewal 5
I	1.216184 (high)	0.187527 (medium)	−0.26613 (medium)	0.342657 (medium)	*−0.81768 (low)*
II	−0.77638 (medium)	1.310429 (high)	*−1.14516 (low)*	0.003979 (medium)	0.607131 (medium)
III	−0.00989 (medium)	−0.77318 (medium)	*−1.0468 (low)*	1.477113 (high)	0.352756 (medium)
IV	0.555644 (medium)	−0.36649 (medium)	0.483523 (medium)	*−1.58071 (low)*	0.908029 (high)
V	*−1.04633 (low)*	0.274414 (medium)	1.53979 (high)	−0.09747 (medium)	−0.6704 (medium)

2.5.3.1 Summaries on the Rules on the Urban Memory Level in the Five Categories of Historic Areas

The rules on the urban memory level in the five categories of historic areas are as follows: memory of Preserving Elements, Characteristic Elements, Renewal Elements, Static Elements, Evolutionary Elements, Temporal Elements, and memory upon Point of Time, Time Section, and Time Axis (Fig. 2.3). The specific rules for these memories are shown in Table 2.5 (using standardized data on urban memory level).

Through the above summary of urban memory levels in historic areas under five categories, the different characteristics in the urban memory of Beijing can be obtained. For each category, different strategies for future protection and specific aspects for continuing urban memory can be proposed according to the different elements of urban memory considered as high, low, or medium. The applicable rules for nine main elements are compared, which yields the following features:

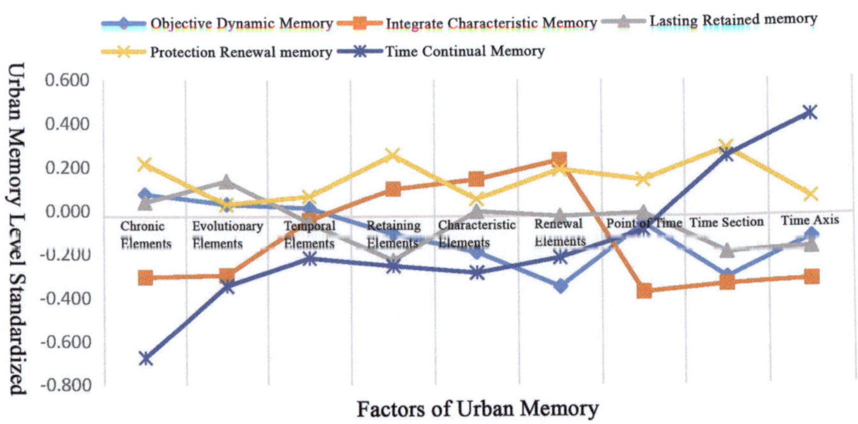

Fig. 2.3 Comparison of rules on the urban memory level of historic areas under five categories (*Source* ©Authors)

Table 2.5 Rules on the urban memory in five categories of historic areas in nine main elements (*Source* ©Authors)

Categories	Static elements	Evolutionary elements	Temporal elements	Retaining elements	Characteristic elements	Renewal elements	Point of time	Time section	Time axis
Objective dynamic	0.077	0.030	0.011	−0.108	−0.192	−0.350	−0.062	−0.308	−0.130
Integrated characteristic	−0.304	−0.296	−0.043	0.100	0.143	0.231	−0.376	−0.339	−0.324
Lasting retained	0.039	0.137	−0.056	−0.229	−0.004	−0.027	−0.014	−0.192	−0.175
Protection renewal	0.217	0.029	0.066	0.255	0.053	0.188	0.139	0.285	0.057
Continuous time	−0.674	−0.344	−0.218	−0.254	−0.285	−0.217	−0.091	0.249	0.431

(1) **Overall rule**
From the perspective of the overall level of urban memory, the Protection Renewal Memory factor ranks the highest, with scores generally higher compared with other types of historical districts. The Objective Dynamic Memory and Lasting Retained Memory factors rank the lowest, garnering negative scores in certain items.

(2) **Balanced rule**
From the perspective of even distribution of urban memory scores among different elements, Protection Renewal Memory and Lasting Retained Memory factors are relatively balanced in distribution with little fluctuation. Meanwhile, the factors of Objective Dynamic Memory, Integrated Characteristic Memory, and Continuous Time Memory are not evenly distributed. For example, the Continuous Time Memory factor of historic areas ranks the highest (0.431) in the elements of Time Axis but lowest in Static, Evolutionary, and Temporal Elements (−0.674, −0.344, and −0.218, respectively).

(3) **Rules for each element**
Objective Elements: A distinct difference is seen in the high and low points in the urban memory level of five categories of historic areas. The Continuous Time Memory and Integrate Characteristic Memory factors score low in the three sub-elements of Objective elements ([−0.674, −0.344, −0.218] and [−0.304, −0.296, −0.043], respectively); the other three categories are higher on the Objective Element Memory level, mostly larger than 0. Objective Dynamic Memory factor scores are 0.077, 0.030, and 0.011, whereas Protection Renewal Memory factor scores are 0.217, 0.029, and 0.066.
Subjective Elements: Among the scores for all five categories of historic sites in three sub-elements of the Subjective Elements, Integrated Characteristic Memory (0.100, 0.143, 0.231) and Protection Renewal Memory factors (0.255, 0.053, 0.188) score the highest. Meanwhile, Continuous Time Memory factor scores the lowest (−0.254, −0.285, −0.217).
Time Elements: Three sub-elements of the Time Element of urban memory show a significant level of difference. Continuous Time Memory (−0.091, 0.249, 0.431) and Protection Renewal Memory factors (0.139, 0.285, 0.057) have the highest scores. The overall characteristics memory shows negative scores (−0.376, −0.339, −0.324), and the other two also score low, with negative values between −0.014 and −0.308.

2.5.3.2 Analysis of Influence Factors on Urban Memory in Five Categories of Historic Areas

The analysis of historic areas in five categories on memory related to Preserving, Characteristic, Renewal, Static, Evolutionary, and Temporal Elements, as well as memory at a Point of Time, Time Section, and Time Axis, is combined with the residents' attribute information. This process generates the relevant influential factors toward the major urban memory for different types of historic areas.

(1) **Type I, Historic Areas with Objective Dynamic Memory**
According to the cluster analysis results, the most salient features (including static, evolutionary, and temporal elements) of historic areas with Object Dynamic Memory are chosen for the analysis of the influential factors (as shown in Table 2.6). The main factors influencing Objective Dynamic Memory is the residents' access to information related to a historical area, where the static elements and information access correlate at the 0.05 level of significance (bilateral), whereas evolutionary elements and information access are significantly related at the 0.01 level (bilateral). These findings indicate that information from life experiences supports the formation of Objective Dynamic Memory.

(2) **Type II, Historic Areas with Integrated Characteristic Memory**
For historic areas with Integrated Characteristic Memory, the most salient features (including the historical cultural elements, important characteristics, and understanding of Beijing's culture) are chosen to analyze the influential factors (as shown in Table 2.7). The main factors influencing urban memory in these historic areas are the age structure of the population, which significantly correlates at the 0.05 level (bilateral) with a Pearson's correlation coefficient of 0.276, in other words, the older the residents, the more profound their Integrated Characteristic Memory.

Table 2.6 Analysis of influencing factors on urban memory of historic areas with objective dynamic memory

Objective dynamic memory		Age	Duration of residence in Beijing	Degree of familiarity	Access to information	Education background	Per capita income
Static elements	Pearson correlation	−0.059	0.145	0.032	**0.302** (*)	0.197	0.092
	Significance (bilateral)	0.677	0.304	0.824	0.030	0.161	0.515
	N	52	52	52	52	52	52
Evolutionary elements	Pearson correlation	−0.102	0.052	0.192	**0.367** (**)	−0.002	−0.013
	Significance (bilateral)	0.473	0.715	0.173	0.007	0.987	0.927
	N	52	52	52	52	52	52
Temporal elements	Pearson correlation	−0.155	−0.087	−0.014	0.226	0.119	0.050
	Significance (bilateral)	0.274	0.541	0.922	0.107	0.400	0.727
	N	52	52	52	52	52	52

* significant of the correlation coefficient
** extremely significant of the correlation coefficient

Table 2.7 Analysis of influencing factors in urban memory of historic areas with integrated characteristic memory (*Source* ©Authors)

Integrated characteristic memory	Age	Duration of residence in Beijing	Degree of familiarity	Access to information	Education background	Per capita income
Pearson correlation	**0.276** (*)	0.166	0.177	0.049	−0.027	−0.172
Significance (bilateral)	0.047	0.241	0.208	0.732	0.849	0.223
N	52	52	52	52	52	52

* significant of the correlation coefficient

(3) **Type III: Historical Area with Lasting Retained Memory**
For historic areas with Lasting Retained Memory, the most salient features (including whether to retain areas, influence of demolition, and necessity of reconstruction) are chosen to analyze the influential factors (as shown in Table 2.8). The main factors influencing the urban memory in these historic areas are mainly the age structure of the residents, which significantly correlates at the 0.05 level (bilateral) with a Pearson's correlation coefficient of 0.314; that is, the older the residents, the more profound the Lasting Retained Memory.

(4) **Type IV: Historical Area with Protection Renewal Memory**
For historic areas with Protection Renewal Memory, the most salient features (including whether renovations reflect the original appearance, whether the original culture is preserved, and whether the original function is preserved) are chosen to analyze the influential factors (as shown in Table 2.9). The main factors influencing the urban memory in these historic areas are the level of education and average income of residents, which significantly correlate negatively at the 0.1 and 0.05 levels (bilateral) with a Pearson's correlation coefficient of −0.357 and −0.296, respectively. In other words, low education and average income levels produce less awareness in memory continuity of protected and renewed historic areas.

(5) **Type V: Historical Area with Continuous Time Memory**
For historic areas with Continuous Time Memory, the most salient features (including point of time, time section, and time axis) are chosen for the analysis of influential factors (as shown in Table 2.10). The influencing main

Table 2.8 Analysis of influencing factor in urban memory of historic areas with Lasting Retained Memory (*Source* ©Authors)

Lasting retained memory	Age	Duration of residence in Beijing	Degree of familiarity	Access to information	Education background	Per capita income
Pearson correlation	**0.314** (*)	0.157	0.014	0.039	0.052	−0.104
Significance (bilateral)	0.024	0.266	0.922	0.782	0.715	0.465
N	52	52	52	52	52	52

* significant of the correlation coefficient

Table 2.9 Analysis of influencing factor in urban memory of historic areas with protection renewal memory (*Source* ©Authors)

Protection renewal memory	Age	Duration of residence in Beijing	Degree of familiarity	Access to information	Education background	Per capita income
Pearson correlation	0.081	−0.027	0.177	0.232	**−0.357 (**)**	**−0.296 (*)**
Significance (bilateral)	0.570	0.847	0.208	0.097	0.009	0.033
N	52	52	52	52	52	52

* significant of the correlation coefficient
** extremely significant of the correlation coefficient

factors are the level of education and familiarity with Beijing, which significantly correlate negatively at the 0.1 and 0.05 level (bilateral), that is, the more the residents are familiar with Beijing, the higher the understanding of the historic area and urban memory level.

2.5.4 *Discussion of Protection and Renewal Strategies of Historic Areas in Beijing*

Based on the analysis of rules for the urban memory related to historic areas in Beijing, as well as the classification of historic areas and analysis of influential factors, the article concludes that existing information on research in historic areas serve as guide to the protection and renewal strategy of historic areas in Beijing (Table 2.11).

Table 2.10 Analysis of influencing factor in urban memory of historic areas with continuous time memory (*Source* ©Authors)

Continuous Time memory		Age	Duration of residence in Beijing	Degree of familiarity	Access to information	Education background	Per capita income
Point of time	Pearson correlation	−0.133	−0.020	**0.303 (*)**	0.139	0.235	0.151
	Significance (bilateral)	0.347	0.887	0.029	0.326	0.093	0.286
	N	52	52	52	52	52	52
Time section	Pearson correlation	0.031	0.135	**0.307 (*)**	0.101	0.103	0.087
	Significance (bilateral)	0.829	0.340	0.027	0.474	0.469	0.539
	N	52	52	52	52	52	52
Time axis	Pearson correlation	−0.157	0.161	0.099	0.111	**0.275 (*)**	0.176
	Significance (bilateral)	0.268	0.254	0.486	0.434	0.049	0.213
	N	52	52	52	52	52	52

* significant of the correlation coefficient

Table 2.11 Summary of features of and influential factors on urban memory of historic areas in Beijing (*Source* ©Authors)

Type		Features of urban memory		Influential factors	Typical area
		Strongest	Weakest		
I	Objective dynamic memory	Static elements	Renewal evaluation	Access to information	Shichahai
		Evolutionary elements	Time section		
		Temporal elements	Time axis		
II	Integrated characteristic memory	Characteristic elements	Objective elements	Age structure	Tanzhe temple
		Renewal elements	Time elements		
III	Lasting retained memory factor	Static elements	Subjective Elements Time elements	Age structure	Nan Luoguxiang
		Evolutionary elements			
		Temporal elements			
IV	Protection renewal memory	Static elements	Evolutionary elements	Education Income	Weiming lake and Yan Yuan
		Preserving elements	Characteristic elements		
		Time section	Time axis		
V	Continuous time memory	Static elements	Point of time	Education Familiarity	City wall in ming Dynasty
		Evolutionary elements	Time section		
		Temporal elements	Time axis		

Based on the summary of the characteristics of historic areas, different strategies for the continued, specific, and differential protection schemes in the renewal and regeneration of historic areas are chosen, according to the strongest and weakest features and other influential factors at the urban memory level. In the following part, three out of the five categories of historic areas are discussed in detail:

(1) **Type I, Historic Areas with Objective Dynamic Memory**

Memory Features: The Objective Dynamic Memory (Static, Evolutionary, and Temporal Elements) are the leading factors in the preservation of urban memory.

Protection Strategy: Focus on the protection of Objective Dynamic Memory, especially protecting weak memory elements, such as time section and time axis, and innovation for differentiated conservation strategies with respect to residents' access to information.

Fig. 2.4 Coordination between modern enterprises and the original cultural atmosphere (*Source* ©Authors)

Protection Example: The Shichahai Historical and Cultural Protection Area (Figs. 2.4 and 2.5).

Continuing Protection: Controlling and protecting features in the overall style of historic areas; coordinating between modern businesses and the original cultural atmosphere.

Specific Protection: Combining the new and existing functional features in Shichahai; planning special festival activities; continuing the original cultural context; carrying out the "Cool Summer," "Water Village in the North," "Former residence of celebrities," and other themed festival activities; and based on existing function, carrying out themed festival activities, such as "Music Bar" and "Creative Culture".

Differential Protection: Increasing people's experience by organizing festival activities; improving the interpretation system related with object information and time clues within the historical area to enhance the experiences of residents from their own perspective.

Fig. 2.5 Shichahai ice stadium (*Source* ©Authors)

(2) **Type II, Historic Areas with Integrated Characteristic Memory**

Memory features: Integrated Characteristic Memory components (memory of Characteristic and Renewal Elements) as the leading factors in the preservation of urban memory.

Protection strategy: Preserving Integrated Characteristic Memory, especially protecting weak memory elements, such as Objective and Time Elements; carrying out differentiated protection based on residents' age structure.

Protection example: The Tanzhe Temple.

Continuing Protection: Protecting and maintaining the overall features and important cultural factors within the historic area to continue the citizens' consensus of Tanzhe Temple as a carrier of urban memory in Beijing.

Specific Protection: Paying special attention to the weak memory elements, such as object and time factors, and controlling the overall style of Tanzhe Temple; through heritage interpretation, enhancing people's recognition of Objective Elements, including Static, Evolutionary, and Temporal Elements, as well as the recognition of major events on point of time, time period, and time axis, such as the overall architectural style and built age (Mandarin: Xi Jin), development (relationship with Buddhism, historical events "Suppression of Buddhism," important characters in history [place where Kublai Khan's daughter got married]).

Differential Protection: Protection and renovation should pay attention to a balance between the preferences among people from different age groups.

(3) **Type III: Historical Area with Lasting Retained Memory**

Memory features: Lasting Retained Memory and Objective Dynamic Memory in good condition (which should be preserved and have positive influence on the urban style of Beijing) as the leading factors in the preservation of urban memory.

Protection Strategy: Maintain the Integrated Characteristic Memory of the preserved historic area; protect weak memory elements, such as subjective evaluation and time elements; carry out differentiated protection based on residents' age structure.

Protection Example: Historical Area of Nan Luoguxiang (Figs. 2.6 and 2.7).

Continuing Protection: Continuing the characteristics of the overall style in the Nan Luoguxiang historical area; strengthening the public's retained synchronic cognition of Nan Luoguxiang and memory of Beijing culture carried by objects.

Fig. 2.6 Nan Luoguxiang memorial archway (*Source* ©Authors)

Fig. 2.7 Chinese scholar tree and traditional architecture (*Source* ©Authors)

Specific Protection: According to the weak memory features of subjective evaluation and time elements, through heritage interpretation, enhance the overall character of the area and important elements, as well as improve the interpretation and popularity of information and major events of time points, time period, and time axis. For example, the "fish skeleton" layout of streets and lanes in Nan Luoguxiang, functions in history "Market in the Back," story about its name (before Qing Dynasty called Luo Guoxiang, also known as the Wugong Xiang).

Differential Protection: Combine the new characteristic into business functions; protection and renewal should pay attention to balance the preferences of people from different age groups.

2.6 Conclusion and Discussion

In the context of globalization and rapid urbanization in China, how do we protect and preserve the rich memory of urban historic areas in fast-changing cities? What are the factors influencing the continuity of urban memory features? What are the elements comprising urban memory, and how can their relative importance be determined? Finally, how can these theories be applied to the maintenance and development of urban memory? This study uses a selection of 367 historic areas within the domain of Beijing in a basic database and 19 typical areas as samples, and then establishes the framework of measurement and application of urban memory of historic areas in Beijing to form a comprehensive method and theoretic guidelines for the preservation of historic areas and continuity of urban memory. The study has reached the following two conclusions:

(1) This work identifies five major categories of urban memory related to historic areas in Beijing, namely, Objective Dynamic Memory, Integrate Characteristic Memory, Continuous Time Memory, Lasting Retained Memory, and Protection Renewal Memory factors.
(2) Based on the extraction of five main factors, the sample historic areas are divided into five major categories. The research summarized the rules and

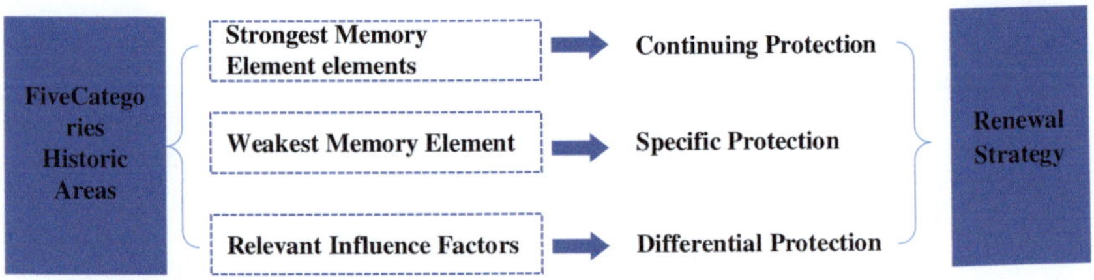

Fig. 2.8 Renewal strategy of historic areas under five categories (*Source* ©Authors)

influencing factors for urban memory in each category, as a reference to historical continuing, specified, and differential protection (Fig. 2.8).

Historic areas are the carriers of physical and mental cultural information. The study on the measurement of urban memory reveals the underlying essence beneath the phenomenon, thus providing a scientific guide to the determination of crucial elements in the protection and renewal of historic areas. The study reflects the features and properties of historic areas per se. In practical planning, a guidance and protective planning project can be created based on the existing memory features. The protection method based on the urban memory measurement proposed in this research is of universal significance, which could serve as a reference to the protection of other historic areas.

Acknowledgment This article is supported by the National Natural Science Foundation of China (Grant No. 51078003).

References

Abramson DB (1998) Neighborhood redevelopment as a cultural problem: a western perspective on current plans for the old city of Beijing. Architectural J 2:014

Abramson DB (2001) Beijing's preservation policy and the fate of the Siheyuan. Tradit Dwellings Settlements Rev 13(1):7–22

Abramson DB (2007) The aesthetics of city-scale preservation policy in Beijing. Plann Perspect 22 (2):129–166

Bacon EN (1974) Design of cities. Thames and Hudson, London

Bélanger A (2002) Urban space and collective memory: analysing the various dimensions of the production of memory. Can J Urban Res 11(1):69–92

Blunt A, Bonnerjee J (2013) Home, city and diaspora: Anglo-Indian and Chinese attachments to Calcutta. Glob Netw 13(2):220–240

Broudehoux AM (2004) The making and selling of post-Mao Beijing. Routledge, New York

Casey ES (2004) Public memory in place and time. Framing Public Mem 17–44

Confino A (1997) Collective memory and cultural history: problems of method. Am Hist Rev 102 (5):1386–1403

Crinson M (ed) (2005) Urban memory: history and amnesia in the modern city. Routledge, New York

De Alba M (2012) A methodological approach to the study of urban memory: narratives about Mexico City. In: Forum qualitative sozialforschung/forum: qualitative social research, vol 13, no 2

Ekici D (2007) The surfaces of memory in Berlin. J Architectural Educ 61(2):25–34

Fang K (2000) Regeneration of Old Beijing City in modern times. China Architecture & Building Press, Beijing (in Chinese)

Forest B, Johnson J (2002) Unraveling the threads of history: soviet-era monuments and post-soviet national identity in Moscow. Ann Assoc Am Geogr 92(3):524–547

Goldman J (2003) From hutong to hi-rise: explaining the transformation of Old Beijing, 1990–2002: (Dissertation for Doctorate). Massachusetts Institute of Technology, Cambridge

Halbwachs M (1992) On collective memory. University of Chicago Press, Chicago

Heath T, Tang Y (2010) Beijing's hutong and siheyuan: conservation of an urban identity. Proc ICE Municipal Eng 163(3):155–161

Hebbert M (2005) The street as locus of collective memory. Environ Plann D 23(4):581

Henneberg V, Clara K (2004) Monuments, public space, and the memory of empire in modern Italy. Hist Mem 16(1):37–85

Huyssen A (1995) Twilight memories: marking time in a culture of amnesia. Routledge, New York

Huyssen A (2003) Present pasts: urban palimpsests and the politics of memory. Stanford University Press, Stanford

Johnson NC (2002) Mapping monuments: the shaping of public space and cultural identities. Visual Commun 1(3):293–298

Jordan JA (2006) Structures of memory: understanding urban change in Berlin and beyond. Stanford University Press, Stanford

Kansteiner W (2002) Finding meaning in memory: a methodological critique of collective memory studies. Hist Theory 41(2):179–197

Ladd B (2008) The ghosts of Berlin: confronting German history in the urban landscape. University of Chicago Press, Chicago

Lahiri S (2011) Remembering the city: translocality and the senses. Soc Cult Geogr 12(8):855–869

Le Goff J (1992) History and memory (trans: Rendall S, Claman E). Columbia, New York

Legg S (2005) Contesting and surviving memory: space, nation, and nostalgia in LesLieux de mémoire. Environ Plann D Soc Space 23:481–504

Liang S (1986) Brilliant work in urban planning. In: Works of Liang Sicheng, vol IV. China Architecture & Building Press (in Chinese)

Liu M (2006) Research on the small-scale gradual and organic renewal mode for historical residential area in Old Beijing: (Dissertation for Doctorate). Tsinghua University, Beijing (in Chinese)

Maden F, Temsiliyet SDK (2009) Libeskind'deBellek, TarihVeMimarlik. Middle East Tech Univ J Fac Archit 26(1):49–70

Matten MA (ed) (2011) Places of memory in modern China: history, politics, and identity. Brill, Leiden

Mowla QA (2004) Memory association in place making: understanding an urban space. Memory 9:52–54

Nora P (1989) Between memory and history: Les lieux de mémoire. Representations 26:7–24

Olick JK, Robbins J (1998) Social memory studies: From "collective memory" to the historical sociology of mnemonic practices. Annu Rev Sociol 105–140

Othman S, Nishimura Y, Kubota A (2013) Memory association in place making: a review. Procedia Soc Behav Sci 85:554–563

Postalcy E, Kuruç Ada A, Özbek Eren Y (2006) The new urban memory. In: Proceedings of the 42nd international society of city and regional planners congress, Instanbul, Turkey

Ringas D, Christopoulou E (2013) Collective city memory: field experience on the effect of urban computing on community. In: Proceedings of the 6th international conference on communities and technologies. Munich, Germany

Ringas D, Christopoulou E, Stefanidakis M (2011) Urban memory in space and time. Handbook Res Technol Cult Heritage Appl Environ 325–340
Rose-Redwood R, Alderman D, Azaryahu M (2008) Collective memory and the politics of urban space: an introduction. GeoJournal 73(3):161–164
Rossi A (1982) The architecture of the city, 1966 (trans: Ghirardo D, Ockman J). MIT Press, Cambridge
Srinivas S (2001) Landscapes of urban memory: the sacred and the civic in India's high-tech city. University of Minnesota Press, Minneapolis
Stangl P (2008) The vernacular and the monumental: memory and landscape in post-war Berlin. GeoJournal 73(3):245–253
Stone A (2008) Farewell to the hutongs: urban development in Beijing. Dissent 55(2):43–48
Till K (2003) Places of memory. A Companion Polit Geogr 289–301
Wang Y (1998) From large-scale reconstructionto small-scale gradual renewal: the renewal planning of fengsheng neighborhood, Beijing. Archit J 8:47–52 (in Chinese)
Whitehand JW, Gu K (2007) Urban conservation in China: historical development, current practice and morphological approach. Town Plann Rev 78(5):643–670
Withers CW (1996) Place, memory, monument: memorializing the past in contemporary Highland Scotland. Cult Geographies 3(3):325–344
Zhang J (1996) Small scale regeneration of urban historic area-the way of "organic regeneration". City Plann Rev 4:14–17 (in Chinese)
Zhang Y (2008) Steering towards growth: symbolic urban preservation in Beijing, 1990–2005. Town Plann Rev 79(2):187–208
Zhu R (2005) Collective memory of city and urban form: (Dissertation for Doctorate). Southeast University, Nanjing (in Chinese)

Author Biographies

Dr. Fang Wang is Associate Professor in the College of Architecture and Landscape Architecture, Peking University and a registered urban planner.

Ms. Wei Li is a master student in the College of Urban and Environmental Sciences, Peking University.

Ms. Yang Liu is an urban planner in the Beijing Municipal Institute of City Planning and Design and received a Master in College of Urban and Environmental Sciences, Peking University.

Mr. Hongru Cai is an undergraduate student in the College of Urban and Environmental Sciences, Peking University.

Chapter 3
New Urbanization and Land Use in China

Changchun Feng, Zhuyun Xiao, Haojing Shen and Lei Zhang

In 2011, China's urbanization rate reached 51.27 %,[1] which indicates that the urban population exceeded the rural population for the first time and marks China's foray into a new development stage of urbanization. At the beginning of 2014, China officially issued the New Urbanization Plan, which made clear the conceptual design and deployment related to the urbanization process (Shan and Huang 2013). The new urbanization is drawing attention from various fields in the industry and academe. Land use is one of the key points of the new urbanization strategy. This strategy needs to determine means for formulating a suitable land use policy and alleviating the contradiction between the supply and demand of land. This research aims to present methods for formulating a land use policy with consideration for locality and in the context of the new urbanization.

3.1 Development Stage and the Characteristics of Urbanization in China[2]

According to the development experience of countries around world, urbanization has characteristic stages. Northam (1979) summarizes the process of the urbanization development approximately as an S curve. In general, the urbanization

[1] *Source* National Bureau of Statistics of the People's Republic of China, http://www.stats.gov.cn/.
[2] Data in this section are taken from the National Bureau of Statistics of the People's Republic of China, http://www.stats.gov.cn/.

C. Feng · Z. Xiao · H. Shen
College of Urban and Environmental Sciences, Peking University, Beijing
People's Republic of China

C. Feng · Z. Xiao · H. Shen
Key Laboratory of Land Planning and Developing, Ministry of Land and Resources, Beijing, People's Republic of China

L. Zhang (✉)
Institute of Geographic Sciences and Natural Resources Research, Chinese Academy of Sciences, Beijing, People's Republic of China
e-mail: zhangl@igsnrr.ac.cn

F. Wang and M. Prominski (eds.), *Urbanization and Locality*,
DOI 10.1007/978-3-662-48494-4_3

process can be divided into three stages: when the urban population is more than 10 % of the entire population, a country enters the initial stage of urbanization, and the urban population grows slowly; when the urban population is more than 30 %, the country enters the accelerated stage of urbanization, with the urban population increasing rapidly; and when the urban population exceeds 70 %, the country enters the late stage of urbanization, with a slow growth or stagnation of the urban population (Northam 1979).

China's urbanization is in line with the general law of the world's development, but it also bears unique characteristics (Fig. 3.1). China's urbanization process can be divided into the following five stages:

First, the initial stage of development is seen in the period between 1949 and 1957. The national economy gradually recovered from the damage of World War II, especially during the "one five" period, when hundreds of large-scale projects came into operation, thereby improving the level of industrialization. The urban population increased, a prelude to China's urbanization. At this stage, the number of cities increased from 136 to 176, and urban population increased from 57.65 to 99.49 million.

Second, the tortuous development stage is said to have occurred between 1958 and 1965. Under the influence of the Great Leap Forward (Mandrin: Da Yue Jin) and natural disasters, the level of urbanization fluctuated considerably. The blind expansion of production in the early years and employment trend in the industry led to an urban population surge of 20 million. Later, the national economy atrophied, attributed to natural disasters. Through the mobilization of urban workers who returned to their hometowns and an adjustment of the town setting standards, the level of urbanization retracted. In 1965, the urbanization level returned to the level in 1958.

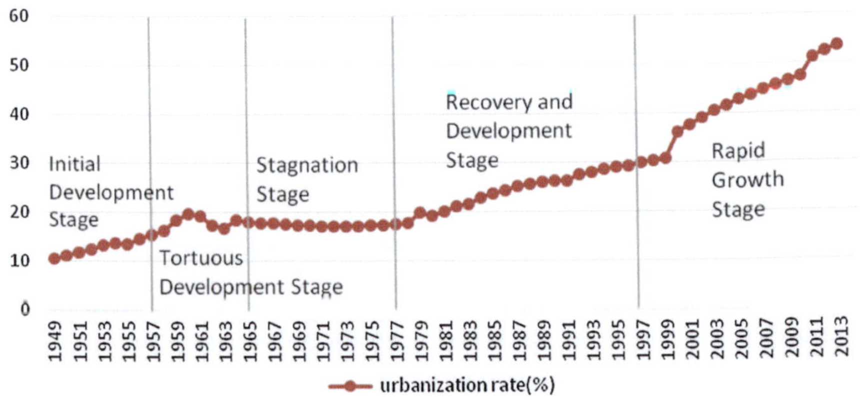

Fig. 3.1 China's urbanization development history (1949–2013). *Data source* National Bureau of Statistics of the People's Republic of China, http://www.stats.gov.cn/

Third, the stagnation stage is observed in the period from 1966 to 1977. During the Cultural Revolution, the national economy remained stagnant, and a large number of the educated youth went to the countryside. The urban population grew slowly, which led to an abnormal regression of the urbanization process.

Fourth, the recovery and development stage is observed from 1978 to 1996. The rural reform finalized in the 1978 Meeting (Third Plenary Session of the 11th Central Committee of the Chinese Communist Party) promoted the development of the rural economy, releasing a large number of rural surplus laborers. The policy of Reform and Opening Up promoted urban economic growth, and the national economy developed steadily. With the Country to City (Mandrin: Xian Gai Shi) policy, the level of urbanization steadily grew. The number of cities increased from 193 in 1978 to 668 in 1996, and the urbanization level increased from 17.9 % in 1979 to 29.4 % in 1996.

Fifth, the rapid growth stage has been underway since 1997. The annual urbanization rate growth is more than 1 %. In 2013, China's total population is 1360 million, with an urban resident population of 731 million and rural resident population of 629 million. The Chinese urbanization rate reached 53.7 %. This predominantly urban society has brought a historic change in China's social structure.

3.2 Problems and Challenges of Urbanization in China

Compared with other countries in the world that have entered a rapid growth stage, China has an especially rapid speed of urbanization. To increase the urbanization rate from 30 to 50 %, Europe and other developed countries required 35 to 70 years, whereas the process took only 13 years in China (1998–2011). The large overall scale and rapid speed of urbanization are the main characteristics of urbanization in China. Compared with developed countries, China's urbanization rate is relatively lower and the urbanization quality is rather poor (Table 3.1).

Table 3.1 Duration of urbanization rate increasing from 30 to 50 %

	Exceeding 30 %	Exceeding 50 %	Duration (Years)
UK	1810	1850	40
Germany	1854	1892	38
France	1864	1931	67
USA	1882	1918	36
PRC	1998	2011	13

Data source The World Bank website, http://data.worldbank.org.cn

3.2.1 Unbalanced Regional Development of Urbanization Level

Overall, within nearly 10 years, China's urban population increased by 207 million people, corresponding to an urbanization rate increase of 14 %. However, regional development is not balanced. The urban population in eastern areas grew quickly and reached a high level of urbanization. At the same time, the gap between the central and western regions is widening. Between 2000 and 2010, the growth of urbanization is the fastest in the Yangtze River Delta, recording up to 15.2 % and reaching an urbanization rate of 65.2 %. The urban population in the northeast area, which is the slowest growing region, increased by only 5.3 % in 10 years, with an urbanization rate of 57.7 %. Other regions, such as the Ring of Bohai, central, northwest, southwest, and Pearl River Delta, have seen an increase between 11 and 15 %. The urbanization level in the southwest is the lowest with only 40 %. Assuming that the urbanization rate increases 1 % per year, the southwest area will need more than 20 years to reach the current level of the Yangtze River Delta (Fig. 3.2).

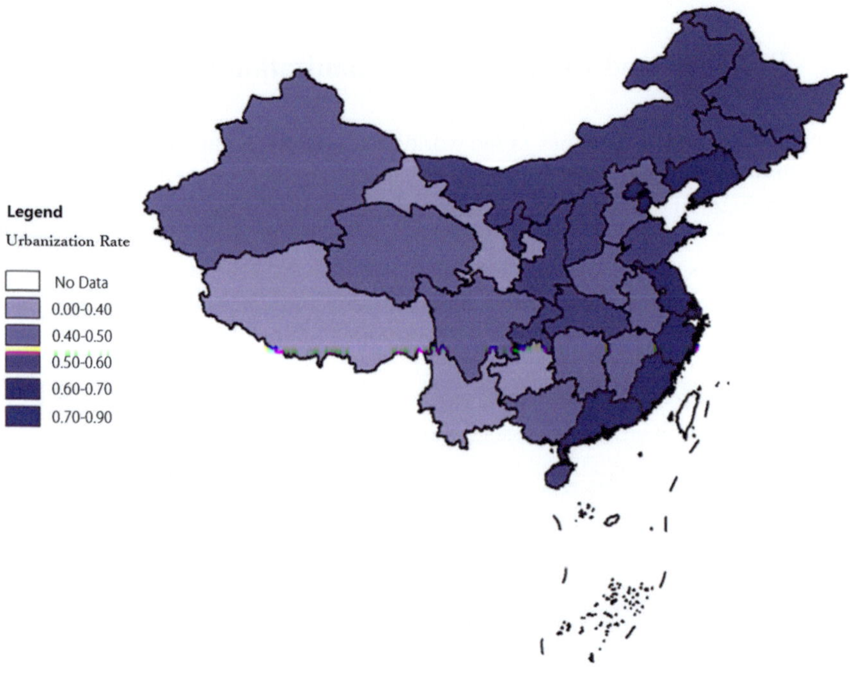

Fig. 3.2 China's urbanization rate spatial distribution (2013). *Data source* National Bureau of Statistics of the People's Republic of China, http://www.stats.gov.cn/

3.2.2 *Widening Gap Between Urban and Rural Areas*

Another manifestation of the unbalanced urbanization is the gap between urban and rural areas. The purported "city biased policy" has benefited industries and cities in the form of surplus subsidies from agriculture. A large number of production factors and capital are concentrated in cities. Indeed, the promotion of industrialization and urbanization causes the widening gap between urban and rural areas. In 2013, the national urban and rural income ratio was 3.03:1. The dichotomy between urban and rural areas leads to various problems, such as the integration of rural residents in cities; non-city residents face difficulties in terms of employment, social security, or housing. Such segregation leads to the rise of shanty towns in cities. If these problems are not handled properly, industrialization and urbanization will be stalled (Fig. 3.3).

3.2.3 *Cities of Different Sizes Facing Different Development Problems*

During urbanization, large cities enjoy social and economic development as well. However, owing to disorderly development, and the prevailing value for economic growth over the environment, and building over service, metropolitans face serious problems, such as traffic congestion, public safety concerns, environmental pollution, low efficiency in city management, insufficient public service supply, and serious social contradictions, considered "urban diseases" (Niu et al. 2013).

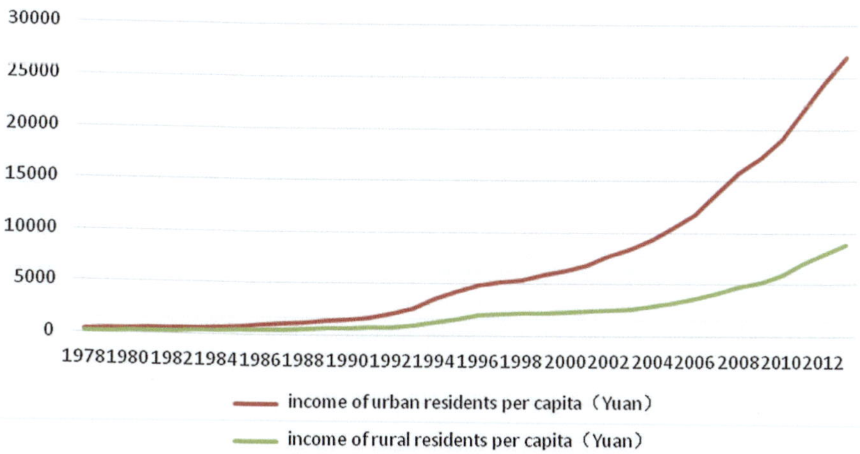

Fig. 3.3 Urban and rural per capita income (1978–2013). *Data source* National Bureau of Statistics of the People's Republic of China, http://www.stats.gov.cn/

Compared with large cities, the urbanization rate and proportion of secondary and tertiary industries in small cities are much lower. Industrialization remains the main goal of development. In terms of basic public services aspects, investments by small- or medium-sized cities are relatively small. That is, the attention to training migrant workers is insufficient, the quality of compulsory education is relatively low, and the coverage of social security level is limited. In terms of infrastructure aspects, small- and medium-sized cities generally face such problems as deficient infrastructure construction, low utilization rate of facilities, and low penetration rate of water supply, power supply, and other municipal facilities.

3.2.4 *Lack of Coordination Between the Economy and Population Urbanization*

The urbanization in both the population and economy needs to be coordinated. If the gap between the two is too large, the overall development of urbanization would be hindered. According to the experience of developed countries, economic urbanization (referring to industrial structure transformation and increased ratio of the tertiary sector) is half a step (about 46 %) faster than population urbanization. The difference between China's economic and population urbanization has reached 1.95, far more than that in developed (1.23) and other developing countries (1.73) (Yao et al. 2010). When economic urbanization exceeds population urbanization, economic development will slow down owing to the lack of strong support. Too much emphasis on economic construction and negligence on the development of social services supply, in turn, will hinder the further development of the economy. The ultimate effect is to impede the process of overall urbanization.

3.2.5 *Low Conversion Rate of Rural Population*

In coordinating economic and population urbanization, the unreasonable economic structure (primary sector: secondary sector: tertiary sector = 1:5:4) results in a low capacity to absorb employment in urban areas, and consequently, a low conversion rate of rural surplus population to urbanization. At the end of 2013, China's urbanization rate reached 53.7 %, increasing by 1.1 % from the previous year. At the same time, the "separation of residents from household registration" population reached 289 million, including a floating population of 245 million, leading to a household urbanization rate of only 35.7 % (Huang et al. 2011).

3.2.6 *Low Efficiency of Resource Utilization in the Process of Urbanization*

From the perspective of energy, urban consumption and emission have become prominent challenges. In 2006, the energy consumption of 287 cities was 1366 million tons of standard coal, accounting for 55.48 % of the total energy consumption. Carbon dioxide emission is 2916 million tons, accounting for 54.84 % of the total emission quantity. The GDP energy consumption is large: 2.2 times the world average in 2010 (Zhang and Zhang 2008).

From the perspective of water, China's resources per capita are only a fourth of the world's average level. In 600 cities in the country, more than 400 face a lack of water, and the daily water deficit reaches 16 million cubic meters. Water scarcity forces cities to improve their water efficiency and apply water-saving techniques (Shen 2013).

From the perspective of land resources, the available rate of land for urban and rural construction is low. In the past few years, the urbanization development corresponded with the extensive use of land. From 1990 to 2000, the growth of land urbanization rate was 1.71 times the population urbanization rate; and from 2000 to 2010, the index rose to 1.85. According to the experience of developed countries, a ratio between land urbanization and population urbanization of 1.12 is more reasonable (Zhang and Zhang 2008).

3.3 Connotations of New Urbanization

New urbanization is a reflection of the previous path of urbanization. In recent decades, China was characterized by high urbanization speed and urbanization rate. The country invested much money in infrastructure construction and real estate development, causing an excessive expansion of cities, wasting precious land and engendering a city landscape characterized by simple piles of reinforced concrete. China advanced the planning and construction of various industrial parks, development zones, and new town areas, which led to "ghost towns" with low population and industry support. The fragmented urban and rural structure led to migrants who lack full rights, compared with those with urban registration. Further, the development results in environmental pollution, without building green ecological and livable cities.

Facing these problems, this research puts forward the connotation of new urbanization as a composition of four basic parts: first, the population; second, resource input; third, industry and outputs; fourth, social services (Fig. 3.4).

Population urbanization indicates people-centered urbanization, compared with previous forms that had focused more about land than the population. In the past, the development of cities has usually been realized by the expansion of scale, but people did not necessarily settle down in the constructed city. The "no settlement" phenomenon refers to "semi-urbanized" population with no household registration, no

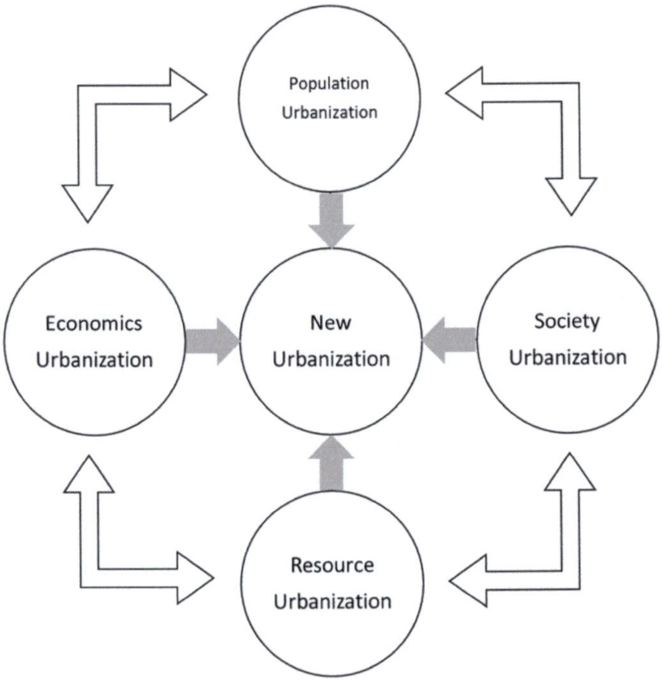

Fig. 3.4 Connotations of new urbanization (*Source* ©Authors)

right to enjoy the same medical insurance and other welfare benefits of urban people. Population urbanization refers to the transformation of semi-urbanized people into actual urban people. Population urbanization can be realized by reforming the household registration system, breaking the barrier between urban and rural areas.

Economic urbanization refers to an adjustment of the economic structure. In developed countries, the tertiary economic sector takes up to 70 %, whereas the economic structure of our country is led by industry, the secondary economic sector. Economic urbanization involves the transformation on the industrial structure and increase in the ratio of the tertiary sector whose output revenue is much higher. Through developing industrial clusters, more jobs and benefits are created to support the incoming population and expansion of the city scale.

Society urbanization refers to the transformation of a rural population into a non-agricultural population. In this process, the local way of life, behaviors, and mental values become "civilized." Social urbanization may be realized by improving the infrastructure and public service facilities, achieving equity in public services, and helping farmers in both the material and spiritual aspects to foster urban incorporation.

Resource urbanization refers to the intensive use of land, water, energy, and other natural resources. This process is the bottleneck of modern urbanization. Cities with water shortage are common, accounting for two-thirds of all cities. Although the total amount of land resource is huge, the available construction land per capita is much less so; over two-thirds of China's total land area is not suitable for urbanization. Energy saving, emission reduction, development of low-carbon businesses, and intensive land use are needed to guarantee the resource supply for urbanization.

3.4 Analysis of Land Resource Demand in Urbanization

As for land use strategies in the context of new urbanization, the core problem is the demand for land resources. Possession or consumption of resources, and exploitation of the environment, in urbanization can be achieved in three ways: direct, indirect and induced.

First, direct possession or consumption generally refers to the demand for resource occupation during the process of development and extension of urban areas, or considered as the demand for survival. Second, indirect possession or consumption refers to the demand for resource occupation to meet the basic material needs of urban daily life, such as various agricultural and sideline production schemes for urban daily consumption, or considered as the demand for food. Third, induced occupation or consumption involves the need for resources to ensure the security of survival and development. For example, for the protection of drinking water, water conservation areas need to be established around a water source and its upstream area. This type can also be considered as the demand for the environment (Fig. 3.5).

Specific to land resources, demand also can be classified into the three types: direct, indirect, and induced consumption. Direct land use means the direct occupation of land in the process of urban spatial expansion. The calculation formula is as follows:

$$DL = BA_c + BA_t + TL$$

In the formula, **DL** represents direct land use, $\mathbf{BA_C}$ is the built-up area of a city, $\mathbf{BA_t}$ is the built-up area of a town, and **TL** is traffic land.

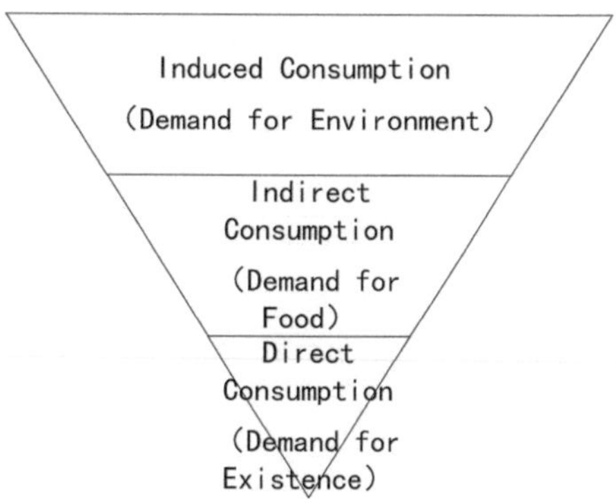

Fig. 3.5 Consumption of resources and environment in urbanization (*Source* Zhang and Zhang 2008)

Indirect land use refers to land consumption designed to meet basic material production for daily urban life. The formulas are as follows:

$$IL = ICL + IGL$$
$$ICL = \sum A_i P / P_i$$
$$IGL = B_i P / TC \times TGL$$

In the above, **IL** represents indirect land use; **ICL** is the arable land occupied indirectly by urbanization; $\mathbf{A_i}$ is the annual consumption of all types of agricultural products per capita in urban areas; **P** is the number of the urban population; $\mathbf{P_i}$ is the production of various agricultural products per acre, including grain, vegetables, and fruits; **IGL** represents the indirect occupation of pasture areas; $\mathbf{B_i}$ is the urban residents' consumption of beef and mutton production per capita; **TC** is the national consumption of beef and mutton production; and **TGL** is the total pasture area in a country.

Induced land use refers to land consumption caused by the protection of the environment intended for survival development. It generally depends on the geographical location and ecological status of an area. Taking into account data availability and ease of calculation, urban forest areas that absorb carbon emission are used to represent induced land use, which is calculated as follows:

$$IDL = C_0 / \alpha$$

In the formula, **IDL** represents induced land use, $\mathbf{C_0}$ the total annual emissions of carbon, and $\boldsymbol{\alpha}$ the average carbon storage of forest land (38.67 ton/ha).

This model can determine land occupation for urbanization at the country (UK, US, and China) and city levels (London, New York, and Shanghai). Urbanization in China in 2005 occupied 43.8 % of the total land area, similar to the situation in the US in 2000, but the rate of urbanization is relatively low in China compared with the US, indicating that the use of land resources need to be more intensive and efficient. From the perspective of the city level, Shanghai's urban population has been far higher than that in London and New York, and land use is relatively intensive and efficient, indicating that the efficiency of large cities relying on land resources has reached a high level (Tables 3.2 and 3.3).

3.5 Land Use Strategy and Practical Reference Under New Urbanization

Land use strategy under new urbanization can be analyzed from the following four perspectives: where do people go, where does land come from, how to manage land, and how to use land.

Table 3.2 Land occupation for urbanization in the UK, USA, and China

	Urbanization rate (%)	Ratio of urbanization occupation to the total land area (%)	Ratio of direct occupation (%)	Ratio of indirect occupation (%)	Ratio of induced occupation (%)
UK (2000)	89.5	80.7	5.17	28.10	47.47
USA (2000)	77.2	44.9	2.43	14.64	27.79
China (2005)	43.0	43.8	1.17	15.43	27.22

Table 3.3 Land occupation for urbanization in London, New York, and Shanghai

	Direct use of land (km^2)	Indirect use of land (km^2)	Induced use of land (km^2)	Urban population (in million people)
London (2000)	622	9640	16270	7.1
New York (2000)	780	55726	61851	8.0
Shanghai (2005)	1344	42026	94845	16.0

Data source Zhang and Zhang (2008)

First, about where people go, the new urbanization requires a scientifically guided migration plan to medium and small cities and towns, along with the promotion of urbanization among farmers. As such, urbanization demand for land resources will gradually increase not only in large and mega-cities but also in small and medium cities. Various cities need to develop appropriate land-use policies, taking into account the economic development and long-term supply of land resources, as well as avoid wasting land resources.

Second, as regards where land comes from, new urbanization requires the diversification of land supply methods according to local conditions, to ease the contradictions between land supply and demand, without compromising ecological security. Methods to be used include regeneration of built areas inside cities, exploitation of low mountains and hills, reclamation and replacement of waste mining land in areas that lack land resources or consolidation of construction land in rural areas.

Third, in terms of land management under the new urbanization situation, land circulation is needed not only to improve the relevant legal system, which can strengthen national macro-management, but also to pay attention to the interests of farmers. By implementing land property rights system reform, the government can empower rural people with the full usufruct of rural land and speed up the establishment of a circulation system of land use rights, thereby promoting the large-scale operation and industrialization of agriculture. A unified urban and rural construction land market needs to be set as well to link immigrants with the land mechanisms.

Finally, about the use of land, given the characteristics of China's land resources, land must be used intensively to improve land use efficiency. China needs to redevelop inefficient land (such as old cities, villages, or factories) and then revitalize the urban land stock.

The Immigrant–Land Linking Policy and Land Intensive Use Policy have entered the practical phase and brought forth practical experiences. This study finds that formulating a fixed policy to manage land use in different place may not be feasible because of the various economic and social features involved. Instead, the authorities should formulate flexible land use policy and respect the local characteristics. The following section will discuss the policy design for land use and management in combination with locality under new urbanization.

3.5.1 Case of Immigrant–Land Linking Policy: Henan Xinxiang Land Management Policy

With the acceleration of urbanization, China's population is experiencing a dynamic restructuring. On one the hand, economic development has been hampered by urban land shortages; moreover, vast areas for rural construction have become fallow owing to population outflow and industrial decline. On the other hand, in certain cities, land urbanization is faster than population urbanization, which has led to an extensive waste of urban land. The scenario points to a lack of balance between population growth and land resources. The Immigrant–Land Linking Policy came into being based on such a socio-economic background. This policy means to link the increased scale of urban construction land with the incoming rural population as well as people from other cities. The case of Xinxiang is used in the following section to analyze the specific policy design of Immigrant–Land Linking.

Xinxiang City is in Henan Province, in the middle of China. The urbanization rate of Xinxiang is above the average level of Henan but below that of the entire country. Compared with developed regions, Xinxiang has much room for further development. Problems of urbanization in Xinxiang include a relatively small scale of cities and towns, with an average population of 8,705 people, and insufficient radiation and influence ability of the core cities.

Immigrant–Land Linking in Xinxiang is designed according to the general idea of "people as the fundamental [factor], industry as the core, land as the base, and money as the guarantee" (Feng et al. 2014). With people as the core, the increase in scale of the land must be according to the population growth. In industry as the core, support to the industrial development in urban areas is necessitated; industries offer jobs to absorb the foreign population. The development of the secondary and tertiary economic sectors to promote employment leads to a concentration of the

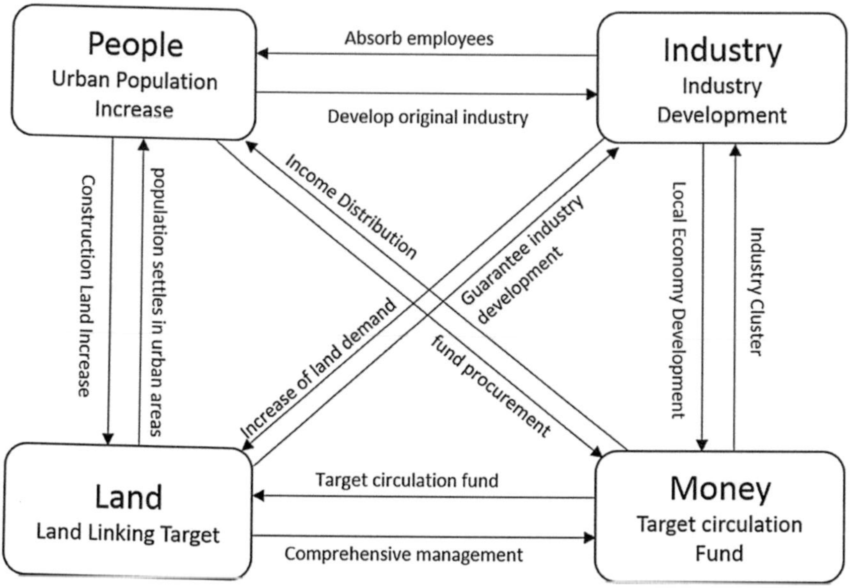

Fig. 3.6 Four elements of immigrant–land linking policy (*Source* ©Authors)

population in urban areas. Land as the base means that the spatial distribution of land development occurs right through the target circulation. Through comprehensive land improvement, the government can increase the amount of arable land and improve farmland quality to ensure food security. Money as the guarantee indicates the expansion of funding channels and improvement of the benefits distribution system. By actively expanding the financing channels, more effort should be made to explore the way to establish a rural residential land use right mortgage system (Fig. 3.6).

Through industry development in urban areas and agricultural modernization in rural areas, migration is led from rural to urban areas, and employment is secured in urban and new rural communities, which promotes human urbanization. Construction land surplus is generated by population movements, land consolidation, comprehensive land management (demolition and reclamation of old land), and construction of new rural communities. Construction land can be transferred between rural and urban areas and between different cities. The distribution of land allows more land to be developed in urban areas to provide space for the development of urban industry and immigration. Benefits from targeted circulation in rural areas could be used for comprehensive land management and agricultural modernization, and in turn, industrial development is promoted in urban and rural areas. The cycle will carry on to realize the goal of land management (see Fig. 3.7).

The crucial aspect of the Immigrant–Land Linking Policy is the amount and price of exchange target, which consists of two aspects: urban land demand estimation (land) and transaction price index measurement (money).

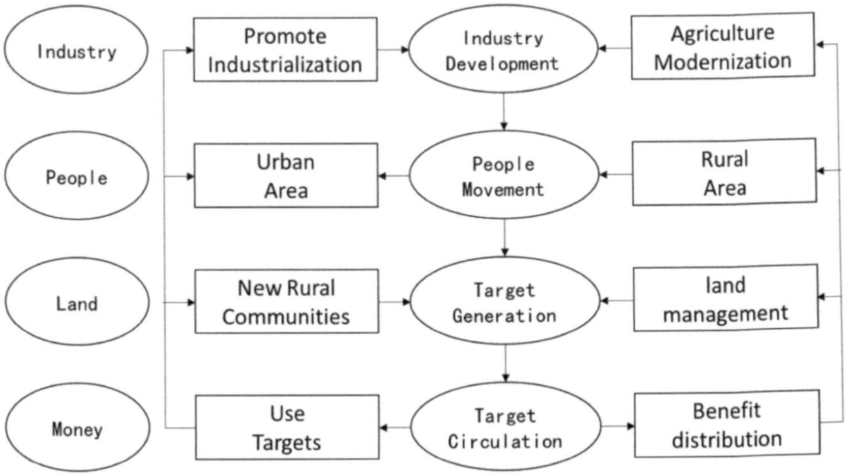

Fig. 3.7 Cycle of immigrant–land linking policy (*Source* ©Authors)

First, as regards the estimation of urban land demand, the existing formula applies to Xinxiang City, to estimate the urban land demand (land):

$$Y_n = M_{n-1} \times B$$

$$\text{Or } Y_n = M_{n-1} \times B + (R_{n-1} - M_{n-1}) \times B \times 0.6$$

In the above, Y represents the actual demand for urban construction land, M the urban household population increase, R the increase of urban residents, B the urban construction land per capita, and n the year. The amount of Immigrant–Land Linking is generated by combining the new urban construction land target and construction land circulation plan between rural and urban areas:

$$A_n = Y_n - (F_n + G_n)$$

A represents the yearly amount of Immigrant–Land Linking, Y the actual demand for urban construction land, F the new urban construction land target, G the construction land circulation plan, and n represents the year.

A problem with this method occurs when the estimation of the annual land supply and demand is not reasonable, which is observed when the increase in population is used to estimate the size in land increase. It does not consider the complex relationship between demand for urban land, urban development, industrial development, and demographic change, resulting in an estimated distortion of urban land demand, which may limit the opportunities for city development. Peking University has proposed four methods for improvement: (1) correction of the original calculation based on economic volatility; (2) urban land classification method; (3) economic–demographic dual method; and (4) employment–land estimation method (Table 3.4).

Table 3.4 Four methods for improvement to estimate the scale of immigrant–land linking

Method	Estimation process	Comment
Correction of the original calculation based on economic volatility	Correct the original estimation method according to industry projects; plan and implement situation	More convenient to integrate with the original plan
Urban land classification method	Calculate tertiary industry output, investment strength, and other industrial and demographic data Based on different types of urban construction land, estimate land demand according to industry land use standards and unproductive land per capita	More comprehensive and scientific
Economic–demographic dual method	Predict land increase scale based on the dual factors of economic and population development, which coincides with the general idea and theory of the Immigrant–Land Linking Policy	More operable
Employment–land estimation method	Calculate the population scale according to the characteristics and employment capacity of different industries Control for land demand based on the increase size of population	More innovative

(*Source* ©Authors)

Second, as regards the measurement of the transaction price index, the price of transaction target measurement consists of two levels:

1. Inner-city transfer phases: during targeted land circulation between urban and rural areas, the construction land target must be excluded from rural land according to the urban–rural discount index to promote the synergy of urbanization between the population and land. A standard cost price for the target should also be set. Calculations are as follows:

$$\begin{aligned} & \textit{urban construction landlinking targetscale} \\ & \quad = \textit{rural collective construction landlinking targetscale} \times \textit{urban} - \textit{rural discount index} \\ & \textit{urban} - \textit{rural discount index} \\ & \quad = \textit{urban construction land area per captia}/\textit{rural construction land area per captia} \\ & \textit{standard cost price} \\ & \quad = \left(\frac{\sum_1^n \textit{cost of target} \times \textit{amount of target } j}{\sum \textit{amount of target } j} + \textit{cost of platform operation}\right)/\textit{urban} \\ & \qquad - \textit{rural discount index} \end{aligned}$$

2. Inter-city transfer phases: Given the different capital intensities in different cities, standards in urban construction land per capita vary. Considering the coordination between the population and land, the scale of transacted construction land targets should be reduced correspondingly. With the total cost price unchanged, and size reduced, the value of unit targets should increase correspondingly. The calculation formula is as follows:

$$\begin{aligned} \textit{inter}-\textit{city discount index} &= \textit{urban construction land area per captia of target inflowing city} \\ &\quad /\textit{urban construction land area per captia of target outflowing city} \\ \textit{inter}-\textit{city standard cost price} &= \textit{standard cost price of inflowing city}/\textit{intercity discount index} \end{aligned}$$

The Immigrant–Land Linking Policy in Xinxiang is intended to achieve the optimal allocation of urban and rural lands, sustainable development of industries, proper movement of the population, and reasonable, long-term operation of the capital chain.

3.5.2 Tapping Inventory Land Potential: Evaluation of Intensive Use Potential of Stock Land in Dongcheng District

In the context of new urbanization, the full utilization and revitalization of stock land are critical. The term "intensive use potential of stock land" refers to the study of the three-dimensional space of an urban built-up area within a period of development for the optimization of the structure and layout of the land. Such a work happens mainly through adjusting the stock land structure, function, and intensity to improve conditions without changing the total amount of land. From this definition, connotations of intensive use potential of stock land include the following: (1) the function potential, referring to the land value increment by changing land-use; (2) intensity potential, referring to the land value increment by increasing the volume rate and building height; (3) location potential, referring to the impact of external factors on the incremental value of land, and when considered with endogenous variables, can be understood as the land value produced by geographic conditions.

The current work uses the example of valuation of intensive use potential of stock land in Dongcheng District. As an important commercial, cultural, and administrative center in Beijing City, Dongcheng has a large number of buildings constructed in late 1950s and 1960s. Tasks for renewal for this old district are important and urgent.

The steps in the evaluation of intensive use potential of stock land are as follows: (1) determine the evaluation unit, (2) establish the evaluation system and determine the weights of each index, (3) use the potential model to calculate results according to the collected data.

In the first step, the evaluation unit is determined to allow scientific comparisons and facilitate workable and convenient land management. The current method used to divide land units includes the grid, road cutting, and parcel methods.

An analytic hierarchy process (AHP) is then used to determine the evaluation index system and their weights. The system is be composed of three levels: the target layer, referring to intensive land use potential; the factor layer, including function potential, intensity potential, and location potential; and the index layer, including land usage, building height, volume rate, GDP density, population density, the distance from subway stations, roads, CBDs, and primary schools. According to the design of the index system, the weights for the three groups need to be determined. The weights can be calculated using the paired comparison method (Fig. 3.8).

The potential model is then used to calculate results according to the collected data. First, through data collection, collation, calculation, and normalization, the value of each index is determined. Second, the paired comparison method is used to determine the weight of each index. Third, separately, according to formulas (1) and (2), the value of the intensity potential and location potential is calculated. Finally,

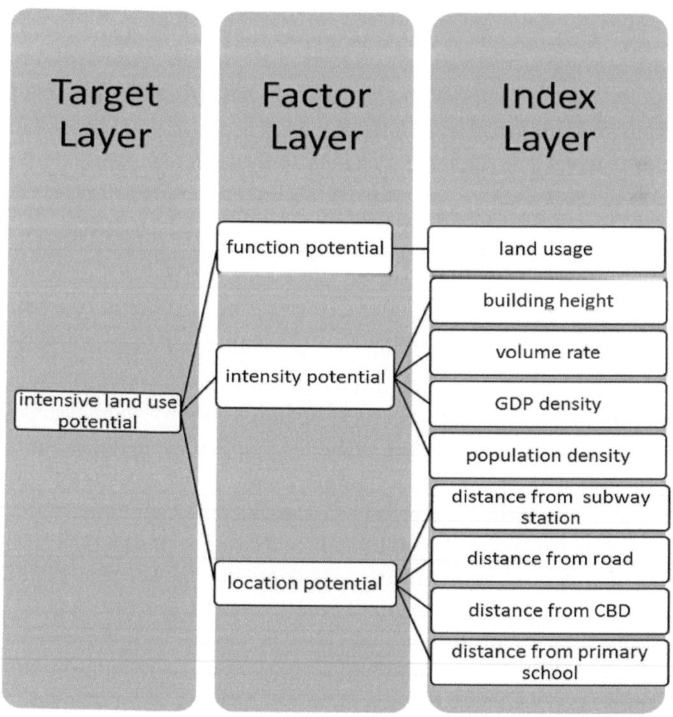

Fig. 3.8 Evaluation index system for intensive land use potential (*Source* ©Authors)

according to formula (3), the intensive use potential value of each stock land parcel is calculated.

Formula (1), value of intensity potential:

$$S_i = A_{i1} \times u_1 + A_{i2} \times u_2 + A_{i3} \times u_3$$

S_i is the intensity potential value of land parcel i; A_{i1}, A_{i2} are normalized scores of building height and volume rate; when i is residential land, A_{i3} represents the population density normalized score, or it represents GDP density normalized score; u_1, u_2, u_3 are their weights, and $u_1 + u_2 + u_3 = 1$.

Formula (2), value of location potential:

$$L_i = B_{i1} \times v_1 + B_{i2} \times v_2 + B_{i3} \times v_3 + B_{i4} \times v_4$$

L_i is the location potential value of land parcel i; B_{i1}, B_{i2}, B_{i3}, B_{i4} are normalized scores of distances from subway stops, urban roads, CBDs, and primary schools; v_1, v_2, v_3, v_4 are the weights of each index, and $v_1 + v_2 + v_3 + v_4 = 1$.

Formula (3), value of intensive land use potential:

$$C_i = U_i \times w_1 + S_i \times w_2 + L_i \times w_3$$

C_i is the value of the intensive land use potential of land parcel i; U_i, S_i, L_i refer to the function, intensity, and location potential values of land parcel i; w_1, w_2, w_3 are their weights, and $w_1 + w_2 + w_3 = 1$.

With this evaluation method for intensive use potential of stock land, the high potential intensive land use can be determined. The result could provide a general guide for the renewal work for this old district to maximize land use potential.

3.6 Summary

By reviewing the urbanization development stages and features of China, this article argues that China has entered a stage of high-speed urbanization since 1997. High speed and large scale are the main features of this stage. Meanwhile, the problems and challenges of urbanization at this stage include the following: unbalanced regional development of urbanization level; widening gap between urban and rural areas; "urban diseases" in large cities and shortage of infrastructure and public services in small and medium cities; lack of correspondence of economic and population urbanization aspects; low conversion rate of rural population; and low efficiency of resource utilization. These problems lead to a poor quality of China's urbanization. This article has likewise discussed the connotations of new-type urbanization, which should include four aspects: population urbanization, economy urbanization, society urbanization and resource urbanization.

When new-type urbanization policies are applied to land use issues, based on the calculation results of a theoretical model for land demand, this study has found that during the process of urbanization, there should be a more intensive and efficient use of land resources. As regards cities, the land use efficiency of China's mega cities has reached a high level, whereas medium and small cities have a large potential for intensified land use. As such, we propose a land use strategy and practice appropriate for new-type urbanization. This work introduces the specific methods of operational practices of Immigrant–Land Linking Policy and Tapping Land Stock Potential Policy.

Under new-type urbanization, appropriate land use policies must be developed to alleviate the contradiction between the supply and demand of land during the process of urbanization, as well as promote a healthy development of urbanization, which is still at an exploratory stage. We hope experts and scholars can explore together the development of suitable land use policies according to current urbanization conditions.

Acknowledgment This work was supported by a grant from the Key Program of National Science and Technology Support Plan during the 12th Five-Year Plan Period (No. 2012BAJ22B04).

References

Feng CC, Liu M, Shen HJ, Hou YS (2014) Research on the problem of transfer of rural collective construction land from the perspective of land development rights: taking Xinxiang City of Henan Province as an example. Urban Dev Stud 3:19–22 (in Chinese)

Huang YP, Chen Z, Xie LR (2011) The feature and trends of the remote urbanization in the context of the new urbanization. Urban Dev Stud 8:11–16 (in Chinese)

Niu XC, Du ZC, Li TS (2013) Evaluation of regional urbanization level based on new urbanization:a case of 10 provincial cities in Shaanxi Province. Arid Land Geogr 2:354–363 (in Chinese)

Northam RM (1979) Urban geography, 2nd edn. Wiley, New York

Shan ZR, Huang YP (2013) An analysis of concept, goals, contents, planning strategies and misunderstandings of new urbanization. Urban Plan Forum 2:16–22 (in Chinese)

Shen QJ (2013) Study on new urbanization based on ecological civilization. Urban Plan Forum 1:29–36 (in Chinese)

Yao SM, Zhang PY, Yu C, Li GY, Wang CX (2010) The theory and practice of new urbanization in China. Scientia Geographica Sinica 6:641–647 (in Chinese)

Zhang L, Zhang SM (2008) Land resources and urbanization. Resour Sci 4:578–584 (in Chinese)

Chapter 4
Urban Interplay

Annette Rudolph-Cleff

4.1 Introduction

The UN estimates that 80 % of the world's population will be living in cities by 2050. Climate change, environmental destruction, and urbanization constantly form new challenges as well as change existing ones. Climate forecasts predict grave consequences from heat waves, floods, heavy rains, and storms by the end of the 21st century (World Bank 2012). The complexity of urban systems and uncertainty regarding the long-term effects of urbanization and climate change will bear a lasting influence on the current understanding of city planning (Leichenko 2011).

Cities are complex, adaptive systems of networked services and infrastructures. The growing urban population, concentration of resources and capital, unclear contingency planning, often inadequate and environmentally unsound water supply and sewage management, menacing continual destruction of ecosystems, and outdated infrastructures and buildings all present massive challenges to city planners.

The shortage of resources has brought the subject of energy supply to the forefront of the discussion. Working to protect the climate and reduce CO_2 emissions requires not only the use of renewable energy sources but also new concepts in applied technologies. Major advances made in energy-efficient buildings are impressive. These, along with the progress in eco-friendly housing developments, solar-powered residential areas, and "Efficiency House Plus" projects, demonstrate the growing importance of building and systems engineering. However, the development of such sophisticated technologies brings many dependencies and a high cost. Only available to a fraction of the world's population, these technological solutions are affordable for a chosen few, and in the event of crises, represent critical sections of the infrastructure that make a city particularly vulnerable (UN 2005).

A. Rudolph-Cleff (✉)
Department of Architecture, Technische Universität Darmstadt, Darmstadt, Germany
e-mail: rudolph@stadt.tu-darmstadt.de

F. Wang and M. Prominski (eds.), *Urbanization and Locality*,
DOI 10.1007/978-3-662-48494-4_4

Blind faith in technological salvation may be a thing of the past, intellectually speaking, but not the question of how to handle technology and its impacts on modern lives. On the contrary, the need to find an answer to this question is growing urgently in the face of global risks.

4.2 Resilience Strategies and Sustainability

Modern planning concepts are built on the assumption that there can be no certitude that future forecasts are accurate, and therefore, long-term reliability in planning might be shortsighted. This view has two effects on cities. For one, it is assumed that there can be no perfect technological solution, only a selection of robust solutions for managing urban risk factors through the intelligent combination of infrastructure and targeted project measures, of technology and ecosystem services. Meanwhile, given that risks will always remain, then cities are responsible for continually improving their information and communication processes, early warning systems, as well as emergency, evacuation, and reconstruction planning (World Bank 2012). The key word is resilience, which "is the ability of a system, community, or society exposed to hazards to resist, absorb, accommodate, and recover from the effects of a hazard in a timely and efficient manner, including through the preservation and restoration of essential basic structures" (UNISDR 2011). Since Holling (1973), the concept of resilience has been a guiding principle that has been further developed through varying interpretations. The resilience of a system is determined by the properties that comprise the dynamics of that system. In socio-ecological systems, these properties are resilience, adaptability, and transformability (Folke et al. 2010, Walker et al. 2004).

Resilience can ensure the safety of citizens and guarantee, to the extent possible, the quality of life in the face of climate change and urban stresses. All cities have different social, ecological, and economical resources as well as political capacities. Therefore, the concept of resilience requires strategies tailored for specific locations. In the current work, key issues are explored for each location in interdisciplinary teams. A location-specific approach is developed to enhance and embrace the qualities of the urban and natural environment and to optimize technical solutions (Shaw 2012).

Water supply systems and flood protection are large challenges that cities face worldwide today. Energy supplies and communication systems dominate considerations at the national and regional level, as do transportation and mobility. Urban infrastructures, including water, sewage, energy, communication, and transport systems, are of crucial importance in crises situations, vital for speedy social and economic recovery. These "critical systems" are currently the focus of urban resilience planning (World Bank 2012: 32).

With the goal of strengthening resilience in mind, there has been a lasting change of perspective in planning. The scope has been broadened from the specialized engineer's viewpoint to an interdisciplinary understanding of interactions and processes within the cityscape. Resilience is an anticipatory principle that transcends risk reduction and intends to mitigate the effects of system failures as well as increase capacities. However, the built urban structures leave very little room for changing spatial constellations or recreating what has been established. Accurate risk and safety evaluation is therefore of utmost importance (World Bank 2012: 5).

The proper choice of method of analysis and the involvement of stakeholders are vital to evaluating risks accurately. Reinforcing resilience in cities relies on investor decisions that are viable in a variety of scenarios. To estimate risks responsibly and plan sustainable urban areas, a balance must be sought between opposing interests to minimize damage and large-scale investments that offer long-term protection from environmental disasters. Investments in new infrastructures, foresight in land management, and sustainable planning of green areas are currently the central planning elements, which can only be balanced locally and individually for each city.

Researchers differentiate between ecosystem and engineering resilience as two different perspectives on the behavior of systems under external influences. Ecosystem resilience, according to Holling, is defined as the ability to absorb external influences through cyclical adaptation while preserving the structures, processes, and identity of a system. Ecosystem research is based on the theory of adaptive cycles, and with the panarchy model, posits a nonlinear, cascading relationship in the behavior toward different variables (Günther 2009). A system can be considered resilient if it possesses capacity buffers that allow it to tolerate discontinuous changes within a stable equilibrium. However, the literature offers no universal categorization of the concepts of resilience, vulnerability, and adaptive capacity (Günther 2009: 134).

Ecosystem resilience is understood as a way of reducing technological dependence and sensibly supplementing the protective measures of urban infrastructures. It is meant to help prevent cities from committing to costly technological solutions whose significance could be lost with future developments (World Bank 2012). Major international studies, such as the Millennium Ecosystem Assessment, have delved into the subject of the capabilities of worldwide ecosystems and warned of the consequences of their eventual reduction or loss. This highly topical subject is being addressed by scientists in many different disciplines. As a result, approaches vary widely, as does the understanding of the terminology and methodology (Grunewald and Olaf 2015).

Ecosystem management can therefore only provide answers to planning goals and site-specific matters concerning ecosystems and landscapes. A wide range of knowledge, careful implementation, and close evaluation and monitoring of all measures are key factors in the meaningful integration of ecosystem services (World Bank 2012: 51).

The following five projects represent planning approaches that integrate concepts of urban resilience and sustainability at various levels, as examples of localized planning strategies.

The first project, "Jenfelder Au," involves a housing development on an abandoned military site that tangibly combines land usage with sustainable water management in a residential context. The second project, "Qunli Stormwater Park," is a Chinese example that convincingly unites landscape architecture with ecosystem services. The third project is an award-winning entry to an international student competition seeking sustainable solutions to the population density issues in Asian cities. The project introduces a new understanding of materials cycles and community-based urban structures. The fourth example sets new standards in city engineering with the infrastructure project “Semizentral.” Finally, the fifth project demonstrates, on the scale of the individual building, how a highly energy-efficient low-tech structure can contribute to social housing.

01 Project Jenfelder Au, West 8

Ongoing since 2005, Hamburg, Germany

The city district “Jenfelder Au” displays ecologically sustainable neighborhood development that intelligently combines urban spaces and green areas. In close cooperation with Hamburg City, the former military complex Lettow Vorbeck was converted under the oversight of West 8 into a new city quarter for residents to live and work in (Fig. 4.1).

Since 2005, the 29-ha area has been developed into rows of brick-walled townhouses and single-family homes grouped around four public squares that serve as parks for the neighborhood, with grass, trees, gazebos, ponds, and water cascades as the main design elements. Rainwater is collected in infiltration ditches, which drain into the water cascades and then flow into a central pond that acts as a rainwater reservoir (Figs. 4.2 and 4.3). Water is thus a defining theme in New

Fig. 4.1 Site plan, ©West 8

Jenfeld. Apart from the ecologically sustainable concept realized via a high-quality design that creates an attractive recreational area for residents of all ages, it is also a hands-on educational project for teaching water management. Additional eco-friendly measures, such as solar panels on the roofs and high standards for energy efficiency, further support the concept. Jenfelder Au received an Award of Excellence from the IBA in October 2013, because "the concept of the project meets the criteria of excellence of the IBA Hamburg; it is characterized by outstanding quality, innovation, and sustainability." (West 8 2015).

02 Project Qunli Stormwater Park, Harbin City, Heilongjiang Province, China

Turenscape and Peking University, Beijing
Qunli Stormwater Park
Harbin City, Heilongjiang Province, China
Client: Qunli New Town Government

Turenscape's project for the Qunli Stormwater Park in Harbin City, China, is a prime example of the importance of landscape architecture in planning flood protection. The Stormwater Park serves as a "green sponge for a water-resilient city" and takes over the duties of collecting, cleaning, and reserving storm water, as well as promoting new groundwater formation and protecting indigenous species and their ecosystems (Fig. 4.4). The planning puts equal emphasis on new impulses in

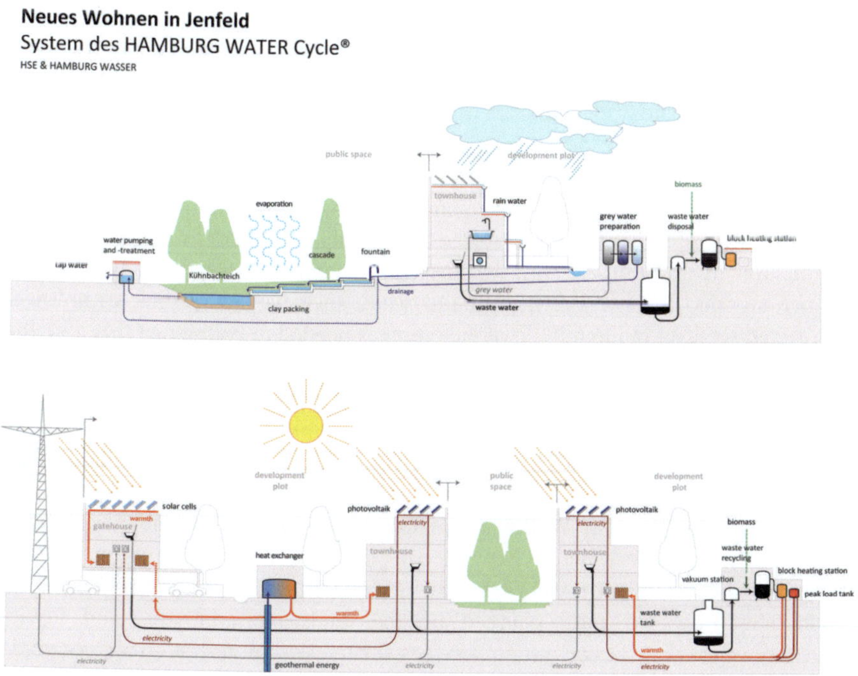

Fig. 4.2 System of the water cycle, ©West 8

Fig. 4.3 Water cascades, ©West 8

urban development by expanding the available recreational options and including new aesthetic experiences for users.

The new park landscape stretches over an area of 34 ha (84 acres) and forms the center of a new city on the edge of Harbin in northern China. The area is surrounded by dense building development and access routes that have spread since 2006 to cover an area of 32 million square meters (344,445,133 sq. ft.) of building floor area. The high percentage of sealed soil in this city district has led the annual precipitation of 567 mm (22 in.) to cause floods and leave stagnant water in the summer months. Meanwhile, the ground water level began to sink ever lower. A protected wetland in the middle of the city was needed to counteract this, one that was separated from its original water supply (Fig. 4.5).

The planning essentially rests on four pillars: the center is reserved for the development of the natural ecosystem. A ring of hills and ponds encircles the wetland in a cut-and-fill strategy and acts as a buffer zone for rainwater filtration and purification. A modulated planting concept reinforces the ecosystem as well as the aesthetic quality of the area. Walkways, platforms, and seating are integrated in such a way as to offer various nature experiences possible for the residents. A skywalk with gazebos and lookout towers offers views of both the cityscape and nature.

The new rainwater park planned by the landscape architects and Peking University offers several ecosystem services for the region and is also a congenial focal point for the district's residents. The new park has several functions: the existing wetland was overhauled while preserving the local flora and fauna. Floods

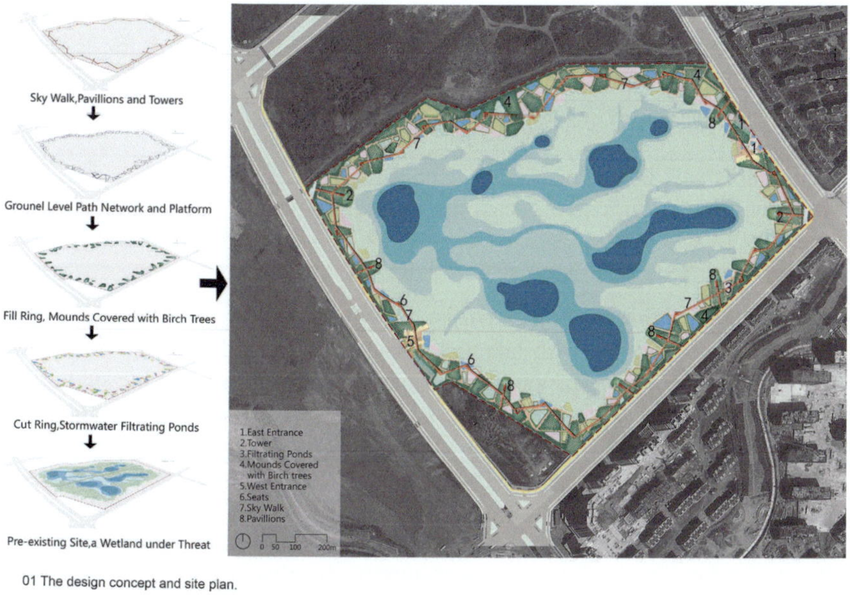

Fig. 4.4 Design concept and site plan, ©Turenscape

Fig. 4.5 Park view, ©Turenscape

are no longer a danger; rains only make the park more pleasing to the eye. The Stormwater Park was recognized as a National Urban Wetland Park for its lasting improvement of the ecological and biological conditions in the area (ASLA 2012).

03 Project Close City, Vertical Cities Asia 2013

Tongji University, Shanghai
Yiru Huang, Philip F. Yuan, Zhendong Wang
Close City Design Team:
Yao Bo, Rui Chen, Yibo Fu, Xun Li, Siyun Shen, Fan Wen

In the competition "Vertical City Asia," held by the National University Singapore in cooperation with international universities and designed to promote sustainable urban development ideas, the first prize was awarded to the submission from Tongji University, "Close City," for its "innovative solution to urban connectivity (NUS 2013)."

The jury honored the project team for its outstanding concept of close-knit neighborhoods and urban connectivity, which is a reflection of the social transformation of urban life in Hanoi. Based on extensive research, the team proposed a self-contained ecosystem for a city as a future-ready urban planning model. Central to the proposed materials cycle are opportunities for urban agriculture and the use of waste material as a resource for energy production and fertilizer for urban farming. The concept takes up the principles of traditional Vietnamese culture and adapts them for a densely populated modern Asian city. The interplay between communal and public spaces in an urban context is particularly well-formulated and shows great sensitivity to the needs of inhabitants. The traditional family structure is part of the concept and a building block of this community-based model for urban living.

A second entry in 2013 from Tongji University is likewise worth noting, in this case for its unique climate simulations. The urban planning concept "Micro Cities" takes typological elements of housing construction drawn from an analysis of historical examples and modernizes them for modern lifestyles. The composition of the city plan is developed using computer simulations for lighting and ventilation. Optimal sun exposure and fresh air corridors are central criteria for the positioning of the various structures within the urban ensemble. "Through a computational aggregation process, well-known architectural typologies [have] emerged in new forms of multi-functional clusters representing different spatial intensities" (Vertical Cities Asia 2013: 690 (NUS 2014)).

Micro Cities, Design Team A
Xuening Li, Jie Xie, Bo Wen Zhang, Tong Xiao, Jia Zhang, Yin Jia Gong

04 Semicentralized supply and treatment systems for fast-growing urban areas
Joint project between the Federal Ministry of Education and Research and TU Darmstadt, Institutiwar, in cooperation with Tongji University, Shanghai

Team
Iwar: Peter Cornel, Martin Wagner, Susanne Bieker
Est: Annette Rudolph-Cleff, Simon Gehrmann, Yang Li

SEMIZENTRAL Germany is an approach to sustainable housing development in fast-growing urban areas (Fig. 4.6). Sponsored by the Federal Ministry of Education and Research and headed by Prof. Peter Cornel at the Technical University (TU) of Darmstadt, this joint infrastructure project is undertaken with cooperation partners from science and the industry. It has received both public and private funding.

After a two-year conception and planning phase, the world's first semicentralized resource and recovery center (RRC), focusing on the recycling of water and material flows was opened on the occasion of the "World Horticulture Exposition 2014" in Qingdao, China. It is the first reference system for the semicentralized, integrated approach to infrastructure building. With a key contribution made by TU Darmstadt, the system will accommodate some 12,000 people. Approximately eight million people live in the burgeoning metropolis of Qingdao, which has been suffering for years under a major water shortage. Only about one-seventh of the average per capita water supply in China is available to the inhabitants here. As in other metropolitan regions worldwide, water and energy play a central role in housing development. In the coming two years of monitoring, the systems and their components will be evaluated and further improved by way of simulations for future projects.

The forward-looking infrastructure approach has decreased the need for fresh water as well as volume of waste water in the catchment area. One example is the use of process water for street cleaning, irrigation, and water reserves for firefighting, which result in significantly greater savings. Biogas and energy are generated from sewage sludge and organic household waste. As a result, the urban infrastructure system in Qingdao has an independent energy supply, and its work is largely carbon-neutral. A key objective of the project is an adaptive, resource-efficient water infrastructure that can grow flexibly along with the urban surroundings.

The special feature of SEMIZENTRAL is its integrated approach. Conventional systems rely on a strict separation of water supply, waste water purification, and waste treatment. SEMIZENTRAL integrates these three sectors in a holistic approach. It enables the sectors to be coordinated with one another, creating synergy effects, such as a self-sufficient energy supply and reduction of greenhouse

Fig. 4.6 View, ©Simon Gehrmann

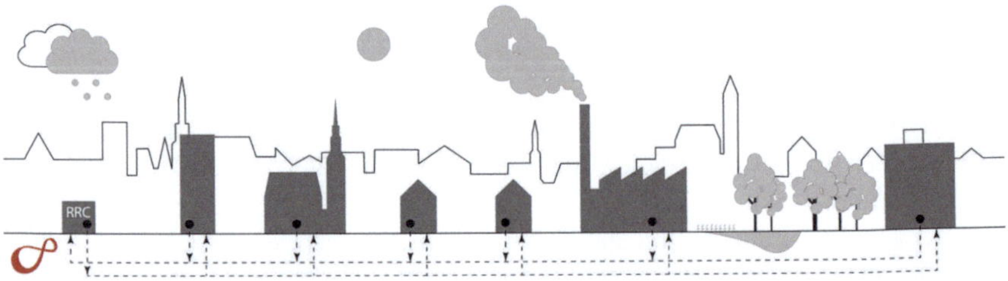

Fig. 4.7 Diagram, @ Simon Gehrmann

gases emission. An advantage over conventional infrastructure systems is the large savings potential: water savings of 30–40 % and more, all energy required for sewage and waste treatment, greatly reduced need for transport, a secure water supply with consistent quality, and high planning security. The same applies on the sewage and waste side (Fig. 4.7). Semicentralized supply and treatment systems offer a future-oriented and resource-saving alternative to conventional central infrastructures (Semizentral 2015).

SEMIZENTRAL Germany has received the GreenTec 2015 award in the category "Urbanization" because it has made an impressive contribution to improving the quality of life in megacities. This award is one of the most highly regarded environmental and business prizes in Europe. The GreenTec award is presented annually to recognize innovative environmental technologies and ecological commitment.

05 Project Solar-Active Skin in Punkthaus, G. Pfeifer and A. Rudolph-Cleff

TU Darmstadt
G. Pfeifer and A. Rudolph-Cleff
Balck + Partner, Heidelberg
Client: GBG Mannheimer Wohnungsbaugesellschaft mbH
Team: Sarah Bein, Simon Gehrmann

In this research project, the TU Darmstadt modernized the typology and energy systems of a 1950s residential building in cooperation with the GBG Mannheimer Wohnungsbaugesellschaft mbH. The project was funded by the German Federal Environmental Foundation (Deutsche Bundesstiftung Umwelt). As a model project, it was viewed by those involved as an important touchstone for determining the extent of economic and aesthetic feasibility of alternatives to conventional procedures and standards for the modernization of (social) housing stock. The current work focuses on the development of a solar collector facade, storing the energy produced, and uniform distribution of heat energy over an entire façade (Rudolph-Cleff and Pfeifer 2010).

Germany has a high proportion of postwar buildings that no longer fulfill current requirements with respect to their typology, energy use, and technical facilities. Builders, planners, and decision makers always face the question of whether to tear down and rebuild or attempt to work with what already exists. Modern requirements for energy consumption as outlined in the respective version of the Energy Saving Regulation (EnEV), which is made more stringent every few years,—force planners and building clients to opt for fast, easy, ready-to-use, tried-and-tested refurbishment methods, requiring in most cases thick, external-bonded insulation elements. Frequently, clients aim only to meet the minimum requirements of the EnEV with the renovation, and their ambition to exceed these is relatively low. The only serious concept in striving to exceed the EnEV standards is the so-called passive house with its stringent requirements and calculation methods according to the Passive House Planning Package (PHPP). However, this is exactly the type of energy modernization that is out of the question for nonprofit builders, particularly in the area of social housing, owing to the high planning costs and major technical effort involved. The present project therefore aims to dispense with the usual full thermal protection and yet achieve with little technical support the same or better energy values as prescribed by the passive house standard (Fig. 4.8).

The apartment building chosen as prototype for energy-oriented modernization has not seen any major renovation or modernization work since its first occupancy in the 1950s. With its uninsulated roof, façade, and balconies, the building had a heating energy consumption of approximately 273 kWh/a. In addition to a sensitive treatment of the building type, the energy concept comprises three additional components that mutually interact to reduce annual heating energy requirements to around 10–14 kWh/a: a climate-active façade in combination with a stonewall storage, controlled ventilation, and heat recovery. The energy concept is to be regarded as a low-tech solution. The results have been monitored since October 2013.

Fig. 4.8 Social housing after renovation in 2014, ©Claudius Pfeifer

The climate-active building envelope consists of a double-skin facade with a solar air collector. A translucent skin of polycarbonate with a U-value of 0.83 W/m K has been added to the existing outer wall, creating an in-between layer of circulating air. This "chimney" is connected via a pipe system to a loosely layered pebble storage mass in the basement and on the roof. In the winter, the resulting closed air system distributes the energy of the sun's rays in the morning (sun in the east) and evening (sun in the west) across the outside surface of the entire building without the need for a mechanical drive. In the summer, the storage mass in the basement can be used to distribute the coolness of the ground evenly across the entire outside surface of the building. The airflow in the gated air collector is supported by a recirculating fan (Fig. 4.9).

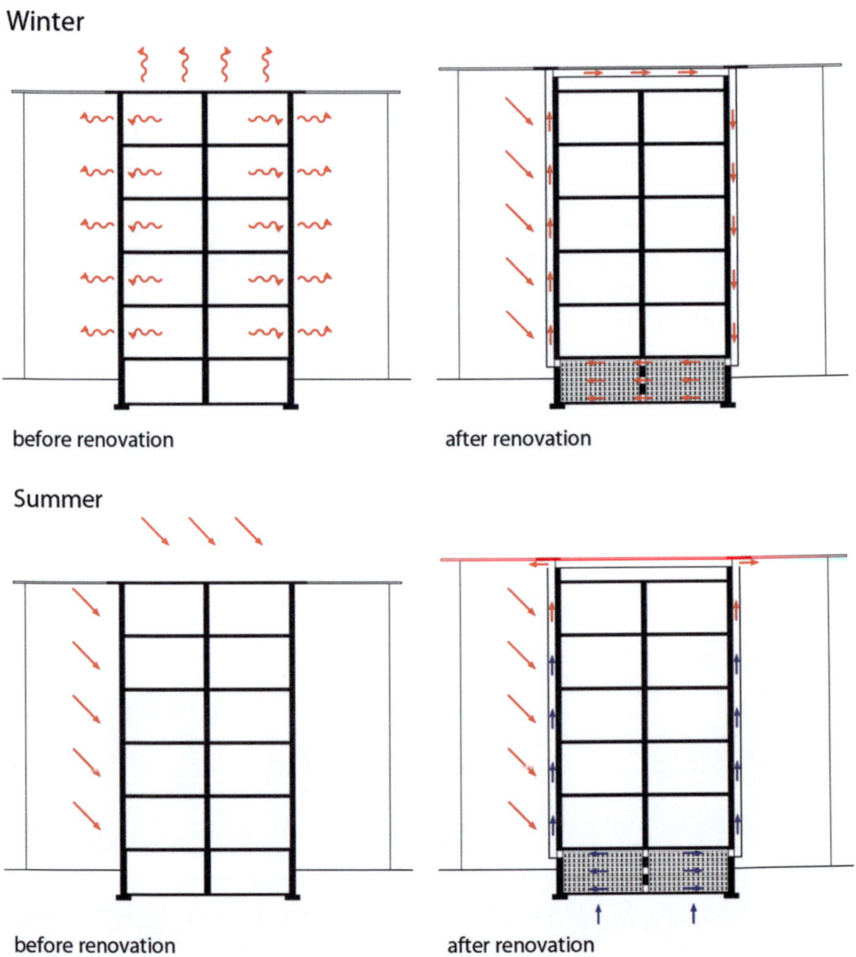

Fig. 4.9 Concept of solar-active skin, ©West, TU Darmstadt

A façade composed of translucent lightweight building components made of polycarbonate sheets has never before been realized in multi-story housing. To comply with the building code, the material first had to be tested by the Materials Testing Institute in Leipzig in a fire test in original scale and certified non-critical in the planned execution. In cooperation with BALCK + PARTNER facility engineering, computer simulations were carried out on different variants to optimize the design. To study and optimize the flow patterns within the collector interspace, CFD simulations of a section of the building were carried out in cooperation with ANSYS Germany GmbH.

The simple energy concept and double-skin collector façade offer an energy-efficient and economical alternative to standard housing modernization. The range of architectural possibilities for façade design is wide, enabling the retention of the typical features of the original period style while updating them to suite present-day tastes: the fine articulation of the façade, conversion of balconies into loggias, and transitions to the building's base and roof edge (Rudolph-Cleff and Pfeifer 2013).

The project was awarded the following: Exemplary Building 2013 by the Chamber of Architects of Baden-Württemberg, Third Environmental Prize of the City of Mannheim, and House, Houses, Quarters award presented by the Working Group of Building Societies in Baden-Württemberg (Arbeitsgemeinschaft of Baden-Wuerttemberg) and the State Government of Baden-Württemberg.

4.3 Planning Objectives and Planning

The importance of interdisciplinary, integrated planning concepts is demonstrated in the range of projects from converting a former military site into a residential development to a landscape planning concept for protecting urban wetlands, and from integrated urban infrastructure systems to examples of climate-adaptive planning. All of these innovative projects are based on integrated concepts that improve the quality of life for residents; ensure access to clean water, air, and energy; and open up transportation and communication pathways, while also providing opportunities for living, working, and partaking in leisure activities within the community.

The projects presented cover a wide range of innovative planning approaches. They differ in their concepts, planning levels, and targets, although all demonstrate in a simple way the importance of integrated and interdisciplinary planning approaches that are closely tied to their respective setting. All of these projects share the disregard for a fixed planning principle or formula; they are based instead on differentiated analyses and an intensive search for responses befitting particular local situations. The idea is to understand the context, formulate plans in terms of that context, and then highlight the potential of a particular city district under consideration.

Every building has multiple interfaces to the urban context, and hence to the urban climate, the ground, the bodies of water, and the surrounding development and open-space typologies. Further, the density of a district and the form taken by the construction there exert a decisive impact on its living conditions and energy needs.[1]

Buildings also have a number of interfaces with a city's technical infrastructure, and hence, with the heating and cooling energy, electrical energy, water, and waste water systems. Building and facility technologies are inseparably networked with the urban technical infrastructure, and therefore, must be developed in parallel with it and reconsidered in terms of usage cascades.

Indeed, buildings and their surroundings have a lasting impact on the microclimate. The redensification of an urban built environment or demolition of individual properties affects the microclimate equivalent to the sealing of surfaces between buildings and color schemes of the buildings themselves.[2]

It is worthwhile to take a closer look at and link current knowledge at the building level with up-to-date urban technology and the urban climate. The interaction between buildings and districts opens up myriad possibilities for improving energy generation and use. Further, the theme of energy efficiency needs to be grasped not as a technological standard but rather as an intelligent solution tailored for a particular location.

4.4 Local Ties

There are distinct goals to be achieved through an integrative contemplation of buildings and districts. The main point is always to design an urban realm with a high quality of life; however, in light of climate change, it is also important to improve the urban climate (ventilation/thermal load/water) and enhance energy efficiency by means of the following:

Cybernetic building models low-tech instead of high-tech that draw on passive solutions for autochthonous building typologies,
The networking of existing facilities,
Harnessing untapped potentials,
Coupling energy-producing with energy-consuming buildings, and
Expanding the network to include regenerative elements.

[1]This impact is estimated at 15–20 %. A comprehensive study of various housing development models is conducted at TU Darmstadt in the research project UrbanReNet under the coordination of Professors Manfred Hegger and Jörg Dettmar.

[2]Light-colored surfaces improve the daylight qualities of both interior and exterior spaces. A lower albedo means a reduction in the heating-up of surfaces, avoidance of microinversion, and improved ventilation of an urban space.

Location and typology are decisive factors in the design of local energy networks. Traditional (autochthonous) building types, such as the Black Forest house or the Andalusian courtyard house, display in their energy concepts a meaningful localization in their particular environment. The distribution of storage masses, arrangement of buffer zones, utilization of cooling effects or of evaporative cooling, and use of solar heat are based on empirical knowledge. New usage requirements have largely superseded these building types, without further developing the wealth of knowledge underlying them. However, with the demands of climate protection and the search for energy-efficient building types, the question of "passive solutions" is being raised anew.

4.5 Energy Potentials: Microclimatic Potentials

Energy-efficient planning calls for a precise analysis of the given conditions, such as the basic climatic conditions and user profile. A building shell, for example, can be considered energy-optimized when it can be ensured that hardly any energy is needed throughout the year and that no elaborate energy supply technology is required. The passive performance of new energy-saving building shells forms the foundation for future-ready energy concepts. Software programs that help monitor and steer planning tasks, ranging from simple energy balance sheets to complex energy and streaming simulations, have been available since the mid-1980s. Heat conduction, radiation, and convection can be displayed in three dimensions and over several zones, taking into account dynamic changes in the external and internal basic conditions (Hegger et al. 2008: 39).

Solar air heating systems have existed since the 19th century (Butti and Perlin 2009) but have since faded into oblivion. Initial construction information and energy balance proposals are available with the final paper issued by Task 19 of the International Energy Agency. Under the title "Solar Air Systems," the paper describes five basic types and provides an extensive catalogue of parts but does not go into details on the architectural and design aspects (Hastings 1999, 2000). Important basic research on architecturally based systems was done by Herzog and Natterer (1985) in their book "Gebäudehüllen aus Glas und Holz" (Building Shells Made of Glass and Wood). Charles Filleux and Andreas Gütermann went on to differentiate between systems for outside air preheating, space heating, and water heating (Filleux and Gütermann 2009). A first systematic account of the planning and assessment of heat-collecting, energetically dynamic building components and spatial structures in residential construction was presented by Tersluisen (2013) in cooperation with the "Fondation Kybernetik" of TU Darmstadt.

Only through the interplay of active and passive measures on all levels (heating, cooling, ventilation, light, electricity, water, and waste water) can energy needs be minimized while also optimizing energy supply. Each component deserves to be scrutinized closely and integrated carefully into the overall system. Open spaces take on great importance in this regard[3]: through cooling effects, integrated rain-water and greywater concepts, and as spaces for geothermal energy, ground collectors, or underground storage (BMVBS and BBR 2009).

4.6 Goals, Not Standards

To open up new possibilities, it is essential to progress from the consideration of individual buildings, facilities, and uses to that of interconnected building clusters. However, although current legal regulations promote the upgrading of energy performance, they also set standards for individual buildings and facility systems. These established standards inhibit the development of innovative concepts that point the way to alternative approaches. Further, technological solutions are doomed to become prematurely outdated, which is opposite of the goals underlying them.

When goals are framed not for an individual building but for an entire housing development or district, greater scope opens up for new concepts, and hence, for ways to strengthen local identities.

The microclimatic conditions at a location, available storage masses, and various uses and different open spaces available vary widely and do not allow for standard answers if their potentials are to be taken seriously. A great opportunity to work against the uniform scene of global standards and find instead local answers that emphasize the special quality of a location without having to rely on historicizing images exists herein.

4.7 Performance and Spatial Ambience

Entrenched images of what the interior and exterior of a home, and of what urban space and open space look like must be expanded. Such an expansion can be achieved by deriving and developing innovative design ideas for new energy-performance functions. Examples can be found in the design of solar-active façades and energy gardens. This scenario is not only a matter of developing the building shells further but also of modifying the building typologies themselves once the energy flow is understood as a three-dimensional system and the necessary storage and buffer zones are integrated as fixed components of the design.

Learning from current experiences with autochthonous building types does not mean taking recourse to earlier building typologies. Instead, the empirical knowledge

[3]BMVBS, BBR: *Nutzung städtischer Freiflächen für erneuerbare Energien*, 2008.

gained from them must be applied to meeting present-day requirements. This step involves more than simply translating passive building models into modern construction, because functions, building practice, and technologies have in the meantime fundamentally changed. The step is nonetheless worthwhile, because it shows a way out of the dead end of high-tech solutions (Rudolph-Cleff and Schaal 2012).

Changed spatial ambiences in architecture and open-space planning also provide a chance, when successful, to find a design balance between cityscape and landscape, between attractive usage offers and energy use along with maintenance and operating costs. The possibilities for combining the classic functions of urban and open spaces with new energy functions needs to be investigated further using technology assessment, and with regard to integrating their design and function (for example, the compatibility of shallow geothermal storage with green areas).[4]

4.8 Urban Heritage

There are also opportunities for integrative consideration in the field of listed historical buildings. Upgrading their energy performance is unfortunately, as a rule, much too expensive.

A modification of a building's appearance is usually undesirable in this case. Alternative concepts are needed for integrating new energy functions in a simple way without destroying the character of the existing building. For example, a solar air collector installed on the roofs of the buildings in the housing complex in Freiburg-Haslach upgraded the energy efficiency of the historic ensemble without changing the building fabric or façades of the listed garden city. The energetic activation of the roof space succeeded in reducing energy consumption to 40 kWh/m^{2}a. Minimal interventions in the floor plans adapted the apartments to suit modern needs (Rudolph-Cleff 2011).

Energy efficiency and infrastructure are of course only two elements in integrated urban development. A vibrant city district must offer much more than merely a sustainable energy concept.

4.9 Community-Based Planning

History has shown that urban planning projects only stand to gain through the participation of a dedicated public. Hard location factors are no guarantee of a positive development. Involving stakeholders and taking advantage of their implicit

[4]For more information, see the research projects undertaken by Prof. Jörg Dettmar, TU Darmstadt, Department of Design and Open Space Planning.

knowledge are often referred to as critical success factors in planning procedures. This fact has changed the role of the planner: what is called for today is not merely a presentation of the context while pointing out potentials for improvement but also the task of facilitating and mediating in the process of civic participation.

4.10 Conclusion

There is hardly a term that is bandied about today in the field of building planning and urban development as often as "sustainability." Ecological and climate-friendly aspects are invoked especially frequently as credo. Meanwhile, however, a city is a complex and multi-dimensional system that disposes over intricately networked structures and few opportunities for large-scale planning. Only an integrated consideration of the setting and a concept adapted to fit its specific conditions could meet the demands of sustainable urban development. Analysis of the relevant parameters of a site is an essential component to any approach. A key task is to identify and take advantage of synergies. New energetic and creative possibilities emerge as soon as the view is not limited to a single building and its facilities but expanded beyond the building envelope to encompass the entire district and the potentials inherent in a composite concept. Different types of open spaces, urban spaces, networks, and buildings can work together as one. With a combination of active and passive measures, holistic approaches offer new spatial and design possibilities in the neighborhood context: for example, for linking energy production and energy consumption within building groups, for integrating storage masses and compensating for peak demand in open spaces, as well as for improving the urban climate (ventilation, heat load, and water retention).

It is not only about creating energy-efficient neighborhoods, however, but also about the residents and their social identification with their quarter. Every urban development measure changes the social environment and alters the place where residents live and work. A sensitive handling of resources and existing qualities is therefore important if the residents and buildings are to be treated with respect and social displacement processes avoided. During the planning phase, an intense engagement with the location is required to lay the groundwork for an attractive and high-quality living environment. Ultimately, the economic level of consideration is also an important focus of planning, going beyond the actual investment costs to include future operating and maintenance costs of a system as part of integrated life cycle planning.

There is reason to be skeptical when standard solutions and easy recipes for energy saving are suggested. Humankind is only just embarking on a turning point in our energy culture; material flows and energy-related business models will continue to evolve at the global level along with our living environments. This paradigm shift will call for many concessions. Apart from political pressure, a wave of media attention and public interest in the topic of climate protection should accompany the changing legal requirements and lend extra weight to the norms and standards. The focus of research and practice is clearly on CO_2 reduction and energy savings. However, the Energy Saving Regulation relieves neither owners nor planners of the responsibility to decide which measures are sensible and which of the targets reasonable. The need for an honest and holistic consideration of each individual situation is obvious. Every planning process must take into account the requirements for the legal and organizational structure of a project as well as the nature of the modernization and system to be applied. Any approach that attempts to divide the work at hand into sub-targets by means of certification steps and checklists will remain stuck at the superficial, formal level. The bundle of criteria resulting from social and cultural, as well as economic and ecological, capital can only be assessed from case to case and the quality of the planning adapted accordingly. When working with existing building fabric, questions as to its substance and appearance, as well as the reversibility of any measures, take precedence in construction decisions. Important for programmatic decisions are the social structure of the inhabitants and mix of available uses as well as the cost-effectiveness of the modernization measures in terms of their social implications. In terms of upgrading energy efficiency, the same goes for single buildings as for district-wide concepts: there is no universal standard solution that eliminates the need for a differentiated consideration of the location and neighborhood. The planning effort is high, but the chance of finding an ideal solution for a particular location is also high.

Efforts should not stop at energy-oriented modernization. Every good example from actual practice involves aesthetic considerations. Although design is not an end in itself, it is the very element that mediates between the technological standard and individual solution, or between the conceptual planning and subsequent use. Here lies the key that architecture places in our hands to mediate between technology and the residents' world of experience. Architecture and landscape architecture can and must build a bridge to the energy culture of individual users.

Only by connecting sociological components, such as a high quality of life and residential amenities, with the technical and ecological dimensions of energy-related modernization can conditions be created that help residents identify with their built environment. They will then be willing to develop a better understanding of the energy system and how it works, and then accept responsibility for its sensible handling. This acceptance is a critical basis for users to feel like a part of the overall system so that they will strive to advocate for its continued quality.

Renewable energies can be obtained in many ways on site. Their use provides new ways to decentralize supply structures. A balance between ambitiously striving for energy-independent city districts and a centralized supplier structure on the energy market can only be found with the help of policymakers. The cost of energy will rise, even if we succeed in reducing consumption. This fact makes the city quarter and the quality of the living environment all the more important: by taking us back to the theme of designing for people.

References

BMVBS, BBR (2009) Nutzung städtischer Freiflächen für erneuerbare Energien. BBR, Berlin

Butti K, Perlin J (2009) A golden threat: 2500 years of solar architecture and technology. Mario Boyards Publishers Ltd., London

Filleux C, Gütermann A (2009) Solare Luftheizsysteme: Konzepte, Systemtechnik, Planung, 2. Aufl. Staufen: Ökobuchverlag

Folke C et al (2010) Resilience thinking: integrating resilience, adaptability and transformability. Ecol Soc 15(4):20

Grunewald K, Olaf B (eds) (2015) Ecosystem services–concepts. Methods and case studies, Springer.

Günther E (2009) Klimawandel und Resilience Management: Interdisziplinäre Konzeption eines entscheidungsorientierten Ansatzes, Trossingen

Hastings R (1999) Solar air systems: built examples. James & James (Science Publishers), London

Hastings R (2000) Solar air systems: a design handbook. James & James (Science Publishers), London

Hegger M et al (2008) Energie atlas. Birkhäuser Verlag, Nachhaltige Architektur, Basel, Boston, Berlin

Herzog T, Natterer J (1985) *Gebäudehüllen aus Glas und Holz: Maßnahmen zur energiebewussten Erweiterung von Wohnhäusern*, 2nd edn. Lausanne. Presses polytechniquesromandes, p 38ff

Holling CS (1973) Resilience and stability of ecological systems. Annu Rev Ecol Syst 4:1–23

Leichenko R (2011) Climate change and urban resilience. In: Leemans R, Patwardhan A (eds) Current opinion in environmental sustainability, vol 3. ScienceDirect, Elsevier, pp 164–168

NUS (2013) Vertical Cities Asia. In: International Design Competition and Symposium 2013, vol 3. Everyone harvest. BBT Press, Singapore

NUS (ed) (2014) Vertical Cities Asia 2013, vol 3. Everyone harvests, Singapore

Rudolph-Cleff A (2011) Energetische Netze im städtischen Kontext, in: dbu (ed.): Denkmalschutz und Klimaschutz- zwei Seiten derselben Medaille ?!, Beiträge der Akademie für Natur- und Umweltschutz Baden-Württemberg, vol 51. Wissenschaftliche Verlagsgesellschaft Stuttgart, pp 98–107

Rudolph-Cleff A, Pfeifer G (2010) Aubuckel. Typologie und Energie. Freiburg

Rudolph-Cleff A, Pfeifer G (2013) Auf den Punkt gebracht. Typologische+energetische Sanierung eines Punkthauses, Freiburg, syntagma-Verlag

Rudolph-Cleff A, Schaal S (2012) Im Kontext denken. Planungsfragen zu energetischen Quartierskonzepten. In: BDA (Hrg): Energetische Sanierung: Denken im Quartier, Berlin 2012:16–20

Satterthwaite D, Dodman D (2013) Towards resilience and transformation for cities within a finite planet. Environ Urbanization 25:291–298

Shaw K (2012) "Reframing" resilience: challenges for planning theory and practice. Plann Theory Pract 13(2):308–312

Terluisen A (2013) Konzept zur Planung und Bewertung wärmeenergiegewinnender, energetisch-dynamischer Bauteil- und Raumstrukturen im Wohnungsbau, syntagma-Verlag, Freiburg

UN (2005) Ecosystems & human wellbeing. Island Press, Washington

UNISDR (2011) Global assessment report on disaster, risk reduction: revealing risk, redefining development. UNISDR Practical Action

URL:http://www.asla.org/2012awards/026.html. Accessed 6 Jan 2015

URL:http://semizentral.de/en/. Accessed 6 Jan 2015

URL:http://www.west8.nl/projects/all/jenfelder_au_formerly_known_as_new_jenfeld. Accessed 6 Jan 2015

Walker B, Holling CS, Carpenter SR, Kinzig A (2004) Resilience, adaptability and transformability in social–ecological systems. Ecol Soc 9(2): 5. [online] URL:http://www.ecologyandsociety.org/vol9/iss2/art5

World Bank (2012) Building urban resilience: principles, tools and practice. The World Bank Group, Washington

Chapter 5
Mountainous Rural Urbanization: Space Integration of Industry and Village

Hao Long, Jiayang Li, Feng Lu and Dongzhu Chu

5.1 Introduction

In the 1980s, Professor Fei Xiaotong discussed three topics in small town research in his (1985) book "Four Texts of Small Towns," namely, rural industrialization, urbanization of population, and economic marketization. After more than 30 years of development, the demographic urbanization rate of China has increased from 21.62 % in 1983 to 54.77 % in 2014 at a considerable speed (Fig. 5.1).[1] Rural industrialization and economic marketization also achieved great development.

However, such urbanization is accompanied by a large population movement from villages to cities. The scale of urban population expands unceasingly, whereas rural hollowing is growing increasingly serious. Meanwhile, the proportion of the primary sector is gradually declining, as that of the secondary and tertiary industries progressively increases, which seems unreasonable in the industrial structure (Zhu 2014). Other problems have become apparent as well, caused by an incomplete land system and household registration system,[2] among other factors. For example,

[1] According to the National Bureau of Statistics of the People's Republic of China (http://data.stats.gov.cn).

[2] At present, China has two sets of land management systems for the city and the countryside, which are independent of each other. If rural land needs to be urbanized, it must go through land requisition formalities. Only the government has the right to land requisition. In the land increment income from the requisition, peasants' compensation only accounts for 5–10 %. Peasants could neither get due land increment income by their land nor buy houses and receive public services as urban residents (urban households) do in cities because they are registered to hold agricultural permanent residence (rural household).

H. Long (✉) · J. Li · F. Lu · D. Chu
Faculty of Architecture and Urban Planning, Chongqing University, Chongqing, China
e-mail: Longhao@cqu.edu.cn

F. Wang and M. Prominski (eds.), *Urbanization and Locality*,
DOI 10.1007/978-3-662-48494-4_5

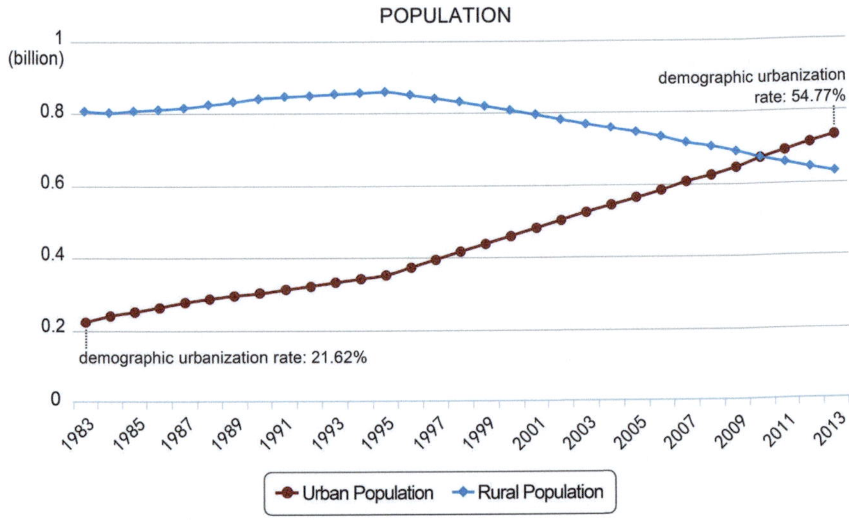

Fig. 5.1 China's urban–rural population statistical chart (1983–2013) (*Source* National Bureau of Statistics of the People's Republic of China)

restrictions of the household registration systems deprive peasant-workers involved in the urbanization process of urban services, such as education, healthcare, social security, and housing. The over-50 % urbanization rate from official statistics actually refers to "half urbanization".[3] The household registration system reflects the disparity between city and countryside, industry and agriculture. If reform to this system can be implemented soon, it can bring land-lost peasants and peasant-workers into the city public service system. Subsequently, they can live and work in contentment, which will promote city development. Otherwise, the disparity between city and countryside will be further widened and bring about larger social contradictions (Zheng 2014).

Therefore, a new understanding of urbanization has come into being from the government to all sectors of society. The new urbanization policy has been explicitly put forward and implemented. The emphasis of urbanization has been changed: the core content is to propel urban–rural coordination and shorten the disparity between the city and the countryside. The main tasks are to attach importance to agriculture and ecology, focus on the peasantry, cover the countryside, realize the integration of urban–rural infrastructure, and enforce equalization of public services.

[3]"Half urbanization" refers to the scenario where a peasant-worker living in a city is counted in the urbanization rate but lacks the same rights and welfare as urban residents (for not owning an urban household).

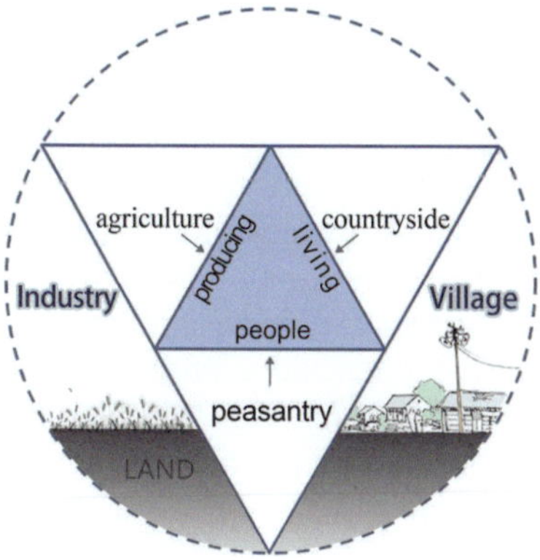

Fig. 5.2 Relationship between industry-village and agriculture-countryside-peasantry (*Source* Study by the authors in 2015)

At the "Academic Conference of Rural Development and Rural Planning" held in Shanghai on January 10, 2015, Professor Shen Guanbao, Fei Xiaotong's student, reviewed his supervisor's topics from the earlier years and put forward his own points. He identified the core problems to be urban–rural integration, citizenization, and equalization in view of the present urbanization. Thus, the goal of rural development should be the modernization of villages and the life of village people. Efforts should be made to realize that residents can be entitled to their houses and working people can be entitled to their occupation. In other words, people should be willing to stay in their hometown for work and residence, entitled to equal public services. The term "Three Agriculture" has shown that all three aspects of countryside, agriculture, and peasantry should be taken into consideration from the perspective of collective consideration for people who are producing output products and living (Zhang 2014). Therefore, attention should be paid to the countryside's dual attribute of producing and living, and toward planning the development of industrial and village spaces as a whole in rural urbanization (Fig. 5.2). This rule is especially important to mountainous villages, where resources differ greatly from those in the plains area and ecological vulnerability is particularly high. Otherwise, the destruction of the ecological environment by unchecked construction will bring out irreversible negative influence.

Therefore, mountainous rural urbanization is not only related to many key issues, such as solving mountainous regions' urban–rural dual contradiction, improving the backwardness of the primary sector, and protecting the ecological environment and human resources. Indeed, mountainous rural urbanization tasks in China should objectively clarify and regard both drawbacks and favorable trends to improve the status and then establish a scientific and reasonable development strategy.

5.2 Plights of Mountainous Rural Development

In recent years, two ubiquitous modes of mountainous rural construction have cropped up: one is design and construction that focuses on improving the rural scene, the other is land functional partitioning. The former can improve the backward atmosphere of mountainous villages in a short time, whereas the latter is intended to divide the production and residential lands in a reasonable and clear manner. However, the former is often characterized by a relative lack of concern for industrial space (Fig. 5.3 shows Lingfeng Village surveyed by the authors in Gaofeng Township, Wanzhou District, Chongqing; the village has a pleasant scenery, but it is undergoing hollowing, low occupancy, and vacancy for most of the houses because of low space integration of the industry and the village). The latter would easily establish a gap between industry and village spaces caused by the clear partition of the two types of spaces together with complex terrains, which may not engender a complementary effect (as shown in Fig. 5.4, in the land use planning of a village in Changle City, industry and village spaces are almost completely separated by a road, and such a clear partition is neither convenient for villagers' daily living and production nor good for the cohesion of rural vitality). Generally, both modes express a lack of proper integration of village space

Fig. 5.3 Lingfeng village, Gaofeng township, Wanzhou district, Chongqing (*Source* Study by authors in 2014)

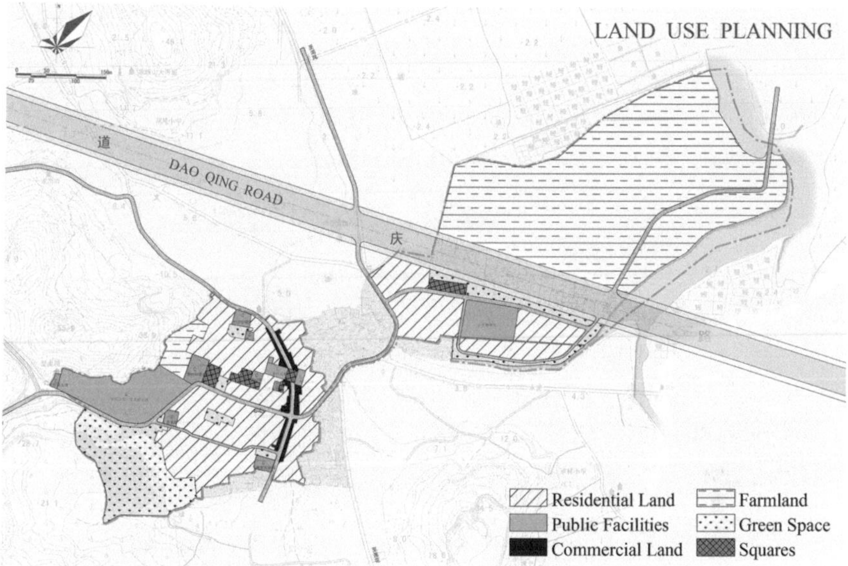

Fig. 5.4 Land use planning of a village in Changle, Fujian Province (*Source* Draw by the authors from Urban and Rural Planning Bureau of Changle City)

construction and renewal with transformation development of the primary sector from a macroscopic perspective. Improvement in the physical space of rural villages cannot be effectively transformed into an industrial and economic motivation for the sustainable development of mountainous villages, which is not useful for the core aim of improving the living and producing level of the countryside.

To achieve the abovementioned aim, we must establish an objective cognition of the relationship between rural industry space and settlement space, and of the development bottleneck for both. Otherwise, they will continuously obstruct each other, which may extremely restrict the progress of mountainous rural urbanization.

5.2.1 Lack of an Overall Industry-Village Development Strategy

The primary factor to the abovementioned drawbacks is the lack of coordination between rural industrial and settlement spaces, which threatens ecological security. Given the various restrictions, only primary processing industries can be introduced to mountainous villages to match with the local agricultural industry. Further, most of them are located in ecologically sensitive areas of mountainous cities, such as water resource and eco-preservation areas. Hence, industry development in mountainous villages has an inconvenient influence on the overall environment.

Fig. 5.5 Environmental damage by a hydropower station (*Source* Beijing youth daily)

In recent years, new industry spaces are expanding and developing at an unprecedented rate, profoundly changing the form of traditional settlements in mountainous villages. However, the different principles and separated management between farming, forestry, water conservancy, construction, planning, land, and other departments, which were previously related to construction in industry and village spaces, pose difficulties to the formation of a reasonable and systematic management mechanism and planning methods. Thus, important problems are difficult to solve owing to the lack of effective communication. Meanwhile, during the promotion of new forms of technology for the rural industry, they tend to be ignored for bringing negative influences to the rural settlement landscape, spatial layout, and natural environment in mountainous regions. This situation may intensify the negative effects on mountainous villages and their surrounding ecological environment (Fig. 5.5 shows the environmental damage by one of the numerous hydropower stations along the tributaries of the Yangtze River).

5.2.2 *Weakness in Industry Space Extension*

Another set of reasons is the low degree of industry compounding, insufficient industry chain, and poor adaptability of the market. At present, the goal of the "Three Agriculture" concept in mountainous areas is to increase peasants' income substantially. However, the relative single industrial structure and small-scale production in mountainous villages face various problems, such as low value-added output, poor market adaptability, and low ecological benefits in the context of long-term marketization. With the promotion of modern agricultural technology and intensive utilization of cultivated land, many agricultural outputs are rising steadily. However, given the insufficiencies of the market segment, the ascension of agricultural output contrarily leads to the state where a higher output does not bring a higher income, which becomes the main bottleneck of agricultural development in mountainous areas.

Thus, changes are urgent in the inherent way of mountainous area development by strengthening the processing, service, logistics, marketing, and other supporting links in the industrial chain, to add value to agricultural outputs. Only by taking such ecological and marketization "value-added" methods can we promote a coordinated development for mountainous rural construction and ecological environment protection.

5.2.3 *Disorder in Village Space Development*

The disorderly development of settlement spaces, prominent contradiction between humans and their land, and lack of long-term effective control mechanisms form yet another set of drawbacks to development in mountainous areas. At present, construction in mountainous villages is seeing an upsurge. However, the lack of long-term development strategies and effective control mechanisms have resulted in the disordered development of many mountainous villages; sceneries and spaces are entering a chaotic stage, and regional characteristics are gradually disappearing.

Given the limited land resources, precious land and space are not efficiently used to fulfill the development needs, thereby intensifying the human-land contradiction, increasing the developing cost directly, and indirectly causing the loss of rural endogenous attractiveness and vitality.

5.2.4 *Solutions*

Thus, the construction of rural industry and settlement spaces is challenged by low integration and coordinated contradiction on account of the absence of an overall industry-village development, along with their own bottlenecks and problems. Further, such contradictions and problems interact with and obstruct one another, thereby impeding development in mountainous villages.

Therefore, taking into account the particularity of mountainous villages, especially ecological vulnerability, attention must be paid to the indivisibility and mutual conditionality of rural industrial space, settlement space, and natural environment. Industry and village spaces must considered as a coordinated whole.

To find feasible solutions, stakeholders ought to rely on the foundation and advantageous trend of the current situation: great importance is attached to urban–rural development.

5.3 Tendency of Mountainous Rural Urbanization

5.3.1 National Policies

Since 2004, the Chinese government gas consecutively issued 11 No. 1 Documents on the theme of the "Three Agriculture" (countryside, agriculture, and peasantry).[4] The government has defined strategic objectives for the overall urban–rural development and construction of new socialist villages, as well as established policy systems to solve issues related to "Three Agriculture," which conform to the requirements of the concept of scientific development. In November 2013, the Third Plenary Session of the 18th Central Committee of the Communist Party of China announced the "Decision of the CCCPC on Some Major Issues Concerning Comprehensively Deepening the Reform." The decision explicitly proposed that the urban–rural dual structure is a major obstacle to the integrated development of urban and rural areas, and as such, new relations must be formed between industry and agriculture and between urban and rural areas, one in which industry promotes agriculture, urban areas support rural development, agriculture and industry benefit each other, and urban and rural areas achieve integrated development. Overall, the ruling established a deeper and more comprehensive deployment of the urban–rural structure and rural land policy, population policy, economic development model, and public resource service.[5]

Corresponding with policy development, China is continuously improving its national and local legal system as well as normative documents. The Urban and Rural Planning Law of the People's Republic of China promulgated in 2008 defines the content and requirements of township and village planning for the first time.[6] Otherwise, improving the synchronous development of urbanization, information, industrialization, and agricultural modernization has been classified as the next

[4]The CPC has consecutively issued 5 No. 1 Documents on the theme of countryside, agriculture, and farmers from 1982 to 1982, deploying rural reform and agricultural development. From 2004 to 2014, the CPC consecutively issued the "Three Agriculture" themed No. 1 Documents to emphasize the most important status of the "Three Agriculture" issue in the period of China's socialist modernization. According to the website of the Central People's Government of the People's Republic of China (http://www.gov.cn/).

[5]According to the "Decision of the CCCPC on Major Issues Concerning Comprehensively Deepening the Reform" adopted at the Third Plenary Session of the 18th Central Committee of the Communist Party of China on November 12, 2013.

[6]According to the "Urban and Rural Planning Law of the People's Republic of China" published by the China Legal Publishing House in 2007.

focus of urbanization by the National New Urbanization Planning (2014–2020) promulgated in 2014.[7] All these will bring profound influences to agriculture-oriented mountainous rural urbanization.

5.3.2 *Support from Present Technology*

Based on a number of science and technology model villages, towns, and counties for new rural construction during the 10th Five-Year and 11th Five-Year (such as Longsha science and technology model town of the national new rural construction in Wanzhou, Chongqing),[8] China has published technical standards for the construction of villages and towns, such as the Standard for Planning of Towns (GB50188-2007)[9] and Technique Code for Village Rehabilitation (GB50445-2008).[10]

Meanwhile, during the 11th Five-Year Plan, the National Science-Technology Support Plan apparently increased investment for rural urbanization research and successively conducted key programs, including the following: rural energy, economical construction materials, services, information technology, ecological environmental monitoring and regulation, space planning and land use, residential planning and construction standards, and key technology integration (such as research on urban–rural environmental protection technology and countermeasures for new rural construction, as well as programs for key technology integration and demonstration).[11]

5.3.3 *Trends in Relevant Research*

Since the explicit proposal of the policy of overall urban–rural development, scholars in related fields have been constantly considering and discussing the many issues of rural urbanization. A number of local mountainous villages have been exploring the modes of urbanization based on their own resource characteristics and development requirements. To perceive mountainous rural urbanization more objectively, there are several aspects to be dissected.

[7]According to the "National New Urbanization Planning (2014–2020)" published by People's Publishing House in 2014.

[8]According to the website of the Ministry of Science and Technology of the People's Republic of China (http://www.most.gov.cn).

[9]According to the "Standard for planning of towns (GB50188-2007)" promulgated by the Ministry of Construction of the People's Republic of China in 2007.

[10]According to the "Technique code for village rehabilitation (GB50445-2008)" promulgated by the Ministry of Housing and Urban–Rural Development of the People's Republic of China in 2008.

[11]According to the website of the Ministry of Science and Technology of the People's Republic of China (http://www.most.gov.cn).

Taking the relationship between rural development and urbanization as the first perspective, rural urbanization and agricultural modernization can be seen to share mutual foundations, premises, promotions, and restrictions for each other. Agricultural modernization depends on urbanization because urbanization is advantageous to the transformation of surplus labor force and rural moderate-scale management. Meanwhile, agricultural modernization is also beneficial to promoting urbanization. The core of agricultural modernization, agriculture's third industrialization,[12] may promote urban–rural industrial transformation, propel urban–rural integration, and help realize complementing advantages and common development (Li 2013).

Further, in the view of town space development in mountainous regions, several opportunities are seen, such as the Western development strategy and establishment of Chongqing Municipality and Cheng Yu Urban–Rural Development Experimental Zone in recent decades. These projects have greatly promoted the level of urbanization in western China's mountainous regions. Nevertheless, problems have arisen, such as the prominent urban–rural dual structure, low optimism as regards ecological security, disorderly space development, contradiction between people and land, and lack of basic control mechanisms. As such, researchers have put forward a number of suggestions as follows. Foremost, planning should be regarded as the guide in taking the appropriate urban–rural coordination mode that would engender holistic urban–rural planning and integration of related planning (Qian 2009). Then, the characteristics of small towns should be highlighted based on their regional conditions, thereby enhancing categorized guidance for small towns. In addition, function needs to be strengthened and economic structure optimized to combine with the adjustment of the rural industrial structure and heighten the accumulation and diffusion effects of towns (Li 2008).

Ecological agriculture is another trend in industry development in mountainous villages, which is a prominent feature of the primary sector. Generally, the breeding and planting industries are the main types of the primary sector. For the breeding industry, quality growth should be formed with organic green livestock products as its core (Fig. 5.6). An ecological farming mode should also be established to develop a low-pollution resource recycling chain (Bai 2008) (Fig. 5.7). For the planting industry, mountainous villages should improve the competitiveness of characteristic crop planting (Zhou 2005). For example, Chinese herbal medicine planting should be produced in better scale and standard. Mixed cultivation and utilization modes should be carried forward, such as planting-breeding (Lin and Zhou 2012), woods-medicine (Hao 2004), grain-medicine (Tang 2010), and characteristic tourism or health maintenance (Cheng 2009).

[12]Quoting Prof. Li Jing's explanation: Agriculture's third industrialization is an extension of agriculture's own service function and enlargement of agriculture's external scale, in order to give full play to the multi-functionality of agriculture.

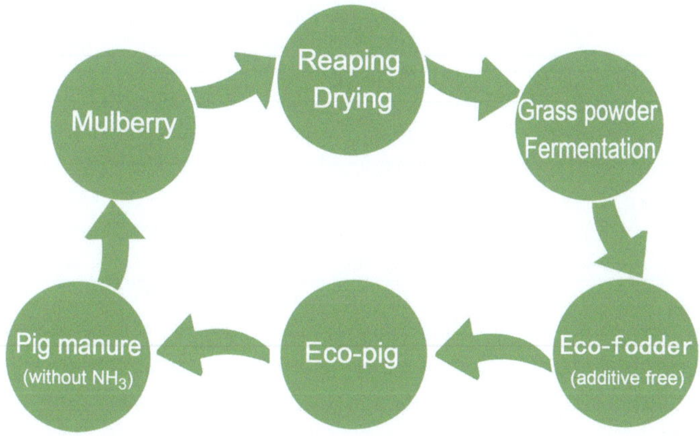

Fig. 5.6 Eco-cultivation (*Source* CQGRIQUAN Agriculture and Animal Husbandry Co., Ltd)

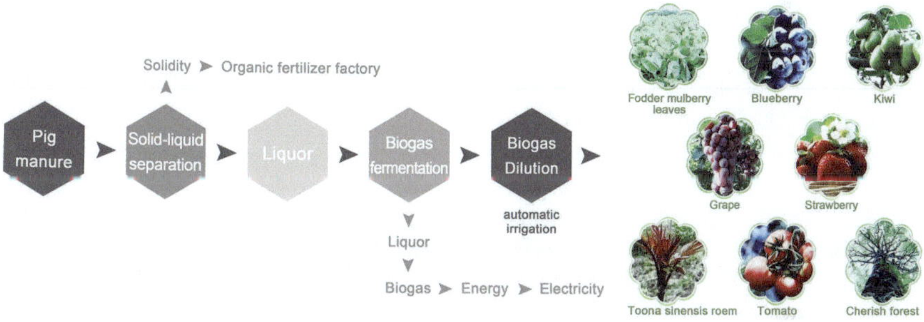

Fig. 5.7 Full-recycle agriculture industry base (*Source* CQGRIQUAN Agriculture and Animal Husbandry Co., Ltd)

5.4 Space Integration of Industry and Village Spaces

Based on the existing favorable foundation and trends, solutions have become clear. The key aims of future mountainous rural urbanization are efficient and intensive utilization of land resources and coordinated development as regards production, daily life, and ecology. The core method for achieving these aims is to optimize the spatial layout for producing, living, and ecology using scientific and reasonable planning control mechanisms. Hence, the following development strategy emerges: spatial integration of industry and village.

5.4.1 Content of Industry-Village Integration

The spatial integration of industry and village considers the space for industry and village as a correlative development community. The development of settlement spaces in mountainous villages is considered together with the long-term objectives of the transformation of the first industry, extension of characteristic industry chains, construction of market systems, revitalization of local cultures, and protection of the ecological environment. New development modes will be explored from aspects of urban–rural overall development, ecological security, and resource integration. It will focus on space research and design practice for mountainous villages, including rural industry space planning and construction, village scene renovation, and ecological agriculture landscape creation (Figs. 5.8 and 5.9). It will build multiple regulatory systems integration, dynamic and orderly control mechanisms, and design systems to guide the coordinated development of mountainous villages and their environment.

Therefore, industry-village integration will achieve practical significance in the implementation of mountainous rural urbanization. First, it can coordinate rural settlements and industrial development within the bearing capacity of the natural environment; second, it can guide the optimization of rural space; and last, it will help support the peasants' income.

Fig. 5.8 Space integration of industry and village in Hongfeng Village, Henghe Township, Wanzhou District, Chongqing (*Source* Applied by Chongqing municipal commission of urban rural development)

Fig. 5.9 Space integration of industry and village in Hongfeng Village, Henghe Township, Wanzhou District, Chongqing (*Source* Applied by Chongqing municipal commission of urban–rural development)

5.4.2 *Key Points of Industry-Village Integration*

To realize the significance above, several key points of industry-village integration should be grasped for the new mountainous rural urbanization.

Foremost is the planning idea of multiple regulatory systems integration, which is an important foundation and precondition to implementing the strategy of industry-village integration. Such integration is expected to break through the segmentation and restriction caused by fiercely independent departments, to ensure the intensive utilization of land and simplification of the management process. Various planning forms should be effectively integrated, such as overall planning for villages and towns, general land use planning, rural tourism planning, mountain agricultural industry planning, and landscape design. In this way, it can promote complementary cooperation between the development of settlement and industry spaces, as well as improve the efficiency and operability of construction management.

The second key point is the framework of mountainous rural planning. To be specific, it should regard the spaces for rural settlement and industry as a whole, based on the indivisibility and mutual conditionality of mountainous villages and the ecological environment. Further, it should focus on the mountainous villages' industrial restructuring and extension, along with the evolution of spatial form and characteristics of the settlement. Subsequently, a mountainous rural space layout and construction technology system should be established, with a restructuring of the mountainous agriculture industry, complementation of space and industry resources, and intensive construction mode as the main parts.

The third key point is the design and control system with the renovation of mountainous rural landscape at its core. On the basis of the integrality of mountainous rural regional culture and how systematic it is, attention should be paid to the public space creation, functional organization, and systematic integration. In addition, macro-scale control mechanism and micro-scale space design should be combined into a conjunct goal and system framework to form a design system and control mechanism with strong pertinence and maneuverability.

5.5 Conclusion

The analysis in this work has focused on mountainous rural urbanization, from its background, disadvantages and advantages, to forming a development strategy. Under the background of national new urbanization development, mountainous villages are faced with unique problems, including the lack of an overall industry-village development, weakness in industrial space extension, and disorder in village space development. Such problems plague mountainous rural development. Finding solutions out of these plights is an essential and urgent issue.

Fortunately, the tendency of China's rural urbanization provides a great opportunity for the current scenario. A series of the national policies provide the direction, and the development of new technology offers a substantial foundation for rural areas that will continuously support rural construction. Relevant research provides plenty of references, helping in the analysis of several important issues in mountainous rural urbanization.

Based on the analysis above, a strategy for mountainous rural urbanization is finally proposed: industry-village space integration. It takes the idea of multiple regulatory systems integration as a foundation, clarifies the content and framework of mountainous rural planning, and establishes a design and control system with the renovation of mountainous rural landscape as its core. Thus, the integrated space that ensures complementary progress for industry and villagers will hopefully promote the sustainable utilization of land, space, industry, and ecological resources in mountainous villages as well as relieve the increasingly prominent contradictions between land and people in mountainous regions. It would raise the marketization degree of mountainous rural industries and drive the ecological cycle of mountainous agriculture development while still protecting the traditional human settlement form and intangible cultural resources in mountainous villages. Therefore, such a form of space integration leads to improved development approach for mountainous rural urbanization, anchored on the premise of reducing environmental burdens.

Acknowledgment This article is supported by the National Science & Technology Pillar Program during the 12th Five-year Plan Period: the Synthesis Technology Integration and Demonstration for the Construction of Suburban "Beautiful Villages" within the type of Industry extension and upgrade (Grant No. 2015BAL01B04).

References

Bai JM (2008) Study on the theory and application patterns for circular agriculture in China. Dissertation for Doctorate. Chinese Academy of Agricultural Sciences, Beijing, p 8. (in Chinese)

Cheng YK, Cheng CY (2009) Discussions of the balance between experimental zone of urban-rural and development of city sightseeing agricultural: the 11th annual meeting of China association for science and technology, session 26 urban modern agriculture seminar. Chinese Agric Sci Bull 100–102. (in Chinese)

Fei XT (1985) Four texts of small towns. Xinhua Press, Beijing (in Chinese)

Hao ZJ, Chen LP et al (2004) A study about development of ecotype urban agriculture in Chongqing. Res Agric Modernization 1:64–67. (in Chinese)

Li H, Xia XL (2008) Strategic thinking for the development of small towns in the context of urban-rural integration. China Collective Econ 5:13–14 (in Chinese)

Li JS, Zhou LY (2013) Suburban agriculture's transformation into tertiary sector and its urban planning in the perspective of new urbanization: the example of Xiaowangmiao District of Fenghua. Time Archit 6:42–47 (in Chinese)

Lin XL, Zhou YH (2012) An empirical analysis on the eco-environmental effect of circulatory agriculture mode of planting-breeding in the paddy field—taking the paddy-fish mode in the southern paddy area as an example. China Popul Res Environ 3:37–42. (in Chinese)

Qian ZH, He B (2009) An analysis on the planning mode of urban-rural integrated in the eastern and western regions. Urban Dev Stud 3. (in Chinese)

Tang J (2010) An empirical analysis on the agricultural industrialization management and land consolidation in the hilly areas of Central Sichuan: taking the example of the modern planting base for the Chinese Medicine of Sichuan Hui Chun Tang Pharmaceutical Company. Econ Aff 5:62–67. (in Chinese)

Zhang SW (2014) Rural planning: characteristics and difficulties. City Planning Rev 2:17–21. (in Chinese)

Zheng FT, Pu MZ (2014) New urbanization: institution shackles and solution paths. People's Tribune Frontiers 6:62–71 (in Chinese)

Zhou FY, Lu FJ, Zhang YL (2005) Problems and counter measures in the development of the Chinese medicine planting. J Agrotechn Econ 2:76–79. (in Chinese

Zhu LT (2014) Study of fiscal policy on promoting the adjustment of Chinese economic structure. Dissertation for Doctorate. Research Institute for Fiscal Science, Ministry of Finance, Beijing, P.R.China. (in Chinese)

Chapter 6
Rural Planning in the New Urbanization Process: The Case of Chengdu, China

Wei Zhao and Jiao Yang

6.1 Introduction

The new urbanization in China has highlighted the significance of developing rural areas and planning for the urbanization of the countryside. A single rural settlement, although small, is widely influenced by policies on planning and construction, along with such factors as political, land, capital, labor, and technological resources. Rural areas are substantially inhibited from sustainable development by the competition for resources between urban and rural areas, lack of clear administrative responsibilities for social governance in townships and villages, continuous environmental deterioration, and socio-cultural structural change and destruction. The current awkward situation can be attributed to the lack of due consideration for rural planning in the past. In the current transitional period of planning and management under a legal framework, rural planning has been given more attention than ever. However, legislation and law enforcement remain daunting.

On the one hand, there is a lack of systematic, comprehensive, and consistent laws governing rural planning. For example, the crucial land policies for rural planning are still under discussion for amendment in a critical period of reform. Meanwhile, governance of rural areas remains challenging, for such areas are widely expansive, backward in social and economic development, and lacking construction technologies, and characterized by a demand for intensive construction and funding. On the other hand, stakeholders need to question how far rural planning should extend and to which level governance should be affected in the rural areas, given that the more remote a rural area is, the fewer the available specialists in urban and rural governance.

W. Zhao (✉) · J. Yang
School of Architecture, Southwest Jiaotong University, Chengdu, China
e-mail: cq_zhaowei@163.com

F. Wang and M. Prominski (eds.), *Urbanization and Locality*,
DOI 10.1007/978-3-662-48494-4_6

6.2 Countryside in Chengdu

Chengdu, a city with a history of more than 2300 years, is unique in its countryside in China. Built in 256 BC, the Dujiangyan Irrigation System continues to play a key role in farmland irrigation and water conservation to nourish the fertile plains of Chengdu. Densely populated at the center, Chengdu is typically resided by rural people scattered in small communities in the rural areas. These parts of Chengdu are well-known for "Linpan," a settlement pattern with a farm courtyard surrounded by a well-established irrigation system, fertile land, and bamboo forest for living and production.

Apart from the traditional settlement pattern and beautiful landscape, the countryside of Chengdu maintains an orderly social system through such agricultural activities as farming, irrigation, and sideline production. The rural area of Chengdu has built a unique rural culture while supporting a dense agricultural population.

In recent years, the proportions of agricultural population and food production have declined. Meanwhile, various business lines developed, the housing conditions of farmers improved, and the per capita net income increased continuously. However, the degree of affluence of Chengdu's countryside remains inadequate in general. In 2013, the rural per capita net income of Chengdu was 12,985 Yuan, ranking lower than most of those in the list of 19 municipalities or sub-provincial cities. Although this outcome is due to the low degree of development in urban areas (the per capita income of urban residents also ranks low), which provides insufficient driving force and radiation effect to the rural areas, the ranking hardly reflects the superior natural geographic and environmental conditions of "The Land of Abundance." Although the urbanization rate has reached 69.4 % (Yuan 2014) in Chengdu City, the income level remains relatively low, indicating satisfactory urbanization. Thus, the development potential and supportive capability of the rural areas are not fully exploited.

6.3 Urban Planning and Management in Chengdu

6.3.1 Planning of Non-urban Construction Land in the Central City

At the beginning of the 21st century, Chengdu began to focus on the issue of non-urban construction land planning in the center of the city; indeed, Chengdu is known as one of the pioneers in the exploration of this issue. Although the concept of non-urban construction land remains controversial, at the time they mainly referred to the green belt, which was intended to address the eco-environmental problems, when designing the layout of the central city. This green belt is a typical principle in urban planning, already adopted in the Overall Plan of Chengdu in

1995. This concept stresses avoiding urban sprawl in a centrifugal concentric pattern by controlling the development of the green belt. Closely tied to the centralized construction area of the city, part of the green belt near the edge of the city has become an "informal" zone where the environment is severely damaged by artificial construction sprawls and the social space is characterized by dilapidated chaos. Referring to the urban land classification standard of the day, the non-urban construction land includes towns and villages. However, the initial planning had taken the ecological factors into account rather than the construction of towns and villages.

In 2002, the completed planning received the National Award for planning and design. However, it was not until the process of rapid urbanization in the following years did the planning managers recognize that, without the demand for green belt areas as well as the consideration of the interests of all parties, the established plan could hardly be carried out. The consequent planning continuously paid attention to the construction problems in these areas and then systematically undertook coordinative consideration for interior spatial planning issues of non-urban construction lands, which gradually helped shake off the yoke of the conventional perception that urban architects regard non-urban construction regions as green patches only to offer ecological barriers to the city. Planning managers began to realize the pressure of village construction in the green belts and the inconvenient truth of rural and urban competition for space. They then formulated corresponding policies and even promoted due legislation.

6.3.2 Urban–Rural Integrated Planning

In 2003, China began to clean up and reorganize numerous development zones to curb blind urban enclosure development.[1] As the scope of development extended to rural areas, concerns on rural land usage rose. In the same year, Chengdu embarked on a market-oriented reform in rural areas and promoted agricultural modernization by accelerating the development of a new rural collective economy. This move helped realize the industrialization of agriculture through large-scale land management, while solving the concentrated living problems and unemployment of farmers to maximize the benefits of resource allocation by attracting private funds for project development. To an extent, the government applied an approach of urban economy development to the rural areas.

The following year, the state council decided in favor of "deepening reformation and strict land management," which promoted the plan-based intensive use of urban lands as well as strengthened the planning and management of rural construction

[1]Notice on Clean-up and Rectification of Economic Development Zones and Further Regulations on Land for Construction (GF [2003] No. 70) released by General Office of the State Council on July 30, 2003 (in Chinese).

lands.[2] Further, under the scientific development perspective of "five balanced plans" (Chi 2004), Chengdu rapidly boosted its urban–rural planning through land consolidation and spatial planning according to "three concentrations": the concentration of industry in centralized development zones, that of farmers in urban areas, and that of land in the possession of large-scale business owners (Research Group of Party School of CPC Shuangliu County Committee 2005). The concentrated development of resources in rural areas succeeded in solving the problem of inefficient infrastructure allocation caused by the decentralized rural development of Chengdu, agricultural modernization problem caused by separated smallholders, and ecological environment damage caused by the spread of rural industries. In 2005, Chengdu enacted an advisory on the promotion of transfer of Rural Land Contractual Management Right,[3] and that on accelerating rural collective economic development in the following year.[4] Reforms were carried out in full swing. By breaking through the constraints of Contractual Management Right, the city aimed to promote rural land transfer, establish a modern enterprise system, and improve diversified business in rural areas. The concentrated use of rural land resources was a path-breaking initiative for transferring space and promoting diverse capital to rural areas.

In this period, the best example of diversified rural development from grassroots to higher levels is the construction of rural tourism spots in the outskirts of the city, such as Hongsha Village, known as "Five Golden Flowers." The project led to a new pattern of suburban rural development in China and attracted attention in the wave of new rural construction that began in 2006.

In 2007, Chengdu approved the establishment of the urban–rural comprehensive reform pilot zone,[5] hence starting a new round of exploration of coordinated and balanced urban–rural development at the national strategic level. According to the overall construction plan of the pilot zone, "Planning and Management" was listed as the first priority among the eight coordinated reforms intended to yield "breakthroughs." The vertically integrated urban planning system laid the necessary foundation for the overall urban–rural thinking. Under the idea of "Overall Chengdu" (Lai 2007), the city conducted systematic comprehensive planning, breaking the boundaries between administrative areas. In the same year, full coverage work of urban–rural planning was rapidly promoted, thereby filling up the planning gaps in certain areas and providing guidance for land use both in terms of planning and legal issues.

---

[2]Decision on Further Regulations for Land Management based on Further Reform (GF [2004] No. 28) released by the State Council on October 21, 2004 (in Chinese).

[3]Opinions on the Transfer of Contracted Land Use Rights in Rural Areas (CWB [2005] No. 37) released on September 7, 2005 (in Chinese).

[4]Opinions on the Acceleration of the Development of Rural Collective Economy (CWB [2006]) released on February 27, 2006 (in Chinese).

[5]Notice on Establishment of the Demonstrative Zone of National Rural-urban Comprehensive Supporting Reform in Chongqing and Chengdu (FGJT [2007] No. 1248) released by National Development and Reform Commission on June 7, 2007 (in Chinese).

Urban planning has thus been successfully transformed into urban–rural planning, with the planning and management in rural areas strengthened, construction sprawl effectively controlled, and construction in certain districts endowed with unique features. However, improvement is still needed in the practices of applying years of experience gained in urban planning to rural areas and creating plans; hurried planning has resulted in unsatisfactory outcomes. For example, farmers had to move into apartments located far from their farmland. Moreover, suitable house types and utilities have been lacking, and many problems related to agricultural modernization have persisted. From the perspective of the earth landscape, the traditional Linpan landscape was heavily damaged by the development of concentration, which brought much controversy.

In early 2008, Chengdu issued Document No. 1[6] with amended provisions on the registration of rural collective land and housing right as well as an update on the farmland protection system to facilitate the transfer of rural contracted land and construction land use rights. This development also helped drive the transfer of house property use rights in rural areas. The vehicle of reform is pulling ahead. With the encouraging innovations in pilot zones, under the guidance of the party committees' documents and thoughtful preparation of planning, various capitalists focused their attention on the feast of development in the vast rural areas.

6.3.3 Post-quake Reconstruction Planning

The western edge of the Chengdu Plain is the Qingcheng Mountain-Dujiangyan scenic area, which is a famous world cultural heritage and natural heritage site, featuring a high quality of mountain rural tourism and leisure resort. Tourist towns, village hotels, and resort residences were developed. Rails were extended to the mountain area, and the magnificent prospect "City March on to Mountains" (Li 2008) was carried out gradually. Document No. 1 has laid a solid foundation for the abovementioned prospect.

Unfortunately, a sudden earthquake in May 2008 severely damaged the construction in rural areas, garnering international attention to Chengdu as regards its post-earthquake reconstruction. In the aftermath of the world financial crisis, with the macroscopic stimulus of central governments as well as strong support and active participation of both local and other regional governments, the less-affected mountain areas recovered rapidly. Under the target of completing the reconstruction in three years and delivering all the work in two years, the post-quake reconstruction was generally completed by the end of 2010 with fruitful results from the

[6]Opinions on Further Reform and Completion of Rural Land and Property Land Right System based on Farmland Protection (Trial) (CWF [2008] No. 1) released on January 1, 2008 (in Chinese).

input of policies, capital, technology, and talent. Indeed, the entire process demonstrated an excellent example for reconstruction.

Under the promotion of the Urban and Rural Planning Law, which was officially implemented in 2008, the post-quake rural planning and construction management in Chengdu was strengthened in a short time with the series of technical regulations and planning guidelines issued. Rural planning and construction developed vigorously in this period. Several principles were clearly put forward, including government guidance, market leading, respect of public opinion, and industrial support. Moreover, several important factors were ensured: site selection, security, per capita construction land, public facilities, and municipal facilities. Construction points of diversity, expansibility, integration, and sharing were also proposed in rural areas (Public Forum of Chengdu Urban Planning 2009). To leave a good impression, the post-quake rural planning and construction especially emphasized the maintenance of the architectural styles and historical and cultural heritage of monuments, such as Chongzhou street, Pingle ancient town in Qionglai, Huanglongxi in Shuangliu, and Luodai in Longquan, resulting in a host of rehabilitation projects of ancient towns.

However, problems persisted during the process owing to the rapid decision making and construction. First, a number of individual houses were destroyed by subsequent earthquakes owing to the insufficient cognition of the complexity of earthquakes and their consequences. Second, the revival level of quake-hit areas was overestimated, and the use of housing, public facilities, and municipal infrastructure were far less than expected in the investment stage. Moreover, with the economic stimulus, a number of industrial projects became oversupplied after completion, causing damage to the rural ecological environment.

6.3.4 *Comprehensive Development of Rural Planning and Construction*

The post-quake reconstruction led to a comprehensive focus on the planning and construction in rural areas and prompted deeper considerations on the relationship between city and village. Chengdu proposed a goal (Ai and Huang 2010) of building a "worldwide modern garden city" in December 2009 based on the core ideas of "natural beauty, social justice, and urban–rural integration." It specifically raised the method of returning to an ideal pattern of constructing classical decentralized cities to explore the possibility of building world-class modern metropolises and rural settlements. Obviously, the core of the city's characteristics lies in the adequate interaction between urban and rural morphology. Thus, the protection and development of the countryside became more pressing than ever.

Specifically, the small towns scattered in rural areas were built and reconstructed. They are deemed as important nodes of the Garden City community, but in the process of urban-concentrated development, many of them began to see decline. In 2010,

Chengdu launched a comprehensive two-year ordinary township reconstruction[7] project to accelerate the function upgrade of small towns, improve people's working and living environment, enhance township development, and promote balanced social and economic development of urban and rural areas. The project involved industrial guidance, farmer concentration, infrastructure improvement, public facilities optimization, and township profile promotion.

In addition, it also pushed forward the construction of the modern garden city by experimenting in demonstrative areas, routes, and spots before expanding from the pilot spots to the entire area toward overall development. Under green eco-innovative efforts, a greenway began was constructed in this period along with the construction of small green towns, which drew unprecedented attention. Wenjiang greenways and Shouan town have become prime examples of successful construction.

6.3.5 Talents and Management in Rural Planning

The experience in post-earthquake reconstruction showed that one of the most deficient resources in rural planning construction was technical experts. In 2010, Chengdu initiated the system of employing rural architects.[8] The implementation of the rural architects system issued by the municipal government ruled that rural architects are recruited, selected, transferred, assigned, and appointed by district and county governments based on uniform standards as full-time architects responsible for towns and villages. Rural architects responsible for problems related to rural planning must have clear opinions. The township party committee and government should welcome and respect the views of the rural architects. Rural architects are hired through recruitment, voluntary organizations, individual volunteering, position transferring, and position attachment; they are required to sign a two-year employment agreement (Chengdu Municipal Government 2014). The plan was to dispatch full-time rural architects in three batches to 196 towns and villages around the city by 2012. In 2010, the number of the first batch was 50.

In 2011, the Planning Administration in Chengdu separated the responsibility of rural planning management from other related offices to establish the rural planning department that would supervise the coordination and management of rural planning, establishment of long-term institutions and mechanisms for rural planning and revision, and improvement of relevant technical standards. The rural planning department is a "centralized" management unit of architects (Wang 2011).

Based on the actual operation, the policy maintained a good continuity and recruited nearly 200 rural architects by 2014. The formation of rural planning,

[7]Opinions on Comprehensive Township Reform (CFF [2010] No. 15) released by Chengdu Municipal Government on March 5, 2010 (in Chinese).

[8]The Notice on the Issue of the Plan for implementation of Rural Architect System in Chengdu (CFF [2010] No. 37) released by Chengdu Municipal Government on September 17, 2010 (in Chinese).

wages of rural architects, and funds for training have all been fully guaranteed every year. Civil servants in the newly established rural planning department strived to deliver the planning and implementation of guidance with rural architects and the staff in district urban–rural planning management departments.

6.3.6 Main Tasks in the Near Future

Unfortunately, another earthquake struck in Ya'an City, Lushan County in Sichuan Province in 2013, affecting five towns and villages in Qionglai City bordering Lushan County. Rural planning yet again focused on post-quake reconstruction. The damage was not as serious as that in 2008, which resulted in less reconstruction support compared with the case of the Wenchuan earthquake. Nonetheless, the Wenchuan earthquake offered lessons and experiences in reconstruction, particularly the need to avoid excessive construction and exercise control in reconstruction.

Support from various financial resources to agriculture brought changes to rural agriculture, which also affected the rural planning and construction. The construction of high-standard farmlands, change of small fields to large ones, land management, demolition and consolidation of courtyards, and land reclamation have all changed the traditional settings of basic farmlands. The traditional living style in Linpan in western Sichuan was further impaired. Amid the new rural construction, the protection and renovation of Linpan has not ceased, but it is extremely vulnerable to the radical policy of land transferring. After 2011, the land transferring efforts in Chengdu began to abate in a major way. The organic agriculture industry and rural experience became entrenched. Subsequently, the value of local land resources was recognized and re-utilized, thereby continuously strengthening the protection and renovation of cultural carriers of the regional settlement of Lipan.

In the entire country, the issue of environmental protection has become so severe that no one is allowed to neglect it, especially the problems regarding the water and atmospheric environment. Chengdu conducted a research and conservation project of non-urban construction land that had been shrinking for 10 years; the city finally formulated laws and regulations to this end, which have been implemented since 2013.[9] The construction of large lakes and wetlands in eco-regions around the city was dedicated to improving the regional water environment, drawing attention to the protection of the river ecological environment. For example, Baitou, a town in Chongzhou, strictly controlled the ecological buffer zone along Qimu River by constructing artificial wetlands, and applied the idea of limited impact development

[9]Regulations on the Conservation of the Ecological Zone around Chengdu (CRF [2012] No. 59) released on November 30, 2012 (in Chinese).

in upstream areas, thus combining the ecological patterns of mountains, water, land, forests, and roads in a commendable form of rural planning.

The effort of searching for characteristics of the regional culture in rural areas is also proceeding as planned. Chengdu is not only an enclave of the diversified settlement culture in the southwest mountain areas but also of the Hakka settlements from the Central Plains, historically. The Hakka once had their own language and folk characteristics, most of which have gone extinct. A number of individual villages attempted to construct the classic architectural morphology of the Hakka through rural planning, although these architectural forms have not been built in local areas. This planning gained the appreciation and support of local governments and administrative departments.

6.4 Conclusion

Under the guidance of a macroscopic policy, broad intervention of the government and department staff, advocacy of professionals, and participation of the public, a series of regulations or normative documents were formulated to facilitate rural planning and management practices, guaranteeing the legality of such planning. Rural planning was further rationalized by the establishment of a special rural planning and management department, which was tasked with improving planning formulation, and a practice-based rural architect system established in advance. Subsequently, the rural planning and management of Chengdu has effectively extended to rural areas, thus providing new planning ideas for the sustainable development of rural areas in China in the process of new urbanization.

From the advocacy of new urbanization at the beginning of the new century to the recent publication of new national urbanization planning reports, Chengdu took the lead in the nation in exploring coordinated and balanced urban–rural development, which has seen fruitful achievements in rural planning and construction. The priority of urban planning also shifted from the city to the balanced development of urban and rural areas, under a more integrated approach of urban and rural planning. Chengdu still has a long way to go to develop urban and rural areas to an advanced level, and extensive efforts should be done for the further innovation and implementation of planning, management, and construction. Although a number of errors were made in the process of exploration, the innovative achievements in rural planning and construction will continue to yield long-term impacts under the well-developed framework in Chengdu.

Acknowledgments The author would like to thank Professor Qing Shen of the University of Washington for his helpful comments and suggestions.

References

Ai ZK, Huang FL (2010) Modern garden city: a case of Chengdu, a new model of balanced rural-urban development. Res Urban Devel 17(3):5–7. (in Chinese)

Chengdu Municipal Government (2014) The plan for implementation of rural architect system in Chengdu [EB/OL] [EB/OL]. http://www.cdgh.gov.cn/hbdt/758.htm. August 13. (in Chinese)

Chi FL (2004) Five holistic arrangements: balanced rural-urban development playing a key role. Party Gov Dig 4:9–9. (in Chinese)

Lai XL (2007) Construction of "Overall Chengdu" by building one city, two zones and six corridors. Chengdu Daily, August 10. (in Chinese)

Li HQ (2008) "Starfish Model" of Overall Chengdu. Acad J Chengdu Text Junior Coll 25(1):5–6. (in Chinese)

Public Forum of Chengdu Urban Planning (2009) Guideline for the planning and construction of socialist new countryside in Chengdu (trial). http://www.cdgh.gov.cn/hbdt/742.htm. January 20. (in Chinese)

Research Group of Party School of CPC Shuangliu County Committee (2005) Investigation and reflection on the initiative of rural-urban integration based on "Three Concentrations" in Shuangliu county. Rural Econ 3:62–65. (in Chinese)

Wang ML (2011) Rural architects are brought under administrative control. Chengdu Daily, February 17. (in Chinese)

Yuan H (2014) The urbanization will be up 0.9 % from the previous year in 2014. Chengdu Daily, August 13. (in Chinese)

Author Biographies

Dr. Wei Zhao is Professor in School of Architecture, Southwest Jiaotong University and a registered urban planner.

Mrs. Jiao Yang is Instructor in School of Architecture, Southwest Jiaotong University and a registered urban planner.

Part II
New Strategies: Locality Preservation and Development in Urbanization Processes

Chapter 7
Integrative Design Computation for Local Resource Effectiveness in Architecture

Oliver David Krieg, Tobias Schwinn and Achim Menges

7.1 Introduction

Architecture has a profound impact on the use of resources. For example, in 2014, the building sector alone was responsible for half of Europe's energy and material consumption (COM 2014). Increasing efficiency will involve all steps from material extraction, to manufacturing, assembly, construction, and usage. Especially in the context of a growing urbanization, utilizing locally available materials and regional fabrication processes, as well as ensuring short transportation routes, will become crucial for a sustainable future. The authors present a research on activating local resource effectiveness by using local wood products in developing efficient wood constructions based on computational design, advanced digital fabrication, and biomimetics. Integrative design computation enables performance-based and material-oriented design methods for a more resource-effective architecture. On the one hand, innovative and adaptive design and manufacturing processes allow for the use of specific material properties while also enhancing architectural quality. On the other, they offer the possibility to access and activate the potential of local resources, especially in the context of lightweight wood construction for urbanization and re-densification.

Utilizing local resources and local fabrication has the potential to strengthen a region's economy, shorten transportation routes, and eventually develop a local identity through differentiated construction methods, depending on the available material. In this sense, the Latin term *genius loci*, or the cultural value of locality, can be extended to engender ecological and social benefits for a region and its community through regional construction enabled by advanced design computation and robotic fabrication.

O.D. Krieg · T. Schwinn · A. Menges (✉)
Institute for Computational Design, University of Stuttgart, Stuttgart, Germany
e-mail: achim.menges@icd.uni-stuttgart.de

F. Wang and M. Prominski (eds.), *Urbanization and Locality*,
DOI 10.1007/978-3-662-48494-4_7

Fig. 7.1 The Landesgartenschau Exhibition Hall is a demonstrator for the potentials of integrative design computation and digital fabrication with local resources (*Source* ICD/ITKE/IIGS University of Stuttgart)

The authors investigate the potentials of integrative design technologies and digital fabrication with local resources through the development, design, and construction of a large-scale demonstrator for lightweight wood construction (Fig. 7.1). Wood is one of the oldest building materials known to humankind. Its exceptional structural strength, positive carbon footprint (Kolb 2008), extremely low embodied energy (Alcorn 1996), and regional availability make the material particularly suitable for the development of more sustainable construction methods. Not surprisingly, the general interest in wood architecture has grown over the last decade. However, industrialized fabrication and construction processes still have to adapt to wood's complex anisotropic behavior (Correa et al. 2013). Current foresting strategies are already responding to climate change and serving as a driver for innovating new wood products as well as for architects and engineers to embrace new wood species for construction. Ultimately, these developments encourage the use of local resources for shorter transportation routes. They likewise stimulate reciprocal relationships between design and manufacturing processes, as well as the available material. In a broader context and in respect to questions of urbanization, the authors argue that adaptive lightweight wood constructions and the use of locally available material will be most suitable for enhancing sustainability in urban extensions and re-densification.

7.2 Biomimetics: A Design Approach for Resource Effectiveness

Newly developed digital design and fabrication methods offer entirely new design possibilities and fields of application. By borrowing functional principles from biology, architectural and structural performances can be increased substantially, whereas resource consumption will be reduced. In comparison to man-made constructions, natural systems exhibit a significantly higher level of morphological differentiation. This variation represents a key aspect for performance and resource effectiveness. In contrast to technology, the metabolic costs of simply adding more material instead persuade natural systems to differentiate a material's shape highly. Geometric complexity is unconstrained by predefined structural systems, questions of fabrication, or aspects of calculability.

Given the constrained and inflexible manufacturing methods for the industrial processing of materials, differentiated and articulated shapes pose a question of energy input, and therefore, of costs. In nature, however, complexity is achieved through the interaction of information in the form of DNA, and the structure, or shape, of material (Vincent 2009). On many different levels, scales, and hierarchies, natural structures are defined by their intrinsic geometry. Differentiation not only results in the highest possible structural performance but also negotiates between different function-based requirements. In this sense, nature differs from modern architecture. Instead of dividing structures into well-defined functions, biology follows the principle of functional integration and forms gradients between geometric articulations. Biological principles of constructional morphology can therefore be transferred into the development of technical applications.

Architecture is similar to biological evolution in the sense that evaluation criteria that necessitate a certain development are constantly changed (Knippers and Speck 2012). Instead of optimizing a system toward a clearly defined goal or function, the system's requirements are many interdependent, at times contradictory, criteria that ultimately describe a multi-dimensional and evolving solution space. Natural systems adapt to these changing conditions through the interaction of multi-layered, finely tuned, and differentiated strategies yielding structures that feature multiple networked functions (Dunlop and Fratzl 2010). They can be described as heterogeneity, anisotropy, hierarchy, multifunctionality, redundancy, and adaptability (Knippers and Speck 2012). All these strategies increase the efficiency and performance of structural systems, and they could potentially be implemented in architectural design.

The possibility of biomimetic transfer and geometric differentiation is one of the many advantages enabled by integrative design computation. In the context of recent developments in foresting strategies, the authors see further potentials for a leap in resource effectiveness and sustainable design through the use of local wood species and newly developed building materials.

7.3 Wood: A Local Resource and Its Future Potentials

Wood is a naturally renewable and fully recyclable resource and building material. In addition to its ecological advantages of negative carbon footprint (Kolb 2008) and low embodied energy (Alcorn 1996), wood has an unrivaled structural capacity in relation to its weight compared with other building materials (Gordon 2003).

MATERIAL	*ENERGY NEEDED TO ENSURE A GIVEN STIFFNESS IN THE STRUCTURE AS A WHOLE*	*ENERGY NEEDED TO PRODUCE A PANEL OF A GIVEN COMPRESSIVE STRENGTH*
STEEL	1.0	1.0
TITANIUM	13.0	9.0
ALUMINIUM	4.0	2.0
BRICK	0.4	0.1
CONCRETE	0.3	0.05
WOOD	0.02	0.002
CARBON-FIBER COMPOSITE	17.0	17.0

Fig. 7.2 The production of a panel with a given compressive strength in wood requires 500 times less energy than in steel (*Source* Gordon 2003)

From the ecological and economic perspectives, steel constructions pale in comparison to wood as they require 500 times more energy to achieve the same structural performance (Gordon 2003) (Fig. 7.2). The demand for a more sustainable and effective building material drives the increased use of wood. However, only responsible and effective utilization of the material will increase sustainability in architecture. The potential of integrative computational design and digital fabrication for higher resource effectiveness in wood constructions must be evaluated in the context of the present and future of Central Europe's silviculture.

In Germany, wood is poised to become a locally available construction resource, given that 31 % of the country's land area is covered by cultivated forests (DHWR 2014) (Fig. 7.3a). Currently, Germany's forests are composed of 41 % hardwood and 59 % softwood species (Mantau 2012). The predominant building materials spruce and pine make up 52 % of the forests, whereas 15 % is beech (Fig. 7.3b). Nonetheless, beech is the most natural species in Central Europe's temperate seasonal climate and would normally make up two-thirds of the forests barring if not

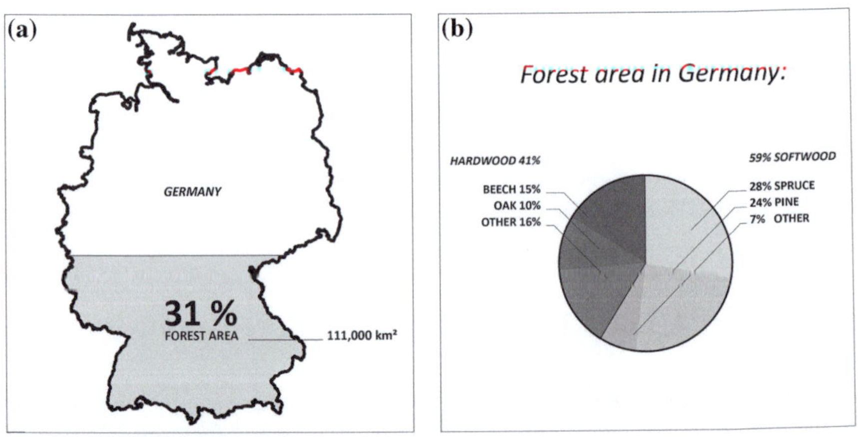

Fig. 7.3 **a** The forest area in Germany represents a stock of 3600 million m^3. **b** Spruce and pine are the most dominant species, whereas beech ranks third (*Source* Mantau 2012)

for the anthropogenic interventions in the past (BfN 2004). Introducing a high amount of softwood, such as spruce and pine, supported the increasing need for a fast-growing resource in past centuries. At the time, the foresting strategy corresponded to the beneficial climate conditions. However, current climate change projections are expected to have a profound impact on average temperatures and precipitation in Europe in upcoming decades (Lozán 2008).

Biologists use the method of a climate envelope to evaluate the most suitable climate conditions for a species to grow and proliferate. Also called a species' ecological potential, the climate envelope describes the favorable average temperature and precipitation. Spruce, the predominant wood construction material throughout Europe, has a climate envelope that is already partially outside of Central Europe's conditions. In the past years, different climate models have calculated possible worldwide temperature changes. Combined, they predict an increase of average temperatures between 1.5 and 4.0 °C (Lozán et al. 2008). More detailed calculations for Central Europe predict that with a rise of only 2 °C until the year 2100, the climate will have unfavorable conditions for spruce; the species would then only grow in mountainous regions at high altitudes (Kölling 2007a, b) (Fig. 7.4a). Although the climate will still be suitable for spruce in Northern Europe, there will be almost no appropriate region left for the species in Germany and other Central European countries. Compared with softwood, however, beech and other hardwood species are more adaptable. Their future potential becomes evident when their climate envelope is compared to that of spruce. Unlike softwood, beech completely overlaps with Germany's current climate and will still almost fully overlap with future climate conditions (Jakob and Hinsen 2012) (Fig. 7.4b).

Germany's forest industry, aware of the climatic situation, has acted accordingly. Current foresting strategies foresee the climate change and have intensified hardwood plantation. At present, 70 % of the forests' juvenile trees are already

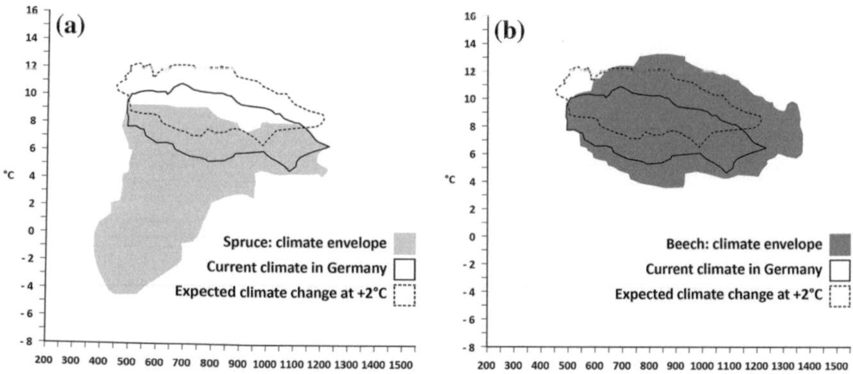

Fig. 7.4 **a** Climate envelope of spruce compared with the current and future climate conditions in Germany. **b** Climate envelope of beech compared with the current and future climate conditions in Germany (*Source* Kölling 2007a, b)

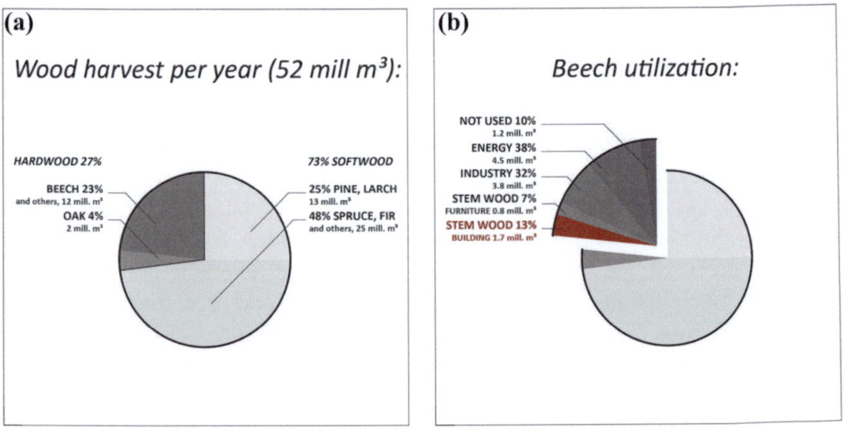

Fig. 7.5 Total wood harvest and amount of beech used for building construction (*Source* Mantau 2012)

hardwood species, eventually transforming Germany's forests back into a more natural state in a few decades (DHWR 2014). Since 2002, the beech population has increased by 5 %, whereas its counterpart, the spruce population, decreased by 7 %.

Germany's forests have the largest stock of wood in all of Europe, pegged at an estimated 3.7 billion cubic meters. However, half of the processed lumber is still imported (Sobiella 2014). Although German forests currently grow by 130 million m^3 of wood annually, only 87 million m^3 are actually harvested (DHWR 2014). Germany's forests have the capacity to satisfy local consumption even under the current wood construction methods. Nonetheless, this imbalance becomes pronounced when looking at the potential of beech as a local construction material compared with its current applications. In contrast to the species' capacity to play an important role in building construction, beech currently makes up only 23 % of the annual wood harvest (Federal Statistical Office 2013) (Fig. 7.5a). In addition, a mere 13 % of harvested beech is used for construction; almost 50 % remains unused or is used as firewood (Mantau 2012) (Fig. 7.5b). In summary, from the overall annual harvest, only 3 % is beech applied in building construction. Although there is enough beech available in Germany that can potentially be harvested in a sustainable silviculture, 50 % of all beech lumber is still imported (Schade et al. 2007). The predominant use of softwood can also be seen in saw mills. From 38 million m^3 of wood processed in saw mills in 2011, only 9 % was hardwood (Mantau 2012).

With an expected abundance of beech in the future, wood manufacturers, engineers, and architects are beginning to look into the material's differentiated potentials. Not only is the climate envelope of beech much more suitable for Central Europe's climate, it also exhibits outstanding mechanical properties exceeding those of spruce and all other building materials (Fig. 7.6) (Pollinger 2014). Its potential as a sustainable and effective construction material becomes evident when seen as a renewable and locally available resource that also represents a recreational

MATERIAL	YOUNG'S MODULUS	SPECIFIC DENSITY	SPECIFIC MODULUS			CHARACT. BENDING STRENGTH	SPECIFIC BENDING STRENGTH
	$E = N/mm^2$	$\rho = g/cm^3$	E/ρ	$\sqrt{E}/\rho$	$\sqrt[3]{E}/\rho$	N/mm^2	Nm/g
STEEL (S235)	210,000	7.85	25,000	190	7.5	235	30
ALUMINIUM	73,000	2.80	25,000	310	15.0	120	44
GLASS	73,000	2.40	25,000	360	17.5	45	19
CONCRETE (C30/37)	15,000	2.50	6,000	160	10.0	4	2
CFRP	80,000	2.00	40,000	450	21.5	900	450
SPRUCE (C24)	10,500	0.45	31,000	720	48.5	24	53
SPRUCE CLT (GL24II)	11,600	0.47	24,500	720	48.0	24	51
SPRUCE PLYWOOD	13,800	0.48	29,000	770	50.0	48	100
BEECH (D35)	14,000	0.68	20,500	550	35.5	35	51
BEECH PLYWOOD	16,800	0.68	25,000	600	37.5	70	103

Fig. 7.6 Although hardwoods have a higher density than softwoods, the bending strength of beech plywood is higher than that of spruce plywood when compared to the material's density (specific bending strength). (*Source* Pollmeier (2014), Gordon (2003), Dong and Davies (2013), BS EN 338 (2003), and DIN EN 1992-1-1)

value. Forests cannot only be seen as a source for building materials; they fulfill different, and occasionally competing, functions. Apart from being a natural habitat for many species and supporting a high ecological diversity, forests are also local recreation areas as well as a material and energy resource. Especially, the ongoing energy transition to renewable energies encourages the use of wood as an energy resource. This tendency competes with wood's function as a construction material and has already led to a threefold increase of wood prices since 2005 (Sobiella 2014). Computational design strategies will enable architects and engineers to utilize the material's structural performance while minimizing its consumption.

While foresting strategies are already adapting to climate change, the building industry still has to familiarize with the material, related building products, and their potentials. The structural performance of hardwood products seems obvious. However, its economic and sociocultural impacts have not been taken into account. Here, integrative computational design can be seen as a driver for exploring and evaluating the material's capacity for promoting sustainable architecture.

7.4 Integrative Computational Design as a Driver for Sustainable Architecture

As a versatile construction material, wood has high potentials in building construction for both large-scale individual structures as well as buildings in the context of renovation and re-densification of urban areas (Cheret 2013). Its suitability is based on the material's ecological sustainability as well as its structural efficiency and low weight, promoting the development of lightweight constructions. In comparison to current processes in architecture, integrative computational design offers the possibility of a holistic approach. This advantage is especially promising for the development of adaptive wood construction systems, for which all aspects of sustainability will ultimately define the system's resource effectiveness.

7.4.1 Adaptive Construction Systems

Established construction systems are characterized by a high degree of standardization and prefabrication. Although they ensure consistent quality and economic efficiency, standardized systems lack geometric flexibility, and therefore, adaptability for differentiated surrounding conditions. Although planning and fabrication methods have been digitalized in the past decades, they only provide limited flexibility as they focus more on the increased efficiency of already known processes. Current developments in computational design, however, aim at providing context and forecast specific solutions that enable variations within or merging of construction systems. Compared with other materials, wood construction most notably provides the opportunity to develop more adaptive and geometrically differentiated construction systems while still being realized with a certain economic efficiency. To adapt a construction system and its building parts to specific structural or architectural situations, it requires a parametric design process as well as direct and automated fabrication data generation, which will allow for further reduction of material use, weight, and manufacturing time.

7.4.2 Integrative Design and Digital Fabrication

Current planning processes in building construction are highly digitalized but also fragmented and often divided into different disciplines (Kieran and Timberlake 2004). On the one hand, digital planning processes allow for more complex buildings. On the other hand, they are currently characterized by a top-down design development where questions of "producibility" and materiality are only answered at a late stage of the design process. This tendency causes not only higher planning costs through changes in the design but also requires more time and effort for manufacturers. The development of interfaces between software packages of the involved disciplines, intended to form a digital chain, optimizes the process and increases efficiency. However, only the integration of manufacturing potentials and constraints in the early design stage and constant feedback between the disciplines will result in a digital loop, through which all requirements of sustainability could be potentially fulfilled. This aspect emphasizes the importance of the early design stage, when most of the cost-relevant choices are made (Kimpian et al. 2009). In practice, the so-called production immanent planning (Brell-Çokcan and Braumann 2010) enables reciprocities between fabrication possibilities, materiality, and the design process. In addition, the development of a computational design process will

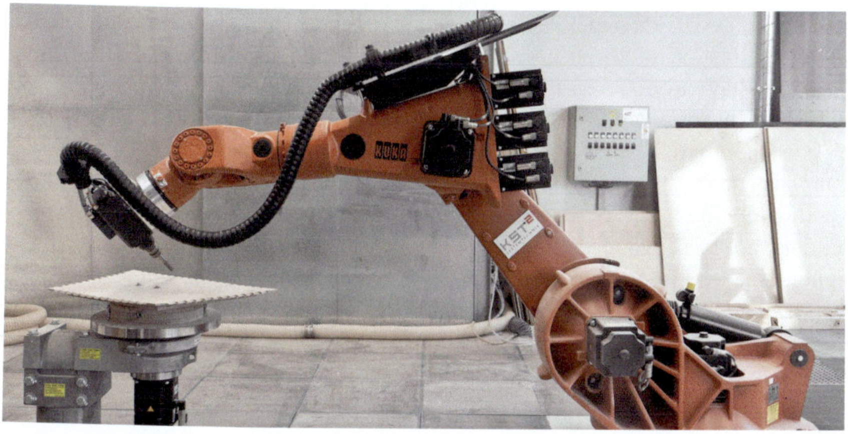

Fig. 7.7 A robotic fabrication setup consisting of a six-axis industrial robot and an additional turn table as external axis (*Source* ICD/ITKE University of Stuttgart)

allow for the integration of more disciplines, such as structural analysis, building physics, project management, and sustainability analysis.

Digital fabrication tools, such as CNC machines, have become well-established in wood fabrication. Their main advantage lies in the automation of individual aspects of production, thus making standardized processes faster and more efficient while also exceeding the quality standards of manual fabrication (Krieg and Menges 2013). However, the rationalization of fabrication processes through automated CNC machines could also lead to a standardization of construction systems in close relation to the machines' range of possibilities (Schindler 2010). In parallel to this development, the automobile industry witnessed the introduction of industrial robots in the mid-1980s. The main difference with process-specific CNC machines in wood construction is the industrial robot's flexibility: The multi-axis robot arm represents a generic platform on which a multitude of tools, or effectors, can be attached. The effectors, or a combination thereof, will ultimately define the variability and potential of the fabrication process. They can be adapted to specific tasks or projects, or enhanced by additional axes and sensors (Fig. 7.7). Further, industrial robots are used in multiple industry sectors and are therefore mass produced, low-cost, and technically refined products. Their potential in wood construction derives from their extended kinematic range that enables the efficient fabrication of complex and differentiated building parts.

7.4.3 *Pillars of Sustainability*

A cultivated forest with finite capacities for the building sector as well as a simultaneous use for recreation requires a sustainable foresting strategy. In this context, lightweight wood construction offers additional advantages through its inherent material efficiency. For validating integrative design computation and digital fabrication in wood construction, its potential in all three pillars of sustainability have to be taken into account.

Ecological sustainability: Wood is a renewable and fully recyclable material with an outstanding CO_2 and energy balance values. Compared with other building materials, processing and transporting wood require much less fossil resources. Additionally, buildings made of wood are ultimately a long-term CO_2 storage. As a building material, wood exhibits excellent mechanical properties. It has a much higher structural performance in relation to its weight, compared with steel. It can absorb high amounts of tension in its fiber direction and still have the same compressive strength as concrete (Gordon 2003). Its regional availability further makes it an ideal material for adaptive lightweight constructions. Through the differentiation of its building parts and integration of additional parameters for sustainability criteria in the design process, an even further increased material efficiency becomes feasible.

Economic sustainability: Another potential of integrative computational design is increased economic feasibility in planning and manufacturing. Wood's suitability for system building can easily be extended by the use of comparatively low-priced industrial robots. Its machinability and low weight make it easy to handle and process into differentiated and complex geometries for adaptive construction. By incorporating fabrication constraints and parameters into a digital loop, a high level of automation and prefabrication for an economically efficient realization of specialized building solutions becomes feasible.

Sociocultural sustainability: Although sustainable silviculture promises ecological and economic sustainability, only the responsible and appropriate use of wood resources can satisfy sociocultural requirements. The history of wood construction is deeply ingrained in Central European culture. Wood is one of the most accepted building materials. Its visual and haptic qualities are experienced as positive and comforting. Additionally, the material has been proved beneficial to human health. At the construction site, prefabricated lightweight wood also enables quick assembly, and therefore ensures minimal disturbance and pollution. Lastly, localized fabrication secures employment and social stability. Using locally available building materials and local high-tech fabrication, surrounding manufacturers and ultimately the regional value-added chain will potentially be strengthened. Additionally, as wood is one of the oldest building materials, a strong culture and sense of tradition within the field of timber manufacturing and construction has developed over several hundred years in Central Europe. Remarkably, the field has always adapted and embraced technological changes while still keeping a strong identity and remaining firmly rooted in a regional economic and cultural context. As an example, many of the leading timber construction companies in Central Europe that operate globally have been family owned for several generations.

The combination of robotic fabrication and lightweight wood construction has particularly high potentials for a truly resource-effective architecture. Adaptive construction systems made feasible through modern fabrication technology promise a high level of differentiation and efficiency and a sustainable use of wood; meanwhile, the local economy and competitiveness will be strengthened. As beech is slowly

Fig. 7.8 The Landesgartenschau Exhibition Hall is a demonstrator building for the research project "Robotics in Timber Construction" (*Source* ICD/ITKE/IIGS University of Stuttgart)

becoming a more dominant construction material fulfilling all aspects of sustainability, its structural and architectural potentials as a local resource were investigated by the authors in the research project "Robotics in Timber Construction." The project, completed in 2014, was funded by the EU and the state of Baden-Württemberg. The demonstrator building "Landesgartenschau Exhibition Hall," which has been developed as part of this research, is the outcome of a computational design process integrating the most up-to-date robotic fabrication technology, material characteristics, structural efficiency, and architectural qualities (Fig. 7.8).

Case Study: Landesgartenschau Exhibition Hall

The aim of the research project "Robotics in Timber Construction" was to investigate how novel methods of computational design and digital fabrication, enabled by the computerization of both the timber construction industry and architectural design process over the last two decades, can increase the resource effectiveness of architectural production and allow novel applications of timber in the construction industry. As proof of concept, a biologically informed lightweight timber shell structure was designed, developed, fabricated, and constructed in collaboration with timber construction company Müllerblaustein Holzbau GmbH. In contrast to Digital Chain, which merely replicates the traditional planning process digitally through the introduction of digital interfaces between the planning stages and its participants as stated above, the objective of this project was to enable a Digital Loop through an integration of the requirements of material, structure, fabrication, and assembly early in the design process, and thereby, to enable higher resource effectiveness compared with the conventional architectural planning process. This effectiveness should be evaluated in terms of reduced planning, fabrication, and assembly effort; reused off-cut and reduced waste during fabrication and assembly; quality assurance of building parts and logistics; the structural capacity of the lightweight system; and finally, in terms of its novel architectural potential.

One of the main limitations of the traditional planning process is the lack of feedback from the later execution stages, such as fabrication and construction, during early design stages. However, it is during these early design stages that most of the relevant decisions are made, as they pertain to energy efficiency, operation, and construction costs, including fabrication and assembly. Nominally, these early stages correspond to only 22 % of the total planning effort (HOAI 2013); however, the design decisions account for 80 % of the economic and ecologic performance of the finished building (Kimpian et al. 2009). Consequently, by developing computational methods for integrating information about material, structural behavior, fabrication, and assembly into the design stage in the form of a Digital Loop, the effectiveness of the planning process as a whole can be increased significantly. The hypothesis is that such a process not only allows increasing the efficiency of the planning process but also enables entirely novel applications, which would not be possible at all without computationally integrated planning. To achieve this goal, the authors pursued a custom approach that synthesizes the morphological study of biological structures, methods of computational design and analysis, and robotic fabrication into one coherent design method.

7.4.4 Biomimetic Design

Biomimetic design is a design methodology that aims at a derivation of design principles from biology (Vincent 2009). Specifically, the premise of constructional biomimetics is that morphological differentiation in organisms is closely related to their performance, i.e., their capacity for survival, as well as their resource efficiency, given that every organism has to build its structures using a limited amount of material and energy. Biological structures exhibit vast variation and differentiation in shape and form. Recognition of such features leads to the design concept of reducing material consumption by strategically introducing more form based on morphological principles derived from biological role models, or in short: “less material through more form.” Consequently, the biomimetic design approach follows a three-step method: (1) the analysis of morphological features of a biological role model as regards morpho-functional relationships; (2) identification and abstraction of performative structural principles; and (3) transfer of those principles into technical applications (Nachtigall and Pohl 2004).

Specifically, the structural morphology of the plate skeleton of sand dollars (Clypeasteroida), a family of the class of sea urchins (Echinoida), which was analyzed in great detail in previous research, served as a role model for the development of a wooden segmented shell structure (Fig. 7.9a). The skeleton of sea urchins is a modular system made of calcium carbonate plates joined by microscopic interlocking calcite projections along the plate edges that are very similar to man-made finger joints (Fig. 7.9b) (Krieg et al. 2011). During the research, the following five morphological principles of the shell of sand dollars relevant to the design of segmented shells in architecture could be identified: (1) differentiation of

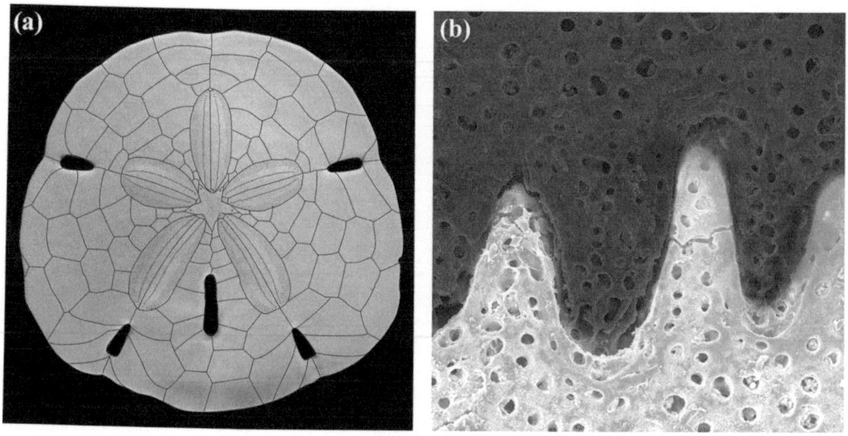

Fig. 7.9 **a** *Top view* of the sand dollar's skeleton. The boundaries of the discrete shell segments have been highlighted. **b** A microscopic view of the calcite projections connecting two plates (*Source* ICD/ITKE/IIGS University of Stuttgart)

plate geometry based on structural and functional requirements; (2) topological principle of three plates meeting at one point, which leads to a structural system where bending moments are translated into shear forces along the plate edges (Wester 1992); (3) microscopic calcite projections, which are ideally suited to accommodate shear forces (La Magna et al. 2013); (4) discrete shell segments, which allow for growth of the plates while maintaining the overall load-bearing capacity; and (5) functional integration of load-bearing structure and envelope. These principles were subsequently abstracted and integrated into the computational design model in such a way that they not only defined the boundaries of a geometric solution space, or the region of possible form, but also described the features of particularly promising areas of the solution space.

7.4.4.1 Agent-Based Modeling and Simulation

To integrate concurrently the various design parameters, including architectural, biological, geometrical, structural, legal (code requirements), material, and fabricational requirements, an agent-based modeling approach was adopted. Agent-based modeling and simulation (ABMS) is a computational methodology for design, simulation, optimization, and decision making that is utilized in a variety of fields, including robotics, finance, logistics, computer games, sociology, and biology. In other words, it is applicable whenever many individual entities interact with each other and the environment according to locally defined rules (Schwinn et al. 2014). In the architectural context, ABMS is predominantly used for simulation purposes, such as when simulating pedestrian and vehicular traffic in urban environments or building evacuation, and in design-oriented cases, but without a focus on materialization. The relation between design and materialization, however, was

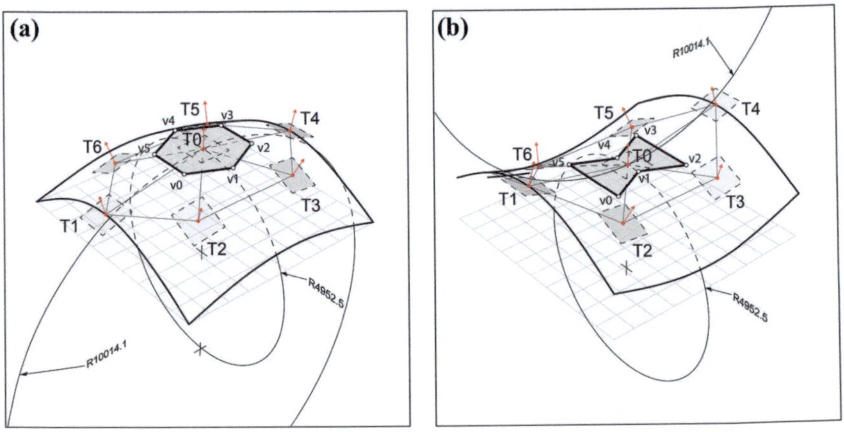

Fig. 7.10 The Gaussian curvature has an effect on the resulting geometry. **a** Positive Gaussian curvature results in polygons with a convex boundary. **b** Negative Gaussian curvature results in polygons with a concave boundary (*Source* ICD/ITKE/IIGS University of Stuttgart)

at the core of the research that led to Landesgartenschau Exhibition Hall (Menges and Schwinn 2015).

Through the definition of steering behaviors, three main aspects were implemented as part of the custom agent system for timber plate structures: (1) the ability to generate approximations of double-curved freeform surfaces through planar polygonal patches, a constraint derived from the chosen building material of beech plywood sheets, in this case (Fig. 7.10); (2) the ability of the system to respond to the spatial limitations of the available machine workspace, and the available dimensions of stock material, including weather proofing and insulation layers; and (3) the ability to control the polygon shape according to minimum and maximum allowable dimensions pertaining to edge lengths, plate sizes, and angles between the plates in response to structural, fabricational, and assembly constraints. The resulting agent system incorporates the design space for each plate in a computational form-finding process such that each plate finds its shape and location in the plate system by itself. Thus, the solutions generated by the agent design system remain within the domain of the solution space defined by the given machining setup, which, in turn, delineates the producible region of form, the machinic morphospace, from the region of possible form (Menges 2013).

7.4.5 *Robotic Fabrication*

Similar to the biological model, the plates in the timber plate structure interlock along their edges in a teethed pattern of finger-joint-like connections (Fig. 7.11a). This large-scale finger joint connection was part of the development of the

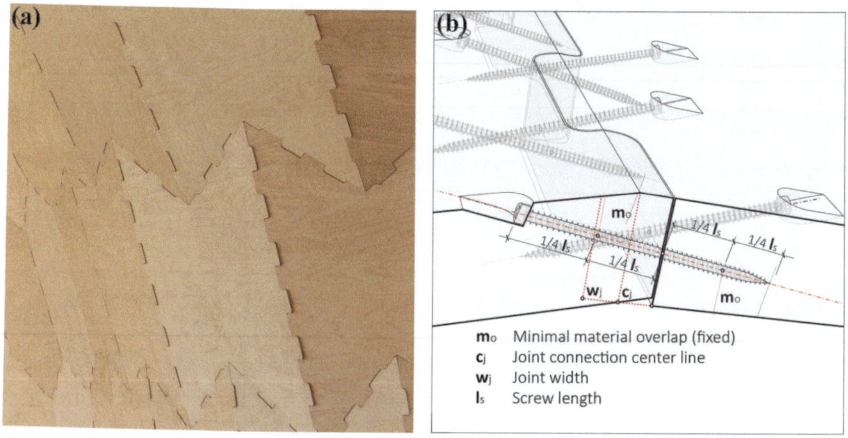

Fig. 7.11 **a** The finger joint connections between the beech plywood plates are visible on the interior. **b** Crossing screws are implemented in the construction detail but invisible on the interior surface (*Source* ICD/ITKE/IIGS University of Stuttgart)

integrative digital design and fabrication process. A major innovation in this development was the integration of construction and assembly details, especially in the context of negative Gaussian curvature areas. Specifically, the finger joints had to meet requirements of on-site assembly as well as building code for connecting plywood plates under different structural load conditions, which led to the development of such assembly-related functionalities as screw pockets and plate insertion vectors, as well as constructional details, such as crossing screws (Fig. 7.11b) (Krieg et al. 2015). This custom joint type led to the following second innovation: the parametric generation of custom tool paths, simulation of the robot movements, and generation of the robot code. The seven-axis robotic fabrication setup provided the additional kinematic range and increased machinic morphospace necessary for the production of the complex joint details (Fig. 7.12a). It also required robot kinematics simulation to avoid collisions, singularities, and out-of-reach points; the simulation allowed the fine-tuning of the robotic fabrication process to ensure that all of the plates were produced as efficiently as possible on the given machine setup (Fig. 7.12b).

Within the overall production sequence of the components of the shell structure, robotic fabrication was used strategically for the accurate fabrication of the geometrically complex finger joints. The production sequence included several steps. First, the stock pieces were cut with oversize from sheets of beech plywood in a three-axis milling process to optimize the packing of the pieces on the plywood sheet and therefore minimize off-cut. Second, the pre-cut pieces were mounted on the robotic turn table and the finger joint details milled robotically; in parallel, the insulation layer made of locally sourced wood fiber board was cut in five axes with mitered joints between the boards to ensure a tight fit; the individually tailored sheets of the EPDM membrane layer were waterjet cut, and the cladding layer made

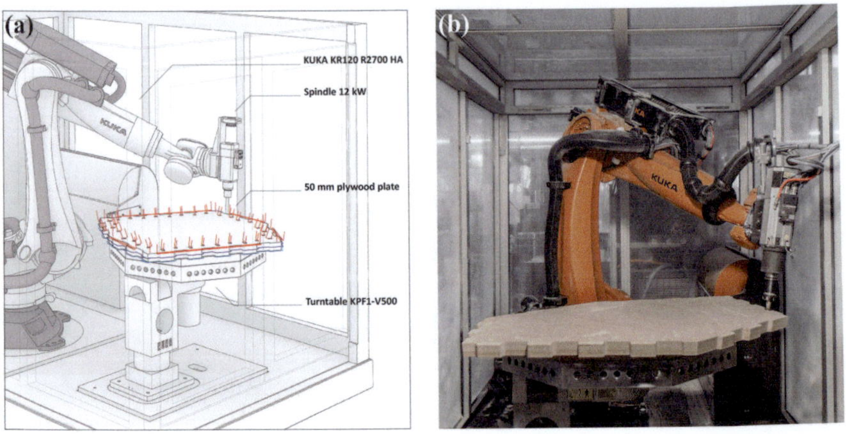

Fig. 7.12 **a** The robotic setup is simulated before the machine code is exported. **b** Robotic fabrication of a beech plywood plate for the Landesgartenschau Exhibition Hall (*Source* ICD/ITKE/IIGS University of Stuttgart)

from locally sourced three-ply larch was produced in a three-axis milling process. The information necessary to produce every functional element in the shell could be generated from the same digital model by writing directly to the respective machine code interfaces. All elements were then pre-assembled in the workshop into sub-assemblies before being shipped 65 km from the workshop in Blaustein, near Ulm, to the site in Schwäbisch Gmünd, and finally being assembled on site. The entire pre-fabrication process took four weeks, followed by another four weeks on site during which the structural shell, sub-assemblies containing insulation and waterproofing, as well as cladding layer were installed (Fig. 7.13).

Fig. 7.13 Assembly of the structural beech plywood plates (**a**) and the insulation and waterproofing layer (**b**) (*Source* ICD/ITKE/IIGS University of Stuttgart)

7.4.6 *Result and Validation*

The Landesgartenschau Exhibition Hall is the first building whose structural shell is entirely made from robotically prefabricated beech plywood plates. All of the structural elements, including the insulation and cladding layers, have been produced from locally sourced and certified wood (Fig. 7.14). Similar to the biological role model, the geometry of each individual building component is unique and adapted to the specific requirements of each element in the assembly. This includes not only the elements' shape but also their connection details, which are adapted to the local structural requirements, thereby resulting in an extremely light-weight and ultra-thin load-bearing plate structure of only 50 mm thickness while spanning 10 m. The structural shell consists of 243 geometrically unique prefabricated polygonal modules with a surface area of 245 m^2, resulting in a structural weight of the shell of only 37.9 kg/m^2. The shell encloses a gross volume of 605 m^3 using only 12 m^3 of beech plywood, while providing a floor area of 125 m^2. In line with the overall goal of maximizing the utilization of the available building material, the off-cut generated when pre-formatting the stock pieces could be reused in the hardwood flooring as parquet lamellas.

The Landesgartenschau Exhibition Hall is a fully enclosed building with an integrated façade system; it is thermally insulated and is waterproofed (Fig. 7.15). During the Landesgartenschau, a horticultural exhibition, the building hosted an exhibition curated by the Forest Agency of the state of Baden-Württemberg; presently, it serves as an exhibition and event space. The interior space is characterized by the visible finger joint connections and transformation of the plate shapes in response to the curvature of the shell. During the progression from the entrance and foyer through to the main space, the visitor experiences a gradient from synclastic

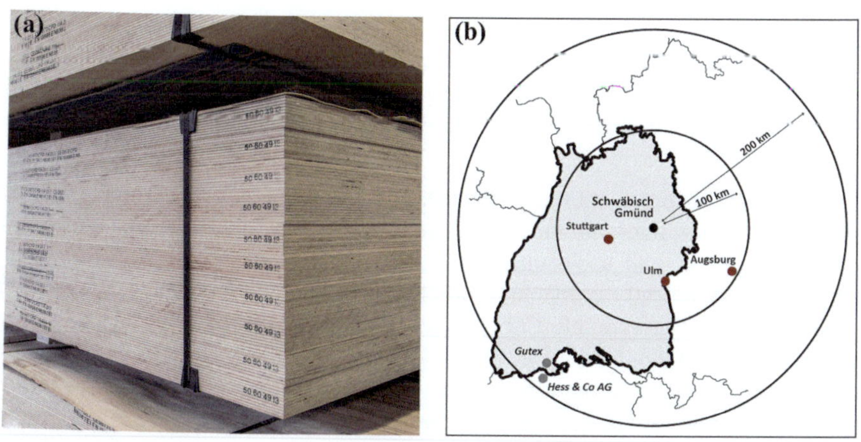

Fig. 7.14 **a** Beech plywood plates before being processed. **b** All structural elements, including insulation and cladding, have been sourced, produced, and processed within a radius of 200 km (*Source* ICD/ITKE/IIGS University of Stuttgart)

Fig. 7.15 The interior lighting highlights the building's architectural qualities. Its thin shell can be experienced from both the inside and outside (*Source* ICD/ITKE/IIGS University of Stuttgart)

to anti-clastic surface curvature reflected in the plate shapes. Ultimately, the view is directed to the surrounding landscaped area framed by the large façade opening.

Similar to the biomimetic design concept of "less material and more form" mentioned above, this project demonstrates how geometric differentiation of building elements can become not only a design feature but also a structural necessity; this particular performance, however, can only be achieved through an integrative computational design process, including locally sourced materials. In this respect, the case study demonstrates how the integration of computational design and digital fabrication can lead to a new synthesis that allows for the design and efficient fabrication of a novel, light-weight, resource-efficient, and socially and locally integrated timber architecture.

7.5 Outlook Urbanity

Innovative wood construction in the context of integrative design computation and robotic fabrication offers promising preconditions for the requirements of an ecological, economic, and sociocultural sustainability in the building industry. The combination of a locally available resource, potential of strengthening the regional value added chains, favorable CO_2 balance, and material's social acceptance is a promising foundation for further developments. Wood construction offers new applications, especially in an urban context, where construction time and pollution are factors. Extension and refurbishment projects as well as re-densification on and next to existing buildings in cities have particularly high requirements for building system planning and production. In many cases, existing buildings are not laid out for high additional loads and provide geometrically complex boundary conditions, to which the construction has to adapt. Advancing technological developments in lightweight wood construction and prefabrication as well as in the design process show great promise for fulfilling these increased requirements, and will be further investigated in the future.

Acknowledgements The work presented in this paper was partially funded by the European Union through the European Fund for Regional Development (ERDF) and the state of Baden-Württemberg through the "ClusterinitiativeForst und Holz" program and is part of a joint research project between the University of Stuttgart and MüllerblausteinHolzbau GmbH. The authors would like to express their gratitude toward their fellow investigators Professors Jan Knippers and Jian-Min Li at the Institute for Building Structures and Structural Design; and Professors Volker Schwieger and Annette Schmitt at the Institute for Geodesic Engineering, University of Stuttgart. The authors would also like to thank their project partners MüllerblausteinHolzbau GmbH, Landesgartenschau Schwäbisch Gmünd 2014 GmbH, ForstBW, and KUKA Roboter GmbH.

References

Alcorn A (1996) Embodied energy coefficients of building materials, centre for building performance research, Wellington

Brell-Çokcan S, Braumann J (2010) A new parametric design tool for robot milling. In: Proceeding of the 30th conference of the association for computer aided design in architecture, New York City, pp 357–363

Bundesamt für Naturschutz (2004) Daten zur Natur 2004, Landwirtschaftsverlag GmbH, Bonn

BS EN 338 (2003) Structural timber. Strength classes, BSI. ISBN 978 0 580 58144 1

Cheret P, Schwaner K, Seidel A (2013) Urbaner Holzbau. Handbuch und Planungshilfe, DOM publishers, Berlin

Correa D, Krieg O, Menges A, Reichert S, Rinderspacher, K (2013) HygroSkin: a prototype project for the development of a constructional and climate responsive architectural system based on the elastic and hygroscopic properties of wood. In: proceedings of the 33nd conference of the association for computer aided design in architecture, Waterloo, pp 33–42

Deutscher Holzwirtschaftsrat DHWR (2014). German Wood Economics Affair Council

Dong C, Davies IJ (2013) Flexural properties of glass in carbon fiber reinforced epoxy hybrid composites. Proc Inst Mech Eng Part L: J Mater Des Appl 227(4):308–317

Dunlop JW, Fratzl P (2010) Biological composites. Annu Rev Mater Res 40(1):1–24

COM, European Commission (2014) Communication from the commission to the European Parliament, the council, the European economic and social committee and the committee of the regions on resource efficiency opportunities in the building sector

Federal Statistical Office (2013) Forest and Wood. [Online] Available from: https://www.destatis.de/DE/ZahlenFakten/Wirtschaftsbereiche/LandForstwirtschaftFischerei/WaldundHolz/Tabellen/GesamteinschlagHolzartengruppen.html;jsessionid=821E2E8329C86CB46249335C5A52E2A6.cae1. Accessed 01 Oct 2014

Gordon JE (2003) Structures: or why things don't fall down. Da Capo Press, Boston

HOAI Official Scale of Fees for Services by Architects and Engineers (2013) § 34 Service profile of buildings and interiors(2) and (3). In: Fachmedien (ed) HOAI 2013-Textausgabe/HOAI 2013-text edition, 5th edn, Springer, Wiesbaden. ISBN 978-3-658-03269-2

Kimpian J, Mason J, Coenders J, Jestico D, Watts S (2009) Sustainably tall: investment, energy, life cycle. In: ACADIA 09: reForm()—building a better tomorrow, Chicago, pp 130–143

Kieran S, Timberlake J (2004) Refabricating architecture. How manufacturing methodologies are poised to transform building construction. McGraw-Hill, New York

Kolb J (2008) Systems in timber engineering: loadbearing structures and component layers. Birkhäuser, Basel

Kölling C (2007a) Klimahüllen für 27 Waldbaumarten. In: AFZ Der Wald, vol 23. Deutscher Landwirtschaftsverlag, pp 1242–1245

Kölling C (2007b) Die Anfälligkeit der Wälder Deutschlands gegenüber dem Klimawandel, Gefahrstoffe-Reinhaltung der Luft, vol 6/2007, p 264

Lozán J (2008) Warnsignal Klima: Gesundheitsrisiken. Gefahren für Pflanzen, Tiere und Menschen, Wissenschaftliche Auswertungen, Universität Hamburg, Hamburg

Mantau U (2012) Holzrohstoffbilanz Deutschland, Entwicklungen und Szenarien des Holzaufkommens und der Holzverwendung 1987 bis 2015, Hamburg

Menges A (2013) Morphospaces of robotic fabrication. In: Brell-Çokcan S, Braumann J (eds) Robotic fabrication in architecture, art and design: proceedings of the robots in architecture conference 2012. Springer, Vienna 28–47

Menges A, Schwinn T (2015) Fabrication agency. Architectural Des 85(5), forthcoming publication

Nachtigall W, Pohl G (2004) Bau-Bionik: Natur, Analogien, Technik. Springer, Berlin

Knippers J, Speck T (2012) Design and construction principles in nature and architecture. Bioinspiration & Biomimetics 7(1)

Krieg O, Menges A (2013) Prototyping robotic production: development of elastically bent wood plate morphologies with curved finger joint seams. In: Rethinking prototyping, proceedings of the design modelling symposium Berlin 2013, Verlag der Universität der Künste Berlin, pp 479–490

Krieg O, Dierichs K, Reichert S, Schwinn T, Menges, A (2011) Performative architectural morphology: finger-joined plate structures integrating robotic manufacturing, biological principles and location-specific requirements. In: Gengnagel, C, Kilian, A, Palz N, Scheurer F (eds) Computational design modeling, proceedings of the design modeling symposium Berlin, Springer, Berlin, pp 259–266

Krieg O, Schwinn T, Menges A, Li J, Knippers J, Schmitt A, Schwieger V (2015) biomimetic lightweight timber plate shells: computational integration of robotic fabrication, architectural geometry and structural design. In: Block P, Knippers Mitra N, Wang W (eds) Advances in architectural geometry 2014, pp 109–125

La Magna R, Gabler M, Reichert S, Schwinn T, Waimer F, Menges A, Knippers J (2013) From nature to fabrication: biomimetic design principles for the production of complex spatial structures. Int J Spat Struct 28(1): 27–40

Lozán JL et al (2008) Warnsignal Klima: Gesundheitsrisiken. Gefahren für Pflanzen, Tiere und Menschen, Wissenschaftliche Auswertungen, Hamburg

Pollmeier (2014) BauBuche: IngeniousHardwood, Informationen, Pollmeier Massivholz GmbH, Creuzberg, Germany

Schade V, Dümmer R, Seume K, Winderscheid B, Bitter W (2007) ZMP-Bilanz Forst und Holz. ZMP Zentrale Markt- und Preisberichtstelle

Schindler C (2010) Die Standards des Nonstandards. GAM—Graz Architecture Mag 06:181–193

Schwinn T, Krieg O, Menges A (2014) Behavioral strategies: synthesizing design computation and robotic fabrication of lightweight timber plate structures. In: Design agency, proceedings of the 34th annual conference of the association for computer aided design in architecture, Los Angeles, pp 177–188

Sobiella C (2014) Das große Gefälle, in enorm Magazin 05/14, SocialPublish Verlag, Hamburg, pp 41–46

Vincent J (2009) Biomimetic patterns in architectural design. Architectural Des 79(6):74–81

Wester T (1992) Structural dualism and sea urchins. In: Natural structures: principles, strategies, and models in architecture and nature (Proceedings of the II. International Symposium of the Sonderforschungsbereich 230, 1.-4.10.1991), Part III. Stuttgart, Tübingen: Vorstand des SFB 230, pp 177–182

Author Biographies

Mr. Oliver David Krieg is a Research Associate and Doctoral Candidate at the Institute for Computational Design, University of Stuttgart.

Mr. Tobias Schwinn is a Research Associate and Doctoral Candidate at the Institute for Computational Design, University of Stuttgart.

Prof. Achim Menges is a registered architect and the founding director of the Institute for Computational Design, University of Stuttgart.

Chapter 8
New Characteristics of Medical Architecture Development in China's New-Type Urbanization

Hui Li

Beginning in the 21st century, economic development in and comprehensive reform of the healthcare system effected significant changes to China's medical and healthcare services. As China has become a middle-income country, and will become an aging society within a short time span (about 20 years), national development strategies and government policies, such as "the urbanization process for the next 20 years" and "basic medical and healthcare services for all," must address the differentiated demand for and content of medical and healthcare services. To satisfy the increasing healthcare demands of the people, the rapid promotion of hospitals that adhere to modern standards in both quantity and quality is currently the crucial task regarding the health service system.

8.1 Great Progress in the Medical and Healthcare Field

Since the past decade, prominent advances have been made in China's healthcare facilities. According to the population distribution, a large number of hospitals and medical service centers as well as clinics at different levels have been set up nationwide, from core cities to remote areas. The main goals of public healthcare service are to fill the gap of requirement for healthcare services and improve the standards of medical facilities (Figs. 8.1, 8.2, 8.3, 8.4, 8.5 and 8.6).

The progress in healthcare services is shown in the following statistics. From 2002 to 2013, over 6000 new hospitals have been opened (excluding community healthcare centers and health clinics), providing over 2.3 million new inpatient beds for the entire country. The average scale of the new hospitals is 380 inpatient beds

H. Li (✉)
Medical Building Engineering Center, China IPPR International Engineering Co. Ltd., Beijing, China
e-mail: lihui@ippr.net

F. Wang and M. Prominski (eds.), *Urbanization and Locality*,
DOI 10.1007/978-3-662-48494-4_8

Fig. 8.1 Peking Union Medical College Hospital, Beijing (*Source* ©Author)

Fig. 8.2 Hebei People's Hospital, Shijiazhuang City, Hebei (*Source* IPPR)

Fig. 8.3 Beijing Chao-Yang Hospital, Beijing (*Source* IPPR)

Fig. 8.4 Peking University Third Hospital, Beijing (*Source* IPPR)

Fig. 8.5 The Hainan Branch of PLA General Hospital, Sanya City, Hainan (*Source* IPPR)

Fig. 8.6 Peking University First Hospital, Beijing (*Source* IPPR)

Table 8.1 Statistics and data analysis of the progress of China's healthcare service in the last 10 years (YEAR BOOK of HEALTH in the People's Republic of China 2013)

	Total number of hospitals	Total number of inpatient beds	Bed number/1000 people (urban)	Bed number/1000 people in Korea	Bed number/1000 people in Japan
2003	17,700	2,270,000	2.39		
2013	24,100	4,580,000	4.55 (urban)	8.6 (2010)	13.9 (2010)

per hospital, which is at the second level of the hospital grade system and far from enough to meet the growing demands of healthcare services. The hospital grade system is classified into three grades based on a hospital's function structure, medical facilities, and technical strength: First-Grade Hospital, which offers basic healthcare services in the community; Second-Grade Hospital, which Functions as a regional medical hub of preventive care and medical education; and Third-Grade Hospital, which is a comprehensive healthcare, medical teaching, and research center in nationwide (Table 8.1).

The number of inpatient beds per thousand urban people has increased from 2.39 to 4.55, which is higher than the standard set in the national and regional planning of the public healthcare system. However, compared with China's neighbors, such as Korea and Japan, the quantity and quality of healthcare services in China is still at a relatively low level.

Basic medical insurance is available to over 96 % of the total population, which is a great achievement considering the large population base, especially in developing rural areas (Fig. 8.7). Even so, as basic medical insurance covers only a small part of medical expenses, people still have to bear the majority of medical costs. Thus, demand for more affordable and efficient healthcare services will grow rapidly owing to the improvement of the medical insurance system.

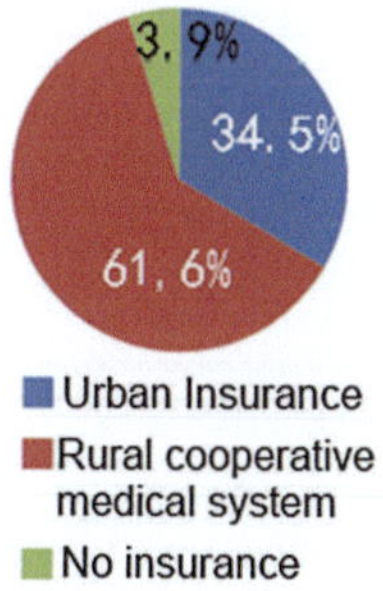

Fig. 8.7 Statistical analysis of population distribution with assorted medical insurance types in 2013. *Data Source* 2013 YEAR BOOK of HEALTH in the People's Republic of China

8.2 Problems in the Development of China's Modern Healthcare Facilities

The modernization of society has made apparent many problems in the medical and healthcare fields. At present, the unbalanced development of healthcare services is worsening between urban and rural areas, and among different types of medical facilities as well.

First, the quantity of medical facilities in rural regions is much less than that in urban areas. The number of inpatient beds per thousand rural people is 1.35, or only a third of that for the urban population. Residents in remote regions can hardly access adequate and timely medical treatment when they suffer illnesses. Second, despite the regional development planning for the healthcare system, medical resources are not distributed reasonably, owing to different regional economic and social situations. Large-scale or high-level hospitals are almost always located in core cities, whereas only healthcare centers and community clinics provide medical services for rural people (Fig. 8.8).

As the map shows, the majority of healthcare resources marked as dots are distributed within the third ring, a few between the third and fourth rings, and the minority in the suburbs. Moreover, given the disjunction between the medical

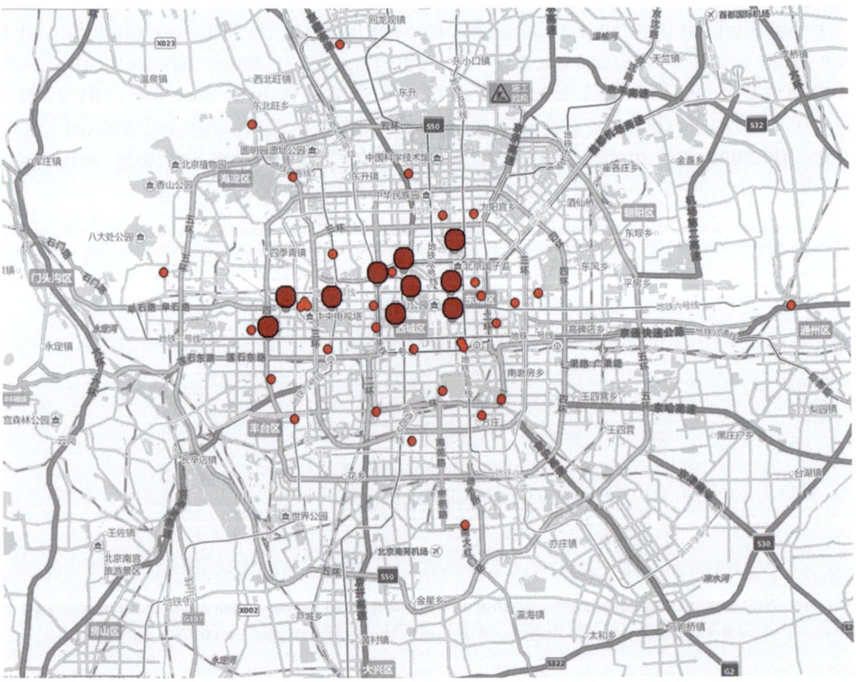

Fig. 8.8 Distribution map of third-grade class-A hospitals in Beijing (*Source* map.baidu.com)

payment and insurance systems, the three-level referral system of medical services lacks efficiency. People can choose hospitals freely based on their own economic condition. Subsequently, high-level hospitals are constantly crowded and overloaded, whereas community health centers are lacking patients (Figs. 8.9 and 8.10).

Therefore, the quality of access to healthcare services for both urban and rural citizens should be one of the main goals of the reform of China's social public

Fig. 8.9 Chinese PLA General Hospital (*Source* IPPR)

Fig. 8.10 Healthcare service center in rural area (*Source* IPPR)

affairs. Further, the central government must put forward new development strategies for the new urbanization process that would prioritize innovation in the medical and healthcare fields in the short term (2014–2020).

8.2.1 Basic Medical Services for All

By 2020, China plans to maintain a basic healthcare system that can provide safe, effective, convenient, and affordable health and medical services to all urban and rural residents. Thus, the new healthcare requirements for the all-encompassing coverage of the medical delivery system that guarantees "basic medical and healthcare services for everyone" call for sufficient and more reasonable distribution of medical facilities (The National Healthcare Service System Plan 2015–2020).

8.2.2 Urbanization Rate of up to 60 % of China's Society

Regarding the differentiation in the medical delivery and payment systems between urban and rural citizens, a new mode and large amounts of facilities with urban-type healthcare services are required for almost 100 million new urbanized people.

8.2.3 New Household Registration System

In urban areas, healthcare services could be shared equally by local registered people, permanent residents, and the urban floating population; the capacity of existing or newly built medical facilities would have to meet the demands of all the different groups. As for hardware facilities, the appropriate corresponding guideline is to plan and construct enough medical facilities with relevant capability in a short period (National New-type Urbanization Plan 2014–2020).

8.3 Planning Guidelines of Medical Facilities in the New Urbanization

Unlike newly built hospitals in urban areas, many social characteristics should be considered in the planning and construction of healthcare facilities in new urbanized regions because they are usually set out from a brand-new beginning and without an existing foundation.

Based on regional development planning, new urbanized areas are usually located close to developed cities with relevant acceptable environmental conditions, which make the rapid city construction and resident settlement possible. Under these circumstances, the medical architectures in these areas reflect only a few aspects of the local environment and new inhabitants.

As to the equalization of the healthcare services provided for either urban or new urbanized residents, the equipment in new medical facilities distributed in new urbanized regions would share the same standards or levels with urban hospitals, which means that healthcare facilities would be planned at a high starting point based on the gradually improving economic and living conditions of newly settled urban people (Figs. 8.11, 8.12 and 8.13).

The architectural variables of medical facilities should be dynamic, as the development and prosperity of new urban regions are always long-term processes. Therefore, to achieve practicability and economic efficiency, the planning and construction of hospitals should be controlled by an overall master plan and implemented by stages. The major considerations in the planning and design of medical facilities in new urbanized regions are as follows: (1) appropriate capability corresponding to the regional population and economic development; (2) optimized distribution of healthcare resources according to orientation and accessibility; (3) in medical services, priority given to new urban regions, extending to the surrounding areas; (4) open and interactive functional mode to promote the bi-directional referral system; and (5) reasonable decision as regards a hospital's scale and development strategy.

Fig. 8.11 Suzhou Science and Technology Town Hospital, Jiangsu (1200 beds), Suzhou City, Jiangsu (*Source* IPPR)

Fig. 8.12 Haihu New District Hospital (2000 beds), Xining City, Qinghai (*Source* IPPR)

Fig. 8.13 Honliv Medical City (5000 beds), Xinxiang City, Henan (*Source* IPPR)

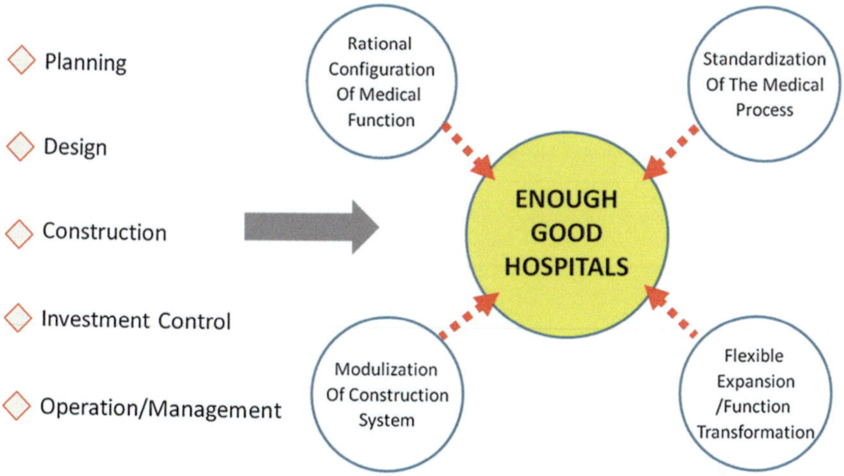

Fig. 8.14 Characteristics of the mechanism of medical architecture, from IPPR

From the view of policymakers and healthcare service administrators, providing enough good healthcare facilities in new urbanized areas within a short period can be achieved by setting up the effective mechanisms of the healthcare architecture during the developing process (Fig. 8.14).

An example of a new hospital in a new urbanized region is Peoples' Hospital of Shifang City, Sichuan Province, which is the medical project during the urban renewal after the devastating 2008 earthquake (Figs. 8.15 and 8.16). The hospital is located at the east side of the new city on a flat site and under convenient municipal conditions. Based on the major design principles considering high efficiency, including half-centralized layout, modular functional framework, grid traffic

Fig. 8.15 Peoples' Hospital, Shifang City, Sichuan (Photo taken on-site, *Source* IPPR)

Fig. 8.16 Site plan of Peoples' Hospital, Shifang City, Sichuan (*Source* IPPR)

system, as well as standardized medical process, the construction time of the hospital with 65,000 m^2 and 600 inpatient beds was compressed to 18 months (March 2009–October 2010), which enabled the public healthcare service system to work promptly and effectively for the new residents.

At the beginning of the new urbanization process in many regions, good effects were achieved by this mode to promote the quality of public healthcare service rapidly. However, the simple quest to shorten construction time and achieve effective mechanisms for medical facilities can sometimes lead to monotony of living environment and lowered attractiveness of the urbanizing region.

8.4 Embodiment of New Urbanization in Healthcare Architecture's New Design Philosophy

In contrast to the development strategy in the previous stages of the modernization process, the quality and humanity of healthcare services has received increasing attention, whereas the hardware conditions in medical architecture have been improving constantly. As one of the most important components of the city's public service facilities, hospital architectures could contribute to improving the quality of living, as well as vigor and vitality, of the community by for offering reliability and accessibility to the settled residents of a new urbanized region.

Thus, the social and cultural attributes of medical buildings have been considered to a large extent and then incorporated with functional elements during the planning and design phase. The historic context, cultural inheritance, local ecological characteristics, sense of belongingness, and people's living habits are reflected directly or indirectly through the design and idea of healthcare buildings. For instance, Hospital of Tianjin Binhai New Area successfully expresses its vernacular identity by incorporating Western classical architectural style into the local building complex (Fig. 8.17). The Chinese Traditional Medicine Hospital of Luzhou City is another perfect example. It not only accommodates the local hilly topography but deconstructs the Chinese traditional architectural form (Fig. 8.18). People's Hospital in Jia County, Henan Province, is a state-of-the-art healthcare community focusing on sustainability and cultural expression (Fig. 8.19). It creates

Fig. 8.17 Hospital of Tianjin Binhai New Area, Tianjin City (*Source* IPPR)

Fig. 8.18 Chinese traditional Medicine Hospital, Luzhou City, Sichuan Province (*Source* IPPR)

Fig. 8.19 People's Hospital, Jia County, Henan Province (*Source* IPPR)

a "healing garden" by providing the sustainable healing environment; moreover, it translates the local culture, including calligraphy and seal cutting, into the architectural vocabulary and appliesit to the façade design.

From the view of different stakeholders, the combined effects and influences of the various forms and styles of healthcare architecture in new urbanized regions can be understood in several aspects. At the governmental decision-making level, the remarkable image of healthcare buildings reflects the ruling ability of the local government and emphasizes the importance of public benefits. Especially for government-invested hospitals, the building character embodies the authority of the government to a degree, in contrast with private- or social-invested hospitals (Fig. 8.20).

Fig. 8.20 Cooperation Hospital, Yichuan County, Henan Province (*Source* IPPR)

For investors and developers of new urban areas, the high quality and inspiring environment of healthcare facilities can improve site habitability and promote the regional value (Fig. 8.21).

To establish medical brand, technical authority, and reputation in a short period, hospital directors and managers aim to impress residents with unique or arresting architectural forms.

Fig. 8.21 Honliv Medical City, Xinxiang City (*Source* IPPR). *The project not only stimulates the development of residential, commercial, and senior living industries but also helps raise the living quality of local residents

For the users of new hospitals, such as the patients, their families, and visitors, the comfortable and attractive exterior and homelike interior provide convenience in the use of medical functions. These aspects likewise promote relaxation and help avoid depression during medical procedures. Meanwhile, this environment also brings benefits to the medical staff and administrators by promoting their working enthusiasm and raising work efficiency.

To the planners and designers, a positive medical environment can be created to enhance the healing effect assisted by medical procedure planning and advanced functional design.

To realize the perspectives of all stakeholders, the architectural form and style of healthcare buildings should embody the sophisticated characteristics of authority, advancement, humanity, communal cohesiveness, and commercial value, apart from the medical functional satisfaction. Given the relevance to all the participants, the planning and construction of healthcare architectures are always the focus of development of new urbanized regions (Fig. 8.22).

The following are two examples that show the concordance of the social and cultural elements with the functional property of hospitals in new urban areas.

8.4.1 Hospital Fitting for Changes Toward the Future

Located in the new developing region of Shunyi District, Beijing City, the branch of Beijing Friendship Hospital has 1200 inpatients beds and a floor space of over 250,000 m^2, planned and designed under the new concept.

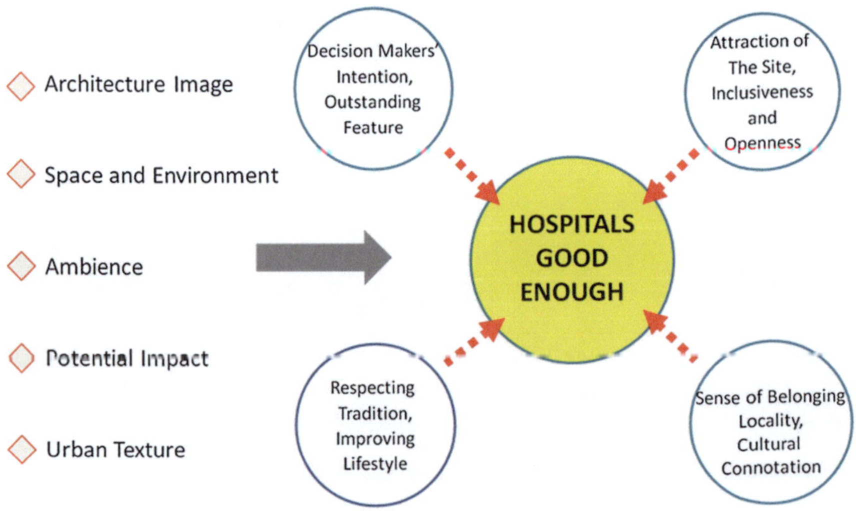

Fig. 8.22 Natural and cultural characteristics of medical architecture in the development of the new urbanization (*Source* IPPR)

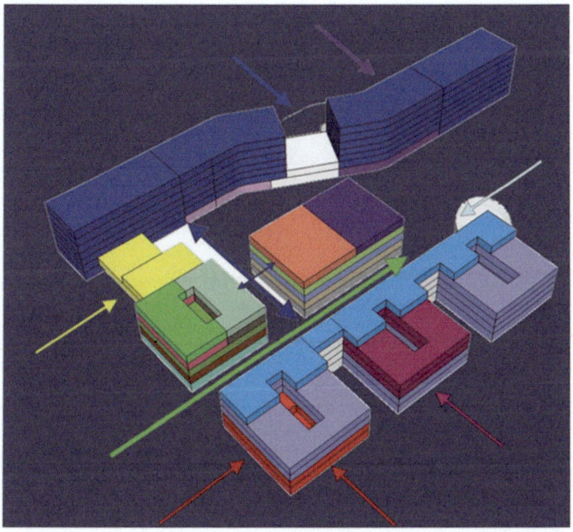

Fig. 8.23 Rational and Clear Medical Function Organization (*Source* IPPR)

Organized in a rational manner and following a clear medical functional framework, the horizontal layout of the hospital creates a convenient and compact medical pattern, which enables effective way-finding experience and shortens the walking distance for patients. The parallel extending trend ensures the feasibility and flexibility of the entire building for future development (Fig. 8.23). Standardized distribution enables medical components to be used in general medical functions as well as specialized ones without disturbing the existing order (Fig. 8.24). Many green technologies have been adopted for energy saving and hygiene quality improvement.

Fig. 8.24 Standardized outpatient sections that easily transform to specialty centers (*Source* IPPR)

Fig. 8.25 Bird view perspective of the Hospital (*Source* IPPR)

Along with social and cultural expression, the hospital brings activeness and affinity to the public. The inner environment is patient friendly, offering patients with a view to diverse courtyards (Fig. 8.25). The unified image establishes a solid recognition for the medical facility in the region. The abstract curve modeling of a peace dove expresses the spiritual symbol of the hospital (Fig. 8.26).

Fig. 8.26 Bird view perspective of the hospital nearby the airport at night (*Source* IPPR)

8.4.2 *Highly Advanced Hospital Integrated into the Landscape*

Under the development strategy of the International Tourism Island, the Hainan branch of The PLA General Hospital is constructed to support the new developing tourism region in Sanya City, Hainan Province. Neighbored by many luxurious hotels and resorts along the seaside, the hospital presents a pure architectural form of an oval ring; this stable and gentle posture makes it stand out from the surrounding environment (Fig. 8.27). Moreover, oriented by the tropical weather near the sea, the public spaces of the hospital are designed as gray spaces open to the surrounding garden in different degrees based on the environmental condition, thereby enabling the breeze from the sea to blow through the building, which significantly reduces the air conditioning energy consumption. In addition, the interior courtyard and natural landscape are linked together by open architectural spaces, which create an attractive impression of a "hospital in a garden" (Figs. 8.28 and 8.29).

Further, the concise layout contributes to the effective functional organization. With the main medical technology departments located at the basement, the medical process of all the patients can be fulfilled conveniently by the multi-level barrier-free transportation system. The rigid and compact but well-organized patient-zone management allows the core medical resources to be shared and utilized conveniently by different types of patients (Fig. 8.30).

Fig. 8.27 Bird's-eye view of the hospital (*Source* IPPR)

Fig. 8.28 Interior courtyard (*Source* IPPR)

Fig. 8.29 Exterior courtyard (*Source* IPPR)

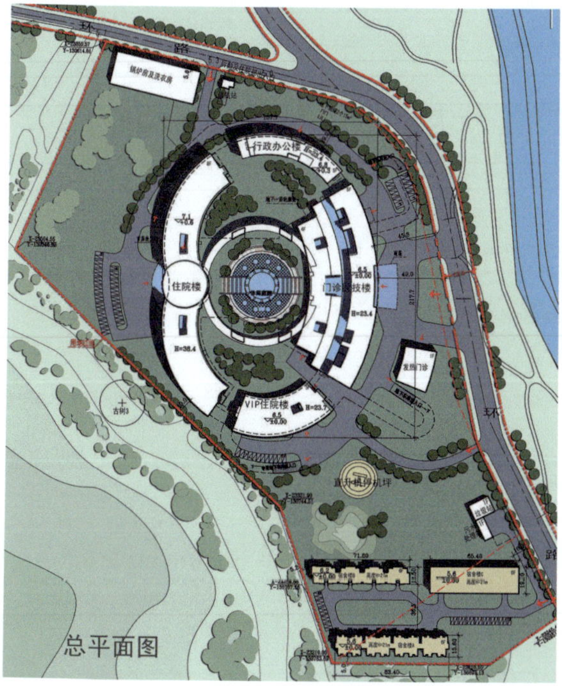

Fig. 8.30 Site plan (*Source* IPPR)

For its outstanding figure and well-operated medical functions, the project of the Hainan branch of the PLA General Hospital won the highest healthcare architecture planning and design award in the National Conference of Hospital Construction 2012. It has become such a holy land of newly constructed hospitals that hospital directors and managers visit to seek inspiration.

8.5 Conclusion

The medical mechanisms of healthcare architecture do not contradict its social and cultural characteristic aspects; all of these aspects comprise an entire project. From the perspective of medical planners and designers, healthcare facilities refer to the medical processes in spatial containers as well as the spatial containers accommodating medical activities (Fig. 8.31).

Especially in new urbanized areas, the requirements for medical services are not only to ensure the effectiveness and efficiency of medical functions but also to realize the high quality of the healthcare architecture and environment, which are evaluated according to all parts related to the development of new regions.

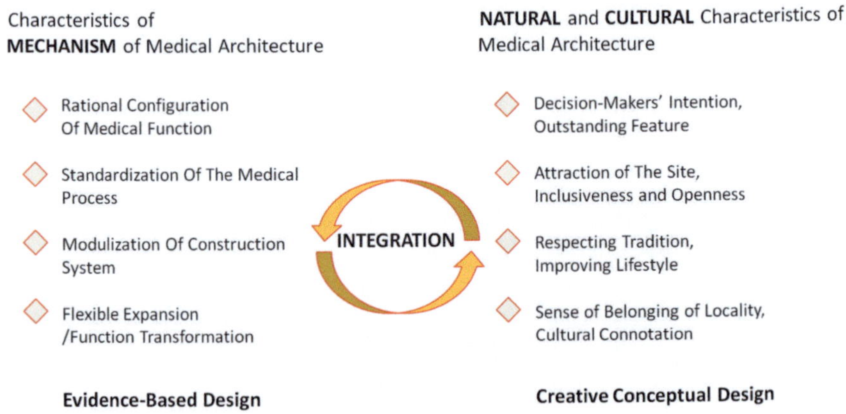

Fig. 8.31 Integrating the medical mechanism element with the social and cultural characteristics of healthcare architecture (*Source* IPPR)

By integrating the medical mechanism element with the social and cultural characteristics of healthcare architecture, enough and good enough hospitals would be designed and constructed to match the rapid pace of the new urbanization process.

References

2013 YEAR BOOK of HEALTH in the People's Republic of China [DB/OL]
National New-type Urbanization Plan (2014–2020) [DB/OL]
The National Healthcare Service System Plan (2015-2020) [DB/OL]

Chapter 9
Study of Vernacular Dwellings and Settlement Renewal

Xiaopeng Fan and Zhennan Wang

9.1 Types of Vernacular Dwellings

Each type of vernacular dwelling has its regional and ethnic characteristics. The structural composition of types is derived from people's production and life needs. It involves many aspects of nature and humanity in the material and morphological characteristics of space and construction, which show the different styles under different actions of various aspects. Closely connected with the local and regional characters, the types of vernacular dwellings constitute the basic styles of regional construction. "Deformation" based on basic types not only dilute the type features of vernacular dwellings, which are precisely the rich, diverse forms that strengthen regional type features of vernacular dwellings, but also form the overall built environment in the region.

9.1.1 Spatial Shaping and Natural Environment

The natural environment and natural resources in a region have a basic critical effect on the spatial shaping of types of vernacular dwellings. In providing the build conditions for residential construction formed by materials, landscape, and climate, the natural environment affects the external form of vernacular dwelling types. Regional natural resources determine local residents' production and life modes through the scale and quality of farmland resources, and thus affect the internal functional components and forms of vernacular dwelling types. Tibet, a place located in southwest plateau area of China, is taken here as an example. Its geographical range spans nearly 2000 km from east to west, and it has an area of

X. Fan (✉) · Z. Wang
Beijing University of Civil Engineering and Architecture, Beijing, China
e-mail: anebony@vip.sina.com

F. Wang and M. Prominski (eds.), *Urbanization and Locality*,
DOI 10.1007/978-3-662-48494-4_9

1.2 million square kilometers, elevation ranging from less than 1000–5000 m above sea level, and diverse natural conditions. It has widely varying natural environments in different regions, such as alpine and gorge region in East Tibet, plain in South Tibet, and plateau in Northwestern Tibet. Construction resources that can be obtained include wood, stone, and earth. Resource conditions have led to a variety of production and life modes, including farming-pastoral, agricultural, and nomadic modes. Accordingly, in residential construction, various local types of vernacular dwellings have been formed, including watchtower, blockhouse, cottage, tents, and caves. Both external forms and internal functional structures reflect the corresponding and shaping relation of dwellings with the natural environment.

9.1.2 Space Layout and Patriarchal Concept

The internal functional composition of local types of vernacular dwellings is determined by lifestyle. Specific to the functional space layout, it corresponds to the regional and ethnic family values. In the traditional agricultural society, the patriarchal concept has formed the fixed social hierarchical system, exerting a profound impact on family life, which has thus correspondingly constituted a rule of hierarchal arrangement of society seen in the spatial layout of vernacular dwellings. That is, the size of residential buildings corresponds to family size, and the layout sequence of residential spatial functions corresponds to the hierarchical order of family members. In the case of the courtyard house, regardless of how large the size is and how complex the form is, its basic spatial layout is composed of principal rooms, back and left seats, and right side rooms, with an obvious axial relation. Among them, the principal rooms are for the family elders, whereas the side rooms are assigned to brothers and their family members, according to the hierarchical structure (Lai 2004). As seen in the courtyard houses at Cuandixia Village of Mentougou District (Fig. 9.1), the courtyard's scale corresponds to family size, with courtyards of the elders as the ordered center. The construction of residential

Fig. 9.1 Layout of Cuandixia Village (*Source* ©Authors)

buildings extends outward along with the growth of the family, forming a vernacular settlement based on quadrangles in northern China.

Corresponding to the self-sufficient natural economy and shortage of natural resources, farmers and herdsmen in the Tibetan plateau area attach importance to independent family life. Thus, the social structure of the population is relatively decentralized. Consequently, there is no hierarchical spatial sequence for types of vernacular dwellings in various regions of Tibet. Instead, the spatial sequence corresponds to the family spiritual life in practice of the universal religion. The layout of the internal space is reserved as space for Buddha and family gatherings at the center. Geographically dispersed vernacular settlements conform to the mutual independence among dwellings.

9.1.3 Construction Mode and Gathering of Materials

Local types of vernacular dwellings are closely related to their construction mode and technology, whereas the construction mode and technology depends on the types of construction materials that can be obtained. The gathering of materials differs according to the regional natural resources. In the Tibetan region, according to the climatic environment, the forest vegetation gradually reduces from the east to the west (Fan 2008). Whereas the alpine and gorge region in East Tibet is relative rich in wood, the central and southern regions are abundant with stone, and the northwest area has a wealth of sandy soil. Thus, vernacular dwellings are mostly made of wood in the southeast mountainous areas of Tibet, and toward the west, they are made of stone and wood, soil and wood, while loess cave dwellings seen in the A-Li area of Western Tibet.

Vernacular dwellings around China generally take wood as the main structure. Most use local materials, especially for the closure structure of residential buildings, owing to the easy availability of this material. Given the inconvenient communication and transportation, construction materials for dwellings mainly depend on yak and human-powered transport in Tibetan plateau areas, which limits the circulation and use of large-scale, heavy-weight, and large-size building materials, thereby forming the dwellings' unique construction modes and forms in the Tibet region. For example, limited by the length of goods shipped by yaks, the flat scale of Tibetan dwellings generally takes a column length as the basic unit size, with a column space of about 2 m; both girder span and purl across are formed from one column, namely, a square planar unit of "one column space." In the areas with wood shortage, most vernacular dwellings are a planar unit of "one column space," which extend and combine with a major structure, and then local soil and stone materials are used to construct building envelopes for the dwellings.

9.1.4 Morphological Characteristics and Climate Conditions

The regional climate conditions have a direct impact on the morphological characteristics of vernacular dwellings—from the transparent, open-pile dwellings in hot areas in the south to heavy, stocky courtyard houses in cold areas in the north, the morphological characteristics are all direct expressions of different climate conditions. In the Tibetan plateau area, relatively lightweight wooden houses only appear at lower altitudes with a mild and moist climate. In Southeastern Tibet, which receives more rain, a sloping roof has to be used. In the vast majority of areas that have a cold climate common in plateaus, that is dry and with minimal rainfall, vernacular dwellings take heat preservation and insulation as important construction aspects, which affect the layout of interior spaces, window sizes and orientation, roof shape, and other aspects of dwellings. Corresponding to the severe cold, dry climate conditions with a large temperature difference between mornings and evenings in winter, most vernacular dwellings in Tibet generally adopt the construction mode of increasing the thickness of building envelopes while reducing the area of windows and doors. The thickness of building envelopes is larger than that in northeast cold areas, whereas the area for windows and doors is smaller. A large window opens to the south in the main space of residential buildings. Small windows are opened along retaining walls of other spaces. A thick and solid flat roof is applied for heat preservation. In addition, limited by building materials, vernacular dwellings in the Tibetan region generally have low head space, which is also conducive to building insulation in response to local climate conditions. The three abovementioned modes jointly constitute the closed, stocky morphological characteristics of vernacular dwellings in most areas of Tibet.

9.1.5 Morphological Characteristics and Religious Belief

As the cultural connotation of people's spiritual world, religious belief must have an external material embodiment in the objective world, such as the worship of entities that carry Buddhist wishes and behaving to pay respect to Buddha, the physical form of concreteness and abstraction carrying the wish of blessing, and the practice of exorcism. Under the profound influence of Tibetan Buddhism, various articles for use in secular life show the form and color that bear strong religious significance on morphogenesis. These aspects promote the lifestyle, customs, and constructions of Tibetan residents, carrying the imprint and characteristics of religious belief.

According to the universal religion in the Tibetan region, the center space of vernacular dwellings is the space for Buddha, constituting the main characteristics of the internal form of residential buildings. Color has its unique significance in Tibetan Buddhism. For example, white is the most sacred color with the most numerous connotations: symbolizing the Goddess of Mercy, sacred lotus, merciful

Fig. 9.2 Colored residential buildings in Sa'gya (*Source* ©Authors)

God, material wealth, purity, and good fruit; red represents the brilliance on Bodhisattva's bosom, irritable deity, and guardian angel of space; and dark blue is a symbol of Vajrapani, standing for fierceness, ferociousness, horror, and curse on evil spirits and enemies. In the use of religious colors in buildings, vernacular dwellings in the Sa'gya area are especially unique (Fig. 9.2). The combination of colors symbolizing Avalokitesvara, Kong Kim, and Manjusri forms significant morphological characteristics for regional vernacular dwellings in the Sa'gya area.

9.2 Construction Rules for Vernacular Settlements

With the growth in the size of populations, vernacular dwellings have gradually developed into settlements. The formation of settlements is not the copy and construction of local types of vernacular dwellings; rules are followed in settlement construction. People with the same production and lifestyle as well as the religious views build their own buildings based on the local types of vernacular dwellings. Local types of residential buildings are gathered to form vernacular settlements according to social organizational relationships and topographic conditions.

9.2.1 Construction Rules and Settlement Shaping

The basic decisive factors for vernacular settlement shaping are natural environmental conditions and mode of production, that is, the topographic condition of a settlement site decides the size of the settlement, whereas the geographic condition determines the spatial structure of the settlement. The range condition of a settlement site and mode of production of the residents decide the functional structure of the settlement. These basic decisive factors constitute the construction rules for vernacular settlement shaping at the spatial level from the two aspects of human–

earth relationship and human–industry condition. For the human–earth relationship, land source and agricultural production play an essential role in an agricultural society. Settlement lands not intended for agricultural production become construction land according to the basic rule for the construction of vernacular settlements. Therefore, land use scale, form, and other natural geomorphic conditions suitable for the construction of vernacular settlements in a site's environment directly determine the shape of vernacular settlements on the physical space, which also gives the vernacular settlement the characteristics of the natural environment. For example, the Jiaju Tibetan villages, located between Big Jinchuan River and the towering peaks of snowcapped mountains at Dadu River, Danba County, have more mountain lands with large slopes, whereas the plains suitable for farming is narrow, shallow, and shattered. Residential buildings are thus constructed on hilly land beside the plain site, and consequently, the overall settlement is spread over lands for farming around the mountains, showing a loose agglomeration of independent residences.

For human–industry relation, as the basis of people's survival and settlement, the mode of production is the core that supports the construction of vernacular settlements, which is another basic rule for the construction of vernacular settlements. Thus, the mode of production should comply with the state of farmland resource, regional traffic, and other conditions in the site's environment. This aspect also determines the shape of vernacular settlements on the space structure. Vernacular settlements are characterized by the use of the natural environment. For example, to fit and be convenient for agricultural cultivation, vernacular settlements in areas abundant with plain farmland resources show a nest-like form; to fit and be convenient for the handicraft industry and commercial transportation, most vernacular settlements in waterway junctions present a banded structure form.

The construction rules for vernacular settlements are derived from responding to natural environmental conditions and supporting people's life, and then condensing these aspects through consensus building in settlements. Residents comply with but not scrupulously abide by the construction rules for vernacular settlements, and in the process, they enrich the forms in settlements while enhancing the regional types of vernacular settlements.

9.2.2 Human Environment and Settlement Characteristics

Vernacular settlements of the same or similar types are distributed throughout China. These settlements in various regions have their own morphological characteristics. The formation of characteristics is closely related to people's social organization, living customs, and cultural tradition. The cultural environment in each state and region determines the formation of characteristics of vernacular settlements, and the characteristics of regional humanities are reflected by the characteristic of the material space of settlements.

The formation of a cultural environment is a long-term process, which begins with the influence of the natural environment and resources, and then developed through the family composition, social structure among crowds, and living customs and beliefs held in common. People differentiate themselves from others in different regions and different ethnic groups in the following aspects: living customs, family relationship, social organization, religious belief, and so forth. Their respective values gradually condense and take shape, thus forming the regional, ethnic differences and characteristics of the cultural environment. Both social structure relations and construction of vernacular settlements formed by a gathering of people are constituent parts of the cultural environment, with the characteristic of regional and ethnic cultural environment. The social relations among residents are reflected in the combination of residential buildings, from individuals to groups, thus constituting the typical characteristics of vernacular settlements.

With blood relationship as the social organization of the crowd, ancestral temples often take the "central position" of vernacular settlements, forming a settlement characteristic of gradual outward spreading. For example, the central position at the top of the site of Cuandixia Village is taken by the dwellings of the clan's ancestors. With the growth of Han families, the organizational mode based on a patriarchal system of settlements has expanded gradually, thus reflecting the obvious centripetal characteristic of the organizational structure of the patriarchal clan system. In addition, settlements of the ethnic minorities have a relationship of religious support. The central position is occupied by ethnic symbolic structures, public spaces, or temple architectures. The characteristics of vernacular settlements reflect the social organizational structure of the gathering crowd, and the characteristic relationship of the crowd is converted into morphological characteristics of the material space. Meanwhile, environmental conditions play an important role. As such, vernacular settlements demonstrate the characteristic of dual influence of the cultural and natural environment (Fan and Li 2010).

9.2.3 Consensus Building and Residential Construction

Residential building and consensus of vernacular settlements stem from the combined action of natural and cultural environmental factors, following the development of history. Consensus building refers to the value orientation of regional or ethnic cultural traditions, and reflects on the concepts, rules, and forms created by dwellings and settlements. Consensus building plays a role on two levels: first, the building of vernacular dwellings; and second, the building of vernacular settlements. The latter can be regarded as the gathering of residential buildings.

The role of consensus building in the construction of residential buildings is to establish a regional residential type, or the basic style for the construction of vernacular dwellings. As the reference of a specific family residential building, the style of residential types can be adjusted according to the family's own size, structure, and lifestyle, among other factors. Thus, although the construction of

Fig. 9.3 Individual dwellings in Jiaju Tibetan Village (*Source* ©Authors)

each vernacular dwelling has its own unique personalized morphological characteristic, it is based on the common regional characteristics (Fan and Du 2012). For instance, individual dwellings in Jiaju Tibetan Village (Fig. 9.3) have three or four layers of detached buildings: the ground floor is for the livestock circle and storage; the second floor is for the kitchen, living room, and bedroom; and the third floor and higher is for the bedrooms and scripture hall. Floor platforms generated by battering in by layer accommodate the functions for daily activities and grain drying. As for residential building materials, wood is used for load-bearing structures and stone for the building envelope. Larger windows are opened at the dayside, and wooden structures are mostly applied in the south-facing part of the top floor. When windows are preferred, small ones are found on the other three thick, heavy stone walls; these windows provide heating in the daytime and heat preservation at night. All residential buildings have approximately the same overall form, albeit slightly different in scale, number of layers, and orientation attributed to differences among families and construction sites. Thus, homes reflect the particularity of the individual family and site.

For Tibetans with a deep religious belief, as an important part of consensus building, religious belief reflects its importance especially in the process of vernacular settlements building. The portal and central constitution of settlements often adopt religious structures as identification of the gathered settlers. In such settlements, individual religious belief reflects the cultural identity of the ethnic groups according to cultural consensus. As such, religious belief also shows the achievement force on residential types. For example, the entrance of residential buildings and the interior and exterior of houses have decorative patterns and designs that hold religious meaning (Fig. 9.4). In specific local settlement and residential building, differences can be observed between the identification and decorative patterns of religious belief, which originate from the personalized pursuit of groups and individuals as regards spiritual life and ideal prospects.

Fig. 9.4 Decorative patterns of residential buildings (*Source* ©Authors)

9.3 Contemporary Renewal of Vernacular Settlements

Established on the basis of a traditional agricultural society, vernacular settlements face an unadaptable situation under the contemporary social and economic environment, such as the decline of vernacular settlements and hollowing out phenomenon. In China, the renewal mode of various vernacular settlements can be basically divided into two types: villagers' self-renewal and planning and construction renewal. These two renewal modes differ especially in terms of implementation.

9.3.1 Self-renewal by Villagers

The subjects of the self-renewal of vernacular settlements are the local villagers. Usually in the site of a homestead, villagers autonomously choose to renew, rebuild, or undertake new construction as regards their dwellings. The government offers guidance in construction, imposes limits, and provides monetary subsidies; affordable housing is also provided in various regions (Fig. 9.5). In such a renewal process, as the subject of renewal, the villagers are both the users and transformers; more importantly, they are the most direct beneficiaries. Self-renewal can best manifest the interest and value orientation of the villagers themselves.

The mode of self-renewal basically continues the construction mode of dwellings in a traditional vernacular settlement. The villagers decide the construction style on their own according to actual demand, economic capability, and other conditions based on the existing homestead, as well as adjust the construction according to actual requirements based on independent styles or design.

In reconstruction based on self-renewal, the object focuses on a specific single residential building, and the range is limited within the existing homestead.

Fig. 9.5 Self-renewal residential building (*Source* ©Authors)

Fig. 9.6 Self-renewal village (*Source* ©Authors)

Therefore, this mode scarcely changes the surrounding terrain and overall scale and form of vernacular settlements (Fig. 9.6).

The self-renewal mode is characterized by a reconstructive and renewing subject, namely, the user, who ensures that the reconstructive and renewing contents tally with the actual demands. Such a bottom-top reconstructive and renewing method can bring up diverse shape changes to and enrich individual vernacular dwellings based on regional residential types, without weakening the characteristic of regional residential types. In the self-renewal mode, with the tight fit between individual buildings and construction site environment, vernacular settlements tend to have the characteristic of regional natural environment, especially suitable for the conservation and renewal of traditional vernacular settlements.

9.3.2 Planning and Construction Renewal

As a bottom-top reconstructive and renewing method, the subject of the planning and construction of vernacular settlements in this mode is the government; examples are new rural reconstruction projects in various regions (Figs. 9.7 and 9.8). Usually,

Fig. 9.7 New rural reconstruction in A-Li area (*Source* ©Authors)

Fig. 9.8 New rural reconstruction in Lin Zhi area (*Source* ©Authors)

the government plans a piece of land and then constructs uniform houses for villagers. Features of this renewal mode are a uniform and planned construction, as well as good municipal and public infrastructure. However, the actual needs of each family tend to be ignored.

In the planning and construction renewal of rural settlements in various regions, residential buildings are usually evenly arranged on newly developed planning and construction land. Although newly built residential buildings meet the functional requirements of local residential types and contemporary villagers' lifestyles, the uniform style has hampered the generation of diversified functional layout and form of old residential buildings. The lack of correlation between newly developed rural construction land and the natural terrain has led to difficulties in planning. Further, constructive rural settlements barely reflect the environmental characteristic of the site selected. For instance, in the new rural reconstruction in Tibet, although the individual form of residential buildings imitates the traditional features of Tibetan dwellings, the established rural settlement overall fails to show the achievement force of religious belief in the construction of settlements.

9.4 Conclusion

In contemporary China, social structural transformation and urbanization development have been promoting the reconstruction and renewal of traditional rural settlements in vast rural areas, along with new rural reconstruction. In the construction process, the most worrying aspect for local villagers is the problem of inapplicable residential buildings. Meanwhile, the most serious aspect for scholars is the problem of the loss of regional or national characteristics.

For the investigation and research on traditional vernacular dwellings and settlements, the core contents are studies on the impacts of the natural and cultural environment on the characteristic creation of vernacular settlements and the influences of construction rules on the characteristic creation of traditional vernacular settlements. Research objectives focus not on the conservation of traditional vernacular dwellings or settlements but on the renewal of contemporary vernacular settlements based on regional residential types and construction rules.

References

Fan XP (2008) The triple construction context of residential buildings—Habitat of vernacular settlements in Tibet Plateau. China Building Industry Press, Beijing, pp 90–96 (in Chinese)

Fan XP, Li BR (2010) Prototype and deformation—structure adjustment of residential building under the form of social structure. Huazhong Arch 01:157–160 (in Chinese)

Fan XP, Du XQ (2012) Social structure and spatial structure in traditional settlements. China Ancient City 03:63–66 (in Chinese)

Lai ZL (2004) Ethical characteristics of traditional social structure in China (Dissertation for Master). Fudan University, Shanghai (2004) (in Chinese)

Chapter 10
Preservation and Tourism-Oriented Use of Cultural Heritage Streets: Case Study of Lhasa's Barkhor Street

Xia Li and Yongzhi Xu

The "reconstruction of old urban areas" campaign, which is common in modern China in recent years, has drawn social concern on the development of historical streets carrying rich cultural heritage. The intervention of the tourism industry and the reactivation of the social, economic, and cultural values of such historical sites become the fundamental driving forces and key methods in the preservation of the majority of cultural heritage streets. Meanwhile, the intervention of the tourism industry has caused a number of issues to such streets, such as over-commercialization, low-level heritage utilization, loss of local residents, or weakened cultural authenticity. This research examines the interrelationship between the preservation of cultural heritage streets and touristic use by taking Lhasa Barkhor Street as a case study example, to identify a win-win solution through which cultural heritage streets are well preserved while the tourism resources contained therein are maximized.

10.1 Components of Barkhor Street's Cultural Heritage System

Lhasa is a famous historical city with a history of more than 1300 years, and Barkhor Street located at the center of Lhasa City is the city's soul and representative street, where the history and culture of this ancient city are fully demonstrated. Known as "Bajiao Street," Barkhor Street consists of Barkhor Street East, Barkhor Street West, Barkhor Street South, and Barkhor Street North, showing a polygonal and annular street block with a perimeter length of about 1000 m covering 35 lanes and 199 residential compounds. "Barkhor" in Tibetan language originally means "Central Circle," and historically, it was a prayer road surrounding Jokhang Monastery. In the 17th Century, the Fifth Dalai Lama established the Gandain Phodrang regime and reconstructed Jokhang Monastery. Eventually, the

X. Li · Y. Xu (✉)
College of History and Culture, Minzu University of China, Beijing, China
e-mail: hismem2002@sina.com

F. Wang and M. Prominski (eds.), *Urbanization and Locality*,
DOI 10.1007/978-3-662-48494-4_10

city of Lhasa became the center of Tibetan Buddhism. Subsequently, Barkhor Street prospered amid the thriving religious pilgrimage to Jokhang Monastery. It then earned renown as the most important pilgrimage and commercial district in the entire Tibetan region. At present, Barkhor Street maintains its original style and features, rich in cultural heritage and bearing multifunctional uses, including pilgrimage, housing, administration, commerce, sight-seeing, and vacation. In 2000, Barkhor Street and Jokhang Monastery, both as expansion items of Potala Palace, were listed in the World Heritage List. In 2009, Barkhor Street was elected as among the first batch in the Top Ten Famous Chinese Historical and Cultural Streets. As such, Barkor Street is highly recognized, with respect to its unique value in the history of Lhasa's urban and commercial development and in the role of preserving and inheriting the splendid culture of the Tibetan nation.

Based on the site investigation and analysis in the present work, Barkhor Street's cultural heritage can be classified into seven categories:

1. **A site for religious culture**. Barkhor Street is prosperous owing to religion. One of major components of the Barkhor Street cultural heritage system is the street's role as a site of religious culture. At present, Barkhor Street is home to 23 religious edifices within Jokhang Monastery, Ramoche Monastery, Gyudmed Tantric Monastery, and Tengyeling Monastery, among others.
2. **An urban public building**. As the political, economic, and cultural center of old Lhasa, it was the site where old Lhasa's governmental offices were located. Thus, a number of urban public buildings are found along Barkhor Street, including the government office for the Minister Resided in Tibet or Tromzikhang Compound, the ancient prison Langzixia, and Lhasa Private School, all of which are important carriers in the study of the history of Lhasa's urban development.
3. **Important private buildings**. Barkhor Street is likewise home to the houses of a number of well-known Tibetans, along with other important private buildings, including the Qujiepozhang (imperial palace of King Srongtsen Gampo), Lazhangningba or the residence of Tsongkhapa (founder of Shamanism), and the private house of Thonmi Sambhota (founder of the Tibetan language). The existence of such ancient houses not only reveals the soul of the architectural culture in Barkhor Street but also displays the unique celebrity culture of Barkhor Street.
4. **A historical site for commercial culture**. Barkhor Street has a long commercial history, lined with a number of old stores and bisecting old business streets. Chongsaikang Market from the ages of Qing Dynasty Emperors Qianlong and Jiaqing attracted Khampa merchants. "Beijing Congkang" was once one of the "Gang of Beiping" shops in the Republic of China era. The century-old shop "Syamukapu" is the most famous Nepalese shop in Barkhor Street. All of these time-honored shops are valuable legacies and important components of the Barkhor Street culture.
5. **Traditional residential courtyards**. The densely distributed traditional Tibetan-style civilian courtyards are the most important components in the

cultural composition of Barkhor Street. At present, there are 56 civilian courtyards within Barkhor Street subject to legal preservation, and the co-existence of modern communities and traditional Tibetan courtyards in Barkhor Street reveals a unique historical scene.

6. **Featured cultural landscape**. The featured cultural landscape in Barkhor Street contains both tangible landscapes, such as Jokhang Monastery Plaza, Songqure Plaza, Monument of Alliance between the Tang Dynasty and Tibetan Regime, Songqure Site, and Tsongkhapa's for Buddhism debate, and intangible cultural landscapes, such as the turning of the prayer wheel and kowtow to pay religious homage to Buddha.
7. **Intangible cultural heritage**. The Makye-ame Legend, Tibetan New Year traditional celebration activities, living culture of traditional clothes, and Tibetan-style furniture that remain popular, along with the Tibetan-style kite hand-making skills, constitute the rich intangible assets of Barkhor Street, representing the dynamic part in Barkhor Street's heritage.

10.2 Preservation of Barkhor Street's Cultural Heritage and Assessment of Its Current Utilization

The rich cultural heritage of Barkhor Street endows value to it on such aspects as history, culture, aesthetics, commerce, religion, and architecture, for which "protection" has become the key word in its long-term development. Since the 1980s, along with the launch of tourism in Lhasa, Barkhor Street has become the most preferred place to visit in Lhasa for tourists from all around the nation. However, while the development of Lhasa's tourism brings new typed of operations, residents, and fresh energy to Barkhor Street, it has also generated a certain degree of impact against the preservation of Barkhor Street's cultural heritage. From the view of the preservation of Barkhor Street's cultural heritage and assessment of its current utilization, four main issues should be considered:

First, the renovation of single building receives significant attention, whereas the overall protection for the cultural space is ignored. Since China's reform and opening up, the Lhasa government has carried out renovation projects for dilapidated houses along Barkhor Street. Further, 29 cultural relics and historic sites as well as 54 preservation ancient building compounds are determined as the core of cultural heritage preservation in this historical street. However, the recovery of the overall situation of the ancient city and preservation of the surrounding environment are overlooked. Moreover, the characteristic functions of many cultural spaces have not been recovered effectively.

Second, the protection of material elements is widely reported, but elements related to intangible heritage are ignored. Since 1992, the Lhasa City government has established policies to set legal protection and scientific standards: the "Detailed Planning of Lhasa Barkhor Street and the Overall Urban Planning of Lhasa City,"

"Historic culture protection zone of the Barkhor Street" with an area of 130 hectares, "Provisional Rules on Preservation of Old Urban Areas of Lhasa City," and "Provisional Rules on Preservation of Historical Street Blocks of Lhasa Barkhor Street." Protection measures and concepts in these documents and planning regulations give more attention to the material elements and material space, such as the choice of architectural color, style, and material, but almost ignore the intangible cultural heritage of the street, thereby resulting in ineffective support to the protection and inheritance of manual skills, living customs, and festival activities.

Third, tourism development is promoted while operation types and quality control are ignored. Tourism development and use have become the predominating direction of Barkhor Street's preservation and development. Thus, the involvement of tourism service businesses boosted the operations within Barkhor Street; hotels, restaurants, bars, and tourist shops have gradually replaced small and unique businesses run by locals to become the main enterprises comprising Barkhor Street business. However, given the absence of effective control on operation quality and type, numerous problems have arisen: insufficient commercial culture connotation, underestimated business value of ethnic culture, proliferation of fake and inferior commodities, and ineffective protection of business heritage.

Finally, the replacement of the residents in the street is a public issue while the formation of the cultural identity of the residents is ignored. For protecting the street appearance and historic structures in Barkhor Street, the relevant administration office has applied measures of relocating functional and residential areas. It encourages residents to move out, which would reduce the protection pressure. Meanwhile, merchants and enterprises engaging in tourism business services have moved in by leasing houses and stores as "new residents" of the street. In this way, problems arise, such as most activities in the street becoming driven by short-term economic interests; the lowered overall cultural sense of belonging, identity, and responsibility; and the challenge to the continuation of the traditional cultural atmosphere and environment.

10.3 Heritage Protection Measures Based on the Tourist-Oriented Use of Barkhor Street

Compared with the traditional cultural heritage's static protection mode, cultural heritage protection of the street's area carried out under the premise of tourist application puts greater emphasis on the use of cultural heritage, focusing on the combination of cultural values with tourism experience and an updated adaptability of the district's function. According to the characteristics of the development of Barkhor's cultural heritage and tourism, the future focus should be on the promotion of the transformation of ideas and protection mode of the district's cultural heritage based on the following four aspects.

First, it means moving from the protection of individual elements to the protection of the district's overall space. "The value of cultural heritage protection is not only constituted by concentrating on particular ancient buildings, it is rather about recreating its overall pattern, traditional style and special environment" (Yang et al. 2004). Beyond the protection of individual buildings, Barkhor's cultural heritage protection should focus on the protection of the surrounding streets and alleys and emphasize the district's temples, streets, shops, courtyards, plazas, and other places of interest. It should involve the coordination of various space elements and maintenance of the pilgrimage, living, and commercial spaces with different cultures mingling together. Further, it should consider building a space that allows the blending of culture protection with tourists' cultural experience, which results in the appropriate separation of culture protection and culture experience.

Second, it should aim at the activation of not only the general but also vector type of building classification. Tourism development of the cultural heritage street should aim to activate all types of cultural heritage aspects. While maintaining the cultural heritage itself, new experience shall be created to maximize the role of cultural heritage in securing social, cultural, and economic benefits. The status of tourism-oriented use of the cultural heritage in Barkhor Street is passive and at an early stage. Thus, the future focus should be the active and gradual promotion of classified activation of historic carriers. Protection and use measures should be established accordingly for different levels of cultural heritage protection, as determined through a comprehensive assessment of the cultural heritage's protection value, degree of damage, and difficulty of use. In the case of Jokhang Temple, as an example for the protection of religious sites, the protection measures shall mainly maintain its original architectural appearance and religious function and then properly control tourist arrivals. For important cultural relics and ancient architectures, the protection measures should be based on reconstruction or fixing and focused on static use, such as the case in Museum Pavilion and Cultural Museum Park, which function as cultural display. As regards normal residence compounds, featured tourism accommodation facility development is recommended to form new cultural spaces for tourists to experience.

Third, updating the measure from simply maintaining the material appearance to reviving the cultural energy of Barkhor Street. Cultural heritage street protection is the protection not only of material heritage but also of the living culture in the street area, or the intangible cultural heritage. "It means to maintain the 'living' in the street, not the 'material form'" (Zhong 2011). The commercial culture, folk culture, and all kinds of manual skills in Barkhor Street constitute the main body of the living heritage of the street. Measures should be taken to establish a proper intangible cultural heritage protection mechanism, carry out protection measures and training for inheritors, set up non-profit foundations, promote productive protection for manual skills, boost the revival of "time-honored brand" businesses, and enhance the inner cultural energy of Barkhor Street.

Finally, move from the improvement of the residents' condition to that of the cultural identity of "new" and "old" residents. Residents in the area are the creators and inheritors of street culture. In other words, protecting the street's cultural authenticity involves preventing the original residents from moving out. Under the condition of tourism-oriented use of the street, residents in the area are commonly replaced, and the entry of "new residents" is not restricted. Although a pressing concern, the focus should remain on the formation of a cultural identity. In the case of cultural identity loss, the historic street will lose traditional lifestyles, customs, and "living authenticity." The focus on the residents in the future should be moved from the improvement of the residents' condition to a consideration of the cultural identity of the new and original residents, thereby encouraging the enthusiasm of the residents to participate in cultural heritage protection and in continuing to live a traditional life as part of promoting the sustainable development of the street culture in Barkhor Street.

10.4 Conclusion: Understanding the Preservation and Tourism-Oriented Use of Cultural Heritage Streets

The cultural heritage preservation and tourism-oriented use of Barkhor Street have unique features while also revealing common issues with respect to all cultural heritage streets in China. The current work has developed an initial understanding of the preservation and tourism-oriented use of China's cultural heritage streets.

First, the preservation and utilization of cultural heritage streets are a complex project, covering the preservation of not only individual cultural relics and ancient buildings but also the traditional style and environment of the entire street, including the street block's spatial structure and interrelationship with mountains, forests, waters, and green spaces. The focus should not only be on the restoration and maintenance of traditional space but also on the expansion and management of new cultural spaces as well as the establishment and restoration of the organic connection among different cultural spaces.

Second, the preservation and utilization of cultural heritage streets comprise a process of keeping pace with the times; therefore, it is impractical to apply "absolute static" protection without considering the residents' real-life demands and modern development. By taking the development of the tourism and creative industries as breakthrough points, the life of old streets may be extended by updating the functions of old streets, ensuring the adequate use of the street cultural heritage, and revitalizing the value of street cultural heritage.

Third, the process of preserving and utilizing cultural heritage streets is related to the process of reactivating cultural heritage. The tourism industry itself has commercial and market features, which frame the commercialization of cultural heritage. Understanding these aspects helps in the adequate promotion of the process of commercialization of cultural relics, without compromising the authenticity of the original street scene and cultural landscape. In other words, street culture commercialization should be controlled within an adequate "degree" to avoid over-commercialization and vulgarization.

Lastly, the preservation and utilization of cultural heritage streets shall be based on the common understanding of the original residents. "The historic street loses traditional life style and custom, that is the same meaning of losing 'living authenticity'" (Ruan and Sun 2001). On the one hand, stakeholders shall strive to retain the original local residents and protect the original cultural gene by improving their living and housing levels; on the other hand, the coming of "new residents" should not be rejected. Instead, a sense of a cultural identity should be established among the "new" and "old" residents, to encourage their enthusiasm toward cultural protection and sense of pride, as well as accelerate the street's mechanism of cultural inheritance and protection. Various means are available, including, but not limited to, broadening residents' participation channels, enhancing publicity and education, and setting up a threshold for incoming residents.

References

Ruan YS, Sun M (2001) A study on various issues concerning China's historical streets preservation and planning. Urban Plann 4:2–9 (in Chinese)

Yang Z, Lu L, Wang L (2004) Tourism development of historical cultural streets—by taking Anhui Tunxi Old Street as the example. Acad J Anhui Univ 5:525–530 (in Chinese)

Zhong HM (2011) Renaissance of historical cultural streets power—by taking Jinan Furong historical cultural street as the example. Modern Urban Res 1:44–48 (in Chinese)

Chapter 11
Sustainable Tourism-Oriented Conservation and Improvement of Historical Villages in the Urbanization Process: A Case Study of Nan'anyang Village, Shanxi Province, China

Ye-Feng Xie, Lu Li, Yan-Dan Guo, Xu-Peng Sun and Yu-Jun Zhang

11.1 Introduction

Among China's 600,000 villages, approximately 3000 are historical villages (Yin 2011). The term "historical village" or "traditional village" was first used in the architecture research field in the 1990s (He et al. 1989; Hong 1987). At present, scholars in the field of historical village research have a different comprehension and emphasis of its concept (Chen 2008; Liu 1997). Despite the lack of consensus on the concept of historical villages, qualitative standards unanimously agree that a historical village has the following features: (a) tangible or intangible cultural heritage reflecting its unique local characteristics; (b) early formation; and (c) the village's original spatial form can be observed from the current conservation situation.

As an important type of human settlement, historical villages carry the ancient wisdom of our ancestors (Wang and Geng 2013). Chinese historical villages are numerous, widely distributed, and distinct from one another. They are precious cultural heritage and convey people's production methods and ways of living (Wang 2013). These historical villages were formed in different dynasties. During China's long history, they appear in different types and styles. The significance of these historical villages can be understood using the following perspectives: heritage, landscape, tourism, and scientific research. **Heritage significance**. As a traditional agricultural country, China's roots are in the villages. Each historical village has undergone a particular development process during the years. In this process, the folk arts, architectural styles, and customs are formed and inherited. All

Y.-F. Xie · L. Li · Y.-D. Guo · X.-P. Sun · Y.-J. Zhang (✉)
School of Landscape Architecture, Beijing Forestry University,
Beijing, People's Republic of China
e-mail: yjzhang622@foxmail.com

F. Wang and M. Prominski (eds.), *Urbanization and Locality*,
DOI 10.1007/978-3-662-48494-4_11

these aspects form the valuable cultural heritage of the human race (Zhang and Bao 2004). **Landscape significance**. The physical landscape and archaic atmosphere are two aspects of historical villages' landscape. The former consists of historical buildings, folk costumes, couplets, and paintings, among others, whereas the latter refers to a cultural atmosphere rooted in the environment of historical villages, abstracted from the physical landscape, natural environment, and human activities. In other words, the archaic atmosphere of a historical village is an intangible complex of tinge, style, and feeling (Feng 2002). **Significance for tourism**. The public desire to appreciate historical villages based on the significance of their heritage, landscape, and ecology. People visit historical villages to sightsee, experience and study the history (Zhang and Bao 2004), as well as engage in a sense of nostalgia (Lowenthal et al. 1981). **Scientific and research significance**. Given the significance of heritage, landscape, and tourism, historical villages attract much attention from scholars in disciplines such as architecture, history, landscape architecture, and tourism. Based on the significance of heritage, landscape, tourism, and scientific and research, along with historical villages' characteristics of antiquity, closure, peculiarity, and fragility (Li and Xiao 2009), conserving historical villages should be an urgent effort in China's urbanization process.

Since the Open Door Policy in 1978, China has entered the era of rapid urbanization. With the increasing urbanization process, contradictions between economic growth and heritage conservation in historical villages have brought challenges (Yu 2006; Fu and Wang 2006; Li and Zhang 2010). On the one hand, traditional architectures in historical villages, especially those in peri-urban ones, have been gradually replaced by modern industrial buildings and real estate houses, and a number of them have given way to "villages-in-the-city" (Mandarin: *chengzhongcun*) and new towns (Smith 2014). Customs and cultural identity have become vague, or even absent, owing to the loss and over-exploitation of traditional architectures. On the other hand, only a few people continue to inhabit a number of historical villages. A majority of the villagers have left their hometown to work and make a living (Xue 2001; Chen et al. 2010; Wang 2005). Others have moved and resettled in new houses built as part of the urbanization, called "new village" (Mandarin: *xinnongcun*), deserting historical villages that are left to decline (Xiao et al. 2011; Chen 2009; Cai and Xian 2009). Thus, in the process of urbanization, how can the decline or disappearance of historical villages be prevented? How can development measures be customized to match each village's condition while maintaining the premise of conservation? Is it possible to strike a fine balance between development and conservation?

To address the above questions, the present research chose Nan'anyang Village as a case study, where we have accomplished a conservation and tourism project. Through this study, three measures to protect and develop historical villages were proposed, including landscape renovation, sustainable tourism development, and community activation. We argue that sustainable tourism could link the conservation of traditional constructions and landscape space, which can effectively ensure the continuity of the locality and value of historical villages, with the development of the industry and economy based on the activation of the community.

11.2 Study Areas

Nan'anyang Village is located southwest of Jincheng City, Yangcheng County, Shanxi Province, China (Fig. 11.1a). As regards the layout of Nan'anyang, it consists of two parts, the old village area and the new village area. The old village area is made up mainly of historical houses, and a few new houses built by the villagers on the site of demolished traditional houses (Fig. 11.1b). The new village area is in the eastern part of the village, constructed in compliance with the guidelines provided in the *New rural development planning Guide of Nan'anyang Village* and shows an orderly layout.

Fig. 11.1 Location and general layout of Nan'anyang Village (*Source* ©Authors based on the planning maps drawn by Chen-Xiao Guo of Conservation and Utilization Plan of Pan's Manor)

As the main component of the traditional houses in the old village area, Pan's manor covers an area of more than 20,000 m^2, with 53 courtyards and 1600 houses. It is made up of 53 courtyards[1] (including the Thirteen Courtyards[2]), two chastity archways, and the alleys among them. The Thirteen Courtyards is the most representative compound of the traditional houses, with an area of more than 6000 m^2 and 390 houses. Being excellently designed and delicately constructed, these 53 Courtyards are of great significance to architectural research and tourism development. Pan's family had a close relationship with the imperial family in history; the two chastity archways and the ancestral hall were constructed under the emperors' orders during the Jiaqing and Daoguang periods (1796–1850). The alleys and roads in the village area were paved with bluestone, and they are well preserved after more than 300 years. On November 23, 2006, given the important value of Pan's manor, Nan'anyang Village was added to the Second Historical and Cultural Village[3] List by the Shanxi Provincial Government.

However, the loss of vitality in Nan'anyang Village is seen in three aspects as follows:

Situation 1: The landscape of the old village area has declined and showed signs of destruction. Attributed to inefficient management, the landscape of the Thirteen Courtyards has declined. Traditional houses in the old village area are valuable historical architectures; however, a number have been demolished and new houses have been built by the owners, who preferred to live in modern residences rather than the traditional ones. Further, other traditional houses, including the Thirteen Courtyards, were damaged during the house alteration projects led by the residents, including installing wall tiles and building houses in courtyards.

Situation 2: The input of talent, capital, material, and technology from outside the village has declined owing to the singularity of the industry structure. Presently, Nan'anyang is an agriculture-based (mainly crop farming and breeding industry) village, with a few private enterprises, which cannot attract talent, investment, and

[1]The 53 courtyards include the Thirteen Courtyards and 40 other courtyards as follows: four Shang and Xia Courtyards, four Hetaoshu Courtyards, three Shufang Courtyards, three Ranfang Courtyards, three Getaipu Courtyards, three Xin Courtyards, three Shang Courtyards, two Duimen Courtyards, two Hou Courtyards, two XingeLue Courtyards, two Qipan Courtyards, one Gongdi Courtyard, one Zhaojia Courtyard, one XuanGelue Courtyard, one Yang Gelue Courtyard, one Chong Gelue Courtyard, one Gengfang Courtyard, one Houhua Courtyard, one Zhangzhang Courtyard, and one Citang Courtyard. Each courtyard has its specific purpose; for example, the Gongdi Courtyard is a residence for servants, and the Citang Courtyard is where the ancestral hall is located.

[2]The Thirteen Courtyards is a compound of the following courtyards: Shikou Courtyard, Zhangfang Courtyard, Xiting Courtyard, Chufang Courtyard, Pu Courtyard, Lao Courtyard, Zhong Courtyard, Mao Courtyard, Niandao Courtyard, Hou Courtyard, East Garden, Middle Garden, and West Garden. The Thirteen Courtyards is well preserved.

[3]China's Historical and Cultural Villages List is approved by the Ministry of Construction and the state bureau of cultural relics. Villages in this list are all rich in heritage preservation and possess commemoration of great historical value or significance. Thus, these villages reflect the tradition and local ethnic characteristics of the historical periods during which they thrived.

other indispensable components for its development. In fact, Nan'anyang has abundant resources that have not been used wisely. This scenario reflects Nan'anyang's vitality loss.

Situation 3: The old village area shows the hollowing out phenomenon. Without residents, most of the historical courtyards are overgrown with weeds and present a lifeless scene. The reason is that most of the dwellers have moved to the new village area after Nan'anyang's new rural construction. Further, a majority of the village's people are working outside or away from the village.

Nan'anyang is a historical village facing various problems caused by urbanization. Thus, it was chosen as a study case for this work. The core historical resources of the village are Pan's manor in the old village area, which is the main study object of this research.

11.3 Study Methods

From 2012 to 2015, members of this study team visited Nan'anyang several times before and during the implementation of the Conservation and Utilization Plan of Pan's Manor. In the process, documentary analysis, interviews, and field investigation were undertaken to determine the basic framework of conservation and utilization, collect the views and demands of villagers and visitors, and adjust the plan according to the feedback. Therefore, this study is dynamic.

Method 1: Documentary analysis. This method was used to summarize the conservation and utilization approaches that have been applied to other historical villages. In the 1990s, scholars began research on historical villages, and then relevant national policies and regulations on preservation and conservation were introduced to the public. The Historical and Cultural Villages in China requires for a conservation plan to be made, which would guide the development of each village. Therefore, before the Conservation and Utilization Plan of Pan's Manor was made, we studied a number of conservation planning textbooks and academic papers on historical villages to form frames and measures to conserve and improve Nan'anyang village.

Method 2: Field investigation. Through field investigation, Nan'anyang's village layout, local chronicle, social economy, population, policies, situation of traditional houses and communities, as well as other basic information about the village were documented. Details of the village's historical buildings and cultural traditions were collected to contribute to the frames and measures formed after documentary analysis into practice (Table 11.1).

Method 3: Interviewing. Villagers and visitors were interviewed. The villagers interviewed are owners of homes in Nan'anyang, and each change in the village closely affects them. In 2012, a majority of the villagers still living in the village were interviewed on issues related to the following: perception of Nan'anyang's historical resources, attitude toward tourism development, willingness to participate in conservation and improvement of the village and to be trained, reasons for their

Table 11.1 Frame of the classification of traditional constructions/structures formed through documentary analysis and field investigation

Classification	Quality	Current condition and harmony with the surrounding environment
Class I	Good (and with great significance)	Good and harmonious (and with great significance)
Class II	Ordinary	Ordinary and harmonious
Class III	Poor	Poor and harmonious (being damaged seriously or only the relics remained)
Class IV	Good	Good but disharmonious

family members leaving the village, reasons for them not wanting to live in the traditional houses, and whether they could take pride in their folkways and traditions, among others. As for visitors, they were the guests and users of historical village tourism products. In 2012, 15 visitors were interviewed on their motivation to come to the village, satisfaction of this visit, expectations for this visit, the type of tourism they want to experience in Nan'anyang, and suggestions to conserve and improve the village. Through the interviews, villagers' and visitors' attitude and ideas regarding the village's conservation and improvement were collected for using in the process of sustainable tourism development and community activation.

11.4 Analysis and Results

As a historical village, Nan'anyang is significant in terms of heritage, landscape, tourism, and science and research. The significance of heritage and landscape is based on locality inheritance, and needs to be conserved. Meanwhile, the significance of the landscape, tourism, and science and research can be improved to contribute to the increase in urbanity. The conservation of locality inheritance and improvement of urbanity increase both help the village develop sustainable tourism. Once tourism industry develops, the landscape can be renovated, and the local community is activated. Thus, Nan'anyang's vitality loss can be changed to reach the goal of conservation and improvement of the village (Fig. 11.2).

11.4.1 Landscape Renovation

Nan'anyang's landscape consists of tangible cultural landscapes, such as traditional construction/structures, alleys, and historical environment elements (ancient wells, stone mills, horizontal inscribed boards, and small building complexes[4]); intangible cultural landscapes, including folkways and festivals; and traditional green space.

[4]Shangma Stones refer to the stones placed near the gate for getting into the saddle more easily.

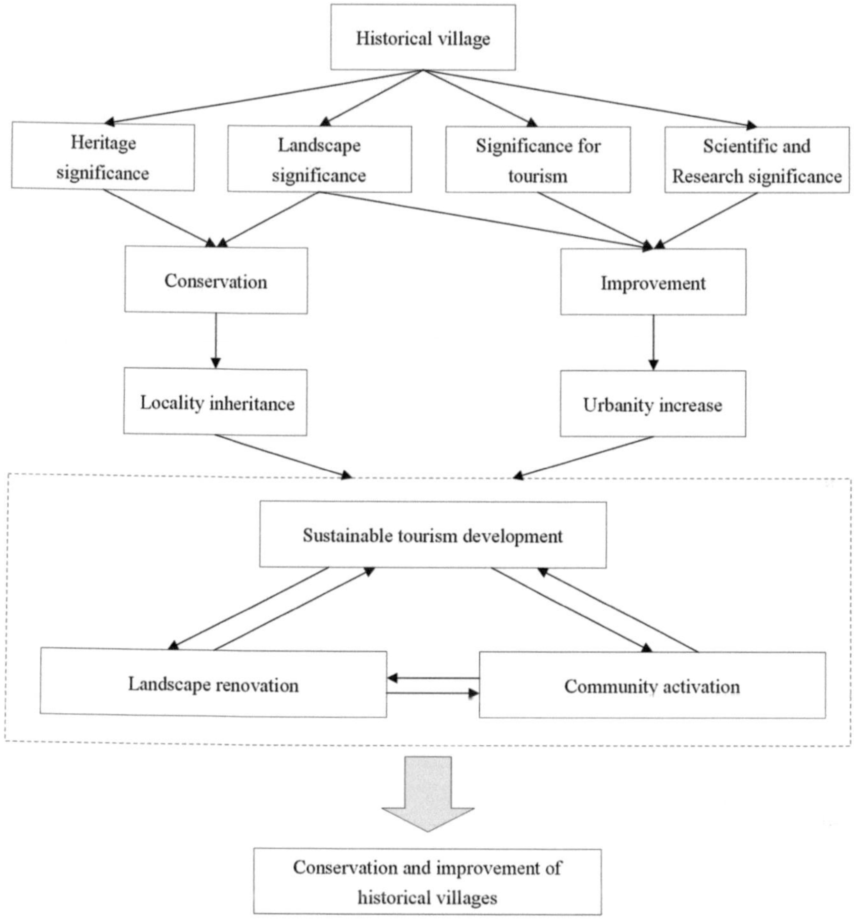

Fig. 11.2 Chart for reaching the goal of historical villages' conservation and improvement in the urbanization process based on significance analysis. *Source* Drawn by the authors

Conservation and preservation are the bases of landscape renovation, which aims at carrying forward and forming the legacy of the landscapes. Ways for renovation are as follows:

1. Classify the tangible cultural landscapes based on the properties, preservation conditions, and elements of the landscapes; apply corresponding improvement methods to the tangible cultural landscape based on the current conditions.

The construction/structures of Pan's Manor include the 53 Courtyards, ancestral hall, and chastity archways. Taking their architectural quality, current condition, and age into consideration, the construction/structures were classified to Classes I, II, III, and IV (Table 11.2).

Table 11.2 Traditional construction/structures landscapes classification of Nan'anyang Village

Classification	Quality	Current condition and harmony with the surrounding environment	Age	Included courtyards and buildings
Class I	Good (and with great significance)	Good and harmonious (and with great significance)	Ming and Qing Dynasties	Lao Courtyard, Mao Courtyard, Shikou Courtyard, Xiting Courtyard, Zhangfang Courtyard, Hetaoshu Courtyard, and Hua Courtyard
Class II	Ordinary	Ordinary and harmonious	Ming and Qing Dynasties	Zhong Courtyard, Niandao Courtyard, Chufang Courtyard, Hou Courtyard, East Garden, Middle Garden, West Garden, Shufang Courtyard, Qipan Courtyard, Gongdi Courtyard, Hou Courtyard, Duimen Courtyard, Zhaojia Courtyard, Zhangzhang Courtyard, XinGelue, Chong Gelue, Xin Courtyard, and Shang Courtyard
Class III	Poor	Poor and harmonious (being damaged seriously or only the relics remained)	Ming and Qing Dynasties	Ancestral hall, Ranfang Courtyard, Gengfang Courtyard, Xia Courtyard, Xiaoshufang Courtyard, Yang Gelue, Xuan Gelue, Getaipu Courtyard, the two chastity archways, and the historical entrance
Class IV	Good	Good but disharmonious	Modern times	Village committee office (former address of Chengtang Temple), a Kindergarten (former address of Pu Courtyard), the primary school of the village, and other disharmonious constructions

Table 11.3 Tourism product system of Nan'anyang

Product structure	Products	Targeted market	Subcategories of products
Core product	Sightseeing in the historical village	Mass tourists	Appreciating Nan'anyang
	Experiencing Shanxi merchants' culture	Mass tourists	Exploring Pan's merchant culture
			Experiencing the commerce history of Pan's family
Important product	Experiencing local culture and customs	Middle-aged tourists; folk culture lovers	Watching historical theatrical performances
			Learning the local culture and customs
			Living in homestays
	Studying traditional architecture	Scholars and students of history and architecture	Studying the architectural art of Pan's Manor
			Exploring Nan'anyang's system and scale
			Researching the development of traditional houses in the Ming and Qing Dynasties
	Relaxing on holidays	High-income people; middle-aged tourists, business travelers	Experiencing the original life in Nan'anyang
			Self-driving tour
			Relaxing in traditional houses
Supporting products	Experiencing the traditional festivals	Mass tourists	Qinglong Festival
			Can'gu Festival
			Photography Festival
			Art Festival
			Harvest Festival
	Artistic creation	Artists, photographers, writers, designers, and art lovers	Focus on Nan'anyang
			Create literary works
			Record the precious moments of Nan'anyang

As to the nine historical alleys paved with polished bluestone in the village, their landscape elements are patterns, elevation, material, and rest space.

The distribution of historical environmental elements are scattered across the village. Recording and compiling information on all of them by general investigation are the basis of improvement and utilization.

According to the landscape classification, improvement methods that correspond to different properties and different situations of the landscape are applied. For example, in the case of constructions/structures, four types of improvement methods (repair, renovation, rehabilitation, and dismantlement) were put forward to improve the different classes of constructions/structures in the corresponding ways.

Repair is the method applied to Class I constructions/structures. Their quality and appearance are both in the upper level, and these constructions/structures have a relatively high value. The constructions/structures have retained their original form, thereby reflecting history truthfully. Raw materials and the original workmanship are used to polish the details that had been damaged. The frames and affiliated structures, such as the eaves, are examined thoroughly and then given the priority when using traditional technology and materials to reinforce stability.

Renovation is the method applied to Class II constructions/structures. These elements are of ordinary quality and appearance. Newly pasted ceramic tiles and cement are removed to reduce the damage on traditional buildings. Raw materials and techniques are used to restore the constructions to their ordinary conditions. Thus, damaged structures, such as handrails, windows, doors, and stairs, are renovated.

Rehabilitation is the method applied to Class III constructions/structures. These constructions/structures are of poor appearance. We rehabilitate the constructions whose foundation still remains but whose upper structures have collapsed. Raw materials and techniques should be used to rehabilitate the structures to their original appearance. For those that no longer exist, we clean the base and plant trees according to the village's historical records, for reconstruction to be completed in future years.

Dismantlement is the method applied to Class IV constructions/structures. These constructions/structures are newly built and are in good condition, but most of them have a negative impact on the village's historical atmosphere. Before dismantlement, a strict survey and assessment would be needed. No historical buildings must be affected in terms of either appearance or frame stability. After dismantlement, the original constructions/structures on the former address need to be restored.

2. Renovate the landscape by bestowing the legacy of the intangible cultural heritage through building an ecomuseum and interpreting the heritage.

The connotation of the landscape could be enriched by building an ecomuseum and using interpretation. Apart from traditional houses, alleys, and historical environmental elements, landscapes could be displayed and interpreted. More important is the inheritance of intangible landscapes. Both tangible and intangible landscapes combine; and renovation goals should be achieved in this context.

3. Renovate the destroyed traditional green space in the East, Middle, and West Gardens according to historical records based on the current construction frameworks.

The backyard gardens were a place for the host to entertain guests, and the wives and children held recreation and entertainment activities there. They are the core components of the landscape in Pan's Manor. The three gardens were divided by two low walls, which were thin and white (Mandarin: *yunqiang*). Each *yunqiang* had a moon-shaped door (Mandarin: *yuemen*) on it. These open doors make a clear and bright visual effect in the space of the three gardens. When the doors are closed, each garden becomes an independent space. Landscape is rehabilitated in the gardens referring both to the words on the plaques on *yuemen* and to historical records.

East Garden: The plaque states "*Geng du chuanjia*," which means that Pan's family revered Confucianism and attached importance to agriculture. Therefore, an atmosphere of simplicity and elegance should be created in the East Garden. The roads are paved with black bricks and pebbles, and bear a pattern of plum flowers pieced together, implying the prospect of leaning shadows and winding roads. In the center of the garden is a pavilion with a hexagonal pyramidal roof, "*Zhan yue*", for appreciating the moon. Peaonia suffruticosa, Malusspectabilis, and Buxussinicaare are planted around the pavilion. At the east entrance of the garden, a short corridor is twined with vines. The corridor provides a resting place for visitors apart from regulating sight lines.

Middle Garden: The plaque here writes "*Shishujishi*," which means the Middle Garden was used to enjoy traditional opera, drink tea, and write poetry. The octagonal fishpond and Tanhualou Building is rebuilt to create a well-arranged spatial effect. The fishpond is designed as a main feature, with a rockery and fish in it. The rockery was built by Taihu stones and had two peaks. Malus spectabilis, Magnolia heptapeta, Salix babylonica, and Phyllostachys propinqua are planted in front of and around the building.

West Garden: The plaque here writes "*Wangxingzhanpu*," which indicates a theme of plants. The garden is designed with lawns and flower beds. Podocarpus macrophyllus, Punica granatum, and Nandina domestica are displayed in the flower beds. Tourists can appreciate the flowers in spring, and enjoy the fruits in autumn. The plant theme is fully expressed in the West Garden.

The complex of the main buildings in the three gardens forms a U shape, and there are two stories. The first floor is patterned after cave dwellings, thereby creating a living space that is warm in winter and cool in summer. A number of villagers live in this space. The second floor, formerly used for admiring flowers and entertaining guests, and then later on as warehouses for grain storage, is presently unused. The structure of the building remains in good condition except for tiny damage in the details, such as the ridge and the dragon-head ornament (Mandarin: *Wenzhou*), as well as the carved window lattices, which are weathered. The building needs repair and conservation, as well as routine maintenance. The Tanhualou Building on the southeast corner of the Middle Garden was formerly used for watching fish and flowers by Pan's female family members. It is currently dilapidated due to bad maintenance. The doors and windows are extensively damaged, whereas the structure continues to remain. The building should be restored based on the historical records.

11.4.2 Sustainable Tourism Development

Landscape renovation is the basis of sustainable tourism development. Sustainable tourism development ensures the sustainability of the landscape. After landscape renovation, the tourism attraction of Nan'anyang would be enhanced, and additional funding and information would follow. The village's infrastructure and service facilities could be enhanced as well. Consequently, the flow of information and tourism industry are activated. Ways to ensure sustainable tourism development are as follows.

1. Integrate and utilize the resources based on landscape renovation.
   For utilization, activated landscape resources are classified as "exhibition" and "experience" based on different forms.
   Exhibition landscapes are further divided into two utilization types: traditional exhibition hall and ecomuseum. The main part of the traditional exhibition hall is the Thirteen Courtyards, whose main function is exhibition, combining public education and a few experience activities. The 40 courtyards around the Thirteen Courtyards form the Ecomuseum, which shows local lifestyles, customs, and abundant historical content of Nan'anyang.
   Experience landscapes are key points and areas in the village's history but no longer exist anymore owing to natural succession or demolition. The landscapes should be reconstructed, and their inner space altered. Homestays should be designed to bear local characteristics, and business streets should display a scholar merchant culture to enhance the sightseeing and shopping experience of tourists.
2. Systemize the tourism products through the wise use of resources.
   A tourism product system should be constructed after the utilization modes of exhibition and experience landscapes are formed (Table 11.3).
3. Provide better facilities on the background of tourism products system.
   After the tourism products are systemized, the village will develop into an attraction. To ensure a healthy development of the tourism industry, the improvement of infrastructure and service facilities is essential.
4. Pay attention to promotion, put forth the development of the tourism industry, and achieve the development goal.
   The core of tourism industry-oriented development is the growth of the tourism industry. By positioning tourism images and promotional means, the sustainable development of the tourism industry could be boosted, and ultimately, development goals could be achieved.

11.4.3 Community Activation

In the activation process of historical villages, the development of the tourism industry will make the village attractive (Chen and Qu 2006). Thus, the villagers could choose to stay in the village to make a living, and the goal of community activation can be achieved. Higher income from tourism would help improve the villagers' conservation awareness regarding traditional landscapes. The development of historical villages can conserve architecture itself; meanwhile, villagers inherit the traditional lifestyle and local customs. In this way, a virtuous cycle of conservation promoting tourism and tourism strengthening conservation can be formed. In practical terms, this process can be carried out through the following aspects.

1. Solve housing problems via the renovation of courtyards and the new rural construction.
   With the improvement of people's living standard, traditional dwellings can no longer meet the needs of their owners, which is one of the reasons villagers leave the village and the courtyards enter decay. To solve these problems, a new rural construction plan was launched in Nan'anyang in 2008, when a new community equipped with modern facilities and appearance was built up near the old village area. To revitalize the old community area, certain courtyards should also be renovated to accommodate their owners or other local residents, thereby revitalizing Nan'anyang.
2. Promote the employment of the local community through the tourism industry.
   At present, villagers in Nan'anyang have a relatively low income level; to conserve and develop the old village, the tourism industry can attract external funding and create jobs to help the local community. Nan'anyang villagers can make a living in the scenic spots of the village or work as guides or interpreters. The following Table 11.4 provides details.
   As the tourism industry develops, more job opportunities can be created. Consequently, villagers who leave to make a living would more likely return.
3. Carry out training programs to improve villagers' employability.
   Different villagers in the community play different roles in the development of the community. As such, different training programs for different roles should be

Table 11.4 Employment promoted by the tourism industry in Nan'anyang

	Job content	Occupation
In Nan'anyang	Nan'anyang's tour line guidance	Guides
	Interpretation of Pan's Commercial Exhibition Hall and other museums in Nan'anyang	Interpreters
	Routine maintenance of the village	Administrative staff, cleaning staff, security staff, green workers, rescue workers, etc.
Related businesses	Travel agencies	Local tour guides, tour operators, etc.
	Hotels, homestays, and other private tour agencies	Operators, servers, managers
	Restaurants, teahouses	Server, managers
	Transportation operators	Managers, servers, drivers
	Gifts and crafts processing, retail	Handicraftsman, vendors

Table 11.5 Different types of trainees, their characteristics, and training points

Different trainees	Characteristics of the different types of trainees	Specific key points of training programs
Village cadres	Participate in significant issues of Pan's Manor in its development; organize training events	Emphasize the improvement of their notion of democracy and leadership for villagers to be willing to participate in tourism; manage skills; emphasize relevant laws and regulations in training courses
Village elites	High educated and with social experience; representative of the community; can negotiate with people representing other social parties	Emphasize the training of elites to be managers and decision makers of Pan's Manor for them to guard against the unreasonable intervention of village cadres and drive the villagers' participation
Staff in Pan's Manor	Direct contact with tourists; offer interpretation service	Emphasize relevant cultural knowledge and service skills
Relative stakeholders in tourism industry	Focus on economic benefit of their own business and overlook the profit of community	Emphasize the significance and necessity of heritage conservation to avoid the notion of seeking short-term economic benefit
Teenagers in the village	Potential of the village's future development; the concept of "Pan's Manor is valuable and the tourism industry is a way to conserve heritage" should be nurtured	Take full use of school courses and combine heritage education with routine courses
Other villagers	Eager to participate in tourism development but lack the skills, experience, and proper understanding of heritage and community	Emphasize the systematic guidance of tourism participation

conducted. The current tourism development of Nan'anyang requires six different roles: village cadres, village elites, staff in Pan's Manor, relative stakeholders in the tourism industry, teenagers in the village, and other villagers. As regards these six types of trainees, their training programs have different key points (Table 11.5).

4. Form an organization that represents the community's interest.
   Such an organization could be formed based on the village committee.
   This organization is tasked to hold meetings or events, such as training programs or activities related to the development of the tourism industry in Nan'anyang. Another organizational obligation is to establish an essential support system to guarantee community participation, including the rules for community participation in planning and decision making, investment and related businesses, the management of Pan's Manor, working for related enterprises, and training programs. The community should be assisted in learning to obey the rules.

11.5 Conclusions and Discussions

With the rapid development of urbanization, combined with complex reasons, such as poor preservation practices and crumbling infrastructure, historical villages in China are facing the widespread and growing problem of loss in locality and vitality. A healthy development of historical villages should demonstrate spatial adaptive reuse via reestablishment and regeneration (Cai 2009), not only to conserve the remaining heritage but also to solve a series of livelihood issues brought by reformation (Yu 2010).

Based on the analysis of Nan'anyang Village, conservation and development measures that are oriented toward ensuring the sustainability of the tourism industry in historical villages are discussed in this work. By analyzing the expression of vitality loss in traditional villages, this study argues that through the development of a sustainable tourism industry, the historical villages' locality and vitality loss problem can be solved, and the goal of overall development can be achieved ultimately. In contrast with general villages, historical villages have a potential to become attractions owing to their rich landscape resources that bear regional characteristics. By integrating activated landscape resources, systemizing tourism products, and paying attention to facility construction and promotion, tourism could be the main business throughout historical village development. The classification and prudent use of landscape resources, including intangible cultural heritage, could promote landscape renovation. Further, the local community is the soul of historical villages. As the main business, tourism provides jobs, attracts local residents back to the village, and achieves long-term conservation and development of historical villages.

There are two main aspects to the driving forces: internal causes and external factors. On the one hand, with its cultural and historical atmosphere, regional and traditional architecture, and pleasant ecological environment, historical villages deserve to be tourism hotspots. The sustainable tourism industry then provides a direction for urbanized construction in historical villages. On the other hand, both the government and industry play complementary roles policy making and financing to ensure the conservation and development of entire villages.

The chief innovation of this research lies in its view of urbanization construction through the lens of conservation as well as development. A balance has been pointed out between these two seemingly contradictory notions, that is, sustainable tourism. We have foreseen the negative impacts of traditional tourism, which recklessly exploits resources and profits from its disrespect for history and locality. We have sought to maintain authentic regional characteristics, and have completed landscape design and renovation, as well as offered service functions premised on conservation. We have offered means to rebuild and revitalize the village (Mandarin: *xiujiurujiu*), with consideration for both the local residents and visitors in the context of regional identity and place attachment.

The methods and results are relevant not only to Nan'anyang Village but also to historical villages in other regions all over China. The approach of sustainable tourism-oriented landscape renovation and community revitalization could provide an alternative perspective on the study of urbanization, along with strategies for urban planners when analyzing policies.

Acknowledgments This article is a Foundation item Project (2012BAJ24B05), supported by National 12th Five-year Science and Technology Support Project. The authors also would like to thank Master Chenxiao Guo for his support in drawing the layout of Nan'anyang Village.

References

Cai MZ (2009) Curing or injuring? The social aesthetic issues in the revitalization of historic sites. J Aesthetics Art 3:37–54 (in Chinese)

Cai YX, Xian TC (2009) Discussion on conservation and development of historical villages: a case study of Nanshe historical village in Dongguan City. Dev Small Cities Towns 12:14–20 (in Chinese)

Chen C (2008) Urban-rural planning under the perspective of ecological civilization: proceedings of annual national planning conference. Dalian Press, Dalian (in Chinese)

Chen G (2009) Conservation and development of historical villages taking community as the core: a study based on field investigation and analysis in Likeng Village. Wuyuan County. J Jianghan Univ (Humanities Sciences) 28(5):86–90 (in Chinese)

Chen L, Qu WQ (2006) Understanding Japan's rural building movement. Contemp Asia-pacific Stud 6:29–35 (in Chinese)

Chen YF, Sun H, Liu YS (2010) Reconstruction models of Hollowed Villages in key agricultural regions of China. Acta Geographica Sinica 65(6):727–735 (in Chinese)

Feng SH (2002) An analysis of the tourist sources market and study of behavior model of travele. Tourism Tribune 6:45–48 (in Chinese)

Fu Y, Wang DQ (2006) The inheriting of folk handicrafts in southwestern minority nationality regions. Guizhou Ethnic Stud 106:11–16 (in Chinese)

He ZY, Ye ZR, Sun M, Sun ZJ (1989) The preservation and development of ancient Village Sinnanxi River Scenic spot. J Beijing Inst Civil Eng Arch 2:26–32 (in Chinese)

Hong TC (1987) Attach importance to the rural residential design. World Arch 3:11–12 (in Chinese)

Li L, Xiao L (2009) Study on characteristics and value of tourism resources in ancient villages. J Shandong Youth Adm Cadres College 6:114–116 (in Chinese)

Li JH, Zhang XG (2010) From vernacular dwelling to settlement: new trend of study on chinese regional culture of architecture: Taking the southwest area as example. Arch J 3:82–84 (in Chinese)

Liu PL (1997) Ancient village: harmonious human poly-space. Shanghai Sanlian Press, Shanghai (in Chinese)

Lowenthal D, Binney M (1981) Our past before us. Temple Smith, London

Smith NR (2014) Change and continuity: chinese villages in transition(IV)—Wanmin Village. China City Plann Rev 23(2):65–73

Wang HL (2005) Study on formation reasons and countermeasures of Hollow Villages. Rural Econ 9:21–22 (in Chinese)

Wang XM (2013) Practice and thought of value assessment and integrate preservation. J Southwest Univ Nationalities (humanities and Social Science) (7):156–160 (in Chinese)

Wang W, Geng X (2013) Study on express of functions of farming-reading culture and landscape-image of ancient villages. Shandong Soc Sci 7:77–80 (in Chinese)

Xiao YX, Lu Y, Xue Y, Xiao X (2011) Vacation tourism development research of hollow history village in the suburb: a case study on Edou village in Guangzhou City. Territory Nat Resour Stud 3:66–67 (in Chinese)

Xue L (2001) Study on the inner-decaying village and the countermeasures with Jiangsu province as the Case. City Plann Rev 25(6):8–13 (in Chinese)

Yin WG (2011) Ancient villages cannot be destroyed [N]. People's Daily Overseas Edition, 09–16

Yu XC (2010) Activation of monuments and sites via tourism: way of achieving the better effect in both conservation and utilization. Arch Culture 5:14–20 (in Chinese)

Yu YF (2006) On application of ecomuseum theory to landscape protection: illustrated by the heritage protection of rural village landscape in Southwest China. Southest University, Nanjing (in Chinese)

Zhang CZ, Bao JG (2004) A literature review of heritage tourism and heritage management abroad. Tourism Sci 4:7–16 (in Chinese)

Chapter 12
The Disappearing Historical Hutongs: Key Issues in Preserving Locality in Old Beijing

Pengjun Zhao

12.1 Introduction

Streetscapes satisfy various human needs in terms of contact with nature, aesthetic preference, and recreation (Matsuoka and Kaplan 2008). They provide a place for people (consciously or unconsciously) to interact with a place by either observation or participation. Streetscapes are also key factors in promoting outdoor activities, whose benefits help maintain the vitality of a place. In particular, streetscapes have significant influences on pedestrian movements (Foltête and Piombini 2007). Historical streetscapes are sites where urban daily life is presented, and where the memory of human culture is manipulated and embedded within the ordinary landscape. As such, historical streets play a crucial role in preserving locality in cities (Drozdzewski 2014).

Historical *hutongs* are a type of narrow streets or alleys (Fig. 12.1). Hutongs are unique heritage sites in old Beijing (Kane 2006), although they are common in old Chinese cities. The term *hutong* first appeared during the Yuan Dynasty. Hutongs are alleys formed by lines of traditional courtyard residences (Mandarin: *siheyuan*). A neighborhood was formed by joining one courtyard with another. The imperial city of Beijing included thousands of hutongs with the Forbidden City at its center. Hutongs used to be the basic units of society. Different hutongs were built according to the social classes of residents. Hutongs in neighborhoods for the aristocracy were wide (10–15 m), but most were narrow (3–8 m).

However, the number of hutongs in Beijing has dropped dramatically since the 1990s. In 1949, upon the founding of new China, Beijing had 3100 hutongs. In 2012, this number had decreased to 900 hutongs, located in the old quarter of Beijing (Fig. 12.2). More than a thousand hutongs were demolished to make way

P. Zhao (✉)
Department of Urban and Regional Planning, College of Urban and Environmental Sciences at Peking University, Beijing, China
e-mail: pengjun.zhao@pku.edu.cn

F. Wang and M. Prominski (eds.), *Urbanization and Locality*,
DOI 10.1007/978-3-662-48494-4_12

Fig. 12.1 **a**, **b** Beijing hutong and courtyard. At *left* is a typical hutong in the old city center of Beijing; at *right* are courtyards bordered by hutongs (*Source* Author)

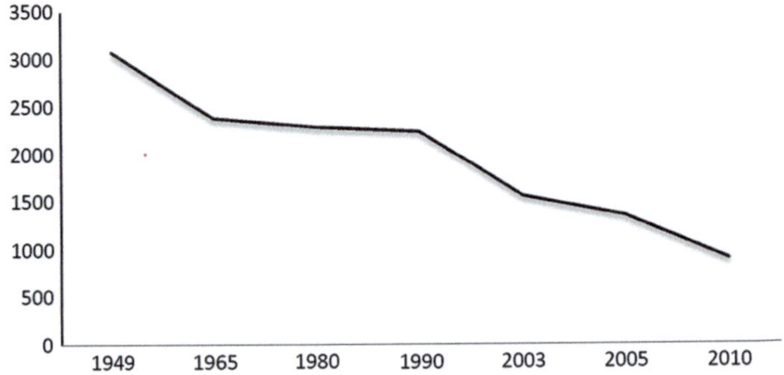

Fig. 12.2 Number of hutongs in Beijing (*Source* Author, edited from BCUP (2008) and BSB (various years)

for new motor roads and new modern buildings. Recently, the importance of historical hutongs to the city culture was generally acknowledged. A historic preservation plan was made in Beijing in 2001. However, the plan only covered 25 zones that were thought to be the most important. Only 600 hutongs were protected by the plan. A large proportion of the historical old city and many hutongs are excluded from the list of areas for conservation. These unprotected zones and hutongs are at a high risk of being demolished in the context of rapid urbanization and market-oriented urban renewal.

The preservation of these historical hutongs amid urban renewal processes has become a key issue in relation to sustainable urban regeneration in Beijing. It has also become a challenging topic to researchers. This study aims to investigate the effects of urban regeneration in Beijing by looking at the Qianmen Dashilan area as a case. An in-depth survey was conducted to examine the gaps between the preservation plan goals and actual urban renewal outcomes.

12.2 Case Study Area

The Qianmen Dashilan area is located just in the front of Tian'anmen, which is the "heart" of Beijing (Fig. 12.3). The region has a total area of 1.26 km^2 and a total population of 57,551, composed of 40,851 local residents and over 16,700 Chinese migrants. The region is rich in historical hutongs. It is one of the most famous historical and cultural areas in Beijing. Most streetscapes in the Dashilan historic district still follow a pattern that was popular in the Ming Dynasty (1368–1644). The pattern is characterized by narrow lanes (0.5–8 m wide), regular courtyards, and low buildings (from one to two stories). One of the most famous pedestrian commercial streets, Dashilan Pedestrian Commercial Street Area, is located in the area. The main street is 275 m in length, lined by more than 100 shops and stores that sell traditional Chinese handicraft, clothes, jewelry, China silk, and Chinese medicines and foods, among others. The Dashilan Pedestrian Commercial Street Area is one of the 25 historical and cultural preservation zones according to the Protection and Control Plan of Beijing Historical and Cultural Area.

In 2002, the municipal government of Beijing made the new Beijing Historical and Cultural City Protection Plan, which covers Dashilan. In the latest edition of the Beijing Master Plan (2004–2020), the Dashilan area was planned as one of the important historic and cultural protected areas. According to the plan, any alteration, expansion, or new activities should be strictly in accordance with the overall historical context in the area.

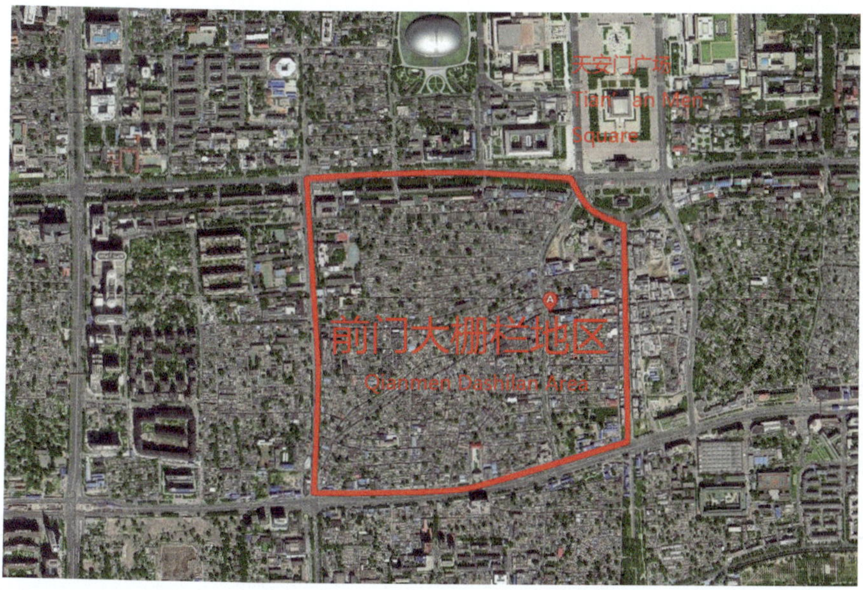

Fig. 12.3 Location of Qianmen Dashilan area (*Source* Author, edited from Google Map)

Fig. 12.4 **a**, **b** The streetscape of Dashilan before and after the renewal in 2007. The *left* photo shows the streetscape before the renewal project (*Source* http://blog.sina.com.cn/zhp); the *right* photo shows the streetscape after the renewal project (*Source* Author)

However, in 2007, before the Beijing Olympics 2008, the municipal government decided to renew the area to showcase a "new" Beijing to the world. A large-scale renovation project was launched in the Dashilan area in May 2007 (Fig. 12.4). It was the largest urban renewal project ever in Beijing. The entire Dashilan Commercial Street Area, including dozens of hutongs, was demolished. Many new buildings and new roads were built in the area. These new buildings have an old-look style copied from their original historical examples. This "tear down and rebuild" mode was strongly opposed by local residents and criticized by the public, planners, and scholars. However, the government insisted on its renewal plan. As a result, many historic buildings and hutongs have gone. Such a large urban renewal project would have significant effects on the historical cultural preservation and locality of Dashilan. The current study investigates the effects.

12.3 Research Method

Previous studies on the impacts of urban renewal on cultural conservation have mostly used the objective evaluation approach. This approach relies on the researchers' observations on the status of conservation. However, the approach ignores the public's attitudes, perceptions, and judgments toward the renewal outcomes. The present study applies a subjective-oriented approach to investigate the effects of urban renewal on local cultural conservation.

In-depth interview data are examined in this research. The data are from the Beijing Urban Renewal Evaluation project, which is funded by the European Union with Peking University as a collaboration partner. The project randomly collected

113 questionnaires from visitors, of which 111 questionnaires were valid (for an effective rate of 98.23 %). 78 questionnaires were collected randomly from local residents, of which 71 questionnaires were valid, with an effective rate of 91.03 %.

Respondents were asked to report their feelings on the degree to which historical culture was conserved in the Dashilan area after the 2007 renewal. For example, they were asked to indicate the extent to which they agreed that the historical style of buildings was conserved using four items on a scale: strongly agree, agree, disagree, and strongly disagree.

12.4 Analysis

12.4.1 Visitors' Perceptions

Table 12.1 shows the score of visitors' perceptions on historical culture conservation. The value of 5 is the highest score, which refers to the highest level of satisfaction with the historical preservation. The results suggest that visitors were mostly satisfied with the colors and old commercial brands in the renewed area. The main reason is that the new buildings were decorated with the same color as the original buildings. As for commerce, after new buildings were built, most original shops moved to the back of the area. Visitors could still see many old-brand shops that sell traditional Chinese handicrafts.

Table 12.1 Visitors' scoring

Elements	Median	Average	Confidence interval of average	Standard deviation	Minimum	Maximum
Transport accessibility	4.33	4.24	4.10–4.38	0.758	2.33	5
Sense of direction	3.5	3.39	3.17–3.62	1.186	1	5
Colors	5	4.26	4.07–4.46	1.042	1	5
Markers	4	3.90	3.66–4.15	1.300	1	5
Monuments	4	3.72	3.45–3.99	1.415	1	5
Buildings	4	3.56	3.31–3.81	1.312	1	5
Streets	2.75	2.82	2.69–2.95	0.678	1.25	5
Time-honored brands	5	4.51	4.37–4.66	0.752	1.5	5
Crowding	1	1.82	1.61–2.03	1.122	1	5
Traditional lifestyle	3.33	3.09	2.91–3.27	0.969	1	5
Traditional culture	4	3.70	3.52–3.88	0.970	1	5
Average visitors scoring	3.59	3.55	3.46–3.63	0.471	2.33	4.55

However, the results of the analysis show that visitors have the second lowest level of satisfaction with the streetscapes. The most important reason that visitors have such an obvious dissatisfaction with the streets is the serious destruction of the historical culture of the streetscapes. Nearly 20 hutongs were demolished and replaced with new roads. New buildings were built along two sides of the new roads. Although a number of hutongs were physically preserved, the historical streetscapes were partly destroyed. For example, the original stone and brick paving was replaced with new ceramic tiles. In the central area of Dashilan Commercial Street, 62.1 % of hutongs' paving had been changed. 86.5 % of the visitors thought that the unchanged hutongs were more attractive than the new ones. In this sense, the renewal project in 2007 had a significant negative impact on the conservation of historical streetscapes and historical context in the area.

Table 12.1 shows that visitors have the lowest level of satisfaction with the population crowding. After the renewal, many new shops were opened in the Dashilan Commercial Street area, including foreign brand shops, such as McDonald's, Starbucks, and KFC. Dashilan Commercial Street became one of the busiest commercial zones in Beijing. The large number of customers brings good business profits to the shop owners. The daily number of customers reached 120,000 on average in 2013. However, this phenomenon has brought overcrowding. The worst impacts of crowding are imposed on the local residents. Their daily life was disturbed by such a huge number of visitors. About 80 % of the local residents agreed that the number of visitors in the area was too high, causing various inconveniences to their daily life.

Visitors indicated a relatively high satisfaction with the new style of old-looking buildings. One of the main reasons is that although they recognized the renovation as copying the original styles, copying was better than a complete demolition of the old original buildings. Before the renewal, the architectural style of Dashilan was dominated by buildings in the style of the Qing Dynasty, the last imperial dynasty in China. In the late Qing Dynasty (the 1870s–1910s), many buildings with a hybrid characteristic of Chinese and Western styles were built in the Dashilan area. In particular, many commercial shop buildings were built with a Western façade. Most of these buildings were two-story houses carved with elaborate Western-style pattern on their doors and façade. In the 2007 renewal, planners paid more attention to recovering the structural masonry, antique-style eaves, and other aspects of the Western style, although the Qing Dynasty style was a primary style for new buildings. As a result, the visitors thought the new buildings may reflect the historical culture despite recognizing these new constructions as "fake old styles."

Traditional lifestyle plays a key issue in relation to heritage conservation in historical areas. However, the results in Table 12.1 show that visitors had less satisfaction with the traditional lifestyle in Dashilan. The urban renewal changed both the local economic and population structure. Large modern shops and new consumption activities replaced old shops and traditional consumption activities in the area. Many middle- and high-income people took the opportunities offered by urban renewal to move into the area. Thousands of original residents were relocated to suburban areas or other districts. The social context in Dashilan changed.

Table 12.2 Typical interview questions

Serial number	Visitors' hometown	Perception of Dashilan before visiting	Perception of Dashilan after actual visit
1	Beijing	Does not look like what I remember in my childhood	Chaotic; only a few real historical buildings; almost no feeling of old Beijing
2	Beijing	The original Dashilan was dirty	Environment improved
3	Beijing	Narrow, crowded, old Beijing style	Loss of old street style
4	Heilongjiang	Quaint old Beijing area	Modern business atmosphere
5	Shandong	There are trams; a lot of time-honored brands; bustling	There are international brands; too many commercial shops; no identity
6	Jilin	A typical area showing streetscapes of old Beijing	Tour of commercial street; few real old buildings
7	Liaoning	I have never thought about it	No historical charm
8	Jiangsu	Historical area	No feeling of being in the old Beijing area
9	Sichuan	Courtyard, alley, gray walls, tiles	Wide and clean roads
10	Shanxi	Colored yellow, like the Forbidden City	Very vibrant
11	Heilongjiang	Old Beijing specialties; a lot of waiters	Distinctive, but not attractive

The traditional lifestyle has been vanishing since the 2007 renewal. This point can be supported by another finding in Table 12.2: visitors did not show complete satisfaction with the conservation of traditional culture.

In this research, the respondents were also asked to report their perception of Dashilan before and after they visited it (Table 12.2). The results of the analysis suggest that many people thought the urban renewal in 2007 failed in terms of historical heritage conservation. For example, one visitor from another district of Beijing said the following:

The area did not look like what I remember in my childhood at all. It is now chaotic. Many old hutongs are gone. Only a few real historical buildings are left. I almost had no feeling of old Beijing when I saw Dashilan.

Visitors from outside Beijing also expressed their disappointment with the conservation of the historical culture in Dashilan. For example, a visitor from Shangdong Province said: "There are trams and a lot of old brand shops. It is bustling. There are international brand shops. But there are too many commercial shops. It does not make Beijing different from other modern cities in China."

The visitors' responses suggest that market-led urban renewal has had negative effects on heritage conservation in Beijing. Since the 1980s, market-oriented reforms have been applied across China's cities. Subsequently, China has been undergoing an obvious transformation, which has at least two fundamental characteristics. The first is that it involves three contemporary and interrelated processes: decentralization, marketization, and globalization (Chow 2007; Wei 2001). The second is that the transformation in China has been a gradual process in which the market and planning systems coexist (Zhu 2000). The transformation process has created new institutional and social contexts for urban development and land development management. In the marketization process, market rules have become important in determining the "rules of the game." Private developers became powerful in the urban renewal process. They are more interested in highly productive commercial development rather than heritage conservation and traditional culture. The developers often ignored the preservation plan of the municipal government. In most cases, the municipal government even changed a preservation plan to meet the developers' requirements.

12.4.2 *Residents' Perceptions*

The questionnaire for residents mainly focused on the comparison of Dashilan before and after renewal. Respondents were asked to report the changes of their perception of Dashilan. Six questions were asked (Table 12.3). Results of the analysis show that local residents thought the renewal improved the living

Table 12.3 Overview of residents' answers

Questions	Median	Average	Confidence interval of average	Standard deviation	Minimum	Maximum
1. I think Dashilan still has many historical streetscapes	3	3.03	2.29–3.98	1.447	1	5
2. I still have a sense of familiarity with Dashilan after the renewal	3	3.19	2.46–4.12	1.403	1	5
3. Shopping is more convenient after the renewal	4	3.68	3.38–3.97	1.240	1	5
4. The living environment has been greatly improved	5	4.23	3.95–4.50	1.161	1	5
5. I hope there will be a similar renewal in future	5	3.77	3.41–4.14	1.542	1	5
6. Visitors disturbed my daily life	3	3.02	2.64–3.39	1.581	1	5
Average residents' rating	3.86	3.86	3.71–4.01	0.644	1.86	4.86

environments in terms of the appearance of new facilities, new shops, new roads, and clean streets. As a result, many residents wished that a similar renewal project would be undertaken. However, they had lower satisfaction with the conservation of historical streetscapes.

Generally, most respondents reported a score below 3.0, which indicates that the renewal did not reach a satisfactory level in terms of heritage conservation. Particularly, 25.4 % strongly disagreed that the new buildings represent the original style. Many residents, mostly elderly people, said they had no sense of familiarity to Dashilan after the area was renewed.

In historical areas, tourists may have negative effects on local residents' daily life. Results of the analysis show that 47.9 % of the residents thought the visitors of Dashilan disturbed their daily lives. Compared with the visitors, the local residents were more likely sympathetic toward urban renewal. One of the main reasons is their hope that living conditions will be improved. For example, 85.9 % of residents believed that the living environment of Dashilan area has greatly improved after renewal. Another reason is that they can receive a high compensation fee when they sell their old houses to developers.

12.5 Conclusion

The preservation of historical streetscapes plays a crucial role in maintaining locality. However, Beijing has been facing severe challenges in preserving historical hutongs in the context of rapid urbanization. In particular, market-oriented urban renewals tend to destroy the historical hutongs. The number of hutongs has been decreasing. Indeed, thousands of historical hutongs have been demolished or replaced with motor roads. Results of the analysis showed that the urban 2007 renewal project in Dashilan drastically destroyed local historical culture. In the core area of Dashilan, the original hutongs and buildings were demolished. New buildings styled after the old ones were built in the same area.

However, it is the visitors who have the least satisfaction with the conservation of historical hutongs and buildings after the original ones were demolished and replaced by new old-looking buildings. Many of them criticized the buildings as being "fake heritage." A part of them stated that the presence of too many commercial shops made the historical area crowded, although the shopping environment was updated. For local residents, they were not satisfied with the conservation of historical hutongs and buildings either, but they were very satisfied with the improvement in the living environment after the area was renewed. The results suggest that the conservation of historical streetscapes in Beijing is also confronted with another challenge: how to achieve a balance between satisfying the local residents' needs for improvement in the living situation and preserving the historical fabric in old historical areas. A more inclusive conservation planning system is imperative in Beijing.

References

Chow GC (2007) China's economic transformation, 2nd edn. Blackwell Publishing Ltd, London

Drozdzewski D (2014) Using history in the streetscape to affirm geopolitics of memory. Polit Geogr 42:66–78

Foltête JC, Piombini A (2007) Urban layout, landscape features and pedestrian usage. Landsc Urban Plan 81:225–234

Kane D (2006) The Chinese language: its history and current usage. Tuttle Publishing, New York

Matsuoka RH, Kaplan R (2008) People needs in the urban landscape: analysis of landscape and urban planning contributions. Landsc Urban Plan 84:7–19

Wei YD (2001) Dencentralization, marketization and globalization: the triple process underlying regional development in China. Asian Geographer 20(1/2):7–23

Zhu J (2000) Urban physical development in transition to market. The case of China as a transitional economy. Urban Affairs Rev 36(2):178–196

Chapter 13
Restructuring the Urban Landscape: A "Critical Reconstruction" of Permanent Structures in Historic Cultural and Urban Landscapes

Sören Schöbel

This study focuses on an important aspect of sustainability: the permanence of the spatial structures in urban and landscape fabrics, which hosts such qualities as social identity and cohesion, cultural heritage and scope, and resource saving and conservation, or in other words, social and ecological stability and resilience. These qualities are bound to site-specific spatial forms. To shed light on the relationship between sustainability and spatial form, the paradigm changes in the European urbanistic discipline are reviewed. These experiences are then transferred to the contemporary challenge of improving the social and ecological qualities of (sub) urban landscapes.

13.1 Dissolution of the City and Landscape

For almost one century, the so-called European city has been in a process of destruction. Starting in the late period of industrialization at the turn of the 20th century, modern architecture and city planning aimed at the dispersal of grown, dense, and mixed city structures. Initiated by utopian models, such as Ebenezer Howard's Garden City of Tomorrow (1902), Bruno Taut's Alpine Architecture (1919), and Le Corbusier's Charter of Athens (1933), the new model called *Stadtlandschaft* meant the dissolution of the city into an endless park that imitated "untouched" landscape. Enforced in many cities by and after World War II, the urban functions of habitation, labor, and leisure became spatially separated; boroughs were cleared up into settlements floated with light, air, and sun; and common road networks were rebuilt into car-friendly traffic systems. The result was a total loss of the historic urban structures. Berlin is an ideal example (Figs. 13.1 and 13.2),

S. Schöbel (✉)
Landscape Architecture and Regional Open Space, Technische Universitaet Muenchen, Munich, Germany
e-mail: schoebel@tum.de

F. Wang and M. Prominski (eds.), *Urbanization and Locality*,
DOI 10.1007/978-3-662-48494-4_13

Fig. 13.1 Ground plan of the inner city of Berlin, in 1940 after World War II (*Source* Senatsverwaltung fuer Stadtentwicklung Berlin, 2000)

Fig. 13.2 Ground plan of the inner city of Berlin, in 1989 after modern renewal (*Source* Senatsverwaltung fuer Stadtentwicklung Berlin, 2000)

as the largest city in Germany. The city considered the total demolition and reconstruction of its complete structure. The medieval, baroque, and Wilhelminian city was blown up house by house, street by street, and quarter by quarter.

However, the landscape, at least the "untouched" parts, did not survive the functionalistic revolution. The European Cultural Landscape, widely the result of a "conquest" (Blackbourn 2006) of nature since the 1750s, was conquered by the process of industrialization. The use of land, especially agricultural land, intensified, the soil fertilized, and the fields machine oriented. Large infrastructures, such as highways and canals, cut through the land. As in the cities, the historic rural structures of the fields and meadows, ways and ditches, and villages and manors, were transformed into functional and homogeneous systems.

In between the dissolving cities and industrialized landscape, suburbia arose: not as an endless park, but as an endless sprawl, formless, unsustainable, and without identity. Although such areas were in many respects optimized for people's needs, they nonetheless feature a dramatic lack of social, ecological, and aesthetic qualities.

13.2 Critical Reconstruction of the City

However, beginning in the 1960s, the urbanistic discipline started to criticize the modern, functional separation of the city, as seen in Jacobs (1961) critique of the deterioration of neighborhoods, Aldo Rossi's manifesto for an urban architecture (Rossi 1966), and Sennett's studies of public space (1974), to name a few. They confirmed empirical discoveries of the social, economic, and environmental benefits of a carefully renewed European city in its historical context, structures, and textures.

The "critical reconstruction" in this sense was an interpretation by a part of the architectural and urbanistic profession of the critical theories of science, policy, and planning of Theodor Adorno, Jürgen Habermas, and especially Karl Popper in his notion of Critical Rationalism. To these experts, the city should not be rebuilt according to dogmatic paradigms but by a principle of trial and error, in small steps, performed with care. Integrated in the historic city textures, a pluralistic society and architecture could be developed beyond the danger of a new urban disaster.

The crucial turning point was the International Building Exhibition (IBA) in Berlin in 1984–87. Its program on critical reconstruction has been, more or less, openly admitted and generally accepted as the guiding principle in an overwhelming number of European cities since the 1990s. Critical reconstruction does not mean the restoration of the living conditions or power structures of the old town. On the contrary, it refers to the liberation of town planning and urbanism from the reckless ideologies of demolition and context-less renewal. The bourgeois European city, as a residential and living place, was thus rediscovered. Its social and ecological qualities, lower land and resource consumption, open and tolerant civilization, and immense power of integration should be lifted in a new social contract, a "third city contract" (Hoffmann-Axthelm 1993).

Critical reconstruction involves a careful renewal of historic forms, but not of their functions or meanings, and a reduction to a few, historically successful and simultaneously changeable types, such as parcel and building blocks, yards, streets, and squares. These structures are not bound to a particular function but to a permanent urban form: the urban "tissue" or "texture." This European urban texture saves resources, and facilitates social integration and civilization by defining high social density and mixture, short distances, and clearly defined private and public

Fig. 13.3 Berlin master plan for critical reconstruction (Planwerk Innenstadt 1999)

spaces. The 1999 Berlin masterplan for the inner city consequently implemented the critical reconstruction approach into the modern urban landscape of Berlin (Fig. 13.3).

The renewed paradigm of the dense and mixed European city today has also been adopted in city expansion projects in the so-called suburban areas. There, however, where no former urban structures exist, critical reconstruction seems to be meaningless. What remains or emerges are the permanent landscape structures. As examples of landscape use to provide structure in suburban spaces, two different approaches of urbanists and landscape architecture are described by the following example of Munich.

13.3 From Landscape to Green System: Town of Cold Air Dynamics

As a typical process of suburbanization in the 1980s, the Munich airport was translocated. The Bavarian State decided to develop a large airport hub in marshlands 40 km north of Munich. The out-of-use airfield at Munich Riem, already surrounded by mushrooming suburbs, was transformed into a so-called trade fair city. A third of the development area was used for a new trade fair, another third for a new urban residential area and commercial center, and the remaining part was designed into a large park of about 2 km^2, the third biggest park in Munich.

How could a new town be built in open spaces, surrounded by unplanned settlements, leftover fields, and new highways? In the early 1990s, the discussion

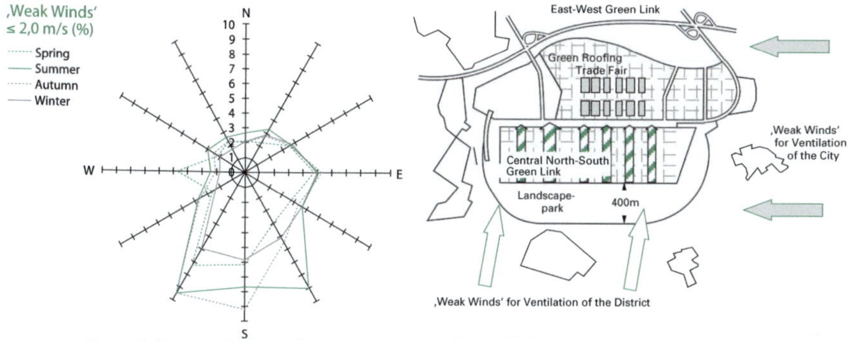

Fig. 13.4 Munich-Riem: The town of cold air dynamics (Landeshauptstadt München (1995)/ transl. by the author)

on ecological urban renewal in Germany focused on air pollution (smog). Despite advanced pollution control regulations for vehicles and industries, the city decided to align the standards in the new city of Riem with urban climate demands, especially in such weather cases as low winds and atmospheric inversion (Fig. 13.4). The belief was that the city and landscape could merge in a structure of green and road strips that strictly followed the prevailing wind direction for "weak winds" and flows of cold air, to lead the airflow into as far as the inner city and new settlements as well. In fact, the structure was planned according to a standardized system of rectangular axes. Even the borders between public and private spaces were formed by this system and by a "graded system of open spaces" but not as an urban "texture." This functionalistic approach led to a strange, alien structure that was neither bound to the historic shape of the former airport nor to that of any other existing structure. In spite of a pressing housing shortage in the Munich region, the demand for houses in the new settlement was comparatively low.

13.4 From Green System to a Critical Structuralism: Park Without Boundaries

Based on this master plan for the city structure, the competition for a new large park was opened for bidding. The winner was the French landscape architect Gilles Vexlard. In contrast to the "landscape-functionalistic" city master plan, his approach can be called "landscape-formalistic." Simply said, he did not design a park but a landscape that could serve as a "structure-giver" not only for the new trade fair city but also for the surrounding suburban landscape as a whole.

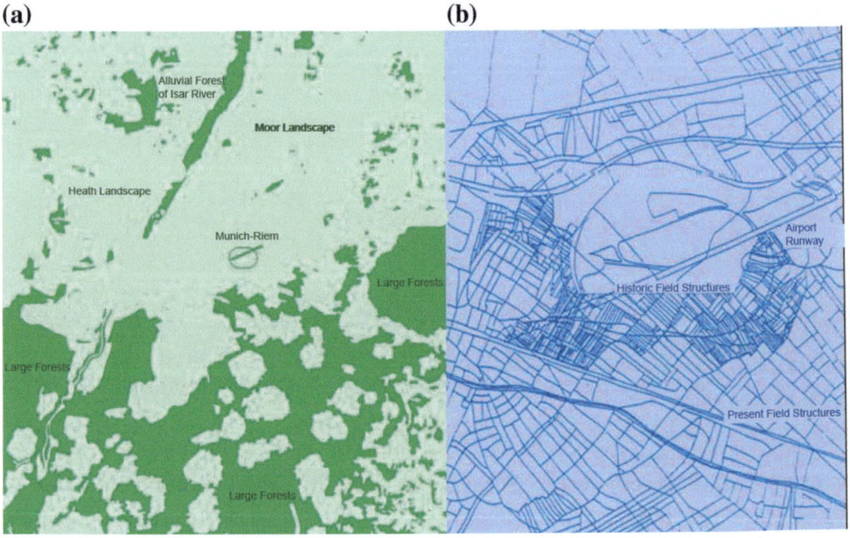

Fig. 13.5 Forests, clearings, and heaths around Munich (**a**), historic field and airport structures at Munich-Riem (**b**) (Gilles Vexlard)

> "Work begins on the context, the scale of a place, its morphology, and the landscape in which it is integrated. The geographical shape of a place for me is like a historic monument. The work in one place is unique because the landscape into which it is integrated is unique. It means to find out what is specific of a place, to work it out, and to get rid of any disruptive elements. We try to lose as little of the concept, design, and implementation as possible, and to rid a place of all that obscures the readability of its landscape and uniqueness. The difficulty in the work of landscape architects is as follows: To show and communicate these encountered qualities, the basic essence of a place. Discipline, determination, and experience are needed to preserve the qualities of a place, from conceptualization through realization, and simultaneously, to anticipate future developments". (Vexlard, transl. by the author).

Vexlard's concept took up the local situation, which is on a regional layer in the junction of the two large-scale landscapes of Munich's surroundings: the forests with large clearings in the south and the cultural landscapes with heath and grasslands in the north. On another layer, he deduced the diagonal structure from the former field boundaries of the area, before it was used as an airport, and rebuilds them as axes in the park (Fig. 13.5a, b). The spatial structure also guarantees cold air dynamics but performs another function as well. The axes have no beginning and no end; they point out to the suburban landscape. By this, not only did Vexlard create a park structure on a grand scale but a framework for the (sub)urban landscape in the surroundings. Vexlard intended to develop parks neither simply for "ecological system service" nor for horticultural quotations or as guidance systems for pastimes but as part of a landscape that would re-connect everything. Beyond park boundaries, the suburban residential landscape offers integration (Fig. 13.6).

Fig. 13.6 Munich-Riem, 2014, http://geoportal.bayern.de/bayernatlas

13.5 From Suburban Green Belts to Urban Landscapes Full of Character: Long-Term Urban Development in the Munich Region

Two decades later, the population growth in the Munich region is, compared with the overall development in Germany, is dramatic. Despite significant efforts in inner-city densification, half the growth is expected to take place in the outer region. To discuss alternatives to typical suburban sprawls, a design studio with students in landscape architecture at the Technical University of Munich strikes a new path.

The students were expected to understand the Munich region not as suburban periphery or even green belt of the center but as distinguished landscapes full of character, as equal partners. In reference to place-specific historic, permanent forms of landscape and settlements, "settlement-appropriate landscape" and "landscape-appropriate settlements" were designed. In a first step, the students identified the different landscapes around Munich (Fig. 13.7). The gravel plain of Isar River with Munich in its center is surrounded by different landscapes by young and old moraines of several glacial periods. They are surrounded by large forests, grasslands, heath lands, and lakes, as well as by extremely different settlement structures. Within the suburban sprawl, old villages still serve as ideational centers.

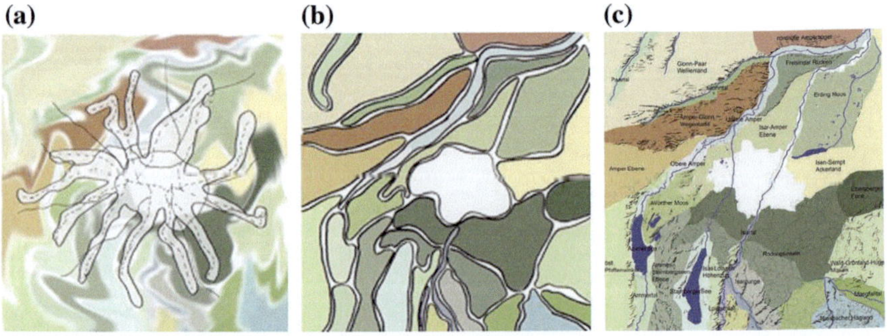

Fig. 13.7 From generic periphery to distinguishing landscapes: the city as an octopus (**a**), the city as a landscape among others (**b**), landscapes named as brands (**c**) (Herrmann, Sihler, Sojka, TUM LAREG 2014)

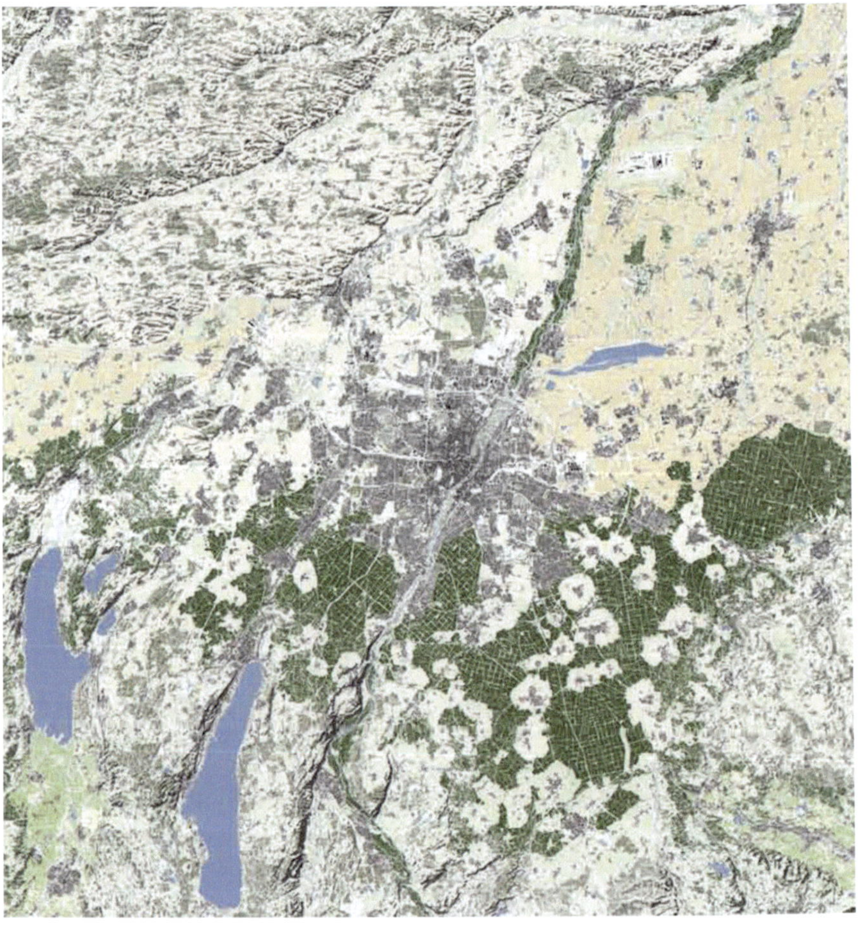

Fig. 13.8 Landscape morphologies and textures, settlement typology (Herrmann, Sihler, Sojka, TUM LAREG 2014)

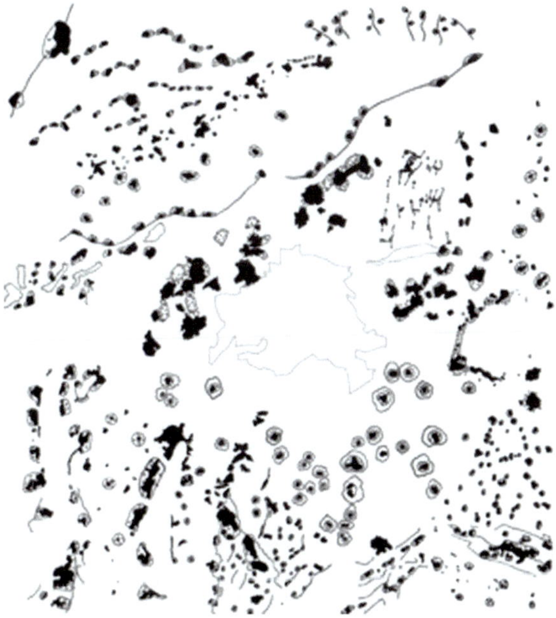

Fig. 13.9 Typology of settlement patterns (Herrmann, Sihler, Sojka, TUM LAREG 2014)

The students worked out the site-specific spatial elements and structures by highlighting differences but without distinguishing between "beautiful" and "ordinary" landscapes (Fig. 13.8). Then, they created a typology of site-specific settlement patterns (Fig. 13.9). As a result, they conceptualized a landscape-oriented spatial

(a) (b)

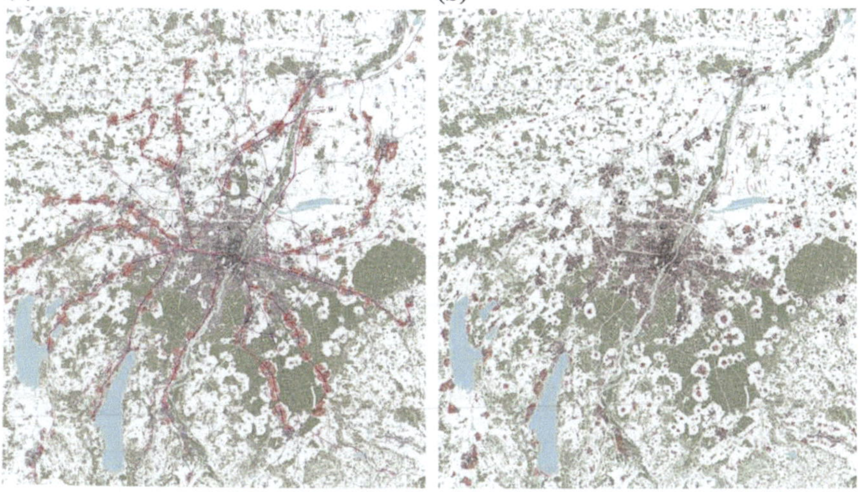

Fig. 13.10 State of radial development along railways (a), landscape-oriented alternative (b) (Herrmann, Sihler, Sojka, TUM LAREG 2014)

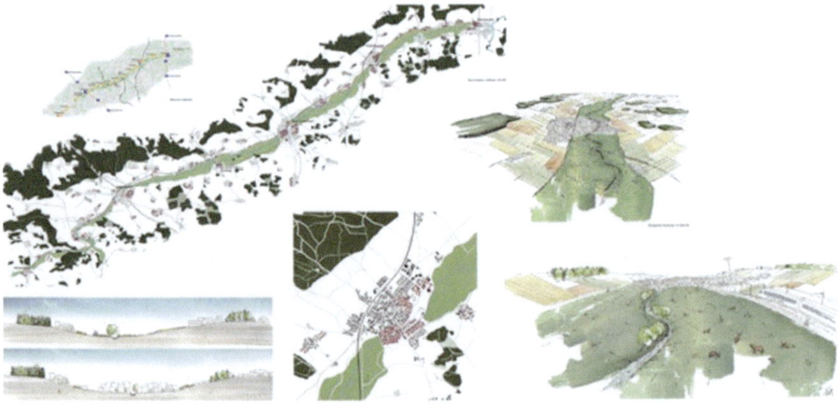

Fig. 13.11 Examples of existing (*black*) and new (*red*) landscape-oriented settlements (Herrmann, Sihler, Sojka, TUM LAREG 2014)

structure of settlement expansions alternative to the state of radial development of settlement corridors along the railway systems (Fig. 13.10). For a selection of sites, they conclude with examples for settlements expansions appropriate to the historic village and cultural landscape patterns (Fig. 13.11).

13.6 Restructuring Urban Landscape: A Critical Reconstruction of Permanent Structures in Cultural and Urban Landscapes

In conclusion, the urbanistic model of a critical reconstruction of the European city might be transferred into urban landscapes, if elements or modules and structures or forms of the historic cultural landscape serve as structure-givers for all the buildings, infrastructures, and land uses that conquer the historic landscapes and cities and turn them into urban landscapes. The land is not a blank foil. "A 'place' is not a given but the result of condensing. In countries where humans have been present for generations, a fortiori for millennia, all territorial accidents are significant. To understand them is to give oneself the chance of making a more intelligent intervention. (…) it is in fact evident that the foundation for planning can no longer be the city but that territorial reserve to which it must be subordinated. It is equally true that development can no longer consider only quantities but must acquire an additional dimension of integrating the shape of the land into design" (Corboz 1983).

As seen in the examples, cities as well as historic cultural landscapes are often rich in visible and hidden elements and structures (Table 13.1) that can serve different functions over time as well as initiate coherence and sustainability in the

Table 13.1 Elements and structures in cities and cultural landscapes that offer permanence to new developments in urban landscapes

PERMANENCES	City	Cultural Landscape		Urban Landscape
ELEMENTS OR MODULES *that can serve for different functions over time*	▪ plot, block, quarter … ▪ courtyard, street, square, promenade … ▪ centers, areas, … ▪ walls, ditches, canals, viaducts …	▪ land lot, farmyard, type of village … ▪ markets, fairgrounds, public pathways, local connections, commons … ▪ shore, beach, edge … ▪ terraces, alleys, fruit gardens, fields with barns, monasteries … ▪ ditches, walls, dikes, channels …	→	Buildings, infrastructures and land uses to be restructured by a *critical reconstruction*: ▪ suburban settlements ▪ business parks ▪ agricultural land ▪ nature reserves ▪ brownfields and wastelands ▪ highways, railway lines ▪ wind farms, solar fields ▪ overhead power lines ▪ …
STRUCTURES OR FORMS *that can initiate coherency and sustainability (identity, difference, integration, hospitality …)*	▪ 'translucency' of the landscape morphology ▪ historical ground plan shapes ▪ fabric of the public open space ▪ building alignments, maximum eave lines, parceling…	▪ massive morphologies of the natural landscape: relief, vastness … ▪ fine structures of the cultural landscape: textures, grids, networks … ▪ historical public rights and ownership structures … ▪ meaningful places: visual axis, landmarks, panoramas …		

permanence of spatial form. Stability, resilience, identity, difference, hospitality, and integration are the crucial qualities of ecological, social, economic, and aesthetic societies.

References

Blackbourn D (2006) The conquest of nature. Water, landscape and the making of modern Germany. W.W. Norton, New York

Corboz A (1983) The land as Palimpsest. Diogenes 31:12–34

Herrmann, Sihler, Sojka (2014) Landschaf(f)t Identität (Landscape creates identity). Design Studio TUM LAREG. Not published

Hoffmann-Axthelm D (1993) Die dritte Stadt. Suhrkamp, Frankfurt a. M.

Jacobs J (1961) The death and life of great American Cities. Random House, New York

Landeshauptstadt München (1995) Messestadt Riem. Ökologische Bausteine. Teil I Stadtplanung. Muenchen

Rossi A (1966) L'Architettura della Città. Marsilio Press, Padua

Sennett R (1974) The fall of public man. Vintage Books, New York

Part III
New Explorations: Site-Specific Planning and Design in the Context of Urbanization

Chapter 14
Providing Urban Ecosystem Services for Human Well-Being: A Comparison of Exemplary Institutional Arrangements in China and Germany

Martin Welp, Natalie Ward, Siegmund Missall, Abdulla Abliz and Ümüt Halik

14.1 Human Well-Being and Urban Greenery

Urbanization is a worldwide phenomenon and a major driver of global environmental change. For example, 75 % of the annual CO_2 emissions are produced in cities and towns. Currently, more than half of the world's population lives in cities. By 2050, this proportion is predicted to increase to 66 % (UN World Urbanization Prospects 2014). In China, this process is particularly pronounced, and the central party has an explicit political goal to raise the urban population to 1 billion people by 2030 (China National Human Development Report 2013), partly by establishing new urban centers (cf. Microcities in this book, Chap. X). In Germany, larger cities grow at the expense of smaller urban settlements. The process of urbanization raises

M. Welp (✉)
Faculty of Forest and Environment, Eberswalde University for Sustainable Development (University of Applied Sciences), Eberswalde, Germany
e-mail: martin.welp@hnee.de

N. Ward · S. Missall
International Master Study Programme, Global Change Management, Eberswalde University for Sustainable Development, Eberswalde, Germany

A. Abliz
Eberswalde University for Sustainable Development, Eberswalde, Germany

Ü. Halik
School of Resources and Environmental Science, Xinjiang University, Ürümqi, China

A. Abliz · Ü. Halik
Catholic University of Eichstätt-Ingolstadt, Eichstätt, Germany

F. Wang and M. Prominski (eds.), *Urbanization and Locality*,
DOI 10.1007/978-3-662-48494-4_14

several questions in the context of a broader sustainability debate: How can cities be built in such a way that they provide a setting for sustainable lifestyles? How can human well-being be improved by good city planning and management? These questions are inherently linked to the quantity and quality of urban vegetation.[1]

Urban and peri-urban greenery provide various ecosystem services (ESS) that directly or indirectly contribute to the well-being of city dwellers. Public parks, urban gardens, peri-urban forests, and other green elements of urban environments provide regulating services, such as heat and dust stress reduction. Urban gardens can offer provisioning services, such as food and raw materials, for urbanites. Additionally, urban and peri-urban greenery provide cultural services, serving as points of identification, giving a feeling of locality and continuity, and providing spaces for community action (MEA 2005). From the perspective of environmental education, urban green spaces are important as well. Young people live in increasingly urban conglomerations. Without urban forests and parks, there would be no "learning laboratory" where children can learn and experience nature or learn about food production systems.

Well-being is a general term for the condition of an individual or group. It can relate to the social, economic, psychological, spiritual, or medical state. High well-being means that the individual or group experience is positive. Although well-being is, to a certain extent, a subjective condition from a sociological perspective, research on human well-being attempts to identify the factors that contribute to a high well-being among the majority of people. Research on welfare and happiness is close to this line of inquiry. Apart from physical well-being, social relationships and the experience of being able to take an active role in the environment are important elements. For a number of people, urban gardening is a form of self-fulfillment. Urban green spaces also provide a possibility to meet and gather with family and friends outside one's own home.

The distributive aspects of availability and access to urban green as factors that promote well-being are not yet discussed by governments in a sufficient way. Nonetheless, many European cities provide threshold values for per-capita urban green spaces or minimum accessibility for a defined area of urban green space (Kabisch and Haase 2014). For instance, Berlin, Germany, aims at 6 m^2 of urban green space per person (Senate Department for Urban Development and the Environment 2013). China is examining ways to provide green space for its people by creating national forest cities with 11 m^2 of public green space per capita (indicators for national forest city). Our case study city in Aksu, China, with a total of 40.3 % forest coverage, provides 9.2 m^2 of green space per person (Aksu yearbook 2012).

[1]The study on urban vegetation in China was conducted within the SuMaRiO-Project (Sustainable Management of River Oases along the Tarim River; http://www.sumario.de). This consortium was formed in 2011 and is funded by the German Federal Ministry of Education and Research.

14.2 Institutional Arrangements that Govern the Establishment and Maintenance of Urban Green Spaces

The present work explores the institutional arrangements that govern the establishment and maintenance of urban green spaces through an analysis of two cases from China and Germany. We refer to institutions as structures or mechanisms of social order. These govern the behavior of individuals within a given community. Institutions are both customs or behavior patterns as well as formal organizations of government and public services. Accordingly, a wide range of institutional arrangements govern the establishment and maintenance of urban greenery. In this context, an institution refers not only to organizations of different kinds but also to laws, rules, habits, and conventions, or to those elements of governance that are decisive to the extent and quality of urban green spaces.

Examples of relevant organizations in Germany include public ones, such as Grünflächenamt (the parks commission) or Berliner Forsten (the state forestry service of Berlin), and non-governmental organizations, such as Gartenvereine (gardening clubs) or WikiWoods[2] (volunteer groups that gather to plant trees and promote environmental awareness). Laws include the Act on Parks. Habits and conventions may include voluntary action, which is based on mutual trust and social control among group members.

These institutional arrangements are embedded in the national legislation and basic principles of public decision making, which range from autocratic or central party system (like in China) to democratic decision making (Germany). There are thus great differences in terms of how urban planning and management of green spaces is subject to the democratic control of people via the election of local politicians. Legal arrangements at the sub-national level are naturally defined by national legislation. For example, in Europe, cities have various acts that govern the management of green spaces.

Cities do not only have public green space but also privately owned or managed spaces. Such elements include trees in yards as well as private gardens. The interplay between private developers (including investors) and the public administration is a decisive feature of such institutional arrangements as well.

Community gardening, which is increasingly popular in many European and North American cities, is governed partly by public authorities (which can provide the space for such initiatives) and by principles of common pool resources management. The institutional arrangements within a community garden initiative usually oversee group membership, delineation of space, appropriation rules, and graduated sanctions (Ostrom 1990). To complete the multifaceted picture, we argue: What can be regarded as alternative greening, the so-called guerrilla

[2]URL: http://www.WikiWoods.org.

gardening, is also governed by institutions, where autonomous action may or may not be tolerated by the public administration.

This research gives insights into two extremely different examples and their institutional arrangements, one from Germany and the other from China. One is based on voluntary action organized according to community-based action, and the other is driven by the public administration. These can be regarded as two ends of a continuum. At one end of the continuum, we find citizen initiatives and community gardening in Berlin, which is taking place without strong interference by the authorities. At the other end of the continuum of management approaches, we find local government-led approaches, which rely on the mass mobilization of people. The city of Aksu, situated at the northern fringe of the Taklamakan Desert in northwest China, is exposed to periodic severe dust and sand storms. In 1986, local authorities decided to establish a peri-urban shelterbelt plantation, the so-called Kökyar Protection Forest. It was realized as a patchwork of poplar shelterbelts and orchards. The maintenance of the plantation is facilitated by a leasing system.

14.3 Two Case Studies from China and Germany

China and Germany are economic drivers in their regions and even globally. Both have experienced rapid industrialization and subsequent environmental degradation. Germany, in certain respects, has entered the post-industrial era, although the ecological footprint of Germany is felt globally. Berlin can be characterized as a creative city with little industrial production. Aksu in China is an example of a multi-ethnic city that is growing rapidly. Both cities are located in the dry parts of the country. While Berlin, as the capital of Germany, is the largest urban settlement in the country, Aksu can be regarded as a second- or third-tier city in China, which in the Chinese context is rather small.

14.3.1 Urban Gardening in Berlin, Germany

Germany's capital city, Berlin, has a history of urban gardening dating back to the mid-1800s. Known to Germans as Schrebergärten gardens, allotment gardens were originally developed to improve the health of urban children and serve as a source of alternative food supply for city dwellers during times of crisis, later on serving as a place of retreat for proletarian citizens (Schug 2005). Given their historical status as a means to support urban citizens with food during critical times, allotment gardens are often (but not always) legally secured by the local government. This garden type is found throughout Berlin (with an estimated 70,000 members) (Wunder 2013) and has a different legal status compared with urban gardens (which are not necessarily legally secured). To protect gardens amid the pressure of expanding development, a law was passed in 1983 to protect allotments by securing low rents (Wunder 2013). Further, allotment gardens are not open to the public: Allotment gardeners pay rent for use of the land and are required to secure one-third of the garden space for food production.

The more recent urban gardening initiatives surfacing in Berlin evoke a cultural orientation different from that of traditional urban allotments (Martin et al. 2014). They are often found in empty, unused areas, such as abandoned parking lots (Prinzessinnengarten), former railyards (Rosenduft intercultural garden), or former airports (Fig. 14.1) (Allmende Kontor in the former Tempelhof Airport). These urban gardens can be categorized as a type of community-based initiative. Also referred to as grassroots initiatives, bottom-up innovations, and community-led projects, community-based initiatives are bottom-up innovations led by civil society (individual citizens or community groups) rather than the government, business, or industry, to generate and implement new ideas in organizing interpersonal activities or social actions to meet one or more common goals (Mumford 2002).

14.3.2 *Origins of Community-Based Initiatives*

The notion of community-based initiatives stems from the non-binding, voluntarily implemented Agenda 21, an action plan for sustainability covering nearly all related

Fig. 14.1 Allmende Kontor garden in Berlin's former Tempelhof Airport (*Source* ©Authors)

aspects from changing consumption patterns, combatting poverty, conservation and management of resources, inter alia, endorsed by the United Nations. Agenda 21 was the main document that stemmed from the UN Conference on Environment and Development in 1992 (the Earth Summit), formally endorsed by all attending governments with the intention of providing governments with guidelines for achieving sustainable development (Hordijk 1999).

The Berlin Senate recognized and commented on the Local Agenda 21 in 2004, which was then restructured, and it later became a legal non-profit organization named Berlin 21. Members include individuals, local associations and initiatives, businesses, and other non-profit organizations. Berlin 21 was not created by politicians but rather emerged from the dialogue with and among citizens (Berlin 21, 2014). Within Berlin 21, members are responsible for overseeing, coordinating, and providing financial support for implementing community-based projects from community gardens to green walkways, among others.

Berlin is situated in the eastern part of the country, and its administrative boundaries extend over a region of more than 89,000 ha. Berlin's population is estimated to have reached 3.5 million by 2012 (Amt fuer Statistik, Berlin-Brandenburg 2013). With urban gardening garnering popularity in Berlin (currently, there are an estimated 96 urban gardens in Berlin), a study was conducted by a Master's student of the University for Sustainable Development in Eberswalde, Germany, within the city's urban gardens (Ward 2015). Questionnaires were distributed to and personal interviews were conducted with a range of garden users (volunteer, intern, manager, founder, researcher, visitor), between May and August 2014 to determine garden users' personal opinions on the gardens' contributions to different categories of ecosystem services.

14.3.3 Provision of Ecosystem Services to the Citizens of Berlin

The study generated responses from 20 urban gardens found throughout Berlin (with 47 questionnaire responses and nine personal interviews conducted) and found that generally, garden users identified Berlin's urban gardening initiatives as providing regulating services (pollination, microclimate and air quality regulation, and noise and wind buffering), and contributing to habitat provision by providing habitats for urban birds and other city-dwelling animals. They provide seasonal fruits, vegetables, and herbs to inner city neighborhoods (with amounts varying on a garden to garden basis). However, the cultural services category (a place for recreation, education, and social relations; providing a sense of place and a retreat within a busy city, inter alia) were identified by garden users as being the high value contributions of urban gardens (Fig. 14.2).

As one garden visitor put it, "The purpose of an urban garden is not to provide biodiversity but rather to offer a sense of community." One frequently mentioned subcategory of cultural services was the gardens' contribution to knowledge

Fig. 14.2 Intercultural garden in *Familiengarten Mitte* (*Source* ©Authors)

systems, such as providing environmental education via seminars, trainings, and workshops, and their contribution to the maintenance of traditional ecological knowledge (passing on experiences from generation to generation), which is crucial amid the rise of urbanization and increasing gap between people the natural environment and food production systems.

Several people interviewed believed that the presence of the garden greatly improved the environmental quality within the area, or that the urban gardens were associated with little or no negative aspects. In addition, both the interview and questionnaire responses depicted peoples' perceptions that self-grown food is healthier than food from the supermarket (safer owing to the use of little or no chemicals compared with the contemporary use of pesticides in agricultural practices). In general, garden users included in the survey tended to state that the gardens were sustainable.

One explanation for the respondents' generally positive perceptions of the gardens' contributions to ecosystem services is that people are enthusiastic about the gardening initiatives in which they participate. This tendency toward high enthusiasm could be indirectly related to cultural services, as it is a sign of the positivity of people involved, which in turn indirectly contributes to their overall positive feelings toward the gardens they tend. Thus, generally speaking, those included in the study are enthusiastic about what they are doing and they find urban gardening to be highly positive, especially in terms of cultural services provision.

Despite the case study and other research findings on urban gardens' contributions to ecosystem services for human well-being, the future of Berlin's urban gardens is not necessarily secure. Reasons include the following: gardens lack the finances to support themselves or provide jobs to full-time garden staff, a lack of local government acknowledgment and support, and alternative use of space for an office building or housing may be deemed more economical. One garden, Prinzessinnengarten, has garnered significant media attention through its well-known website. It attracts tourists with its beer garden and restaurant that serves vegetables from the garden, although its representatives also confirm doubts on the garden's future. Another garden, Allmende Kontor on Berlin's former Tempelhof Airport, officially opened in 2011, and its initial permit only granted a three-year land lease; however, the lease has been extended until 2016 (Wunder 2013). For many of Berlin's urban gardens, this aspect of temporary existence seems to be a common theme.

The results of this case study contribute to research on developing quantitative methods for assessing ecosystem services provided by urban gardens. Generally speaking, garden users who took part in the case study were perceived as enthusiastic about what they were doing and they found urban gardening to be a highly positive activity to take part in, especially in terms of the cultural services it provides. The results achieved from these types of methods could lead to informing urban gardeners on designing their gardens in a way that most benefits people. For example, a garden more focused on cultural services than food production could highlight the cultural aspects, such as education and community building, by providing a center or common area for learning and sharing of gardening experiences, and placing the salad-growing corner, for example, further away from the entrance.

14.3.4 Kökyar Afforestation Project in Aksu, Northwest China[3]

The data for the following description of the Kökyar Protection Forest are drawn from existing literature, a socio-economic household survey on Kökyar farmers conducted by the authors in 2012, and additional interviews conducted in 2011 and 2012. Further, a pilot survey among Aksu citizens was conducted in 2012. Only 20 people could be interviewed, and thus, the result of this survey needs to be treated with care.

[3]This section on Kökyar is based on an article published in earth system dynamics by Missall et al. (2015).

Aksu is a city of about 314,500 inhabitants (Akesu Shi Renmin Zhengfu 2012). It is the capital of Aksu Prefecture, lying in the west of China's huge northwestern Xinjiang Uyghur Autonomous Region, close to the borders of Kyrgyzstan. At a geographical position of 41°10′ north and 80°15′ east and an altitude of 1100 m above sea level, it is situated on a long, slight slope between the Tian Shan mountain range in the north and Taklamakan Desert in the south (Fig. 14.3). An evaporation rate of 1868 mm and precipitation of merely 75 mm per annum indicate an extremely arid climate (Kökyar Annals Compilation Committee 2006: 32). However, Aksu's proximity to the mountains guarantees runoff water from glaciers and snowmelt, feeding into the Aksu River and other smaller streams, thereby ensuring the possibility of agriculture and making Aksu the center of a huge river oasis (ca. 1000 km^2, including Awat and Onsu Counties; Halik 2003: 83).

However, the arid environment becomes very tangible whenever the regular hot and dry north winds blow down from the Tian Shan Mountains (Foehn effect). Maximum wind speeds are reached in springtime with 15 m/s (Yoshino 1992). Raising dust and sand from the barren areas north of the oasis, the north winds cause an annual average of 11.5 sand storm days (visibility less than 1 km) and 25.7 floating dust events (visibility less than 10 km) in Aksu City (Kökyar Annals Compilation Committee 1996). The severe dust and sand storms of Aksu blacken the sky, making respiration difficult, covering everything inside and outside of

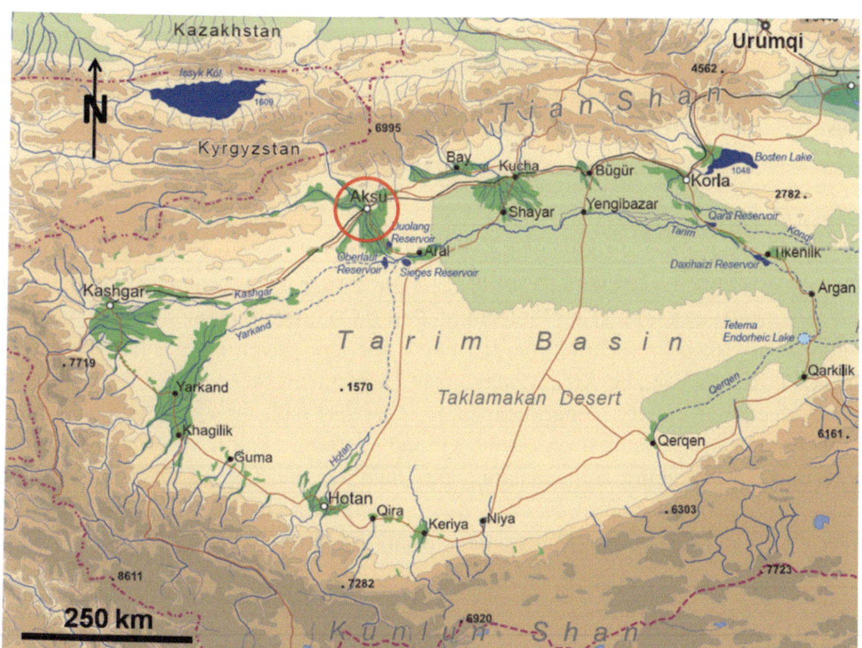

Fig. 14.3 Aksu City is located in the Tarim Basin in northwest China (*Source* Adapted from Paproth and Pietsch 2011)

houses with brown dust, inhibiting traffic, and disrupting public life (Aksu Prefectural Forestry Department and Kuqa Television Station 2006; Aksu Prefectural Greening Committee 2006; street interviews with random Aksu citizens in 2011).

During the 1980s, the dust and sand storms were increasingly perceived as major problems for the city. There are two probable factors for this change. First, in previous decades, Aksu City had undergone rapid socio-economic changes. The composition of the population shifted from a nearly 100 % autochthonous Uyghur society to comprise a majority of Han-Chinese settlers, and the city transformed from a small rural oasis town into a regional industrial and service center (Halik 2003; Intercontinental Pan-Chinese Network Information Co. Ltd. 2008). A different environmental and cultural background of the settlers and shifted ideas of the living standards in cities may have fostered this new perception. Second, the immigration-based growth and economic development of oasis cities in the Tarim Basin usually brought degradation of the natural vegetation at the fringes of the oases, thus compromising their regulating ecosystem services and contributing to the aggravation of dust and sand problems (Halik 2003).

In 1986, the Aksu Prefectural Party Committee decided to respond to the dust problems by establishing a peri-urban protection forest. The first plot to be afforested was an area of 1308 ha in the north of Aksu City that extends from the suburbs of the city to the Great Revolution Canal. It is an old fluvial terrace with an elevation of about 20 m above the core of Aksu City. Its surface is composed of sand, silt, and clay. As it used to be predominantly devoid of vegetation, it was regarded as a major source of wind erosion, with its soil particles blowing right down into the core of Aksu City (Kökyar Annals Compilation Committee 1996; Aksu Prefectural Forestry Department and Kuqa Television Station 2006).

14.3.4.1 Main Actors

The establishment of the Kökyar Protection Forest was organized in a clear top-to-bottom structure. The Prefectural Party Committee, which is the highest authority in Aksu Prefecture, charged two important governmental organizations, the Aksu River Drainage Area Management Department (*akesu heliuyu guanlichu*) and Prefectural Forestry Department (*diqu linyechu*) with the afforestation project. Each organization founded an on-the-ground working station specifically for the purpose of establishing and managing the planting: the Kökyar Greening Project Water Management Station (*kekeya lühua gongcheng shui guanzhan*; from here on referred to as the Water Management Station) and Kökyar Greening Project Protection Forest Management Station (*kekeya lühua gongcheng fanghulin guanzhan*; from here on referred to as the Forest Management Station) with a staff of about 50 persons each (Kökyar Annals Compilation Committee 1996; Interview with the former head of the Forest Management Station, Ibrahim Yusup, October 14 2012). The main task of the River Management Department and its local Water Management Station lay in preparing the planting ground through spatial planning, bulldozing the terrain, establishing a road network, building irrigation canals and other hydraulic engineering for water irrigation, and installing drainage canals to depress the saline groundwater level (Kökyar Annals Compilation Committee 1996; interview with I. Yusup), whereas the main task of the Forestry Department and its local Forest Management Station lay in forest design planning, provision of cuttings and saplings, and afforestation management (Kökyar Annals Compilation Committee 1996).

Many other governmental organizations or government-owned enterprises, such as the Prefectural Traffic Department, Prefectural Road Construction Group, state-owned Experimental Forest Site, and state-owned Red Flag Slope Farm, contributed to the establishment of Kökyar Protection Forest with expertise, labor, resources, or funds. However, the main promoters were the River Management and Forestry Departments with their corresponding on-the-ground stations (Kökyar Annals Compilation Committee 1996; interview 1). Given the lack of funds, none of these institutions were provided additional financial support by the local government. Therefore, they had to restructure their regular annual budgets to mobilize funds for the project (Kökyar Annals Compilation Committee 1996; interview with I. Yusup).

14.3.4.2 Obligatory Labor

The lack of funds also encouraged the application of a legal regulation adopted in 1981 obliging all Chinese citizens to participate in National Obligatory Afforestation Campaigns (Halik 2003; interview with I. Yusup). Based on this regulation, beginning from 1986, the Aksu Prefectural Party Committee called "all citizens, no matter the ethnicity, military or civilian" to participate in obligatory labor on the fields, including leveling the terrain, preparing the ground, and planting trees (Kökyar Annals Compilation Committee 1996; interview with I. Yusup). Consequently, about 70 different organizations and enterprises sent thousands of workers twice a year, for periods of 8, 12, or even 30 days at a time (Fig. 14.4). For one day in 1988, 8459 people worked on the desert plateau (Kökyar Annals Compilation Committee 1996). For each day's shift of hard physical labor in a hot and dry environment, people had to provide for their own transportation, tools, and food (interview with I. Yusup).

14.3.5 *Structure of the Plantation*

The forest plantation was established as a raster of shelterbelt strips consisting mainly of white poplar (*Populus alba* 'Pyramidalis') with fruit plantations in between. Between 1986 and 1990, 686 ha of poplar shelterbelts and 623 ha of orchards were planted, totaling 1308 ha and 1,085,000 trees (Kökyar Annals Compilation Committee 1996).

Fig. 14.4 Obligatory labor on the Kökyar fields (*Source* Kökyar Annals Compilation Committee 1996)

The infrastructure backbone of the plantation is formed by a vertical main canal and a parallel main asphalt road that interlink the Great Revolution Canal in the north with the city of Aksu in the south, providing the area with water and easy access. This main axis has a length of 15.8 km, and it is protected by a 100-m-wide shelterbelt strip at each side. The areas east and west of it are crisscrossed by a regular grid totaling about 125 km of dirt roads and a hierarchical system of subordinate irrigation canals. Shelterbelts, planted in single or double rows, protect the dirt roads and subordinate canals, forming a checkered pattern over the area (Fig. 14.5). The rectangular fields in between are filled with orchards. Hundreds of small farm houses are scattered all over the orchards. The area is equipped with all the necessary technical infrastructure, such as water gates, waterlocks, overflows, bridges, drainage canals, water tabs, power lines, telephone lines, and administrative buildings (Kökyar Annals Compilation Committee 1996).

Fig. 14.5 Aerial view of the northern edge of Kökyar I (*Source* Adapted from Aksu Prefectural Greening Committee 2006)

Since 1991, the project has been enlarged to cover three additional project areas. They are scattered over the most problematic dust fields to the north and east of Aksu City. Their layout follows the basic design of Kökyar I, but they tend to have smaller shelterbelt areas compared with the total area (Aksu Prefectural Greening Committee 2006).

14.3.6 Orchard Leasing System

In 1981, China's State Council began promoting private forestry on a leasing basis through "Resolution on Issues Concerning Forest Protection and Development" (for backgrounds cf. Delang and Yuan 2015). In 1987, when the Kökyar afforestation work was in the early stages, the Forest and Water Management Stations reacted to this resolution and to the dire financial situation of their afforestation project, with the introduction of a leasing system that is fundamentally still in force at present: Plots of already planted orchards and plots ready for planting were leased to private fruit farmers (Kökyar Annals Compilation Committee 1996). Leasing contracts guarantee them, for a period of about 10–15 years, a small section of orchard land (mostly between 0.5 and 1 ha, which may include single- or double-row poplar shelterbelts on one or two edges of the plots), regular irrigation water supply, and technical advice in fruit production (information from a socio-economic household survey conducted in 2012). The leasers, in return, have to pay a substantial lease and irrigation water fee. Additionally, they have certain duties and prohibitions. The main duty is to attend 7–50 days of obligatory labor annually, which is mostly maintenance work on the shelterbelt plantations and irrigation canals. They are prohibited from causing damage to the poplar plantations by cutting trees or branches (even if they overshadow fruit trees) or grazing. The leasers have to compensate any loss of poplar trees in their area. Certain contracts further contain bans on changing the cultivation from fruit trees to field crops, although the former is economically the most promising to cultivate (household survey).

This system of economic incentives and regulative norms, as is fixed in the lease contracts, guarantees the cultivation and persistence of vigorous orchards among undamaged poplar shelterbelts, provides free labor for the maintenance of the infrastructure and poplar shelterbelts, and ensures an income to the lessor organizations that they can reinvest in the plantation. The project leaders soon recognized the leasing system as an instrument to transform Kökyar from a purely government-sponsored protection forest into a self-supporting protection forest (Aksu Prefectural Greening Committee 2006). Consequently, they try to set the lease prices as high as possible, without the leasers backing out (interview with I. Yusup; household survey). From the perspective of the fruit farmers, the actual conditions still seem to be promising, as during a socio-economic household survey conducted in 2012, nearly all of them were optimistic about the future and declared themselves willing to sign up for the next leasing period.

14.3.6.1 Provision of Ecosystem Services to the Citizens of Aksu

Shelterbelts in drylands are generally known to provide vital regulating ecosystem services: they humidify and cool the air by their evapotranspiration; as a natural barrier in the landscape, they slow down wind speeds and thus reduce storm damages; they filtrate dust and sand from the air and deposit it on leaves, twigs, and soil; finally, they fix the soil and protect it from wind erosion (Yimit et al. 2006; Halik 2003; Chokkalingam et al. 2006). Among these, air filtration and soil fixation are of the greatest relevance for Aksu City, as these ecosystem services have the effect of dust and sand storm mitigation, the primary reason for which Kökyar Protection Forest was initiated. The specific extent of the regulating ecosystem services provided by the Kökyar Protection Forest has not been investigated systematically. However, an improvement of the dust and sand storm situation of Aksu City after the establishment of Kökyar Protection Forest is claimed by the Kökyar Annals (Kökyar Annals Compilation Committee 1996) and has been perceived and described by Kökyar farmers (household survey 2012) and Aksu citizens who were randomly interviewed on the streets of Aksu in 2011 (also cf. Halik 2003). Further, the Kökyar Protection Forest is a source of provisioning ecosystem services, especially fruits from the orchards, such as apple, pear, jujube, walnut, and grapes, but also timber, fuel, fodder, and many self-subsistence items.

Finally, the Kökyar Protection Forest provides cultural ecosystem services. Probably induced by the massive participation in obligatory labor, among Aksu citizens there is a widespread personal identification with the Kökyar Protection Forest and a conviction of its usefulness (Aksu street interviews; household survey). Driving into the greenbelt and having a farmer's meal in an orchard environment is a common local recreational activity. Prefectural politics aim to intensify the relationship of the people to the Kökyar Protection Forest by publishing illustrated books and establishing a memorial hall in Kökyar, which is regularly visited by school classes and local tour groups. Both publications and memorial hall charge the Kökyar project with symbolic meanings, such as uniting different ethnicities and social ranks, and creating a positive societal momentum, the so-called Kökyar Spirit. The symbolic value of Kökyar is underscored by its classification as a Patriotic Education Site, Environmental Education Site, and its inclusion in the Global 500 Role of Honour for Environmental Achievement of the United Nations Environmental Programme (Kökyar Annals Compilation Committee 1996, 2006).

14.4 Conclusions

The two examples, community gardening initiatives in Berlin and the Kökyar-shelterbelt forest in Aksu, illustrate the range of approaches to provide key ecosystem services in urban and peri-urban locations. Between these ends lie many possibilities for participatory planning of green spaces, public–private partnerships, mobilization of people through education, and "nudging" people to contribute in one way or another to maintain and increase vegetation in cities. Numerous examples worldwide should also be assessed in a more systematic way.[4]

Although the two case studies in this work are context specific and deeply embedded in their respective socioeconomic reality and institutional frameworks, they provide interesting reference points in at least two ways. First, the greening efforts in both cases are widely recognized by the local people. Both have strengthened the feeling of locality of urban dwellers and identification with a particular urban (respective peri-urban) space. Berlin's urban garden users frequently referred to the "sense of community" offered by taking part in urban gardening initiatives.

In Berlin, urban community gardening is increasingly popular and receives regular media attention. The older *Schrebergärten* has certain parallels to the Chinese case. Schrebergärten areas were initially established with food production in mind. They are structured in small quadratic lots and are subject to more regulations compared with urban gardens, which offer much more leeway for its users. Community gardening is a new form of community action, which fits well into the efforts toward making cities and city living more sustainable. Beyond private ownership, it provides possibilities to act together even in the highly urbanized central parts of the city. As an example of voluntary arrangements, the WikiWoods initiative can mobilize hundreds of people for planting trees on a voluntary basis.

In the case of Aksu, the locals are highly aware of the long-term and intensive greening efforts. Most of the interviewees were confident of the positive effects of greening as regards relieving dust stress. This awareness is partly owing to the accompanying education and propaganda efforts. Meanwhile, the Kökyar Protection Forest is a popular destination for short recreational trips for Aksu citizens, contributing to the immediate experience of nature.

Local farmers, who provide the ecosystem services as a side effect of their economic activity, see a sustainable basis for farming and want to continue with their farming activities in the future. The leasing system operates on a sustainable market-economy basis, without any compensatory payments (payments for ecosystem services, PES). The exhibition hall in the Kökyar greenbelt is a popular destination for school classes and other groups and a manifestation of the joint efforts to increase well-being in the city. A considerable share of Aksu citizens have worked in the area, or know a friend, colleague, or relative who has worked for its establishment.

What works well in Germany does not automatically work well in the Chinese context, and vice versa. Based on the two case studies, we draw four main lessons or strategies for urban planning and urban green space management:

First, public administration needs to recognize the importance of ecosystem services for urban well-being. Awareness of the causal relationships with regard to

[4]For example, Kumasi City in Ghana, previously famous for being a garden city, has a political goal to gain back this status by planting 1 million trees in the next few years. Currently, the city is exploring possibilities for interagency cooperation, school involvement in tree planting, and sponsorship for tree planting activities.

ecosystem services is not always particularly pronounced throughout the city government (Frank 2014). From a systems dynamics perspective, cities and their surrounding rural areas need to become the topic of a careful analysis; water availability, recharging of groundwater, healthy soils, reduction of dust stress, and pollination are essential for human well-being. Global climate change poses additional stresses and risks for the delivery of key ecosystem services.

In the case of Aksu, well-being was directly impacted by heavy dust stress, particularly in spring time, when winds bring small particles from a higher lying plateau. For many other cities, human well-being can be directly linked to temperatures during heat waves; if cities act in a timely manner, they can create green spaces and corridors that reduce the urban heat island effect. Cities should perform systematic assessments of these services, which are highly relevant for human well-being.

Second, planners should give leeway and secure a legal framework for voluntary and community action that aims at increasing the amount and quality of urban green spaces. The urban population is increasingly interested in dedicating time for gardening or for planting trees (cf. WikiWoods). The motives can be a combination of many aspects: sustainable lifestyle, engaging in group activity (friends, family, and neighbors), physical exercise, and aesthetic pleasure, among others. Giving individuals and groups the opportunity to co-create urban green spaces is also in line with the goal of making planning more participatory. In addition, in times where public funds for establishing and managing parks is scarce, voluntary initiatives that contribute to urban greening can cut local government spending. Market-based approaches may complement the range of institutional arrangements. In the case of Aksu, the city created the necessary infrastructure for arable land (irrigation channels, roads), which were then realized by leasing land to small-scale farmers. In an analogy to this, Berlin's Schrebergärten worked in a similar way (initially, food security was a key aspect of such arrangements). The strategy of setting up of a coordination center for urban gardens can also support the gardens' existence, and in turn, achieve ecosystem services contributions, which directly influence human well-being.

Third, cities need to be planned in such way that there is available space for public-, private-, or community-driven urban greenery. In densely built areas (which is ideal for avoiding urban sprawl), vertical structures and rooftops can be used. Former industrial spaces are available in many cities, as in the case of Berlin's Tempelhof Airport. If permanent space cannot be provided, mobile gardening (such as raised beds) is one option to provide people with possibilities to be involved in gardening. Essentially, the provision of such areas requires integrative planning, including transport and traffic. In new cities, urban green spaces can be integrated in the planning from the early phases on.

Fourth, vegetation in urban areas tends to be vastly different from natural vegetation. Artificial (non-natural) vegetation structures can nevertheless provide key ecosystem services. In arid regions, a crucial issue is water consumption. In recent expert elicitations, different trees and shrubs were identified and compared in terms of their water consumption (Frank 2014). In the future, urban vegetation must possess the important features of drought resistance and heat wave mitigation, especially in arid and semi-arid regions. Mimicking natural processes and natural vegetation may provide resilient urban greenery, providing key ecosystem services. Our experimental field research in China within the SuMaRiO project (Rumbaur et al. 2015) addresses the following question: How can key ecosystem services be provided under changing climatic conditions?

Ecosystem services for human well-being can be delivered through different institutional arrangements. Urban planners can increase awareness, commitment, and ownership regarding urban green spaces through encouraging people's initiatives and determining the preferences and expectations of citizens (e.g., through surveys, interviews, focus groups, and various large group methods). Public participation and stakeholder dialogues enable individuals, communities, and households to have a say in issues related to their immediate green environment (cf. Welp et al. 2009). Further, local knowledge on important places and historical structures should be integrated into visions of city development. Awareness of the historical layers reflecting the different epochs of urban development can contribute to feelings of locality and ownership.

In the process of learning by implementing and co-creating urban green spaces, people can become involved in the sustainability transition in cities. In the social learning process, locality can be seen in the context of a global "greening" process, which includes improving well-being locally, such as through urban gardening, without exploiting natural resources from far away. If embedded in a participatory learning process, urban greening can contribute to an increasing awareness on local and global human–nature interactions of urban dwellers.

References

Akesu Shi Renmin Zhengfu (2012) Akesu Shi Qingkuang Jianjie, Akesu Shi Renmin Zhengfu. www.akss.gov.cn/lsyg/405.jhtml. Accessed 20 Feb 2015

Aksu Prefectural Forestry Department and Kuqa Television Station (2006) Lüse zhuangju: jinian Kekeya jianshe 20 nian, Wulumuqi Jitai Keji Youxian Gongsi. Urumqi

Aksu Prefectural Greening Committee (2006) Lüse de Kekeya, Hengyuan Zhonghui Caise Baozhuang Youxian Gongsi. Aksu

Amt fuer Statistik, Berlin-Brandenburg (2013) Statistik Berlin-Brandenburg. www.statistik-berlin-brandenburg.de/home.asp. Accessed 28 June 2014

Berlin 21 (2014) Berlin 21. www.berlin21.net. Accessed 27 June 2014

China National Human Development Report (2013) Sustainable and liveable cities towards ecological civilization

Chokkalingam U, Zhou Z, Wang C, Toma T (2006) Learning lessons from China' s forest rehabilitation efforts. Center for International Forestry Research (CIFOR), Chinese Academy of Forestry Research Institute of Tropical Forestry (RITF), State Forestry Administration Afforestation Department, Jakarta. www.cifor.org/publications/pdf_files/Books/Bchokkalingam0603.pdf. Accessed 20 Feb 20 2015

Delang CO, Yuan Z (2015) China's grain for green program: a review of the largest ecological restoration and rural development program in the world. Springer International Publishing, Cham

Frank S (2014) Expert-based Bayesian Network modeling for environmental management. Dissertation for Doctorate. Frankfurt am Main. Goethe-Universität

Halik Ü (2003) Stadtbegrünung im ariden Milieu: Das Beispiel der Oasenstädte des südlichen Xinjiang/VR China. Technische Universität Berlin, Berlin

Hordijk M (1999) A dream of green and water: community-based formulation of a local agenda 21 in peri-urban Lima, Peru. Environ Urbanization 11(2):11–30

Intercontinental Pan-Chinese Network Information Co. Ltd. (2008) Akesu Shi gaikuang www.chinaxinjiang.cn/xjgk/rkcs/t20080131_320342.htm. Accessed 28 Apr 2013

Interview 1 with Ibrahim Yusup in Urumqi, 15 Oct 2012 (Head of the Kökyar Greening Project Protection Forest Management Station in years 1986–1995)

Kabisch N, Haase D (2014) Green justice or just green? Provision of green spaces in Berlin, Germany. Landscape Urban Plann 112:129–139

Kökyar Annals Compilation Committee (1996) Kekeya lühua gongcheng zhi, Xinjiang Renmin Chubanshe. Urumqi

Kökyar Annals Compilation Committee (2006) Kekeya lühua gongcheng zhi (Oct 1996–May 2006). Urumqi, Xinjiang Renmin Chubanshe

Martin G, Clift R, Christie I, Druckman A (2014) The sustainability contributions of urban agriculture: exploring a community garden and a community farm. LCA Foods 2014. The American Center for Life Cycle Assessment, San Francisco

MEA (2005) Millennium ecosystem assessment 2005. Ecosystems and human well-being: synthesis. Island Press, Washington D.C

Missall S, Welp M, Thevs N, Abliz A, Halik Ü (2015) Establishment and maintenance of regulating ecosystem services in a dryland area of Central Asia: the Kökyar protection forest, Aksu, NW China, as an example. Earth Syst Dyn 6

Mumford M (2002) Social innovation: ten cases from Benjamin Franklin. Creativ Res J 14 (2):253–266

Ostrom E (1990) Governing the commons: the evolution of institutions for collective action. Cambridge University Press, Cambridge

Paproth F, Pietsch C (2011) Tarim Basin, Available at: http://www.sumario.de/image/image_gallery?uuid=75b70ae9-355b-457e-8466-3e0f577d0c77&groupId=10544&t=1303204620940 (last access: 1 July 2015)

Party Committee of Aksu (2012) Aksu yearbook, p 455

Rumbaur C, Thevs N, Disse M, Ahlheim M, Brieden A, Cyffka B, Duethmann D, Feike T, Frör O, Gärtner P, Halik Ü, Hill J, Hinnenthal M, Keilholz P, Kleinschmit B, Krysanova V, Kuba M, Mader S, Menz C, Othmanli H, Pelz S, Schroeder M, Siew TF, Stender V, Stahr K, Thomas FM, Welp M, Wortmann M, Zhao X, Chen X, Jiang T, Luo J, Yimit H, Yu R, Zhang X, Zhao C (2015) Sustainable management of river oases along the Tarim River (SuMaRiO) in Northwest China under conditions of climate change. Earth Syst Dyn 6:83–107

Schug W (2005) Urban agriculture: its impact on the food security of urban population. In: Kracht U, Schulz M (eds) Food and nutrition security in the process of globalization and urbanization. Münster, LIT

Senate Department for Urban Development and the Environment (2013). Berlin Environmental Atlas 06.05: Availability of Public, Near-Residential Green Space., Available at: http://www.stadtentwicklung.berlin.de/umwelt/umweltatlas/eda605_01.htm (last access: June 1, 2015)

L.I.S.T. Stadtentwicklungsgesellschaft mbH Berlin (2011) Handbuch zur Partizipation. Berlin, Senatsverwaltung fuer Stadtentwicklung und Umwelt

United Nations (2014) World urbanization prospects. Department of Economic and Social Affairs, Population Division

Ward N (2015) The case for green space: Berlin's urban gardening initiatives and their contribution to ecosystem services. Master thesis at the Eberswalde University for Sustainable Development (University of Applied Sciences)

Welp M, Kasemir B, Jaeger CC (2009) Citizens' voices in environmental policy: the contribution of integrated assessment focus groups to accountable decision-making. In: Coenen FHJM, Paterson R (eds) Public participation and better environmental decisions: the promise and limits of participatory processes for the quality of environmentally related decision-making. Springer, Netherlands

Wunder S (2013) Learning for sustainable agriculture: urban gardening in Berlin. Ecologic. www.ecologic.eu/de/10307. Accessed 17 Apr 2015

Yimit H, He L, Halik W, Giese E (2006) Water resource development and its environmental effects in the Tarim River floodplain. In: Hoppe T, Kleinschmit B, Roberts B, Thevs N, Halik Ü (eds) Watershed and floodplain management along the Tarim River in China's Arid Northwest. Shaker Verlag, Aachen, pp 91–107

Yoshino M (1992) Wind and rain in the desert region of Xinjiang, Northwest China, Erdkunde. Arch Sci Geogr 46(3/4):203–216

Author Biographies

Prof. Dr. Martin Welp is Chair of Socioeconomics and Communication at the Faculty of Forest and Environment, Eberswalde University for Sustainable Development (University of Applied Sciences).

Ms. Natalie Ward is a graduates of the International Master Study Programme Programme Global Change Management at the Eberswalde University for Sustainable Development.

Mr. Siegmund Missall are graduates of the International Master Study Programme Programme Global Change Management at the Eberswalde University for Sustainable Development.

Mr. Abdulla Abliz is project researcher at the Eberswalde University for Sustainable Development and Ph.D. Student at the Catholic University of Eichstätt-Ingolstadt.

Prof. Dr. Ümüt Halik is professor at the School of Resources and Environmental Science, Xinjiang University and Mercator visiting professor at the Catholic University of Eichstätt-Ingolstadt.

Chapter 15
Research on IMGE^{SB} in Sustainable Building Design Process

Dongzhu Chu and Shuxiang Wei

15.1 Sustainable Building: Integrated Design Generation and Evaluation

Integration Mechanism of Generation-Evaluation for Sustainable Building (IMGE^{SB}), known as Integration Mechanism of Generation-Evaluation, is a design mechanism, with emphasis on the full participation of evaluation concerning sustainable building design, including design generation and evaluation for a synchronous fusion development as well as interactive design principle and model.

Discussion on sustainable building has a long history. As a composite concept derived from sustainable development, sustainable building is not only concerned with the environment, ecology, and resources but also stresses the harmonious coexistence of society, economy, and nature. Sustainable building can be understood as the highest stage of green building (Liu et al. 2010). Sustainability as an existential attitude of building came into being for thousand years (Fig. 15.1), and comprises numerous clever coping strategies (Bill 2007). In essence, the concept of sustainability emphasizes the symbiotic relationship between building, nature, and people, rather than the mechanically measurement of given indicators (Fig. 15.2).

D. Chu (✉) · S. Wei
Faculty of Architecture and Urban Planning, Chongqing University, Chongqing, China
e-mail: c.dz@vip.163.com

F. Wang and M. Prominski (eds.), *Urbanization and Locality*,
DOI 10.1007/978-3-662-48494-4_15

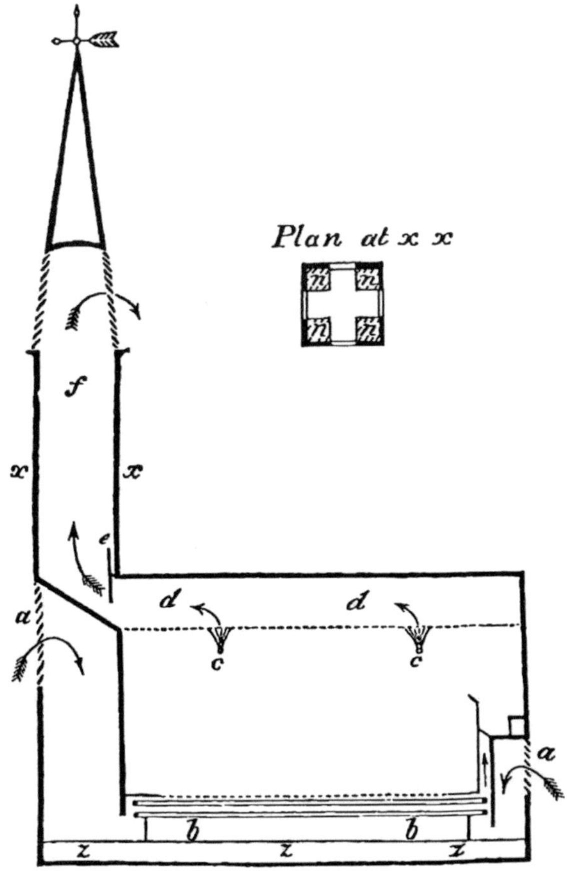

Fig. 15.1 Section of European classical church that shows the natural ventilation system. *Source* Addis (2007). Building: 3000 Years of Design, Engineering and Construction London, 1837 (*Source* Dongzhu chu)

A basic question arises: How is a sustainable building designed (Bax and Trum 2010)? Sustainable building is not an entirely new type of building. Thus, its design methods will naturally be non-disruptive. The level of sustainability can be measured using a more concise concept: sustainable performance.[1] Improving the sustainable performance of design has naturally become the soul of this building design approach (Korkmaz et al. 2010). While reasonably inheriting the traditional design methods and procedures, sustainable building design interprets the building–

[1]The so-called Performance of Sustainability is the "effectiveness and capabilities manifested in various building aspects to support or meet the requirements of sustainable development." Different countries have proposed a variety of indicators in the Green Building Rating System. For example, Japan's Comprehensive Assessment System for Built Environment Efficiency (CASBEE) rating system takes building environmental efficiency (BEE) as the core data. The "Performance of Sustainability" in this research is associated with this system but does not completely overlap. In actual operation, the "Performance of Sustainability" is not an indicator that can be quantitatively compared with a single number, but rather a dynamic system.

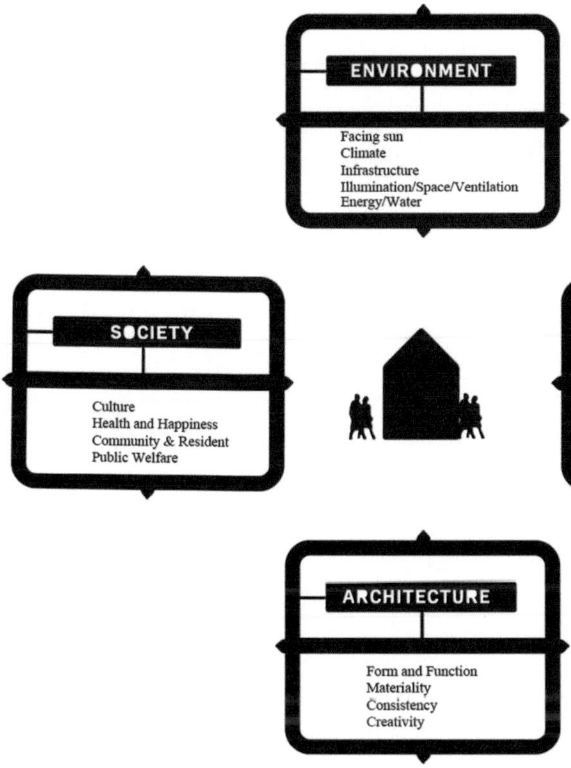

Fig. 15.2 Four factors of sustainable architecture (*Source* Schmidt Hammer Lassen Architects (http://shl.dk/eng/))

nature–people relationship into such specific factors as building, environment, economy, society, and input to build a three-dimensional coordinate system (Fig. 15.3). The level of sustainable performance is specifically embodied in the comprehensive balance of the above factors and applied throughout the life cycle of the building.

The construction of any building stems from the pursuit of a certain value, and consequently, the evaluation is injected into the design process. Performance acts as the other side of value. The two are integrated into design results and constitute a clear interface, associating users and designers together (Fig. 15.4). Value is proposed based on users, that is, the satisfaction degree of the users as regards the building. Simply put, evaluation is a subjective process to find, reveal, and judge the value; value is always connected with evaluation. The subjectivity can be confirmed: the designer cannot fully control how users use and evaluate the buildings; what he/she can control is the performance level in the design outcomes. Although the enhancement of design performance cannot absolutely increase the

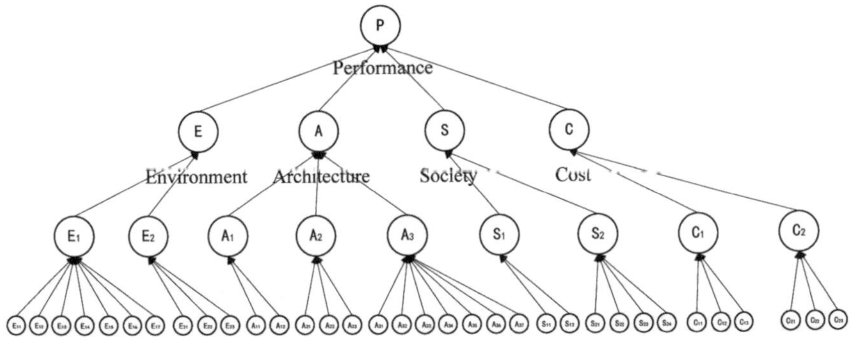

Fig. 15.3 Tree structure of the evaluation index system. E_1 Outdoor environment; E_2 energy; A_1 resources and materials; A_2 infrastructure; A_3 indoor environment; S_1 image and culture; S_2 requirements and value; C_1 efficiency and benefit; C_2 life cycle input (*Source* ©Authors)

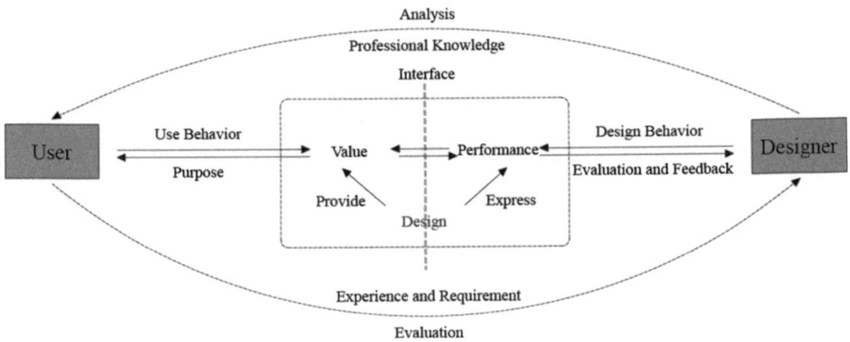

Fig. 15.4 Relationship between designers and users based on design as medium (*Source* ©Authors)

value, the architect must take performance enhancement as an objective and evaluation in the process as a means to enhance the design value.

Proposing the concept of sustainable building leads to the enhancement of requirements for various indicators, and thus promotes the development of a design evaluation method, index system, and aiding tool. With a wide variety of digital-aided design tools, their effective use in the design process has also become an important issue in the context of building that is moving toward sustainability. Therefore, to achieve the sustainability goals of building, evaluation approaches must be rationally and effectively integrated into the design generation process in multiple aspects, from design thinking to design process, to ensure that the evaluation behavior not only has determining force but also brings greater productivity (Thompson 1998; Pearl 2004; Habraken 2010). Therefore, the proposition of the integration of generation and evaluation in sustainable building design is naturally raised.

15.2 Responses: Programming Model of the IMGE^{SB} Ideology

Building design is a process of constant interaction between subjective creation and objective reality, and it is also a coherent and systematic process. Formulating ways and objectives in early, middle, and late stages demonstrate different characteristics. IMGE^{SB}, based on the basic characteristics, divides the design process into four executive modules: Information Importation and Management Module (IIM), Concept Generation and Development Module (CGD), Strategy Test and Optimization Module (STO), and Decision Making and Integration Module (DMI). These four modules are mutually related albeit relatively independent. According to the mode of thinking of the different modules as well as the objective requirements of all levels, the design generation and evaluation methods are organically integrated into one (Table 15.1).

IMGE^{SB} is first manifested as a design ideology, that is, the ideology of integration, dynamics, and timely evaluation in sustainable building design. It is not geared toward subverting the traditional design process. Instead, based on sustainable development objectives and requirements, it is a tool to re-examine the interaction between generation and evaluation in the design process, and to propose paths toward sustainable building design, while adhering to rational design development as the main focus. It emphasizes the role of subjective consciousness and integrates it into the different design stages for analysis, to establish an integrated model based on the individual creative state of architects. Figure 15.5 is a representation of IMGE^{SB}.

Table 15.1 Comparison of the four modules in IMGE^{SB} (*Source* ©Authors)

	IIM	CGD	STO	DMI
Thinking model	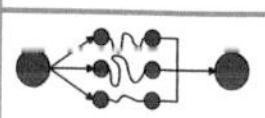	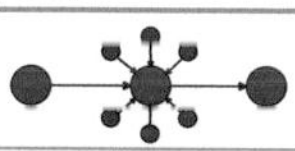	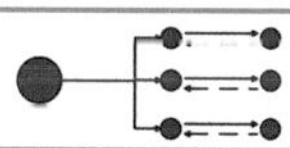	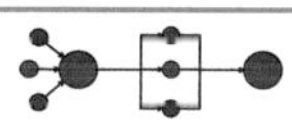
Thinking characteristics	Integration	Qualitative thinking	Quantitative thinking	Integration
Evaluation of characteristics	Preference evaluation	Embedded evaluation	Targeted evaluation	Diversity evaluation
Key means	• Architect experience • Architect personality • Mathematical statistics	• Architect experience • Architect personality • Precedent research	• Performance simulation • Mathematical statistics	• Digital tools • Architect experience • Architect personality
Stage results	Accurate position of sustainable performance targets	Choose the best program	Optimize contents	Performance maximization program

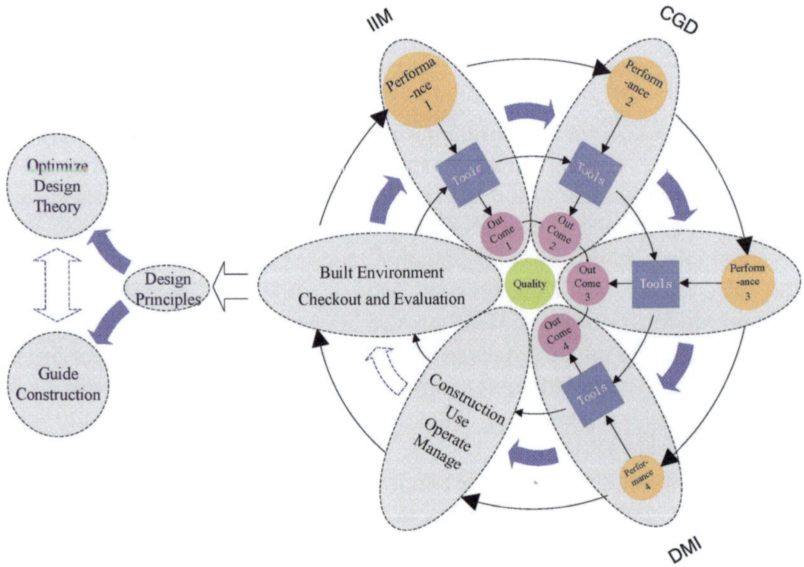

Fig. 15.5 IMGE^{SB} design framework (*Source* ©Authors)

In the model of IMGE^{SB}, the location and timing of "positioning" and "target" in the design process are given with a more detailed expression. According to the rational requirements of sustainable building, the default positioning and target based on the designers' experience need a more rational evaluation in the initial design stage; that is, a more accurate and appropriate improvement through the planning analysis stage (Fig. 15.6).

Different stages of the design process in shall involve evaluation at different depths. The early-stage evaluation system is relatively vague and macro, but gradually becomes concrete and specific in the middle and late stages. In the final design stage, the initiative of the designers must play a dominant role in the evaluation methods; partial evaluation results must be integrated to return to the basic issues of the building, that is, the comprehensive treatment of function, space, form, and the resulting psychological perception. Several important but implicit key issues are encompassed by the IMGE^{SB} model, such as sustainable performance objectives, design specifications, and design tools. These three elements are involved in the process of design and play an important role in the development and quality of the design: the "objectives" lead the ultimate direction of design, in which "specifications" and "tools" are like the two wings of the design process, providing both the development path of design and promotion of the design process.

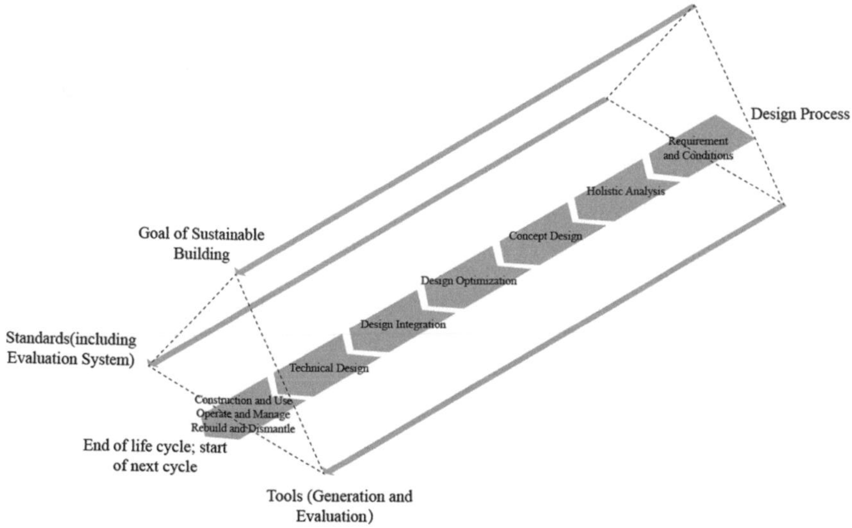

Fig. 15.6 Important and implicit key issues in the IMGE^{SB} model (*Source* ©Authors)

15.3 Experiments: IMGE^{SB} Model Application in a Sustainable Building Design

Aiming at a summary and optimization of the theoretical study, the author experimentally applied it to the design project of Chengdu Cold-Chain Logistics Warehouse.

15.3.1 Project Overview and Design Starting Point

The project base is located in Qingbaijiang Logistics Park, Chengdu, and will serve as the corporate headquarters of the owner, including the office, food inspection center, drivers' apartments, banks, and other functions, with a total construction area of 9422 m^2. In the east are the trading and residential areas. The cold storage and truck parking areas are in the south, whereas urban roads are found in the west and north (Fig. 15.7). In this project, the demand is mainly from the government and the owner. In addition to high quality, the project should also reflect the characteristics of the owner and the entire industrial park; and conditions contain many factors related to the design, ranging from the urban layout, regional architecture culture, and environmental climate, to the surrounding environment.

As one of the key factors determining the design direction, the professional attitude and design interest of the designer play an essential role in the subjective control of the direction of design development. The design team must strive to

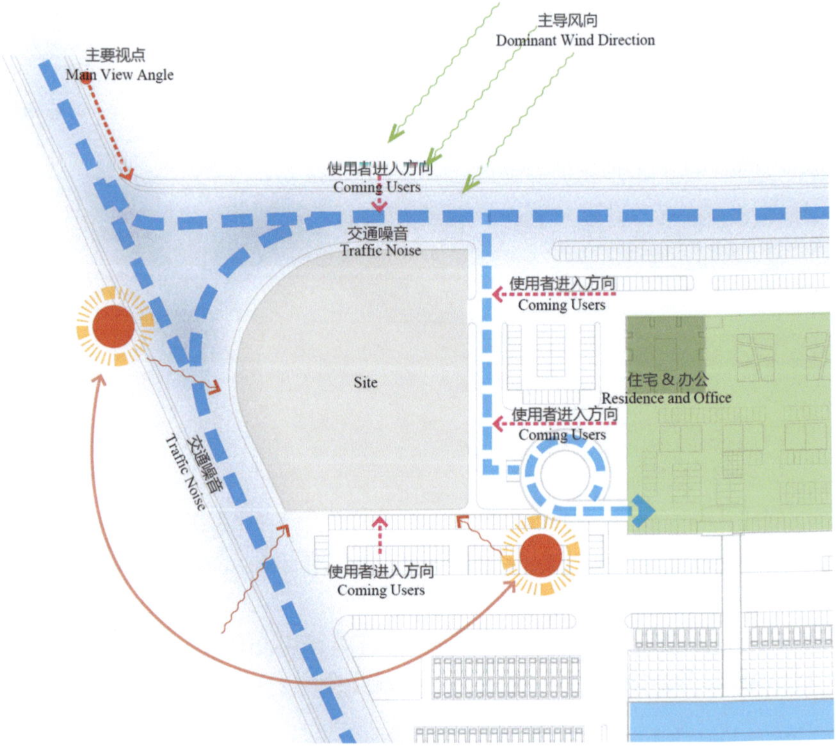

Fig. 15.7 Site layout (*Source* ©Authors)

demonstrate through the design the pursuit for the common interests of sustainability and spatial quality. The proposed building should adhere to a simple, fresh, and modern style, and not blindly following the so-called exotic trend, while putting a high degree of emphasis on the comfort and practicality as well as basing the building quality on green ecological measures.

In the design, the mastery of basic information is only a necessary but not sufficient condition of the design; it cannot logically achieve satisfactory design results. In other words, it cannot establish the simple "investigation → analysis → conclusion" logical model. The common roles of Demand, Conditions, Designer, and Precedent have become common catalysts in the initial design stage.

15.3.2 Implementation Steps

Based on the IMGE^{SB} model, concrete design steps are in accordance with the four program modules, summarized as follows:

1. ***Information importation and management***

Under the overall objective of sustainable development, indicators such as energy conservation and low carbon production do not serve as the fundamental purpose of building construction. While satisfying such technical performance indicators, building construction should denote an exploration of perceived quality from a human-oriented perspective (Akin 1986). Indeed, construction should serve as an important approach in response to long-term sustainability (Christopher et al. 2009). Research frameworks in building design are gradually shifting from technical to spiritual perceptive in nature (Chu 2012).

At this stage, access to as much related information as possible should be secured. With repeated evaluation, value judgments and an orderly organization of information should be undertaken. Specifically, based on the evaluation, information that will affect sustainable performance needs to be integrated and matched with the developed sustainability objectives, to establish the primary performance objectives and design basis positioning (Wei 2013).

After completion of the design for the experiment process, the architecture team posed the following questions in consideration of the basic knowledge during the experiment:

(1) What are the climate characteristics in the Chengdu Plain?
(2) What is the perimeter environment?
(3) What is the social environment in Chengdu?
(4) What are the needs of the owner?
(5) What are the needs of the government?
(6) What are the needs of different users, respectively?

The design team collected information through multiple channels: (1) several rounds of interviews with the owner before sorting and documenting the records; (2) observation of the surrounding environment to gain in-depth understanding and then embody the urban environment for the purpose of integrating the urban culture into the building while investigating the courtyard spaces with distinctive characteristics in the Chengdu Plain; and (3) use of Cadna\A, Winair, Ecotect, and other simulation software to obtain preliminary information on the local climate and surrounding environment. NVivo is used for the preliminary analysis of the aforesaid information before the needs of the owner and main basic conditions could be summarized (Fig. 15.8).

Playing a leading role in the entire sustainable building design process, architects have to start out from macro design ideas to handle the implementation of the process. In addition, scientific and rational views are explored to look into the development of the computer information technology. Meanwhile, the practical features of the project are taken into consideration for the selection of and reference to the advantageous software used in other disciplines to deal with problems encountered during the design process.

Most of the information management work is carried out simultaneously with data collection. During the data analysis stage, information imported to the NVivo

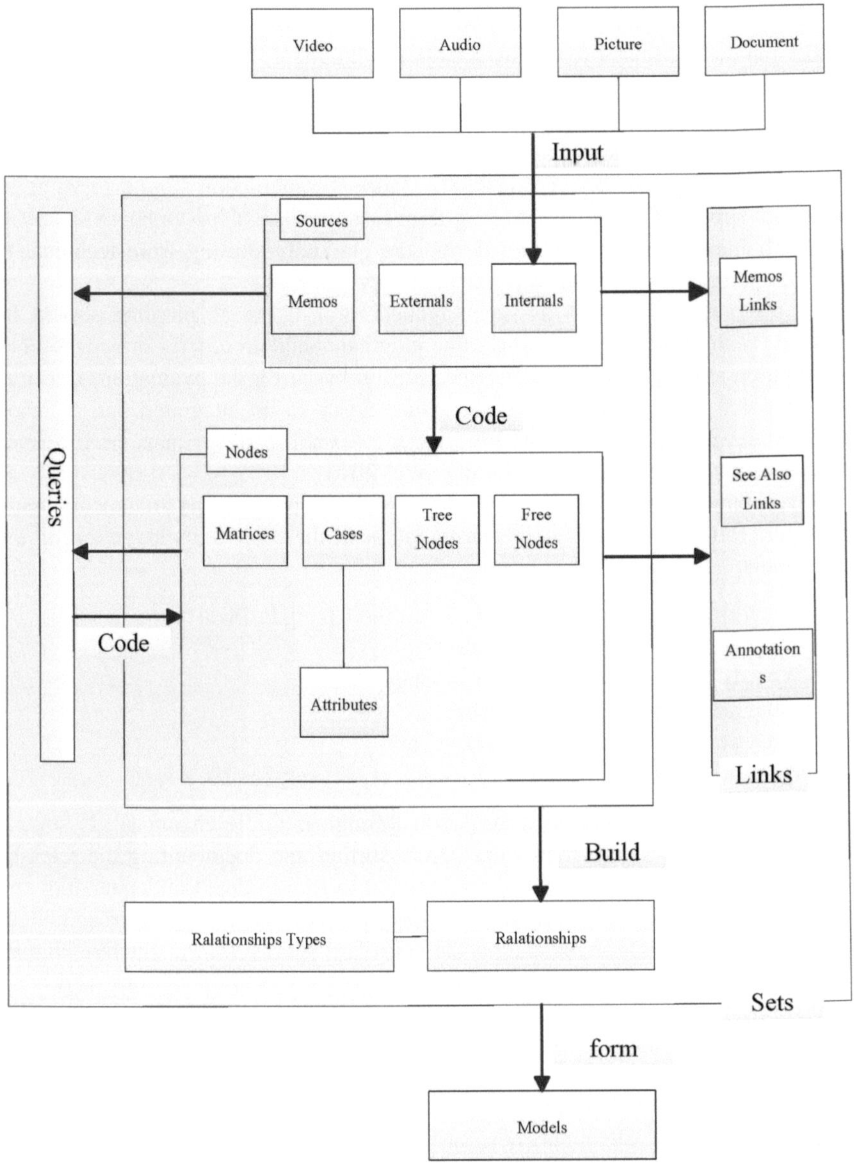

Fig. 15.8 Process of analysis in NVivo (*Source* ©Authors)

original database is duly considered with their sources to understand further the design conditions and demands and thus lay a solid foundation for the next steps. Codes are stored in nodes. The original sources of encoded paragraphs are then made available. In accordance with the principles of the organizational tree node proposed by Richards, and accounting for the current experiment as well as core concept of Human–Architecture–Environment in sustainable building design process, the codes are classified into four categories in structuring the tree node: human, building, environment, and economy. If free nodes and tree nodes are treated as Level 1 codes, the relation node becomes the Level 2 code. After completion of tree node encoding, the relationship between these nodes are treated. This experiment takes the request as the relation node to set up the relation model that reflects the requirements of the building, environment, economy, and human, as in Fig. 15.9, which serves as the most critical part of the experiment. In NVivo8, conditioned code query is generally used for triangular validation. The design team conducted triangulation between the interview draft and documents to seek

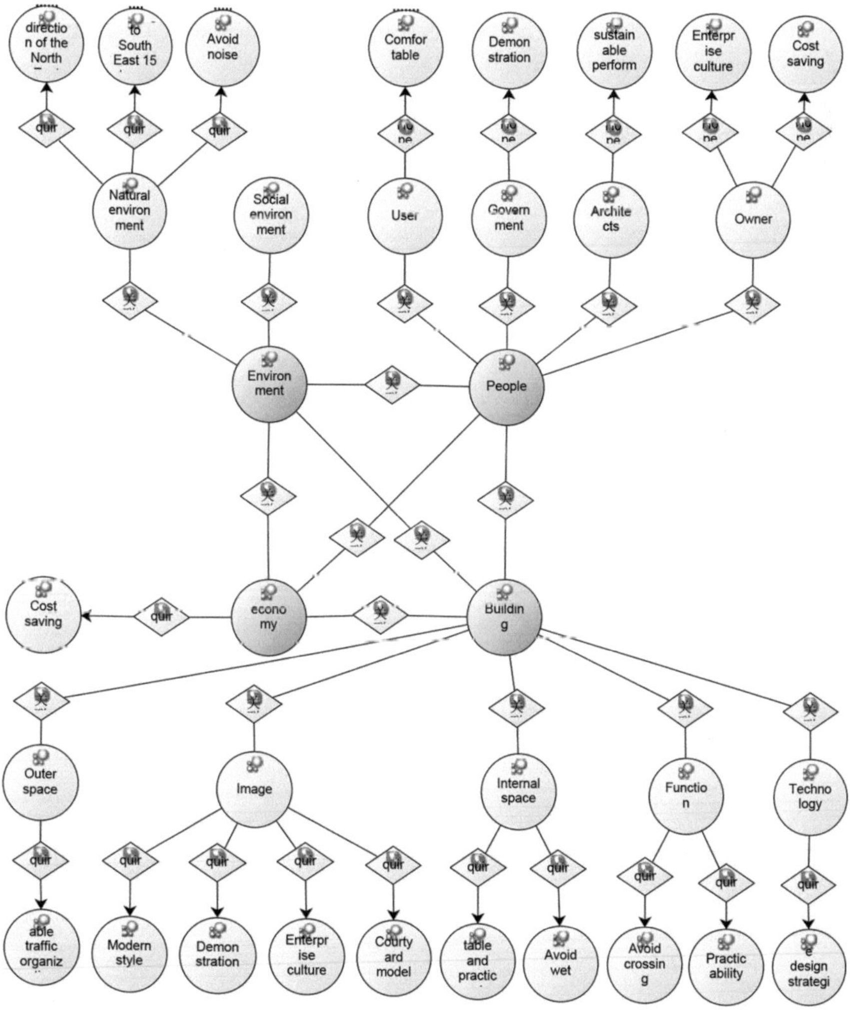

Fig. 15.9 Relationship model. *Source* Working interface of NVivo (*Source* ©Authors)

overlapping between the interview draft and observations or ideas of the architects. The final validation results confirm the effectiveness of the relation model. In contrast with traditional qualitative analysis, the qualitative analysis results from sustainable building design process can only clearly lay down the results with guiding significance based on specific requirements. The relation model set up in this experiment serves as the qualitative sustainable building design strategies from four levels, namely, human, architecture, environment, and economy (Fig. 15.9).

2. ***Concept generation and development***

The concept generation stage in the design generation process is the most difficult to describe. It is related to both the characteristics of the designer's thinking and design condition analysis. At this stage, evaluation is involved in the design generation in implicit and multiple ways, including image detection of the accuracy of the process design and building design.

Based on the study of local culture, urban patterns, and industrial features, this project follows three design directions (Fig. 15.10). Under the premise of maintaining communication with the owner, the design team selected an optimal

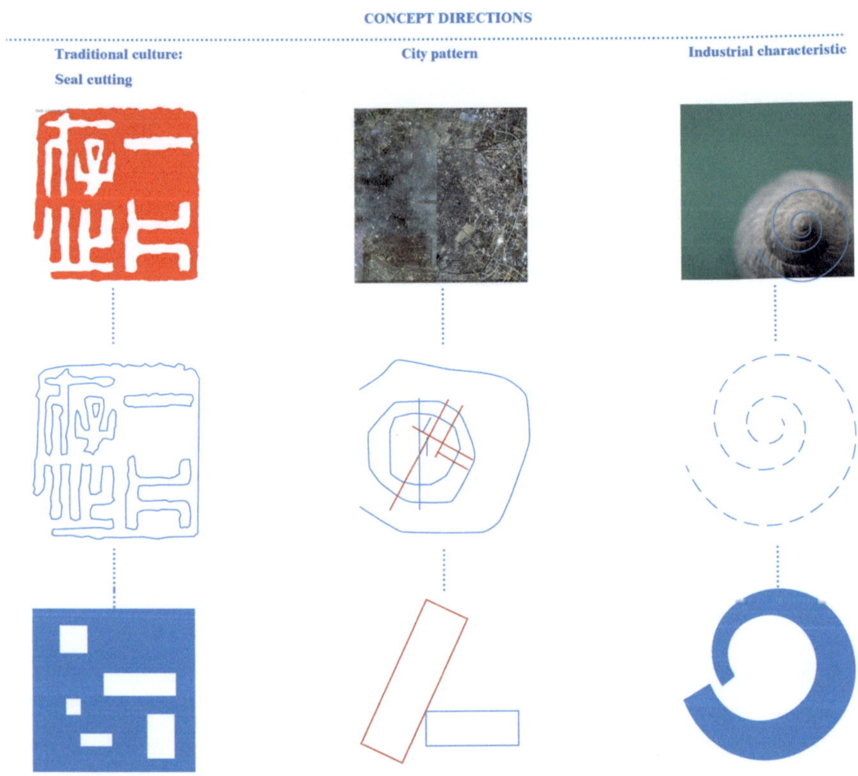

Fig. 15.10 Three different ideas from three inspirations (*Source* ©Authors)

solution through analytic hierarchy, in which the first direction based on traditional culture was chosen as the optimal program.

The basic objective of the program is to create a quiet office space in a noisy environment. Specifically, it takes the form of a courtyard. Based on this requirement, the design team establishes a simple design concept following the principle of high sustainable performance to create a comfortable working environment that features energy efficiency and low-carbon emission, while focusing on enterprise culture. The program applies the minus approach in the traditional stone carving culture to evoke space experiences by contrasting the real and the imaginary. To improve the relevance of the performance optimization module, the designer filters the sustainable strategy of the optimal solution, and then adjusts and optimizes it (Figs. 15.11 and 15.12).

3. ***Strategy test and optimization***

Based on the overall sustainable objectives, the designer at this stage changes the design method based on the experience and stresses the comprehensive qualitative and quantitative evaluation of the object in physiological, psychological, social, and cultural terms. The designer is concerned with the relations between the time and space of phenomena and cultural historical context.

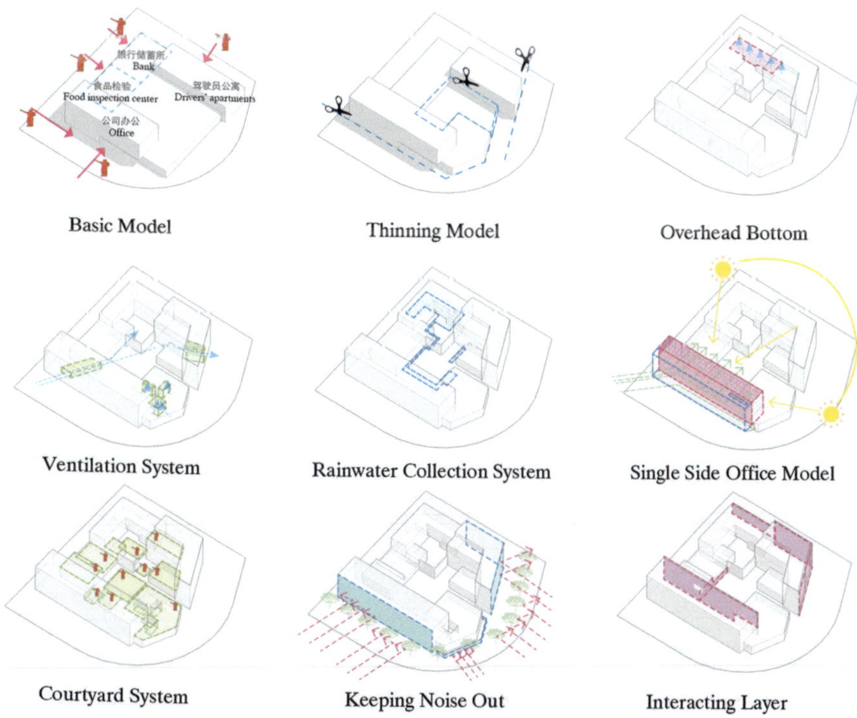

Fig. 15.11 Space design based on sustainability goals (*Source* ©Authors)

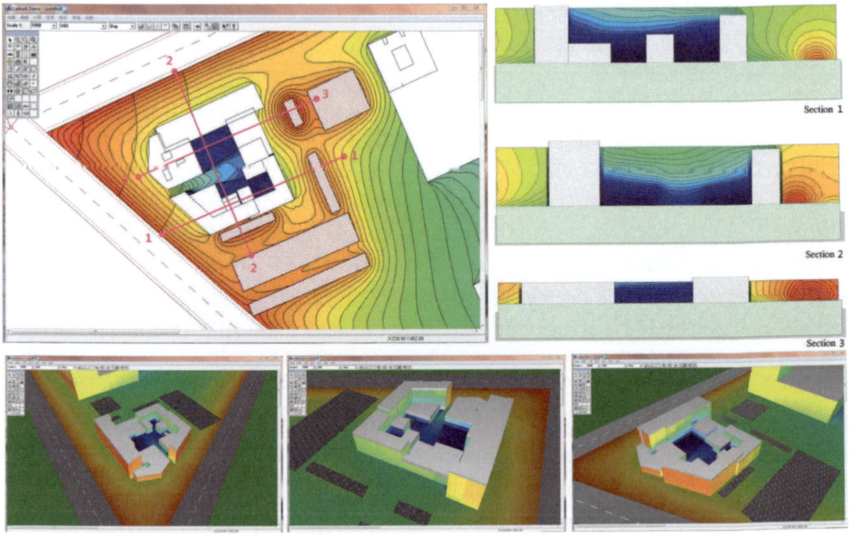

Fig. 15.12 Noise analysis by software Cadna\A (*Source* ©Authors)

Progressing in the design process, the building increasingly grows toward a complete and inseparable whole. Although the module is targeted at partial issues, the designer cannot blindly pursue the high performance of an evaluation factor; the relevant factors should be considered as a whole. The openness of the courtyard in this case will have an impact on the wind and acoustic environment. To block traffic noises, an external structure is used in the concept generation stage to establish a synthetic shield, thereby creating a quiet environment within a space. Therefore, in this module, the architect uses Winair and Cadna\A software to conduct a reciprocating evaluation simulation on the wind and sound environment, to balance the requirements of the building for natural ventilation and quiet environment (Fig. 15.13).

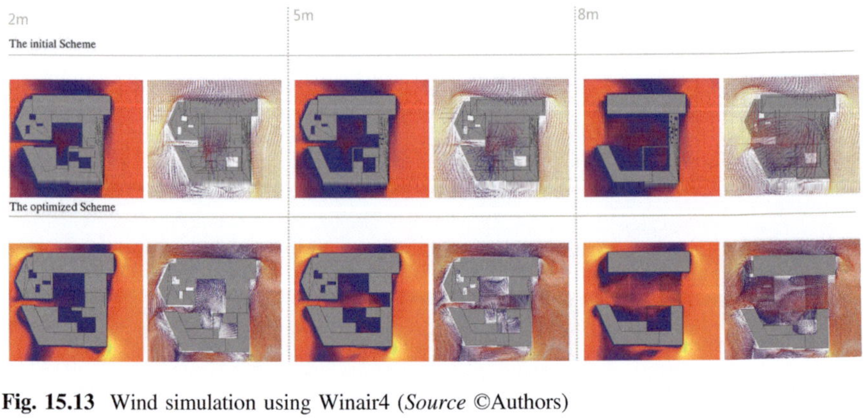

Fig. 15.13 Wind simulation using Winair4 (*Source* ©Authors)

After performance optimization, the outcome of the optimization needs to be evaluated to verify the optimization results. The experiment uses the hierarchy analytic process and fuzzy analysis method for the evaluation. The results indicate that the sustainable performance of the building has been improved significantly.

4. ***Decision making and integration***

This module requires the architect to have a high level of overall control as well as spirit of self-testing. Comprehensive decision making allows for maximum efficiency through the integration of different perspectives and information.

In the concept generation module, the development of the building toward the direction of the multi-courtyard is determined, and in the next module, complex problems related to the courtyard occur: the room facing the courtyard should have large windows as much as possible to allow users to appreciate the landscape of the entire courtyard. If the room facing the west has large windows, additional measures must be taken for shading, which does not meet the sustainable concept. Therefore, in the integrated decision-making stage, the designer, from a macro perspective, makes an integrated adjustment of many elements that produce contradictions through sustainable strategy in the design process (Fig. 15.14), and ultimately enhances the building's integrated sustainable performance. This procedure also reflects the game feature of IMGE^{SB}.

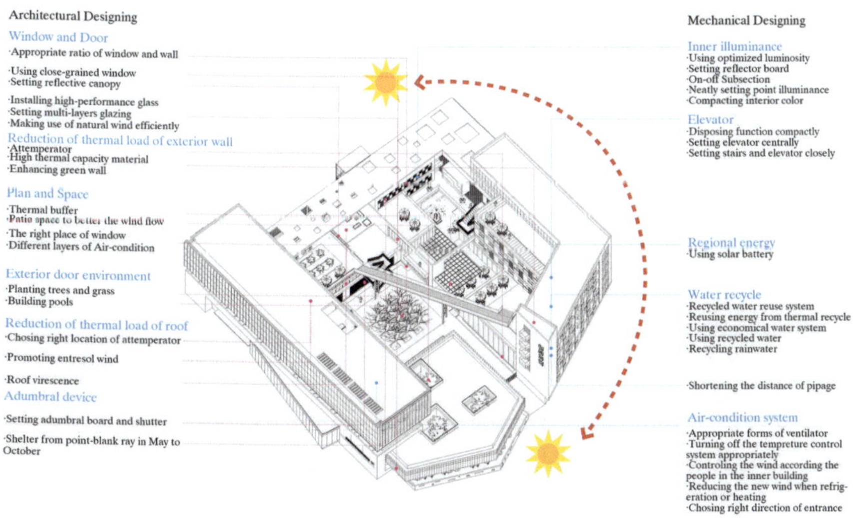

Fig. 15.14 Sustainable basic strategy summary (*Source* ©Authors)

15.3.3 IMGE^{SB} Application Summary

The above design experiments further define the design process based on IMGE^{SB} and feedback, thereby providing corrections to theoretical studies. The following key concepts need urgent attention: (1) IMGE^{SB} is manifested as a design idea in practice rather than a set of rigid rules; (2) IMGE^{SB} puts emphasis on the organic combination of the rational and emotional in practice; (3) IMGE^{SB} in practice needs to focus closely on the objective of sustainable performance and the possibility of flexible amendment; (4) IMGE^{SB} in practice needs to address the successive relationship between modules and strengthen the self-examination and inspection of the design results; and (5) IMGE^{SB} needs strong emphasis on the game and coupling features of sustainable elements.

15.4 Power of the Process

IMGE^{SB} is one of a number of ways for exploring sustainable (green) building design. It is designed to regard evaluation as an important and dominant tool in the design process to achieve more high-quality design performance, and ultimately enhance the value needed by users. Sustainability is integrated and dynamic, and rigid rules cannot be used to restrict the design, but the overall objective is clear. Exploration of the design process helps in determining the path of realization of the building and also identifies the building's ultimate level of quality. Of course, process is neither a master key nor an abstract concept. It is a collection of all relevant elements related to the design generation path. The strength of the design process is an action map for exploring sustainable building design theories and methods.

The generation of building quality is a general mobilization from thought to action. Additional local methods cannot be used easily to solve problems, and this generation process cannot achieve warm welcome in one place at the expense of icy reception in others. The connotation of sustainable building is adjusted with changes in time and space, and enhances as much as possible the ability to meet the various requirements of human beings under reasonable restrictions agreement, which may be understood as a moderate quality (Fig. 15.15). Studies on sustainable building (design) generation are geared toward achieving better quality. Humankind has no way to return to the age when people dressed simply and crudely, although the energy consumption of buildings at the time was almost zero.

IMGE^{SB} as a way of moving toward sustainable building design can solve a number of current problems. However, true to the essence of sustainability, the design method itself must also be sustainable. Under the framework of mechanics and rules, a richer and more flexible approach is required to suit the local conditions. This study intended to offer such an attempt.

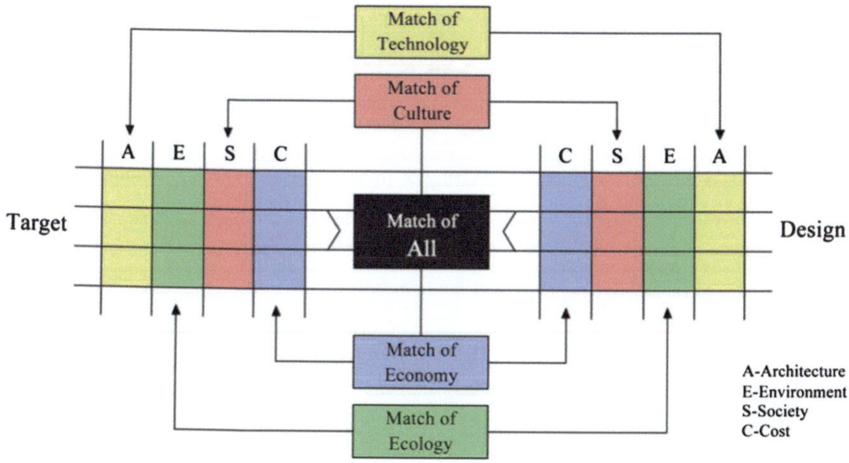

Fig. 15.15 IMGE^{SB} model's integrated view (*Source* ©Authors)

Acknowledgment This article is supported by the National Natural Science Foundation of China (Grant No. 51478055) and the Foundation and Frontier Research Project of Chongqing (Grant No. cstc2015jcyjA00047)

References

Addis B (2007) Building: 3000 years of design, engineering and construction. Phaidon Press, Vienna

Akin O (1986) Psychology of architectural design. Pion, London

Bax T, Trum H (2010) A building design process model: according to domain theory. In: Design research in the Netherlands, pp 19–30

Christopher SM, Sinem K, Leidy EK, David RR (2009) A design process evaluation method for sustainable buildings. Archit Eng Des Manag 5:62–74

Chu DZ (2012) A study of integrated mechanism of generation-evaluation in sustainable building design process. Dissertation for Doctorate. Chong Qing University, Chong Qing (in Chinese)

Habraken NJ (2010) Methods, metaphors, and tools: research in support of design the thematic approach. In: Design research in the Netherlands. Eindhoven, pp 11–14

Korkmaz S, Messner IJ, Riley RD, Magent C (2010) High-performance green building design process modeling and integrated use of visualization tools. J Archit Eng 3:37–45

Liu J, Dong L, Sun S (2010) An introduction to green building. China Architecture & Building Press, Beijing (in Chinese)

Pearl D (2004) An integrated design process (IDP). Can Archit 49(6):32–35

Thompson A (1998) Architectural design procedures, 2nd edn. Architectural Press, Oxford

Wei SX (2013) Study and application of qualitative evaluation in building design process. Dissertation for Doctorate. Chong Qing University, Chong Qing (in Chinese)

Author Biographies

Dr. Dongzhu Chu is Professor in doctoral supervisor of Faculty of Architecture and Urban Planning, Chongqing University and a registered urban architect.

Mr. Shuxiang Wei is Ph.D. candidate of Faculty of Architecture and Urban Planning, Chongqing University.

Chapter 16
Locality as Co-production of Common Ground: Urban Interventions by the Academy of a New Gropiusstadt

Jörg Stollmann

This study reflects upon our chair's activities in cooperative research and design since 2011 in Gropiusstadt, a modernist mass housing development in the south of Berlin. The Academy of a New Gropiusstadt (AnG) is an academic trans-disciplinary laboratory, in which policymakers, local authorities, owners, and residents discuss and negotiate future urban developments of the settlement. The AnG functions as a platform for temporary and long-term projects. Housing agencies and public authorities aim at an improvement of the conditions and the "image" of Gropiusstadt. As planners and researchers, we aim at an understanding of the everyday reality of the place. Mass housing settlements have created specific localities over time, defined by buildings, vegetation, animals, and people. These localities are lived realities for the inhabitants but hardly recognized by planners and officials.

Gropiusstadt is a mono-functional settlement with a population of 36,000. Originally conceived by Walter Gropius and his office, The Architects' Collaborative (TAC), in the early 1960s, it was predominantly financed by the federal social housing program. Since the early 1990s, the increasing retreat of the public sector in housing provision and maintenance of public spaces challenges the spatial as well as social cohesion in those developments. Being prone to a similar process renders Gropiusstadt an exemplary case study. In a series of consecutive and parallel projects, we attempted to test the settlement's current and future potential for socially and environmentally sustainable development. By means of urban interventions, the AnG aimed at redefining and fostering a common agency to accept and negotiate conflicting agenda. Partly a story of failure, partly of success, this quest of a new common ground is rooted in the specific locality of the place. In strengthening modes of co-production with the inhabitants, the AnG aims at redefining popular architecture.

J. Stollmann (✉)
Institute for Architecture, Technische Universität Berlin, Berlin, Germany
e-mail: joerg.stollmann@tu-berlin.de

F. Wang and M. Prominski (eds.), *Urbanization and Locality*,
DOI 10.1007/978-3-662-48494-4_16

16.1 Popular Architecture

In the German planning discourse, mass housing settlements constitute a puzzling challenge. Although late modernism is increasingly fancied in youth culture and the arts, architects and urban designers have a difficult time designing and intervening in the existing modernist settlements.[1] Their landscaped urbanity, large-scale housing typologies, and open spaces, as well as the corresponding design principles, differ substantially from current planning and design practices. They represent a design culture that has been lost as it was made responsible for social decay and urban crisis. Critiques on modernist mass housing schemes have been voiced since the 1970s, especially focusing on segregation, including the ghettoization of the urban poor, which was caused by the state's social rent policies. Nonetheless, these late modernist settlements constitute the living conditions of a large number of residents. Gradually, the inhabitants have changed. At present, they come from diverse ethnic and cultural backgrounds and form a user group difficult to grasp as a whole. However, they are definitely challenging the bourgeois middle-class ideals, which form the cultural background of most design professionals. Thus, in education as well as in practice, there is plenty to learn about who actually lives in mass housing settlements in the first place, which everyday routines and practices make up the good life within them, and what the spatial, economic, and ecological qualities are in reality. Such a re-evaluation seems especially relevant in the context of current discourses on climate-adapted and energy-efficient urban design. Mass housing settlements provide small, space-saving apartments, and large unsealed open surfaces. As their proprietors operate a respectable number of buildings, energetic optimization measures can be implemented efficiently. Thus, rehabilitating this late modernist heritage seems worthwhile. To do so, the gap between the residents' everyday lives and professional designer's inadequate knowledge about them has to be bridged, an endeavor the AnG, as an academic laboratory, wants to take on.

With the decline of the German welfare state, which provided for affordable rents since WWII, only few states remain able to afford social housing programs. Rent controls on subsidized housing stock are terminated, and entire neighborhoods have been privatized and are now part of the portfolio of profit-oriented real estate companies. This scenario is not only a challenge to the individual in terms of increasing rents but also to the settlement as a whole, as it affects the maintenance of community facilities, common spaces in and around the buildings, and shared open spaces; that is, the visible manifestation of a common ground. In critical areas, the state program SozialeStadt[2] (Social City) finances local neighborhood

---

[1]For a closer inspection of the rising popularity of late modern architecture in youth culture and the arts, see Harnack (2012).

[2]The program "SozialeStadt" was introduced in 1999 by the German federal government to support urban development in socially or economically weaker city quarters. Aiming at better social cohesion, the program comprises a wide range of measures and instruments: urban, open space, and infrastructure improvement and the support of a large number of small- to middle-scale

managements, but these operate with short-term financial support initiating small-scale projects that hardly have a chance to enjoy a long-term run. As architects and urban designers, our clients are the administration and the property owners. As an entire culture of provisioning has been erased from our society, we have to extend our professional agenda in research and practice. How far can the inhabitants of mass housing settlements be recognized as responsible and empowered co-producers of the city? Which type of governance ensures the required planning security to both the public and the private companies?

This co-production is a negotiation of power. According to Chantal Mouffe's understanding of democracy, a society is defined on the basis of how agonistic interests are continuously fought about and negotiated. To do so, a common ground on which to fight is a prerequisite.[3] Translated to planning and design, this means that we cannot easily replace the former consensus or common sense of the welfare state with another consensus between civil society, state, and private sector. Instead, we will have to accept that a dynamic struggle for power will have to be orchestrated in the field of urban design, and that to advocate for the weaker parties in the struggle, the designer has to develop an agency supporting the economically and politically weak without patronizing them. This agency permeates our activities within the AnG, and admittedly, all participants have to learn via trial and error. While designers and planners negotiate a battlefield of conflicting interests and propose strategic solutions, the inhabitants navigate differently. They operate, consciously or unconsciously, via tactics, using and misusing spaces. Translating Michel de Certeau's reading of cultures of ordinary language to the culture of living in mass housing, we want to suggest that a popular use of the existing Gropiusstadt has modified its functioning largely below the radar of both planners and owners.[4] While carefully assessing whether to make these everyday practices public, gaining

(Footnote 2 continued)

neighborhood projects on social integration. In 2014, state funds have more than tripled from 40 M Euro in 2013 to 150 M. Further information is available on the government website: www.staedtebaufoerderung.info/StBauF/DE/Programm/SozialeStadt.

[3]With her concept of agonistic democracy, Mouffe argues against the democratic models of deliberation based on information and conciliating participation, and instead introduces conflict as a basis of democratic decision making. Still, political fighting has to be based on a shared common ground (economy, culture, etc.), as she explains in the case of her reading of the European Union: "DamiteinesolchekonfliktäreKonfrontationstattfindenkann, muss eszwischen den europäischen-Bürgernallerdingsetwas 'Gemeinsames' geben, was den Rahmen des 'konflikthaftenKonsens' absteckenkann, der füreineagonistischeKonfrontationVorbedingungist." (Mouffe 2014, Chap. 3, Sect. 5, paragraph 4).

[4]This understanding of "popular" is closely related to Michel de Certeau's understanding of popular culture and his reading of tactics employed in everyday life to subvert a dominant order: "More generally, a *way of using* imposed systems constitutes the resistance to the historical law of a state of affairs and its dogmatic legitimations. A practice of the order constructed by others redistributes its space; it creates at least a certain play in that order, a space for maneuvers of unequal forces and for utopian points of reference. That is where the opacity of a "popular" culture could be said to manifest itself: a dark rock that resists all assimilation." (de Certeau 1988, Kindle file, Chap. 2, Sect. 2, paragraph 6).

knowledge on these forms of use is the basis of an alternative development of mass housing neighborhoods: a truly popular architecture and urban design. Planners and designers have to acknowledge existing strategies and tactics to understand how locality is not an "image" but the result of (lucid or clandestine) appropriation and co-production processes. Further, conflicting agenda are at stake. Especially within fast urbanization processes, where in general very little attention is laid on inhabitants' participation, the only way to create locality and a sense of belonging lies in the engagements in popular production for and with the inhabitants. Popular architecture is one that is produced according to the needs and desires of the people as well as with their active engagement.

16.2 Planning History of Gropiusstadt

In 1959, Walter Gropius' TAC was commissioned with the overall design for a large-scale housing settlement called Berlin-Britz-Buckow-Rudow. The first TAC plan, clearly alluded to the model of the Horseshoe Estate (*Hufeisensiedlung*) by Bruno Taut, Martin Wagner, and Leberecht Migge, 1925–1933. In reference to the curved layout of the Horseshoe Estate's central open space around a pond, the TAC plan provided 12 green open spaces, framed by circular apartment buildings. In addition to the three commercial zones, those open spaces were denominated as serving and defining 12 specific neighborhoods within the settlement. The other linear apartment blocks followed the main streets in orientation and defined open courtyards in between. This articulate definition of open spaces supporting neighborhood building was a major quality of the original urban design.

For various reasons, the final layout moved away substantially from this spatial concept.[5] Berlin planning authorities and TAC's local representative Professor Wils Ebert advocated a functional orientation of the building blocks in strict North-South or East-West orientation, independent from the major street layout. The circular open spaces were reduced to one. The settlement's open space concept changed toward a single, continuous landscape. The overall landscape design guidelines were developed by Walter Rossow, who structured the extensive spatial continuum via topographical modulations, a geometric path layout, and associations of trees. The erection of the Wall in 1961 made the Berlin Senate aware of the limited spatial resources in West Berlin and in the mid-1960s, the general planning paradigm shifted to "Urbanity through Density" (*Urbanität durch Dichte*). Building heights were raised, and towers and large housing blocks were introduced. Finally, the settlement comprised 19,000 units instead of the originally planned 14,500, reaching a density of roughly 14,000 residents per square kilometer. Each housing company commissioned their own architects, resulting in a high variety of building

[5]The detailed planning and building history of Gropiusstadt is well documented in Bandel and Machule (1974).

types and designs. Although Gropiusstadt can claim to be an outstanding example of a modernist landscaped mass housing settlement, Walter Gropius repeatedly voiced critique to the alterations to TAC's original design intentions remains valid: the lack of identifiable small-scale neighborhoods within the large-scale settlement is one of the major drawbacks of Gropiusstadt.[6]

16.3 Academic Urban Interventions

Current and historical examples of urban interventions in academic learning and teaching range from projects of community-based planning to DIY projects, and even artistic interventions in urban spaces. All these projects have a common denominator: they are in close contact with the local users and producers of space; they explore modes of cooperative research, design, and production; and they aim at redefining academic education. Currently, this approach is met by a surprisingly supportive response from German local authorities, even if it often remains rhetoric. Although projects are highlighted as exemplary, the governance sector is missing the adequate tools and regulations to support them. In recent years, there has been a continuous rise in the number of initiatives and publications evaluating a huge variety of projects, their methodology, and outcomes.[7] Discussing our experiences within the framework of the AnG, I want to illustrate how our Chair for Urban Design and Urbanization at the Technical University Berlin, in cooperation with other chairs, students, experts, users, and designers, employs spatial interventions as part of a research agenda on everyday life, conflicts, and common ground in mass housing settlements.

Teaching urban design is an increasingly complex task. On the one hand, we have to pass the technical, historical, and creative basic knowledge to our students. On the other hand, we have to anchor an interdisciplinary manner of learning and teaching in cooperation with partners from civil society, politics, and the economy as part of our academic work. This requirement especially applies in our understanding of urban design as a platform for negotiating future forms of urban life and society. Cooperating with actual stakeholders demands great efforts from all parties

[6]I do not go deeper into the media reports of Gropiusstadt as a hotspot of social deprivation. The 1981 biographical novel *Christiane F.: Wir Kinder vom Bahnhof Zoo* describing a girl's unhappy childhood and her later struggle with heavy drug addiction has coined Gropiusstadt's image. This image of the settlement does not correspond to the inhabitants' perspective today. Parts of Gropiusstadt have a rate of unemployment and state-benefit recipients above average, but in general, Gropiusstadt is a sought-after housing destination without noticeable dramatic social indicators.

[7]Parts of this essay were first published in Transforming Cities. Urban Interventions in Public Space. This publication encompasses a broad range of permanent or temporary projects in the urban space as a contribution to a more sustainable development. The 47 European projects are contributions to the Urban Intervention Award Berlin, an award offered by the Berlin Senate in 2010 and 2013. For further readings, see Feireiss et al. (2015).

involved. A precise formulation of the task given by the clients would be as desirable as advance sociological studies concerning the situation on the spot. Additionally, the motivation of all partners to commit to a project beyond their basic professional obligation is obligatory. Still, it is only in parts realistic to meet these requirements while considering the university's research and teaching schedules, as well as the requirements of the professional partners involved. Thus, it is extremely important to communicate upfront which possibilities and limits determine all the stakeholders' work.

The AnG is one of many practice-related research and design projects at the Department of Architecture at TU Berlin. In contrast to design-build initiatives on the object-scale, such as "baupiloten" or "CoCoon" (CoCoon: sector for contextual construction), the AnG's urban design interventions engage in the urban fabric to make visible and discuss contentious research and planning tasks. Depending on the task and partnership, the AnG's urban interventions are integrated into preparative studies, design or master-planning projects, workshops or exhibitions, or they become full-scale temporary versions of long-term realizations. The conception of participatory formats of discussion and production are crucial in all these projects. In some, the user groups who provide the funding and/or want to continue the project afterward are involved directly. Other projects are aimed at a broader public audience to collect feedback. The latter hints at a major challenge that pertains to critical projects on the urban scale. Only rarely, sociological studies are at hand. Still rarely, resident groups have been organized to address a larger scale, especially in mass housing settlements. Designers and architects can only provide limited community building. Thus, a powerful "client" from the resident side is missing. Here, the interventions in public space and 1:1 models have proven extremely beneficial in attracting residents to the AnG's events and activating awareness and discussion.

In the close connection between research and practice, between reflection and production, partners generate knowledge on the local conditions, resident's tactics, and scope for action needed to involve economically or politically weaker partners in the planning and realization. Apart from these rational criteria, urban interventions have another purpose: They can entice stakeholders to abandon the factual constraints of the status quo and its obvious limited alternatives, and instead envision a better common future. AnG's projects aim at developing those tools, either to envision a common ground on which the future development should be based or to empower the residents and users of the spaces and engage within this development.[8] The following outlined descriptions of five urban installations will give insights into the work of the Academy of a new Gropiusstadt.

[8]For further information on the founding of the AnG and its first projects, see Stollmann et al. (2013a, b, c).

16.3.1 Task Force Climate: Monster's Tracks on Campus Efeuweg

AnG's first project and our introduction into Gropiusstadt was Campus Efeuweg. Three schools, a kindergarten, a youth center, and a sports venue founded an education network and asked us to support their pedagogical aim of setting up consecutive, all-day schooling by designing and programming its grounds. Despite the site's potential for creating a large common space, the individual properties were separated by high fences, poorly maintained, and scarcely inviting. To shift the focus toward cooperation, a series of workshops on the topic of sharing was run. What can each partner contribute or make available: classrooms, undeveloped areas, teaching units, or labor? Undreamt-of forms of space and organization became possible: shared spaces inside and outside, a temporary opening of the fences, and joint design projects that regard the campus as a common urban space opening up to the neighborhood. Sixteen design projects were developed by students and discussed repeatedly in workshops with 70 representatives from the educational network, pupils included. A successful result of this cooperation is the master plan for Campus Efeuweg by the architectural practice "kleyer.koblitz.letzel. freivogel," approved in June 2014.

Part of the preparation work for this master plan was achieved by direct field work with the local pupils of the schools. This work was coordinated in the course of our research project "Task Force Climate: Shaping the City with a Plan" (SokoKlima. Stadt gestalten mit Plan).[9] Financed by the German Ministry of Environment, the research aimed at developing a collection of tools and methods for German school classes to discuss urban development with pupils as well as to test their possibilities to become involved. One successful format developed for this toolbox is the workshop "Monster's Tracks" (Fig. 16.1), in which boys and girls masqueraded as monsters and had to discover wild animals and their territories on and around the campus grounds. Instead of experiencing only the conflicts between them and the older teenagers, they also learned that they share their schoolyard and Gropiusstadt with a multiplicity of species: The fox and its den as well as the squirrels' territories became the starting point for the redesign of the schoolyard in the successive participatory planning process, which was put into practice in the summer of 2014.

16.3.2 AnG Headquarters and GROWPIUSlab

In the summer of 2012, a vacant supermarket in the central Lipschitz Square was transformed into the headquarters of the AnG's Summer Academy. It was used for exhibitions, as a working room, and as the venue for a public forum, including

[9]For further information on SokoKlima, please visit: www.soko-klima.de.

Fig. 16.1 Task force climate: who do we share our city with? Where does the fox live? Subsequent to the mapping out of the school grounds, the pupils discover the area surrounding the schoolyard (*Image* Ines Schaber)

workshops on the everyday life in and future development of Gropiusstadt. One of the student projects on display, called GROWPIUSlab, suggested transforming the supermarket into a teaching and learning space on urban gardening and ecological farming in combination with an inhabitant-run shop and a café (Fig. 16.2). The students offered soil, seeds, tools, and containers for growing plants as well as thematic workshops and discovery trips to cultivatable areas in Gropiusstadt and the surrounding region of Brandenburg. The installation (Fig. 16.3) and activities were conceived as proposals for the future use of the supermarket, once the AnG headquarters moved out again. The participating residents were enthusiastic about the concept of a self-run place to meet one another, but they could not imagine acquiring the initial funding and securing its long-term maintenance. When they were asked whether they would prefer a self-organized shop or a regular supermarket to move into the building, most of the local people voted for the supermarket. Here, the design and programming ideas were developed to test the inhabitants' determination to engage in generating common agenda for a community space. We discovered, however, that they felt overburdened. A community-building process parallel to our design proposals was missing. Meanwhile, despite extensive advertising and cooperation with local partners, the composition of the voters was not representative for Gropiusstadt. In this workshop series, mostly older German first occupants participated; younger migrants and families were not represented.

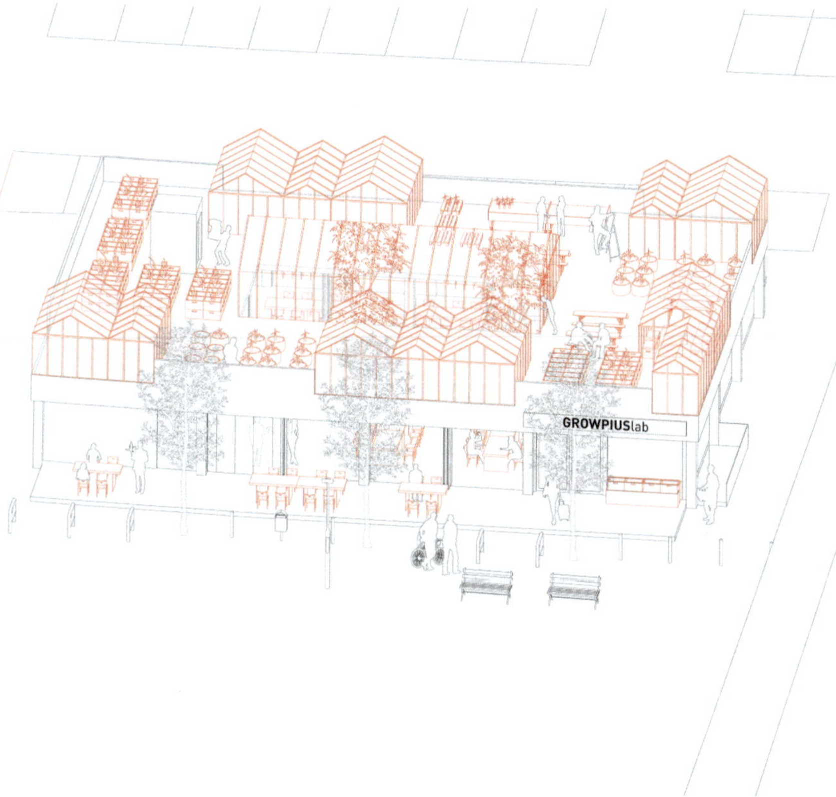

Fig. 16.2 The site of the exhibition is also an object of the students' transformation project. The vacant supermarket is to be turned into a resident-run community center with a marketplace, café, and rooftop terrace with greenhouses and vegetable patches (*Drawing* Mathias Burke, Mandy Held, Vadim Pancenko, Luisa Schäfer, Julia Wyn-Willis)

16.3.3 U-Rangery

The relationship between the residents of Gropiusstadt and "their" extensive green areas is ambiguous. On the one hand, the continuous, park-like surfaces areas are highly popular. On the other hand, there is a feeling of insecurity at nighttime, which is stronger in parts that show low maintenance. The student project U-Rangery was based on the observation that the underground's ventilation shafts, whose tracks ran underneath the neighborhood's central green area, were popular places for children to play. In the framework of the project, a greenhouse was constructed on top of one of the shafts (Fig. 16.4). The air pushed into and out of the underground shaft was used for heating and cooling, respectively, depending on the weather (Fig. 16.5). Simultaneously, the shivering plants created a place of observation, care, and positive social control. The temporary installation in the

Fig. 16.3 In AnG's exhibition during the summer academy in 2011, students explain their projects to the residents and run workshops on practical issues, such as the "Urban Gardening" workshop organized by the GROWPIUSlab team (*Image* Ines Schaber)

public space remained almost undamaged, although it was unguarded and freely accessible. For about 3 weeks, residents, the neighboring kindergarten, and the pupils of the schools in Efeuweg used the installation in the course of the project "Task Force Climate: Shaping the City with a Plan." After the AnG Summer Academy 2012 had ended, the U-Rangery was handed over to the nearby Lise-Meitner-School at Campus Efeuweg, where it will be re-erected.

16.3.4 Car Park Upgrade

More than 20 partly unused multi-storey car parks are situated at the intersections of streets, residential areas, and green open spaces. A group of students learned that these spacious, vacant, and dark buildings contribute to a large extent to the residents' unease in the open space at night. They suggested breathing new life into the car parks by installing a mix of offices, manufacturing industry warehouses, sports venues, and artists' studios (Fig. 16.6). The reuse would enrich the offer of leisure activities and jobs in the area and stimulate the use of the neighboring green areas. Another effect might be the reinforcement of social control, especially by artists and student who would use the studios in the evening. AnG used one of the car parks' rooftop close to the Lipschitz Square for the Summer Academy 2013 (Fig. 16.7).

Fig. 16.4 The U-Rangery serves as a learning space and as a resting place for passers-by. When an underground train passes, a current of air is pushed upward from the shaft into the U-Rangery that causes the plants to shiver (*Image* Ines Schaber)

During the exemplary installation as a neighborhood garden and bar as well as a place for work and discussions, the residents' reactions were revealing. People living in distant areas appreciated the new offer to gather and use the roof. Despite the informative posters and flyers that were used to invite residents to use the space and participate in the events, the direct neighbors experienced the activation of the area and the presence of unknown neighbors as disturbance, regardless of the fact that the noise pollution and temporary occupation of (even informal) residential parking spaces was very low.

16.3.5 We Make Lipschi

In the summer of 2014, undeveloped areas between the extensive green belt of Gropiusstadt and the central Lipschitz Square were to be redesigned in cooperation with the Community Center (Gemeinschaftshaus) Gropiusstadt, intercultural meeting place IKT, and adjacent housing associations. In December 2013, AnG tested the drafted measures in the form of temporary installations in preparation for a voting involving the potential stakeholders of the new design. The accessible 1:1

Fig. 16.5 The first design idea was continuously developed. Both the 1:1 construction of the installation and sponsorship were organized by the students. Permission for the construction on top of the underground shaft was granted after negotiations with the local authorities (*Drawing* MalteHeinze, Paul Künzel, Stefan Liczkowski, Sara Lusic-Alavanja, Zara Pfeifer, Johanna Streicher, Salomé Wackernagel)

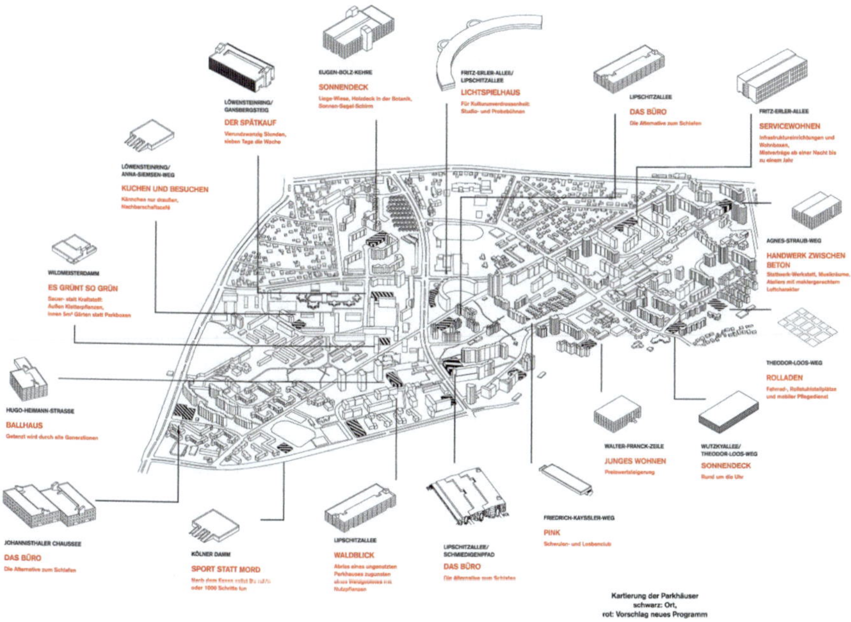

Fig. 16.6 Taking local examples as models, Car park upgrade proposes to reprogram large portions of the parking buildings to achieve a better functional mix in the neighborhood and activate specific vacant and disconcerting spaces (*Drawing* Annette Donat, Annabelle Eicker, Konstantin Richter)

models on the spot made the project's spatial consequences become literally tangible so that conclusions could be drawn for the subsequent planning process (Fig. 16.8). One project partner remarked that only a couple of screws had to be loosened to rearrange the square's furnishing, which aimed at making sitting more comfortable and communicative. Funding for the interventions and maintenance of the newly developed areas was discussed on the spot as well. As we reached the vote on the maintenance, we realized that the initiative, the intercultural meeting place IKT, had no long-term financing scheme. They were, however, the supporters and lynchpin of the self-organization and maintenance of the new facilities. Thus, we decided together to design the interventions in the most robust way and thereby make the necessary maintenance as easy as possible.

Instead of the originally planned extensive urban gardening and DIY projects, three interventions (Fig. 16.9) were planned and realized: three slowly growing nut trees with "sitting nuts" (walnuts, hazelnuts, and almonds) (Fig. 16.10), a door opening for the Community Centre toward the public green area with concrete sitting blocks that can also be used as a temporary café (Fig. 16.11), and a gilding of the square to be carried out together with the residents (Fig. 16.12). The new square was opened in September 2014.

Fig. 16.7 Car park upgrade: the rooftop of one of the multi-storey car parks became the venue of the AnG Summer Academy in 2013. This campaign was a trial run for the conversion of car parks in Gropiusstadt (*Image* Ines Schaber)

Fig. 16.8 The link between the intercultural meeting place ITK and the green belt was discussed and developed using several 1:1 models on the spot (*Image* Dagmar Pelger)

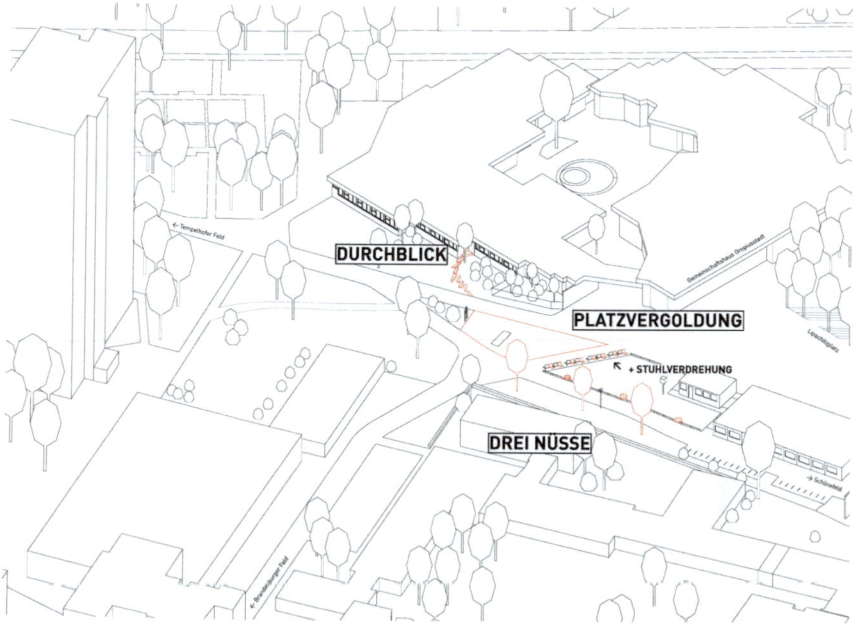

Fig. 16.9 The three interventions depicted together. The Community Center Gropiusstadt is in the upper half (*Drawing* Cornelia Halbach, Anja Leßmann, Björn Lotter, Franziska Polleter, Simone Prill)

16.4 Locality: Co-production of Common Ground

Each of the urban interventions generated new findings. Initial assumptions and challenges were re-formulated throughout the development of each intervention. A number of projects were altered and adopted by the residents, whereas others were totally dismissed. Residents, housing associations, and administrative representatives contributed their skills. Realizations were brought underway, and we as organizers of AnG understood with and for whom we were planning. We were the most successful in realization, when the residents had already formed associations and in the best case, had commissioned us directly, as was the case for the project at Campus Efeuweg or Lipschitz square. However, in all projects, we learned as architects and urban designers that the large scale of Gropiusstadt comprises a multiplicity of urban realities, and thus, localities. There is a vast variety of uses and appropriation of open spaces. They do not necessarily manifest permanently, but are in close relation to seasons, climate, and the diverse cultural backgrounds of local user groups. A certain low definition of the open spaces facilitates their temporal appropriation.

The promise of welfare state provision of services and maintenance is inscribed into mass housing settlements such as Gropiusstadt. Whether civil society engagement can or should make up for the shortcomings of the public sector is

Fig. 16.10 Trees grow slowly. Seating sculptures invite passers-by to sit down (*Image* Jörg Stollmann)

uncertain, but it can contribute to shedding light on how cities in the future should be developed. Even within state-initiated or state-led development projects, practices of participation or co-production will have to be considered, not for the shrinking state resources in provision but for the sake of another idea of place. If we

Fig. 16.11 The intercultural meeting place IKT is supposed get a door leading onto the green belt, which would contribute to the openness and accessibility of the community center (*Renderings* Cornelia Halbach, Anja Leßmann, Björn Lotter, Franziska Polleter, Simone Prill)

Fig. 16.12 We Make Lipschi: in summer 2014, residents and AnG covered the square in gold (*Renderings* Cornelia Halbach, Anja Leßmann, Björn Lotter, Franziska Polleter, Simone Prill)

aim for locality as a sense of place within large-scale development processes, then a functioning neighborhood will most likely be achieved by the continuous co-production of its inhabitants. Living in a place leaves traces, may they be individual and temporal or common and lasting. Design and planning processes that allow for the co-production of common ground, how conflict-laden they might be notwithstanding, will prove the more successful in the long run.

However, how could such a juncture be arrived at? Each AnG intervention pointed to one overall problem: an initiative advocates and asks for shared responsibility in urban development. The fundamental prerequisites are politically active, responsible citizens who want to co-produce and shape their city and assume responsibility. Shared responsibility goes hand in hand with shared power toward decision making. Without the support of housing associations and policymakers, the negotiations are at risk of remaining at a merely pacifying level of participation. Especially in neighborhoods such as Gropiusstadt, where most of the buildings originally built by state-owned housing companies are now largely privatized, new tools are needed to support initiatives, with regard to public law and the administration. It is not only about a "more beautiful" city but about a city that is a common ground, where co-creation and co-responsibility can be practiced through active participation. The future ecological and social resilience of neighborhoods require a new definition of the existing attribution of power.

Academic Team

Technische Universität Berlin

Chair for Urban Design and Urbanization, Prof. Jörg Stollmann
Research Associates: Sandra Bartoli, Katharina Hagg, Mathias Heyden, Anita Kaspar, Mari Pape (kubus TU Berlin), Dagmar Pelger, Fee Kyriakopoulos
Tutors: Dorothee Hahn, Philippa Dierson, Daniela Mehlich, Florian Müller, Kathrin Schömer

Chair for Design and Construction, Prof. Donatella Fioretti (cooperation „Campus Efeuweg")
Tutor: Daniel Bruns

Chair for Art, Prof. Stefanie Bürkle (cooperation „We make Lipschi")
Artistic Associates: Alex Gross, Janin Walter, Su-Ran Sichling

Zentraleinrichtung Wissenschaftliche Weiterbildung und Kooperation (ZEWK) – Kooperations- und Beratungsstelle für Umweltfragen (kubus)

More than hundred Students in Architecture and Urban Design

Partners and Funding Partners:
degewo AG, local council Neukölln, Interkultureller Treffpunkt (IKT)

In Cooperation with:
Neighbourhood Management Gropiusstadt, schools and educational institutions at Efeuweg, Lenkungsrunde 50 Jahre Gropiusstadt, Kulturnetzwerk Neukölln, Gropiuswohnen GmbH

Supported by:
Senatsverwaltung für Stadtentwicklung und Umwelt Berlin, Stiftung Deutsche Klassenlotterie Berlin

Soko Klima. Stadt gestalten mit Plan, Research Project funded by the German Federal Government, Ministry of Environment
Partners: Unabhängiges Institut für Umweltbildung (UfU) e.V., ZEWK – Kooperations- und Beratungsstelle für Umweltfragen (kubus) TU Berlin, Chair for Urban Design and Urbanization TU Berlin, Institut für Energie und Umweltforschung Heidelberg (ifeu)

References

AnG Publications of the Chair

Bandel H, Machule D (1974) Die Gropiusstadt. Der städtebaulichePlanungs- und Entscheidungsvorgang. Kiepert, Berlin

de Certeau M (1988) The practice of everyday life. University of California Press, Berkeley and Los Angeles

Feireiss K, Hamm OG, SenatsverwaltungfürStadtentwicklung und Umwelt (2015) Transforming cities. Urban Interventions in Public Space. Jovis, Berlin

Harnack M (2012) Rückkehr der Wohnmaschinen. Sozialer Wohnungsbau und Gentrifizierung in London. Transcript Verlag, Bielefeld

Mouffe C (2014) Agonistik. Die Welt politisch denken. SuhrkampVerlag, Berlin. http://www.suhrkamp.de/buecher/agonistik-chantal_mouffe_12677.html

Stollmann J et al (2013a) Akademie einer neuen Gropiusstadt. Die Gründung – Machen. Universitätsverlag der TU Berlin, Berlin

Stollmann J et al (2013b) Akademie einer neuen Gropiusstadt. Die Gründung – Denken. Universitätsverlag der TU Berlin, Berlin

Stollmann J et al (2013c) Campus Efeuweg – 36 Tools füreinneues Quartier. Universitätsverlag der TU Berlin, Berlin

Author Biography

Mr. Jörg Stollmann is Professor for Urban Design and Urbanization at the Institute for Architecture, Faculty VI Planning Building Environment at the Technische Universität Berlin and registered architect in Berlin/Zurich.

Chapter 17
Ecological Plan: City Covered by Green Roofs

Linfei Han and Jianmin Guo

17.1 Background

17.1.1 Worsening Global Pollution

Since the 1980s, with the development of China's economy, the country has experienced environmental problems with global influence, which have become increasingly prominent. Apart from regional environmental pollution and ecological destruction, a wide range of global environment crises has emerged, such as the greenhouse effect, ozone depletion, global warming, acid rain, species extinction, land desertification, forest decline, trans-frontier pollution, marine pollution, wild species reduction, tropical rainforests reduction, and soil erosion, which pose serious threats to human survival and development.

In developed countries, the ecological environment is gradually being restored after many years of mismanagement, but in developing countries, the problem remains serious. Taking China for example, haze has become the most important environmental problem in northern China (Fig. 17.1a and b). The harmful effects caused by haze, such as the high incidence of respiratory diseases, highway closure, airport lockout, halt in construction work, and school suspension, are turning environmental problems into political and international problems.

L.F. Han (✉)
School of Architecture and Design, Beijing Jiaotong University, Beijing, China
e-mail: hanlf@bjtu.edu.cn

J.M. Guo
School of Civil Engineering, Beijing Jiaotong University, Beijing, China

F. Wang and M. Prominski (eds.), *Urbanization and Locality*,
DOI 10.1007/978-3-662-48494-4_17

Fig. 17.1 **a** Smog in Beijing. *Source* www.chinafeatures.com. **b** Smog in Beijing. *Source* Baidu images

17.1.2 Accelerated Urbanization in China

In China, the environmental problems in cities are comparatively graver than those experiences in rural areas. Consequently, the discussion of whether China should follow rapid urbanization has arisen.

Fig. 17.2 Expected urbanization rate in China. *Source* Drawn by the author based on data from the National Bureau of Statistics of China

In 2013, the new Prime Minister Li Keqiang again put forward the promotion of China's urbanization. Li pointed out that, "The Chinese urbanization rate has just reached 50 %. It's only 35 % if it is calculated by the household registered population. This number is far less than the average of developed countries (80 %). However, the gap is the driving force." The "new urbanization" is expected to be a driving force of the next round of Chinese economic growth, and it will has long-term effects on the Chinese modernization process (Fig. 17.2). However, the environmental problems the cities face will hinder the progress in this regard.

17.1.3 Existing Environmental Problems for Urban Development

The experiences of developed countries show that urbanization is an inevitable product of development. Therefore, the main emphasis of China's urbanization has been on improving the urban ecological environment effectively. Urban development in the country continues to face many other environmental problems:

(1) Urban land use has increasingly intensified, natural vegetation has decreased, urban forest coverage has been depleted.
(2) The cities lack an urban ventilation corridor; the urban heat island effect is increasingly severe (Fig. 17.3).
(3) Haze weather frequency has increased; air pollution is aggravated.
(4) High energy consumption.
(5) Poor drainage facilities.

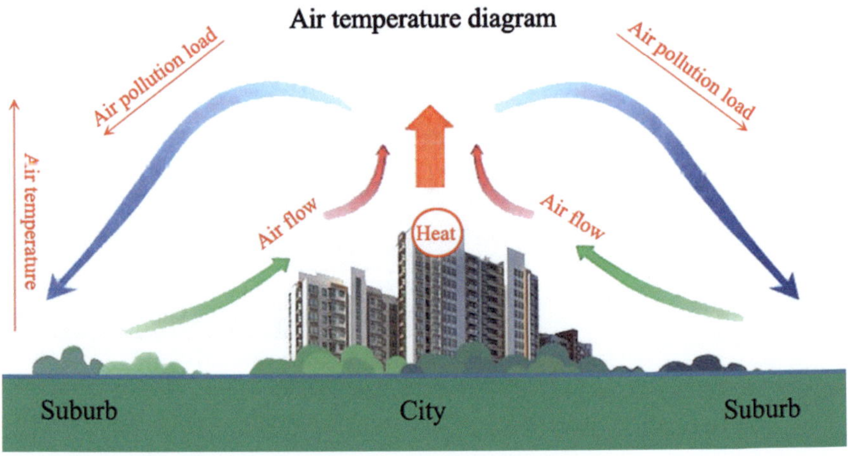

Fig. 17.3 Air temperature diagram. *Source* Drawn by the author based on http://www.fogchina.com/Product/HIndustry.html

17.1.4 Building Roofs, the Only Large-Scale Unused Space Resources in Cities

With the acceleration of Chinese urbanization, urban construction land use has intensified, and large green areas are impossible to construct in urban built-up areas. Building roofs provide unique potential resources in cities as spaces that have not been developed and used on a large scale.

For domestic building roofs already in use, their utilization forms vary, mainly including roof greening (Fig. 17.4a), parking, heliport (Fig. 17.4b), solar energy (Fig. 17.4c), rooftop rainwater harvest, and roof stadium (Fig. 17.4d).

17.2 Green Roof Efficiency Analysis

The concept of green roofs originated from ancient Western Asia. The earliest green roofs were the ziggurats built in ancient Babylon in 2000 BC. According to records, the cultivated base material of these structures was soil. A historical green roof that matches the current notion is seen in the Hanging Gardens of ancient Babylon (Fig. 17.5), which is known as one of the seven wonders of the ancient world (Wang 2005).

Green roofs have the following qualities: (1) carbon fixation and oxygen release, by taking in carbon dioxide from the air and producing oxygen; (2) air cleaning, by absorbing noxious gases in the air and reducing dust in the air; (3) adjusting the urban climate and reducing the city heat-island effect; (4) water conservation, by reducing stress on ground drainage.

Fig. 17.4 **a** Roof greening. *Source* http://www.miao717.com/a/cyfx/cyjj/2012/0309/498.html. **b** Heliport. *Source* http://www.gzsfzh.com/c704.html. **c** Solar energy. *Source* http://www.xintehongye.com/plus/view.php?aid=888. **d** Roof stadium. *Source* http://photo.chengdu.cn/bbs/forum.php?mod=viewthread&tid=368865

Fig. 17.5 Image of the Hanging Gardens of Babylon. *Source* http://www.topit.me/item/16216905

17.2.1 Ecological Benefits

The ecological benefits of green roofs include the following (Han and Guo 2014):

(1) Carbon fixation: 1 m^2 of lawn can absorb 146 kg of CO_2 every year.
(2) Oxygen release: 1 m^2 of lawn can release 105.85 kg of O_2 every year.
(3) Noxious gas absorption: 1 m^2 of green roof can absorb 0.0031 kg of SO_2 every year.
(4) Dust reduction: 1 m^2 of gardening green roof can absorb 12.3 g of dust every year; the basic form can absorb 8.5 g of dust every year, and the average is 10 g.
(5) Energy conservation: 1 m^2 of green roof can save 20 kWh of electricity every year.
(6) Water conservation: 1 m^2 of green roof can conserve 27 kg of water every year.

17.2.2 Economic Benefits

Green roofs have high economic value as well. The value of carbon fixation relates to the Swedish carbon tax rate; the value of oxygen relates to the current price of oxygen generation; the value of noxious gas absorption relates to the SO_2 in the pollution charge schedule; the value of dust reduction relates to the average of coal-fired furnace air contaminants pollution discharge schedule; the value of energy conservation relates to the current electricity price for residents; and the value of water conservation relates to the current water price for residents (Zhang 2010).

According to the above references, green roofs can bring the following annual benefits per square meter: CO_2 abatement, 5.8 USD; oxygen release, 8.5 USD; energy conservation, 1.58 USD; and water conservation, 0.02 USD. According to the above, green roofs can bring benefits worth 15.9 USD per square meter each year.

17.2.3 Social Benefits

The social benefits of green roofs are mainly characterized by the following three aspects:

(1) Close the distance between people and nature
In the context of the modern city, which features tall buildings and compressed space for outdoor activities, green roofs can provide a place for people to keep in touch with nature. They also provide a place for outdoor communication, enabling interactions among residents.

(2) Conducive to social harmony
Green roofs have great ecological benefits. Apart from improving the urban environment effectively, they also address complaints on environmental pollution, and provide a relaxed and pleasing atmosphere for people. Green roofs can improve the image of the government, which is conducive to social harmony and stability.
(3) Promote employment
Green roofs involve many industries, such as garden planting, architectural design and construction, and waterproof materials. The implementation of green roofs can greatly increase the demand for gardening and materials, thereby promoting employment.

17.3 Development Status of Green Roofs in China

17.3.1 Shenzhen

Shenzhen is one of the earliest cities to promote green roofs in China. In 1999, the city's municipal government issued "Shenzhen city roof beautification and greening implementation measures." This policy provided the measures of planning, implementation, inspection, supervision, and evaluation of green roofs. Shenzhen proposed methods in the form of unified deployment over the entire city, multi-party funds, and phased implementation. It also required that where technology and other objective conditions are available, roofs, especially of high-rise buildings, must be green. In 2004, the responsible department of Shenzhen's municipal government introduced three policies to support the rectification of old residential districts: on the industrial level, ensuring the improvement of green roofs development and considering it as a significant part of housing industrialization; on the economic level, appropriating a series of measures, such as taxation and interest rates reduction, or supporting and guiding real estate and property management companies in ensuring green roofs development; on the technological level, implementing technical standards for green roofs to solve a range of issues, such as level of waterproofing and anticorrosion.

In 2013, Shenzhen established the "Work action plan for urban greening promotion," and pointed out that green roofs must be implemented in the new buildings with government investment.

17.3.2 Chengdu

Chengdu promoted the concept of "green roofs" in the 1990s. People then grew vegetables and lotus roots on the roofs. At present, the plants have already evolved into flowers and grass. In the past, Chengdu citizens used to eschew green roofs, saying they look like hats, but presently, people are scrambling to install their small hanging garden. In 2012, the area of green roofs in Chengdu was more than three million square meters.

To develop the green roofs, Chengdu's municipal government put forward a large number of policies to stimulate initiatives by real estate developers, parties, and individuals. Chengdu has made special rules, e.g., new buildings under 12 floors and under 40 m, in the five urbanareas of Longquanyi, Qingbaijiang, Xindu, Wenjiang, Shuangliu, and Pixian, must have green roofs. The government has banned the registration of property formalities for violators. Further, buildings completed in the last 20 years, which have clear established ownerships and meet the safety requirements, can have green roofs. The government has also introduced incentives: Developers are allowed to build out by one square meter if they add one square meter of roof gardens, but not more than 20 % of the approved construction area.

17.3.3 Beijing

The green roof area in Beijing has increased by 100,000 m^2 each year since 2005.[1] Extensive green roofs have always been the dominant trend in Beijing. One reason is that extensive green roofs are low cost, easy to manage, water saving, effective, and secure; another reason is that the extensive green roofs are best for a number of the existing buildings.

In 2011, Beijing installed 11,000 m^2 of green roofs; in 2012, the number was 17,000 m^2.[2] However, the green roofs coverage rate in Beijing still fell at less than 1 %. The green roofs are mainly in the Chaoyang and Haidian Districts (Fig. 17.6).

17.4 City Covered by Green Roofs: Case of Beijing

17.4.1 Expanse of Beijing's Building Roofs

According to the preliminary estimation of 2010 sampling statistics data from Beijing's Municipal Land Resources Bureau, the area of the city covered 16,807.8 km^2: the downtown area was 1368.32 km^2, and the built-up area was 1289.3 km^2. Beijing Evening News argued that the roof area in the entire city was about 322 km^2; Beijing Green Roofs Association provided the more conservative number of 180 km^2. According to the comprehensive evaluation of the author, the roofs area is about 220 km^2 in the downtown area, of which 70 % is available for

[1]The Forest Coverage of Beijing Reaches 40 %, Green Roof is burgeoning, 2013 http://www.jzfsonline.com/roofonline_articles_20130922084017.html.

[2]Beijing Municipal Bureau of Landscape and Forestry.

Fig. 17.6 Green roof in Beijing. *Source* http://www.cqla.cn/chinese/news/news_view.asp?id=26414

green roofs. Among the available roofs, such facilities as equipment rooms, pipe shafts, and lightning rods account for about 5–20 % of the roof area. The available area for green roofs in Beijing will be about 131 km^2 when calculated by 15 %.

17.4.2 Beijing's Green Roofs Coverage Benefits

If half of the 131 km^2 is covered by green roofs, the effective green roofs area would approximately be 58 km^2. The ecological benefits of this area would be the following: absorbing about 8.47 million tons of CO_2 each year, releasing about 6.14 million tons of oxygen, absorbing about 1.8 million tons of SO_2, reducing about 5.8 million tons of dust, and conserving 1.57 million tons of water by measures such as rainwater collection. Further, green roofs also protect building roofs, extend the service life of roofing materials, reduce the city heat-island effect, absorb heat energy, promote heat dissipation, provide innovative spaces of activity and relaxation for residents, and increase urban natural elements (Fig. 17.7).

17.4.3 Number of New Building Roofs in Beijing Each Year

In recent years, Beijing's annual conversion of construction land and building volume has remained stable, except for the year 2009 (owing to the 2008 Olympic Games). The annual permitted construction land is about 5500 ha, and the building volume is about 53 million square meters. In 2012, the total scale of the projects

Fig. 17.7 Roof garden in Beijing. *Source* http://www.chla.com.cn/htm/2011/1208/108046_2.html

issued through the project site selection of Beijing's government reached 2855 ha, whereas the projects with construction land planning permit reached 5497 ha (Han ana Guo 2013). If calculated by 30 % of the permitted land scale, the new roof area in Beijing is about 1650 ha each year.

Beijing's permit construction engineering scale in the period 2009–2012

Years	Permit land use volume (10,000 m^2)	Permit building volume (10,000 m^2)
2009	14,646	4950
2010	5451	5473
2011	5695	5364
2012	5497	5212

Source Beijing Municipal Commission of Urban Planning

17.4.4 Coverage Benefits of Beijing's New Building Roofs Each Year

According to the Urban Eco-environmental Plan of Beijing, "30 % of the high-rise buildings and 60 % of the low-rise buildings should implement green roofs," and about 40 % of the roofs in Beijing need greening. Each year, 21.2 million square meters of green roofs need to be implemented. If we calculate the effective area by 88 % of green roofs, the effective area in Beijing is about 5.81 million square meters each year.

17.4.5 Green Roofs Coverage Zoning Guidance

The central district area in Beijing's urban is huge. According to the Beijing Urban Master Plan (2004–2020), the central district area covers 1085 km^2. The number is 1088 km^2 when the regulatory plan is completed. Regional development is imbalanced in terms of planning, as the east and north are more developed than the west and south. Based on the different situations of each region, different strategies should be adopted when the green roofs plan is implemented.

The Beijing Central District Regulatory Plan has divided the central district into 33 areas (Fig. 17.8), based on Beijing's city layout characteristics. The 01 area is the old city. Areas 02–08 are the core areas around the center of the old city; 09–18 are 10 edge groups that surround the center areas; 19–33 are green-isolated areas. Except for the 15 green-isolated areas, 18 areas are key areas for roofs space implementation for ecological use.

According to the Code for Roof Greening in Beijing, the green roofs coverage zoning guidance is as follows:

Area 01 (within the Second Ring Road): The area is about 63 km^2. This area is home to many ancient buildings, parties or state organs, courtyard houses, and new multi-storey and high-rise buildings built in recent years. Except for the cultural relics, green roofs should be given top priority when making use of roof space.

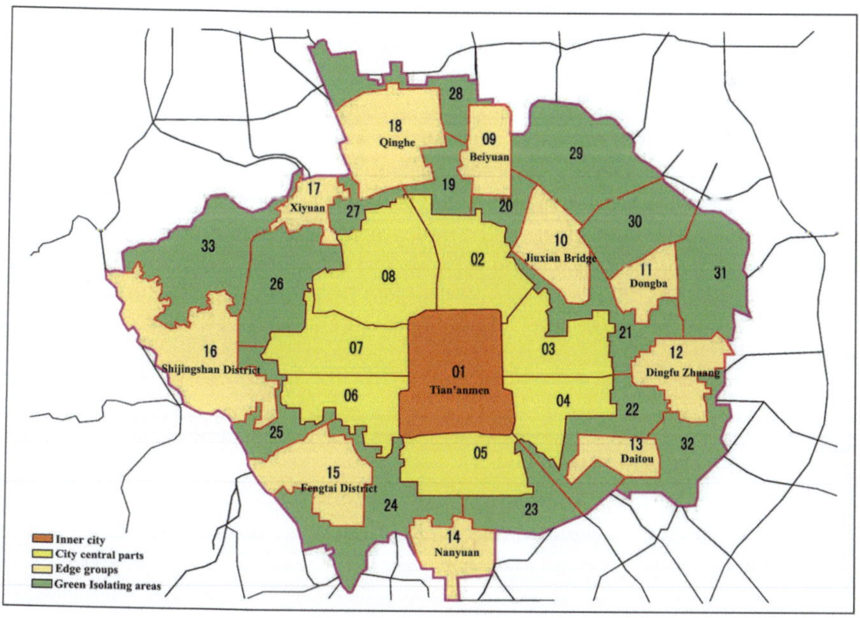

Fig. 17.8 Zoning map of Beijing central areas in the Regulatory Plan. *Source* Beijing Municipal Institute of City Planning and Design

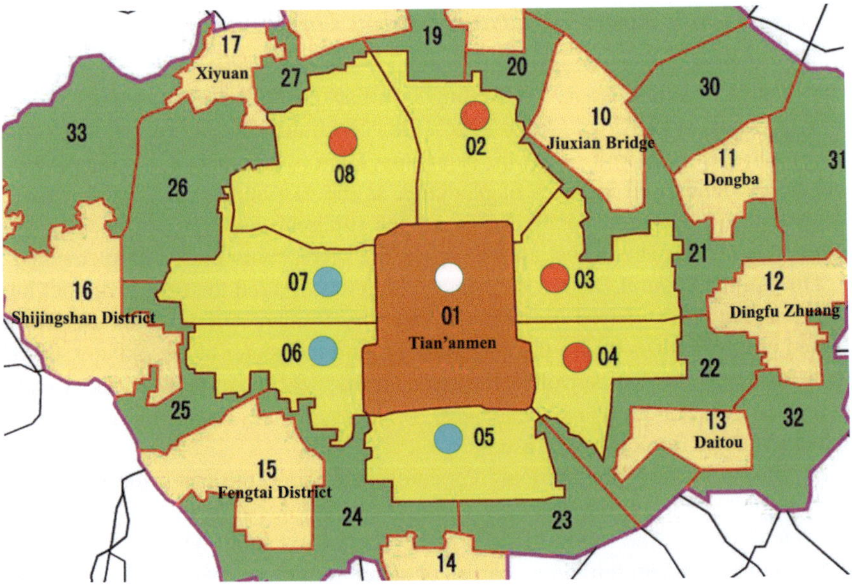

Fig. 17.9 Areas 01–08. *Source* Beijing Municipal Institute of City Planning and Design

Areas 02–08 are adjustment and optimization areas, which are reserved for evacuation, adjustment, and optimization functions of the population in the center of the old city. In these areas, construction intensity must be limited, and the living environment should be improved.

Areas 02, 03, 04, 08: These areas are economically developed. The total area is about 162 km^2. In these areas, green roofs should be given priority (Fig. 17.9).

Areas 05, 06, 07: The total area is about 105 km^2. In these areas, equal attention should be paid to green roofs and other means.

Areas 09–18 are moderate improvement areas. Transportation and public service facilities need to be improved, and employment and living should be actively promoted.

Areas 09–18 areas: These 10 areas are located in the periphery of the central city. The total area is about 287 km^2. Green roofs should be taken into consideration (Fig. 17.10).

17.5 Policy Suggestions

(1) Green roofs coverage and architectural design plans should have synchronous approval

For new buildings, green roofs should be considered in the architectural design. The green roofs coverage plan should be an important part of the completed building. The design should merge green roofs coverage and architectural design to achieve an

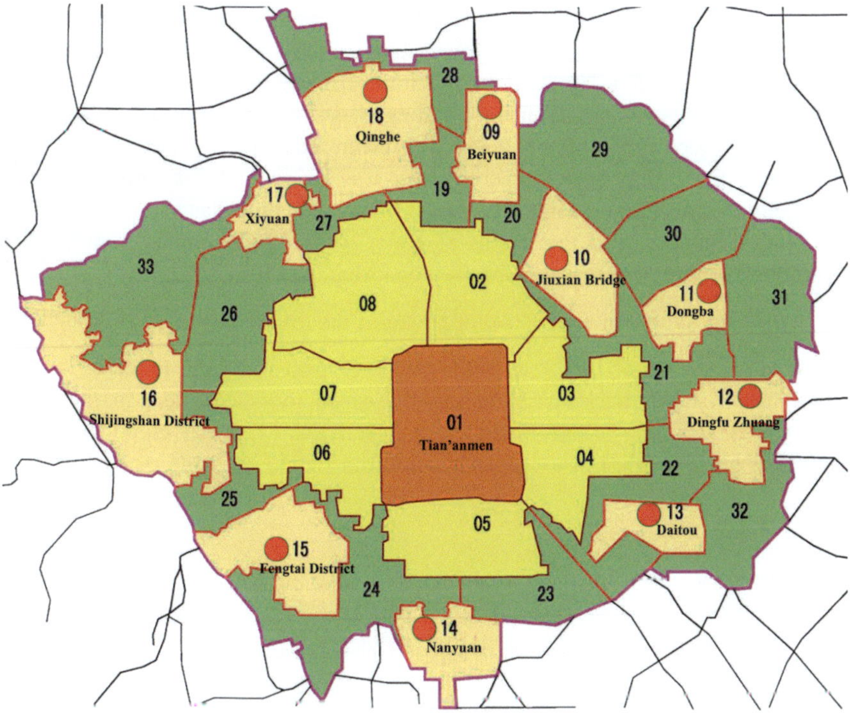

Fig. 17.10 Areas 09–18. *Source* Beijing Municipal Institute of City Planning and Design

integrated design. The green roofs coverage and architectural design plans should have synchronous approval throughout the formalities of relevant planning and construction for building projects.

(2) Fully implement the green roofs coverage plan for eligible buildings

The green roofs coverage plan should be based on construction security. Authorities should ensure that the buildings can carry a certain amount of load. Full implementation of the green roofs coverage plan combined with construction functions for eligible buildings is encouraged.

(3) Areas with green roofs can appropriately increase the volume rate of construction

The government should introduce measures to encourage green roofs coverage. For example, developers can be presented with a higher volume rate as reward for constructing green roofs.

(4) Improve the reduced rate between green roof areas and green land areas

At present, the ratio between green roof areas and green land areas is relatively low. In Beijing, the 2011 "Opinions on promoting the urban space vertical planting construction work" stated that "when the greening rates of the new and reconstruction projects' attached land are lower than the requirements of planning, while the greening area without underground facilities has reached more than 50 % of the requirements, more than half of the building must have green roofs. In this way, 20 % of the green roofs can be included in green areas of the attached land."

Along with the experience of other cities, it is necessary to improve the rate of the green roof area included in the project with attached green land area. Up to 30 % is more appropriate, and the height of green roofs should not be limited. This regulation should be written into the Beijing Urban and Rural Planning Ordinance.

(5) Including the green roofs coverage plan in the urban development planning

The implementation of the green roofs coverage plan is a long process. Its execution needs strong backing. Including the green roofs coverage in the urban development planning is one of the most effective ways to safeguard the development of green roofs. For example, green roofs should be made mandatory.

References

Han L, Guo J (2013) The ecological use of roof in Beijing is coming. Urbanization 62(9):76—77 (in Chinese)

Han L, Guo J (2014) Green roofs is an important method to governance Haze. China Build Waterproofing 11:24–27 (in Chinese)

Wang L (2005) A brief history, present situation of green roof and ways to develop it. Chin Agri Sci Bull 12:304–306 (in Chinese)

Zhang S (2010) Economic analysis of roof greening in Beijing. Beijing Forestry University, Beijing (in Chinese)

Chapter 18
Urban Formation Based on Environmental Performance Simulation

Philip F. Yuan, Shuyi Huang and Chao Yan

18.1 Introduction

In recent decades, rapid urbanization has become a topic of increased discussion. Urbanization in China has become one of the most influential issues that will shape the world's development during the 21st century. Meanwhile, in the process of rapid urbanization, the locality of cities and towns is confronted with the challenges of variation and dissolution. On the one hand, acute human-places conflicts and serious environmental deterioration are obstacles to sustainable development. On the other hand, monotonous homogeneous urban fabrics that lack site-specific identity exacerbate the ongoing phenomenon of diversity deficiency.

It is widely accepted that cities and towns, as the major consumers of energy and resources, stand at the forefront of the global sustainability agenda. Amongst academics and practitioners working in the fields of urban planning and design, there has been an on-going discussion regarding the relationships between urban morphology and environmental sustainability. Under these circumstances, how to turn challenges into opportunities and develop an operative design methodology that leads to sustainable and site-specific urban design has become a worthy topic.

In traditional urbanization practices, the locality of cities and towns can be understood as operating in three domains: history, culture and environment. The former two, which are directly related to the social context and attribution feelings, are generally treated as the main starting points in traditional urban design paradigms. Meanwhile, although it appears to have long-term impacts on our living conditions, the environment, owing to the difficulty of measuring and simulating it, is merely an evaluation criterion in the design process but is not a design generator.

P.F. Yuan (✉) · S.Y. Huang · C. Yan
College of Architecture and Urban Planning, Tongji University, Shanghai, China
e-mail: philipyuan007@tongji.edu.cn

F. Wang and M. Prominski (eds.), *Urbanization and Locality*,
DOI 10.1007/978-3-662-48494-4_18

Recent developments in computational techniques have made it possible to design highly performative urban spaces from environmental simulations, bridging the gap between simulation data and form generation strategies.

18.2 Background and Review

Throughout history, in the process of adapting to environments, human beings have maintained the tradition of focusing on environmental elements such as climate and energy. For example, the geomantic omen theory derived from Chinese Taoist philosophy is a symbol of rules for survival summarized by our ancestors under generations of environmentally adaptive practices. In this theory, many principles of site selection and architectural layout directly reflect people's recognition and utilization of natural phenomena. For example, the folk adage "hide wind and gather gas" emphases the importance of ventilation and wind proofing. Additionally, "return wind and inverse gas" offers a way of preventing and improving local strong wind conditions (Chen 2015).

In contemporary practice, there are an emerging number of environmentally driven design studies. Doctor Andrew Marsh from the University of Western Australia noted that generative and performative designs have become potential novel directions for environments in order to achieve high levels of efficiency and performance. Performance-based morphology reflects the control and balance of environmentally responsive aspects. The environmental parameters thus serve as a driver in the earliest, most conceptual stages rather than evaluation criteria late in the design process (Marsh 2008). Professor Rivka Oxman from the Israel Institute of Technology presented and discussed various models of performance-based designs and concluded that in creating simulation environments for performance-based design, both generative and evaluative capabilities can be integrated into performance-based simulations (Oxman 2009). Harvard professor Inaki Abalos notes that formalizing energy in architecture and its presentation under certain weather conditions is a new research direction beyond traditional tectonics. Introducing the concept of energy into the ontological logic of architecture and viewing city systems as energy systems in order to construct environment-based ontology formalizations and regional expressions of urban and architecture is consistent with the core agenda of sustainable development (Abalos and Ibanez 2012).

The previously presented research demonstrated that environmental simulations conducted in the earliest formative conceptual stages can improve the local responsiveness of urban morphology. This paper builds upon the existing body of research to further expand the understanding of how environment can influence urban planning and design to strengthen the locality and identity of cities. Environmental design drivers such as wind and solar radiation, based on platforms of performance simulation, parametric programming and three-dimensional modeling, enable the interaction of information data and the generation of design proposals. Through emphasizing the particularity of site-specific elements and responding to those elements, urban morphology and environments can be anchored tightly, forming a city's unparalleled inner traits.

18.3 Methodology

The novel urban design paradigm explored in this chapter aims to redefine the meaning of environmental performance in urban morphology. In this way, the simulation of urban environmental performance serves no longer as an evaluation system but as a design-generating tool. The environmental data, based on collection, analysis and manipulation, can be digitally evolved to geometry parameters and urban form. This self-organizing multi-agent system based generative methodology for evolving sustainable urban morphology in time, based on the impacts of associative environmental elements, typically take the following four steps: environmental parameter extraction, environmental performance simulation, geometric form generation and urban morphology optimization.

18.3.1 Environmental Parameter Extraction

Environmental parameter extraction is the starting point of this workflow. By collecting dynamic contextual information and understanding the environment, climate and other conditions of the site, we can obtain quantitative and qualitative information that is relevant to the urban design. On one hand, the site's climate information can be obtained from city meteorological departments. This type of information includes prevailing wind conditions (directions, pressure, speed, frequency), intensity of solar radiation, solar altitude and other factors. On the other hand, a series of custom-made tools, e.g., a low-cost commercial weather station, scientific measuring probes, electronic sensors and development platform (Arduino) constitute a system to quantify and visualize environmental parameters. Through a selection of the above tools, we can develop a system to collect and visualize climate data from public space (Moya et al. 2013). All these data can subsequently be applied on the Processing platform to be read and addressed.

18.3.2 Environmental Performance Simulation

After defining the climate identification, the aforementioned data sets can be imported into working platforms and software which have developed maturely to simulate buildings at urban scale. Software such as Autodesk Ecotect Analysis, Autodesk Vasari and ANSYS Airpak enables designers to visualize and simulate a building's performance within the context of its environment (Clarke 2001). Based on the city's environmental characteristics and objective requirements for radiation, wind and other environmental factors, environmentally responsive strategies can be proposed. For example, in coastal cities that are heavily influenced by wind, wind has the most intimate relationship with the urban morphology. Therefore, the simulated wind data can be applied to control the forms of architectures, guiding the direction of airflow. When designing cities that have strong radiation, such as tropical cities, the simulated radiation data can be used to adjust the urban layout and building orientations.

18.3.3 Geometric Form Generation

Based on the environmentally responsive strategy developed in the second step, digital tools can conduct data organization, manipulation, computation and transformation. With the use of parametric software and plug-ins such as Rhinoceros and Grasshopper, environmental simulation data can be transformed into geometric controlling parameters. Furthermore, parametric design thinking and modelling enables relational, i.e. correlative, integral and explorative design processes (Menges 2011). The process from mathematics (environmental parameter) to geometric (formal parameter) data and to geometric form (building form) is the main logical path of computational formation. This geometric transformation of non-geometric data is the most important core logic in parametric urban formation design methodology. For example, the particle movement simulation of wind makes it possible to visualize wind phenomena around buildings and obtain related wind pressure data, forming primary urban morphology.

18.3.4 Urban Morphology Optimization

Finally, after achieving the multiple primary urban proposals, genetic algorithms can build a computing framework to make iterative calculations of ecological performance so as to evolve optimum urban forms driven by environmental performance (Wang et al 2005). In this optimization analysis, some environmental parameters are selected as evaluation criteria: for example, for high-rise buildings, we can set the wind pressure at a certain height or the wind speed at pedestrian level as the criterion. Iteration can increase the possibility for finding higher performance designs through the notion of design exploration of both geometric and their non-geometric variables according to established design objectives and constraints (Shea et al. 2005). With the analysis from the simulation platform, the simulation data will affect the direction of the next generation (Malkawi and Augenbroe 2004). Therefore, optimal solutions can be calculated in reasonable generations through multi-agent weight coefficient distribution and reasonably defined convergence rules (Fig. 18.1).

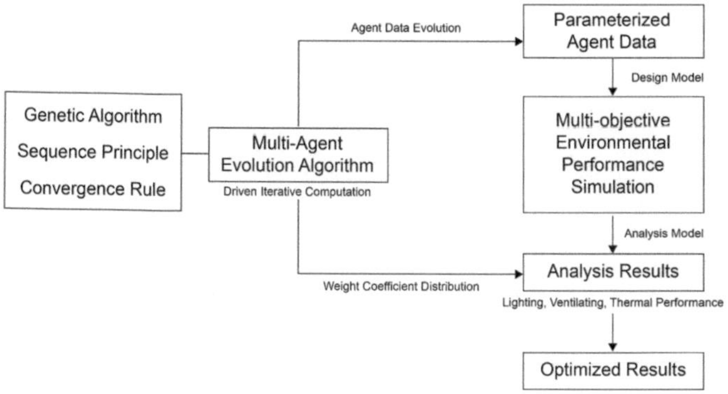

Fig. 18.1 Diagram of the performance optimization process driven by genetic algorithm (*Source* Philip F. Yuan)

Following the steps above, from the environmental analysis and simulation to the urban formation and optimization, geometry becomes the key medium linking performance parameters and environmental strategies. As a consequence, the urban morphology is no longer a subjective definition from designers but the objective outcome of related environmental strategies based on local conditions. Meanwhile, urban morphology driven by environmental performance serves as a modifier to improve the urban environment and to facilitate ecological and livable civic environments in return. Eventually, a new pattern of sustainable urbanization will be formed in which urban morphology and environmental performance can penetrate through and optimize one another and are mutually interactive. Two representative projects will be explored in the next chapter: one involves creating an adaptive urban morphology with diversity and dynamics by adopting ecological strategies based on wind and solar performance; the other treats wind performance as the main driving concept of urban formation.

18.4 Case Study: Micro City

18.4.1 Background Overview

Micro city is an entry in the Vertical Cities Asia International Design Competition 2013 from Tongji University students. This competition aims to focus on the unprecedented opportunities as well as immense challenges led by the rapid urbanization in Asia, address the problems of urban sprawl, congestion and pollution and put forward sustainable development proposals and innovation patterns for future high-density urbanization.

Micro City is the application of urban design methodology, integrating environmental performance simulation with contemporary ecological strategy (Fig. 18.2). In Micro City, the urban morphology and urban environment can be a

Fig. 18.2 Render view of one cluster (*Source* Philip F. Yuan)

mutually beneficial, natural element—for instance, wind and sun generate and optimize urban form, and the new urban form will in turn feed back to the environment, leaving long-lasting impact. This project actively responds to the human-place conflicts of urbanization in Asia, undoubtedly an important reference for China's urbanization.

18.4.2 Environment as Driving Factor

The site selected for competition in 2013 was a rural space 17 km from Hanoi, Vietnam. The competition aims to create novel city plan proposals within 25 km^2 of land and with one square kilometer of land as a testing field. The participants should perform detailed urban plan design, proving jobs, housing and services for 100,000 residents.

The design process for "Micro City" started with the record and research on the environmental elements of Hanoi. From an environmental point of view, connecting design methodology to the specific site features contributes to understanding the inherent nature and extrinsic characteristics of the city. In this way, the design team was able to extract key parameters that determined the city's internal structural logic, analyzing those parameters and interrelations.

Through a study of the historic data of the site we found that Hanoi is in a tropical, hot-humid monsoon climate with four distinct seasons. In summer, the air temperature reaches its highest value and the solar radiation is at its most intense: the solar altitude angle approaches 90°, resulting in hot climate conditions. Meanwhile, in winter, the average air temperature ranges between 14 and 18 °C with a 45° solar altitude angle. In summer, the prevailing wind is southeasterly and comes from the sea, with high humidity, whereas in winter, the prevailing wind is northeasterly, dry and cold as it passes over the vast continent. The local climatic conditions led to the unique Tube-House typology: this house reveals a strip structure, grows vertically, and conducts passive ventilation with its inner courtyard. The Tube-House consists of typical high-density blocks in Hanoi that impede the city's natural ventilation (Fig. 18.3).

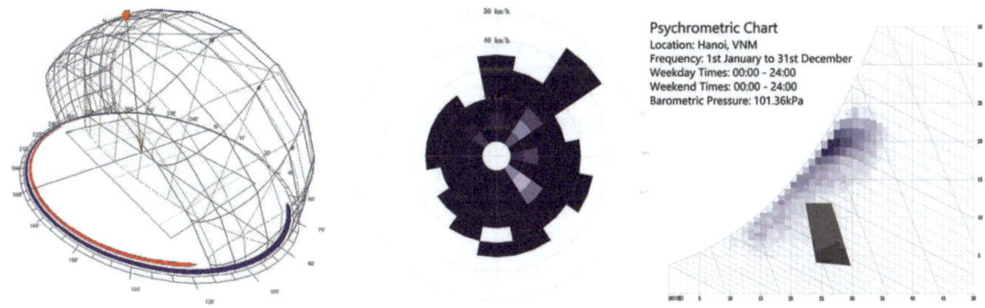

Fig. 18.3 Environmental analysis showing different weather conditions in Hanoi, e.g., daily radiation, wind speed and frequency, psychometric chart (*Source* Weather Tool)

After all these analysis, the next question will be how urban morphology could react. Psychometric chart, which presents physical and thermal properties of moist air in a graphical form, serves as a general guide to understand how passive sustainable technologies could help in hot-humid monsoon climate. As we can see from the chart, among all possible sources of environmental elements in the urban context, the wind and sun, both scalable phenomena, are probably the most influential and predominant. Therefore, the design team proposed three topographic strategies through environmental simulations of the local climate operated at three different scales: urban, cluster and building.

18.4.3 Urban Layout

In traditional urbanization processes, a large amount of farm land is converted into construction land, resulting in uneven urban density. The high density of buildings on the central streets makes them unsuitable for natural ventilation. Therefore, an urban-scale environmentally responsive strategy is to develop multiple micro clusters that consist of the central city and surrounding agriculture, that achieve balanced planning and facilitate natural ventilation.

With the simulation of multi-agent systems, we define rural urban patterns, natural landscape and population density as the key morphological influence parameters and conduct a dynamic simulation of the evolution of Micro City. Different performative parameters are weighted differently in the fitness function according to the design initiatives. The original simulation points are built upon strongholds called "seeds for new urban settlements" which represent the city's locality and adaptability, including cultural heritage sites, potential industrial bases and raw landscape locations. Growing from those points, adynamic density is generated and clusters inheriting urban conditions are formed. Multi-agent simulations help in intelligent function assignment within the city clusters and track the proper functional proportions between different cluster functionalities. At every stage of the simulation, each cluster of the micro city reveals a harmonious relationship between city functions and the surrounding environment. This is a type of dynamic relationship that can adapt itself to current environmental conditions.

The final outcome of the simulation is interpreted as a non-hierarchical continuous urban space based on high-potential developing points. The site is a myriad of functions and open space, interweaving a high-density urban area with its accessory low-density agricultural extension. There is no formal boundary between urban and rural: transitions and spatial organizations are achieved gradually and with soft boundaries. The urban level configuration and spatial distribution networks generated from this simulation trigger the wind to penetrate through the city. Inserting environmental elements such as soil, plants and water into original homogeneous streets and buildings can improve the city's overall environmental performance, with buildings interspersed by green areas of different sizes. Farm-land and the eco-landscape have high penetrability, and high-speed wind that pass through these area scan be slowed down by the environment. In addition, the so called garden city can facilitate thermal transmission: heat can be rapidly dissolved through convection with the surrounding landscape in summer, forming comfortable thermal urban space (Fig. 18.4).

This is the Micro City composed of micro clusters distributed over 25 km^2. This new style of urban-rural integration not only can preserve the city's diversity, but also demonstrates great thermal environmental performance.

Fig. 18.4 General bird's-eye view of the city (*Source* Philip F. Yuan)

18.4.4 City Cluster Prototype

In the selected one square kilometer of the site, the requirement to house 100,000 people contributes to the densely populated urban spaces; the city therefore fundamentally needs a lot of wind for thermal relief and comfort in the built-up areas. For better ventilation in such a dense, hot-humid city, ventilation corridors along major prevailing wind directions would allow cooler air drained from outlying areas to flow through the more built-up areas, removing excess heat, gases and particulates (Dekay and Brown 2014). Thus, the strategy we adopt is to introduce wind corridors aligned primarily along the prevailing wind direction routes, using the wind as the main tool used for cutting the urban fabric, dividing clusters into parcels to loose urban pattern, forming wide breezy streets for wind flow. The dominant wind corridor ranges from 40 to 80 m, which encompasses ecological parks, agricultural lands and irrigation systems. It constitutes a branch of the urban ecosystem, helping to modulate the micro-climate. Having begun with the three different analytical models, appropriate cluster and landscape scale is finally achieved through the experimental selection of a genetic algorithm based on Computational Fluid Dynamics (CFD) simulation results with the landscape percentage and urban footprint as variables (Fig. 18.5).

Three different types of wind corridor are finally calculated: one shows the case of inserting the wind corridor following a diagonal direction and the other two divide the main flux in two, with a 90-degree angle. Influenced by wind direction, wind speed and wind corridor width, under the same plot ratio, the city cluster reveals completely different performance, including landscape percentage, architectural

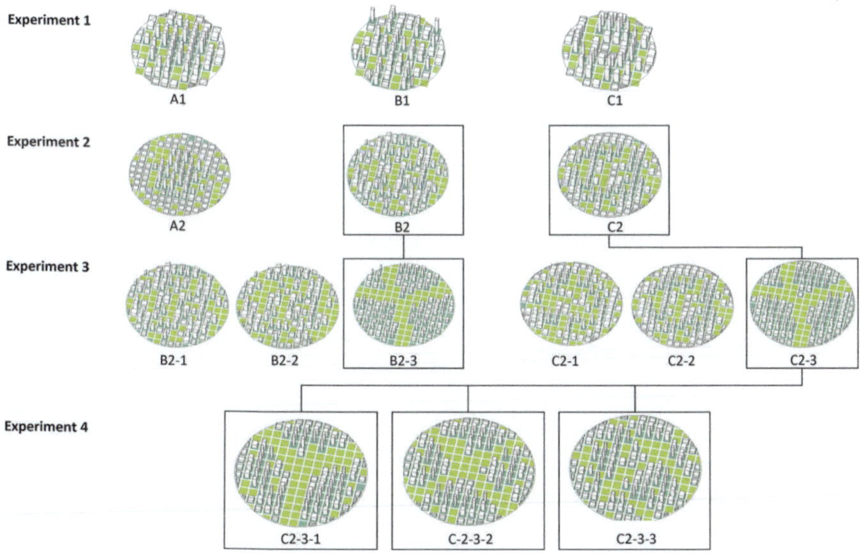

Fig. 18.5 Genetic algorithm-based experimental process (*Source* Philip F. Yuan)

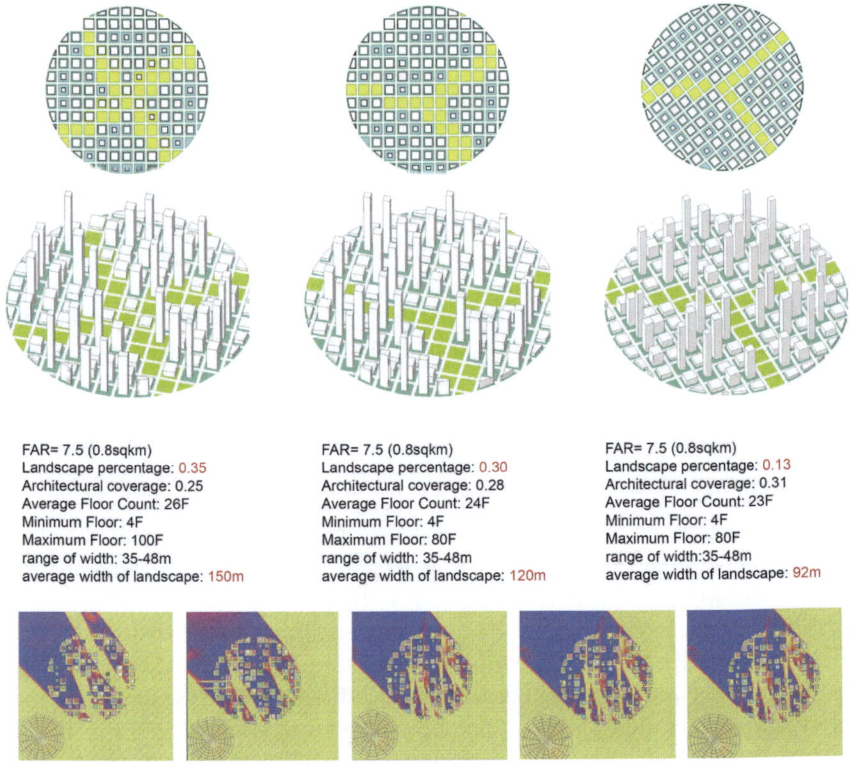

Fig. 18.6 Wind analysis comparisons (*top*) and wind simulations of one cluster showing different wind paths (*down*) (*Source* Philip F. Yuan)

coverage, building stories and landscape scope (Fig. 18.6). With the design of the main wind corridor in the selected city cluster, based on function and landscape planning, a high-density urban morphology with a plot ratio of six is formed. Based on this volume, a secondary wind corridor is inserted into the streets, facilitating the air flow between single buildings. The secondary wind corridor follows the street and road direction, that is, the path of the prevailing wind.

18.4.5 High-Rise Prototype

High-rise prototype uses aerodynamic performance and solar radiation performance as form generators and optimizers. Ecological urban spaces are formed from the collaborative effects of these two environmental drivers in terms of podiums and upper towers.

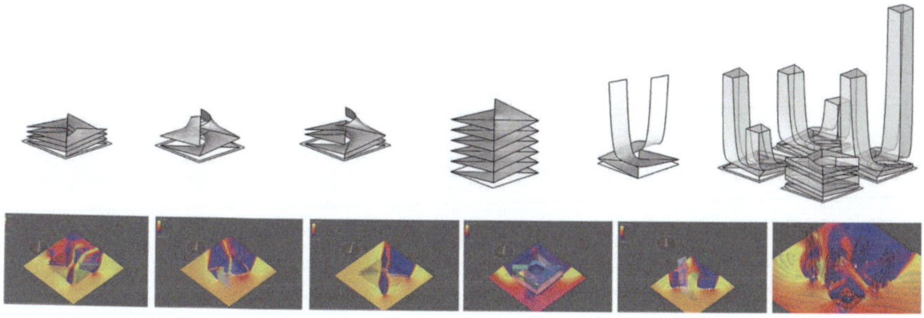

Fig. 18.7 Diagram of the wind-driven high-rise building generation process (*top*) and related CFD simulation images (*down*) (*Source* Philip F. Yuan)

To enhance air circulation for dispersing heat and pollutants, thus creating comfortable pedestrian environment, it is critical to increase the permeability of the podiums at the street level. Based on CFD simulations, podiums with compact volumes are particularly impeding air movement. As a type of fluid, wind can be decreased gradually when it is followed by a spiral podium surface and passes through the building at a moderate speed. The wind-induced streamlined form can deflect the wind, reducing its pressure on the structures and skins of high-rise buildings (Raydan and Steemers 2003). It can facilitate natural ventilation because of the stack effect; and creating comfortable pedestrian zones. Candidate geometries with different helix angles are converted into CFD format to generate the optimum podium form (Fig. 18.7).

In high-density urban space, natural lighting between upper towers is a great challenge as adjacent buildings reduce the availability of daylight and solar radiation. As we know, the energy efficiency of the urban texture relies notably on the buildings' form, which characterizes its capacity to take profit of the solar potential. With the sun, the most important factor is the angle between the direction of sunshine and the building surface in light. The greater the angle, the more radiation the building surface receives and vice versa. Thus, the solar incident angle in winter is used to optimize the tower height of high-rise buildings, lowering the block height in southern directions. The building itself reveals a slope roof, enabling the irradiation of daylight to the northern surfaces to meet the basic demands of living conditions. Additionally, multiple roof terraces and indoor buffering zones cultivated with plants can serve as a self-shading system, largely decreasing the amount of direct solar radiations. The porous structure forms different types of corridors and public spaces which would help wind deflection and avoid air stagnation (Figs. 18.8 and 18.9).

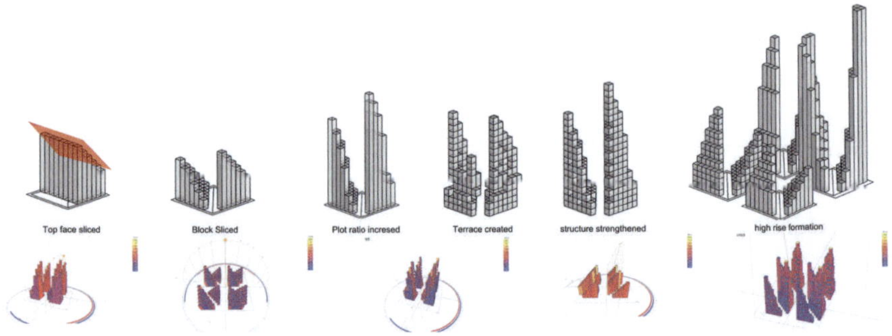

Fig. 18.8 Diagram of the radiation-driven high-rise building generation process (*top*) and related solar simulation images (*down*) (*Source* Philip F. Yuan)

Fig. 18.9 Render images of the high-rise building, showing the solar influenced garden roof and the spiral podiums (*Source* Philip F. Yuan)

18.5 Case Study: City of Breezes

18.5.1 Background Overview

The following example, which reflects environmental performance as a new local identity that affects the contemporary urban formation process, is our design in the recently announced international competition "Shenzhen Bay Super City". In this competition, we proposed a project called the "City of Breezes" in which we attempted to use wind performance as the main concept driving the design process.

Fig. 18.10 Render image (view from Shenzhen bay) (*Source* Philip F. Yuan)

Using the wind as a form generator and the form as a wind modifier, both take advantage of one another to approach a new cityscape (Fig. 18.10).

The project site is located at the central area of the Shenzhen Bay ring, which will become the most important city area in the Shenzhen-Hong Kong metropolitan region. As one of the goals of this competition, three four-hundred-meter high-rise buildings will be proposed in this area to improve the local urban function both economically and culturally. As such, the main task of the design is to balance the development's economic requirements and the local environmental performance at the same time to establish a new urban locality for this area.

18.5.2 Environmental Driving Factor

Starting with the environmental analysis, the local wind temperature and frequency, average rainfall and optimum sunlight orientation were drawn to provide a basic understanding of the environmental identity of this particular area. On the one hand, the average temperature and humidity in both summer and winter far exceed the

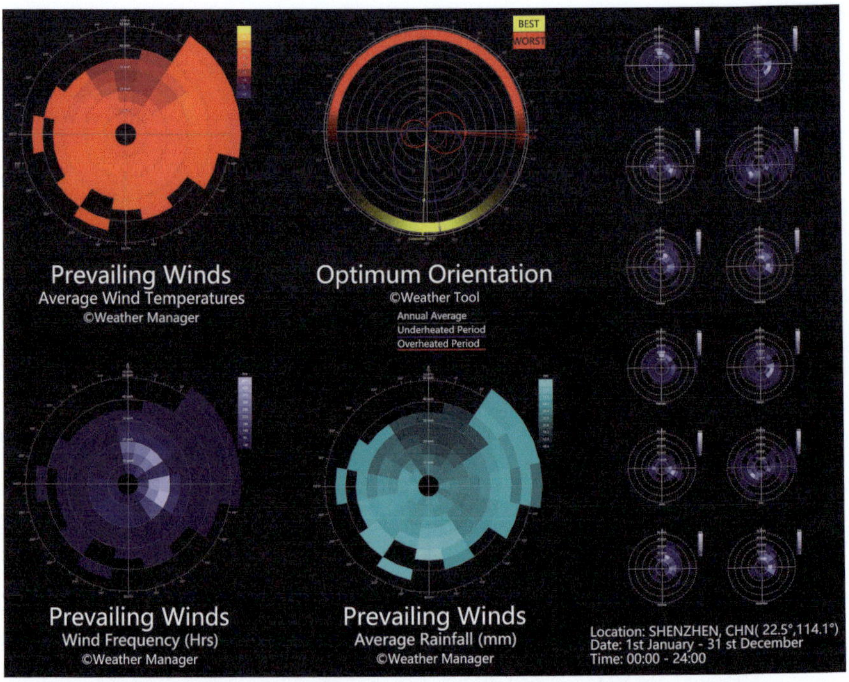

Fig. 18.11 Environmental analysis showing different weather conditions in Shenzhen, e.g., wind temperature and frequency, average rainfall and optimum sunlight orientation (*Source* Weather Tool; Weather Management)

human comfort zone; on the other hand, the annual leading wind direction is fairly constant, with the south wind from the open water area of Shenzhen bay prevailing in summer and the northeast wind from the mountain prevailing in winter. Based on these two climate situations, the main concept of the environmental strategy was to create a comfortable environment by manipulating the form and distribution of the urban space to increase the wind speed in summer and decrease it in winter (Fig. 18.11).

As the local wind performance became the main influence on the urban formation, the design method unfolded into three different aspects, and each explained the relationship between wind performance and urban form in a specific scale: landscape system, building form and skin treatment.

18.5.3 Landscape System

To create a highly wind-controlled zone for urban public activities, all of the buildings were initially distributed to the east and west of the design area; the central part was left empty as a wind tunnel to connect the south water-front and the

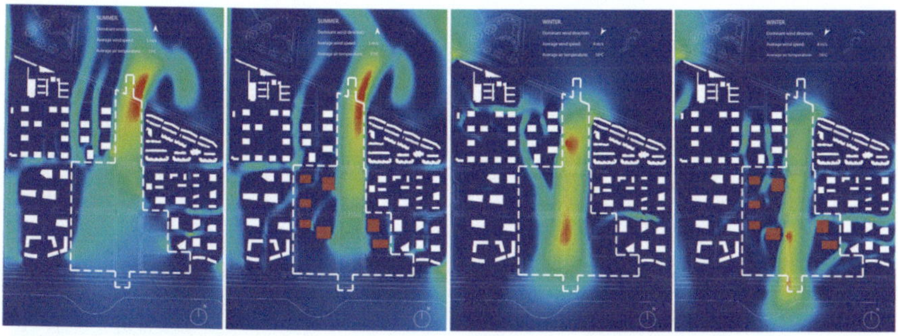

Fig. 18.12 Wind analysis showing wind speed and pressure at different points along the site (from *left* to *right* summer without building, summer with building, winter without building, winter with building) (*Source* Philip F. Yuan)

northern mountains both environmentally and functionally. After the buildings were located in the area, the gradient map showing the wind speed and wind pressure at different points along the site was drawn from the wind analysis at urban scale (Fig. 18.12).

Using the gradient wind field as the main parameter to generate the landscape form of the central area, the interrelation between the city landscape and environmental performance was realized at ground level. By creating a green carpet system, in which the hills, slopes and disposition of the trees and lakes were distributed based on wind depressions and high-pressure areas, the wind speed and direction can be modified and managed, combining with the cooling effect of the lake's evaporation to achieve the desired comfort zones along the park.

In summer, the wind flow from the south water-front will be slowed down first by the bumps in the green surface; then the wind direction will be modified to cross the lake area of the central landscape. After the wind is cooled down by combining the effects of sun irradiation and water evaporation, the air will be forced by the stack effect of the tower's double skin system and begin to speed up to improve the surrounding thermal comfort zones. In winter, because the double skin's stack effect will be turned off to preserve the heat in the building interior, those bumps on the landscape simply become shields to lock the northeasterly wind and slow it down to create outdoor comfort areas behind the shields (Fig. 18.13).

18.5.4 Building Form

In the strategy of the high-rise design, each building contributes to enhancing the site's wind performance by applying different formal and technical functionalities.

At the ground level, the podium of each tower twists itself. Inconsequence, a rotating pass system for both people and wind traveling upward and a public space system between each two floors of the podium are established, which will improve

Fig. 18.13 The landscape topography generated by wind analysis affects the ventilation of the site in turn (from *left* to *right* summer conditions, winter conditions) (*Source* Philip F. Yuan)

the urban environment synthetically. The outdoor space system created from the twist can be considered as a part of the urban space, and thus, to create a continuous landscape system for the city, the green carpet will be pulled out with a deformation technique at some particular spot in the park, such as the hills over streets, to reach all of the podium spaces. Once the central carpet is connected to the podium, the cooling wind will also be guided to those outdoor spaces by the continuous surface and forced upward by the tower's stack effect. Additionally, because of the podium's twisting form, the wind always flows along the public spaces in a rotated way so that the cooling effect will be maximized.

At the top of the tower, the wind erodes the prismatic volume, converting it into a system of "small fingers". The high-rise, as a vertical object, creates air friction, which usually generates great wind pressure on the building skin. In this project, rather than blocking the wind, the tower's formadapts itself by dividing into multiple small volumes to reduce the wind pressure on the curtain wall and stabilize the wind field in the surrounding area. The conditions at the top are important not only for the space outside the building, but also for the inside. Spatially, the dividing top increases the amount of ventilation, views and sunlight required by functional uses at the top of the tower, such as hotels and residential spaces. Structurally, the outrigger structure is no longer needed because of the smaller floor area, and instead it is transformed into a braced rigid-frame system (Fig. 18.14).

18.5.5 Skin Treatment

The skin of the main part of the towers, where the offices are located, was designed as a highly controlled passive ventilation system, which dissolves the isolation of the high-rise's interior space by creating an adaptive comfort zone in this area. As a sequence, the public space inside the tower will become a semi-outdoor space that can be understood as an extension of the urban landscape.

To create this adaptive comfort zone, the main part of the high-rise is divided into groups of 15 floors by multiple technical levels which associate with the outrigger structure. Each group has a vertical open space in between the office space and the tower facade where a double skin system was proposed to generate a buffer space outside of the tower. Thus, the energy transmission between the vertical space and the exterior is based on the buffer's air energy exchange efficiency, and the thermal effect of the interior can be highly controlled in different seasons (Fig. 18.15).

This double skin system has one intake (at the lower technical floor of the group) and one outlet (at the top technical floor of the same group), the opening of which can be controlled mechanically. During summer, these apertures are opened to turn the buffer zone created between the two skins into a solar chimney. On one hand, the outer skin absorbs the energy from the solar radiation to heat the air inside the buffer and force it upward through the outlet. Because of the stack effect, the cooling air from the ground landscape will be forced into the buffer through the intake to reduce the heat in that area. On the other hand, the inner skin of the tower is an active element that closes the tower to the wind and at the same time offers the possibility of being permeable for ventilation. Therefore, the cooling air from the ground level will eventually be ventilated into the vertical open space inside the tower. As a result, a controlled stack effect is produced inside each group, generating continuous natural ventilation of interior space.

In winter, because of the differences in temperature between the interior and exterior, the intakes and outlets of the double skin system will be closed. Then, the buffer zone between the two skins becomes an air chamber. By slowing down the

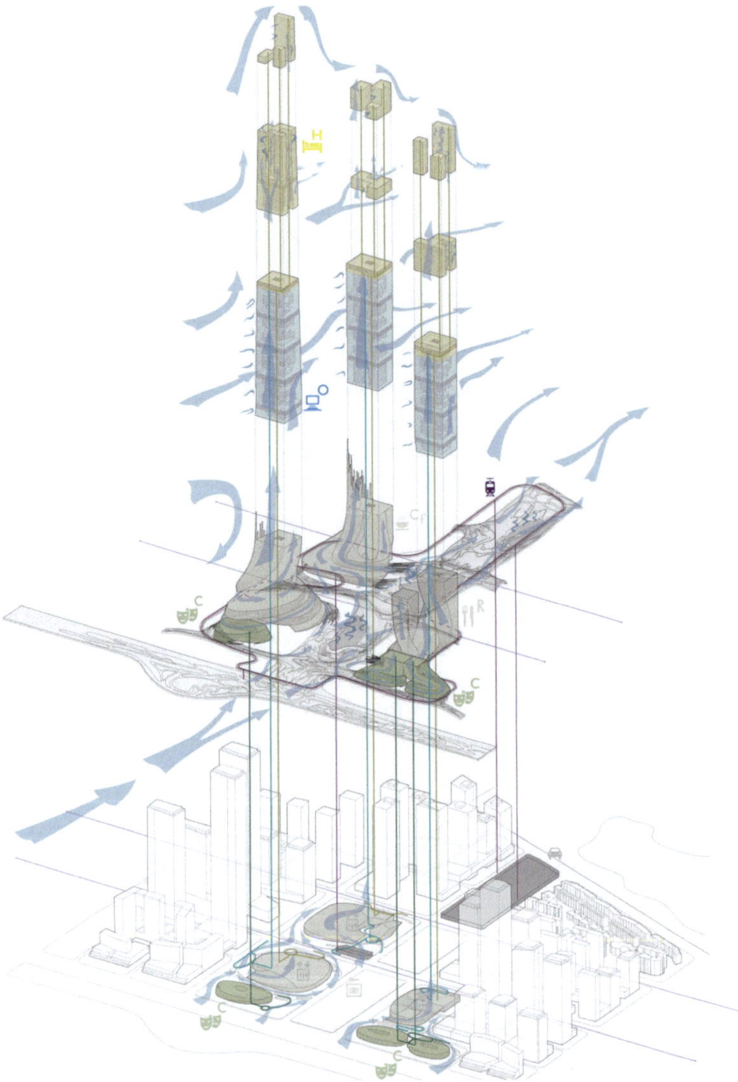

Fig. 18.14 Diagram showing the relationship between the high-rise's form strategy and the ventilation of the urban space (*Source* Philip F. Yuan)

energy exchange between interior and exterior, the heat inside the open space will be preserved.

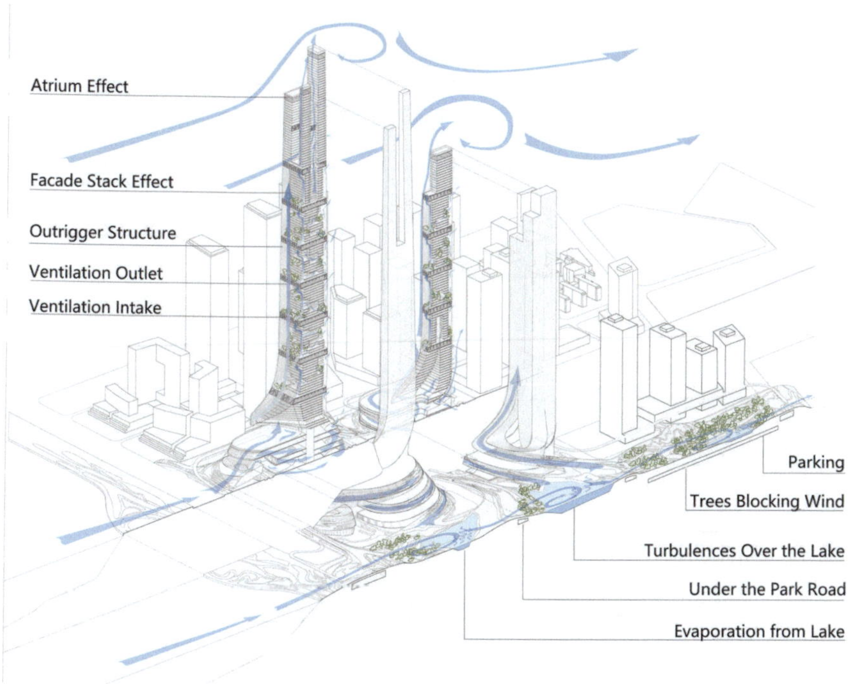

Fig. 18.15 The stack effect from the double skin system enhances the ventilation of both the building interior and the urban public space (*Source* Philip F. Yuan)

18.5.6 Synchronized System

The thermodynamic thinking based on the relationship between natural ventilation and form was applied at different scales to the systems of this urban project. However, these systems are not isolated from one another; rather, they work as a synchronized system. The stack effect of the tower skin affects the ventilation of the central park, which will in turn determine the landscape's topographyand the podium's form. The wind is forced and guided by the thermal effect and the urban form, passing through the whole vertical landscape, to achieve a comfortable urban environment as well as to establish a new local identity for the Shenzhen bay area (Figs. 18.16 and 18.17).

Fig. 18.16 Photo of the physical model showing the central landscape (*Source* Philip F. Yuan)

Fig. 18.17 Photos of the physical model showing the surface system, including the urban landscape, the podium and the tower skin (*Source* Philip F. Yuan)

18.6 Conclusion and Discussion

This article explores a new urban formation methodology based on environmental performance simulations. This performance driven generative design approach filled with its reliance on locality is thus deemed an effective way to understand our built environment and to generate sustainable and specific urban morphology from bottom-up. A multi-disciplinary mode of operation to integrate cutting-edge computational and environmental design tools for the sake of identity and sustainability is thus seen as a vital outcome of the design methodology.

Meanwhile, in the whole workflow, much remains to be improved. First, at present stage, most environmental performance simulations rely on digital tools such as CFD simulations. Although we admit that digital simulation tools have opened up new possibilities for design and research by introducing environments in which we can manipulate and observe, the computational power constrains limit its availability when simulating performance in dense urban spatial context. In this situation, a combination of digital and physical simulation tools (custom-made wind tunnels) would be the future directions for simulations. With the open-source platforms, direct feedback from simulation results and digital design will become a reality, optimizing the simulation experience and the overall workflow.

References

Abalos I, Ibanez D (2012) Thermodynamics applied to highrise and mixed use prototypes, 1st edn. Harvard GSD, Boston

Andre P, Kummert M, Nicolas J (1998) Coupling thermal simulation and airflow calculation for a better evaluation of natural ventilation strategies. In: Liege: proceedings of the system simulation in buildings conference, Belgium

Asadi E, Silva MG, Antunes CH, Dias L, Glicksman L (2014) Multi-objective optimization for building retrofit: a model using genetic algorithm and artificial neural network and an application. Energy Build 81:444–456

Attia S, Herde A (2011) Early design simulation tools for net zero energy buildings: a comparison of ten tools. International Building Performance Simulation Association, Sydney, Australia

Barry RG, Chorley RJ (2009) Atmosphere, weather, and climate, 9th edn. Routledge, London

Bazjanac V, Maile T, Rose C, O'Donnell J, Mrazovic N (2011) An assessment of the use of building energy performance simulation in early design. IBPSA Building Simulation, Sydney

Chen W (2015) Chinese environmental aesthetics. Su F (trans), Cipriani G (ed). Routledge, London

Cheng V, Steemers K, Montavon M, Compagnon R (2006) Urban form, density and solar potential. In: Geneva: the 23rd international conference on passive and low energy architecture, Switzerland

Clark JA (2001) Energy simulation in building design, 2nd edn. Butterworth-Heinemann, London

DeKay M, Brown GZ (2014) Sun, wind and light: architectural design strategies, 3rd edn. Wiley, New York

Givoni B (1998a) Climate consideration in building and urban design, 1st edn. Wiley, New York

Givoni B (1998b) Climate considerations in building and urban design, 2nd edn. Van Nostrand Reinhold, New York

Kolarevic B (2005) Architecture in the digital age: design and manufacturing, 1st edn. Taylor & Francis, New York

Lechner N (2014) Heating, cooling, lighting: sustainable design methods for architects, 4th edn. Wiley, New York

Malkawi AM, Augenbroe G (2004) Advanced building simulation, 1st edn. Spon Press, London

Marsh A (2008) Generative and performative design: a challenging new role for modern architects. In: The Oxford Conference, Oxford

Menges A (2011) Integrative design computation: integrating material behaviour and robotic man-ufacturing processes in computational design for performative wood constructions, ACADIA2011–Integration through Computation, Banff, Alberta, pp 72–81

Moya R, Salim F, Williams M, Sharaidin K (2013) Flexing wind: aerodynamic study of architectural windbreak. In: Delft: the 31st international conference on education and research in computer aided architectural design in Europe, Netherlands

Oxman R (2009) Performance-based design: current practices and research issues. Int J Arch Comput 6(1):1–17

Raydan D, Steemers K (2003) Building form and environmental performance: archetypes, analysis and an arid climate. Energy Build 35(1):49–59

Ritchie A, Thomas R (2013) Sustainable urban design: an environmental approach, 2nd edn. Taylor & Francis, London

Santamouris M (2006) Environmental design of urban buildings: an integrated approach, 1st edn. Routledge, London

Santamouris M, Papanikolaou N, Koronakis I, Livada I, Asimakopoulos D (1999) Thermal and air flow characteristics in a deep pedestrian canyon under hot weather conditions. Atmos Environ 33:4503–4521

Shea K, Aish R and Gourtovaia M (2005) Towards integrated performance-driven generative design tools. Automation in Construction 14(2): 253-264

Wang W, Zmeureanua R, Rivard H (2005) Applying multi-objective genetic algorithms in green building design optimization. Build Environ 40(11):1512–1525

Yi YK, Malkawi AM (2009) Optimizing building form for energy performance based on hierarchical geometry relation. Autom Constr 18(6):825–833

Chapter 19
Nature Conservation as Part of a Multifunctional Use of Suburban Landscapes

Michael W. Rode

19.1 Introduction

Since the first application of agricultural practices, humans have altered most of the world's landscapes and adapted them for their own utilization (Lambin et al. 2001, 2003). Initially, the yield function of the landscape for food production was the major driver of this development. It was driven by increasing demands produced by growing urbanization and technological development, which intensified changes through the increased utilization of other landscape functions. Examples are increasing the supply of urban population with drinking water, energy, and raw material for pre-industrial production, as well as the disposal of wastes. The increase in population necessitated an agriculture that optimally exploited the given site conditions for food production to meet the growing demand for food. Local and regional variations in site conditions resulted in a diverse use of natural resources and varied land management (Vos and Meekens 1999). To an extent, different parts of the landscape were used in a multifunctional way (Vos and Meekens 1999). Nevertheless, overexploitation occurred, which, combined with the degradation of agricultural land, was followed by regulations for the protection of livelihoods (Simpson et al. 2001; Thomson and Simpson 2006).

With the onset and progression of industrialization, urbanization continued to increase. This trend has particularly accelerated since the mid-20th century. New requirements arose for landscapes surrounding cities and in rural–urban relationships. For instance, landscapes should provide recreation, infrastructure, and improve the urban climate. This requirement is connected with changes in the natural and land-use systems, in the regional flow of materials, and in the ways landscapes are used by other land uses (Decker et al. 2000; Rode 2005a).

M.W. Rode (✉)
Institute of Environmental Planning, Leibniz University of Hannover, Hannover, Germany
e-mail: rode@umwelt.uni-hannover.de

F. Wang and M. Prominski (eds.), *Urbanization and Locality*,
DOI 10.1007/978-3-662-48494-4_19

Meanwhile, the mechanization of agriculture, introduction of artificial fertilizers, and use of pesticides reduced the dependence of agriculture on natural site conditions. As a result, the impact of nutrient enrichment, particularly nitrogen, and pesticides on the environment increased to the same extent as did erosion and soil compaction. The structure, and with it the diversity, of the landscape decreased, which has negative consequences for biodiversity and the overall appearance of landscapes (Haynes-Young 2009; Swift et al. 2004; Lautenbach et al. 2011; Ruschkowsky and Wiehe 2008; Wiehe et al. 2009). Currently, global warming, which is predominantly caused by the use of fossil fuels, places additional demands on the landscape to provide renewable energy and store climate-active substances (Buhr et al. 2013; Metzger et al. 2006; Saathoff et al. 2013).

The greatly expanded demands on different landscape uses create strong competitions for the functions provided by the landscape, which concerns both the competition for space and for the intensity and type of use (Termorshuizen and Opdam 2009; Walker et al. 1997). Thus, direct and indirect competitions can be distinguished (Rode 2009).

Direct competitions arising from competition for space are primarily caused by the following utilizations: production of food and animal feed, production of renewable energy and material utilization (e.g., paper production), nature conservation (e.g., protected areas, nature protection by agreement), extension of settlements and infrastructure, and raw material extraction.

Indirect competitions arise primarily from the intensity of land use by agriculture, forestry, recreation, and energy production and are mainly attributed to the following utilizations of the landscape: drinking water extraction, nature conservation (biotop networks, changes in landscape structure, indirect effects on protected areas), local recreation and landscape-related tourism, and flood control, among others.

Each of these competitions includes feedback effects as well as competitions between the different indirect land use types. The greater the variety of demands placed on landscape use and the greater the intensity of these uses, the more frequent and intense is the competition. The growing demand for different landscape uses contrasts with the finiteness of available space. For the landscape to fulfill the various demands placed upon it, the functions offered by a landscape must be used in a multifunctional way. Various functions must be simultaneously provided in a landscape and within the same area (Ling et al. 2007; De Groot et al. 2010; Zasada 2011). However, different uses frequently have contradictory aims (Klug 2007). This scenario raises the question of what and where the conflicts and limits of multifunctional land use are. In addition, how can the multifunctionality of a landscape be optimally exploited?

Against this background, the limits and possibilities of multifunctional land-use, in terms of the implementation of nature conservation objectives, are examined and discussed using examples based on different research projects at the Leibniz University of Hannover. The limitations of multifunctional land-use arising from direct competition for space are most evident in the suburban area. The need for and possibilities of multifunctional land use are apparent from the growing indirect competitions with numerous ecosystem services, which arise from the increasing intensive use of agricultural land not only in suburban landscapes but also in the countryside.

19.2 Multifunctionality in Suburban Areas

Different demands on the landscape cumulate in suburban areas. Thus, the surroundings of urban areas are exposed to enormous utilization pressure compared with landscapes located far from urban sites (Kroll et al. 2012; Walker et al. 1997). Controlled and uncontrolled expansions of built-up and paved areas create suburban communities that are often characterized by a disturbed countryside (Strubelt 1997; Thomlinson et al. 1996). Remaining unbuilt portions of the countryside are used intensively for recreation or agriculture to produce food for urban inhabitants (Kroll et al. 2012). In this way, natural and extensively used ecosystems are often either completely destroyed or reduced. As is the case with other heavily used landscapes, "biodiversity is most often completely subordinate to production objectives" (Vos and Meekes 1999) or recreational activities. The potential for successful nature conservation, which is one of the (economically) weakest land uses, is extremely low. Therefore, nature conservation in suburban areas exists only in small and strongly protected areas. In the remaining large portions of undeveloped countryside, intensive use contradicts and prevents efforts for nature protection.

Nonetheless, undeveloped landscapes within suburbia, which are used for agriculture and recreation (in nature), are also endangered by the expansion of land development (Tan et al. 2005). New nature conservation concepts that are based on multifunctional, integrated land use, in conjunction with recreational and agricultural land uses, are thus necessary (Termorshuizen and Opdam 2009; Zasada 2011; Rode and Haaren 2005; Haaren and Rode 2010). Based on the above, the main hypotheses to be tested by nature conservation-related scientific investigations are as follows:

Within suburban landscapes, the integration of nature conservation into multifunctional land use with agriculture and recreation is possible.

The integrated, multifunctional use of unbuilt landscapes enhances the conservation possibilities of selected precious landscapes and natural environment within a suburban area.

19.2.1 Situation

The increasing demand for residential, industrial, and commercial sites leads to a reduction of undeveloped land and decrease in adequate sites for agriculture, recreation, and nature conservation; disruption and fragmentation of the remaining countryside, and intensification of the use of the remaining open spaces and agricultural areas (BfLR 1996; Thomlinson and Rivera 2000; Antrop 2004; Lovell and Johnston 2009; Kroll et al. 2012).

As a result, competition for the remaining open spaces among recreation, agriculture, and nature conservation land users increases, and the fragmentation and isolation of populations and habitats restrict the opportunities for nature conservation in suburban areas. This case in turn has negative consequences for biodiversity and population dynamics within the landscape (Findlay and Houlahan 1997; Whited et al. 2000).

For the most part, the remaining undeveloped areas within suburbia show a mono-functional use as either agriculture or recreation or nature conservation (Beckmann 1997). In other words, one type of use dominates within one part of the landscape.

Recreation is concentrated in parks and green spaces. Recreation in suburban agricultural, forestry, or nature conservation areas is restricted to corridor zones (paths, roads, etc.), their borders, or to special sites. The remaining open landscape is experienced indirectly, through scenic views of the landscape.

Agriculture (and forestry) is a land use driven by economic principles and does not allow for the use of fields and meadows by people for recreation. Ecological farming promotes nature conservation, but the production principle is more important than, for example, species or ecosystem protection.

Nature conservation is often restricted to special protection areas, in which agriculture and forestry play only a minor role and are not motivated by economic principles. Nature protection and/or development principles dominate.

The decreasing availability of open areas; parceling of the landscape; segregation of mono-functional land uses; and competition and conflicts among recreation, agriculture, and nature conservation uses impede the protection of suburban open landscapes as well as obstruct the development of nature conservation potentials (ARL 1997; Koenigs 1993). Consequently, "the urbanization process is more powerful than the process that creates good ecological conditions" (Schrijnen 2000) and the efforts that protect open spaces.

Nevertheless, sustainable development of suburbia requires effective protection of open spaces to ensure social (e.g., recreation), economic (e.g., higher environmental quality to attract businesses), and ecological functions (protection of biotic and abiotic resources) (Schmidt 1997; Schrijnen 2000). To give nature more space, new concepts for the protection of open areas and nature conservation within suburbia are necessary.

19.2.2 Integrated Multifunctional Land Use

One particular land-use concept is being tested in the Kronsberg suburb of Hannover. It is a plan for the coordinated recreational, agricultural, and nature conservational use of open areas in the suburban landscape to alleviate competition among the three types of land uses. It also aims to lead to positive synergistic effects in the area of nature conservation and better protection of the open spaces against continued expansion of built-up areas. For this concept to function and to achieve optimal synergistic results, recreational, agricultural, and nature conservational land uses must be equally prioritized. In principle, three types of coordinated land uses are imaginable (Fig. 19.1, cf. Brenken et al. 2005; Haaren and Rode 2007, 2010):

- Total integration of land uses in each site, with recreation, agriculture, and nature conservation all taking place in one site (**total multifunctionality**)
- Partial integration of land uses in each site, two of the three land-use types occurring in each site (**partial multifunctionality**)
- Spatial separation of land uses at the site level, where only one type of land use occurs within each site but the sites are well mixed and within close proximity of one another in the same landscape; integration of land uses occurs at the landscape-level (**tessellated multifunctionality**)

Based on these theoretical considerations, a concept for combined integrated land-use strategies is being developed and tested in the suburb of Kronsberg, a settlement southeast of Hannover (Brenken et al. 2003; Rode and Haaren 2005; Haaren and Rode 2010). The project "Nature conservation-oriented suburban development at Kronsberg, Hannover" is carried out by the Parks and Open Space Department of Hannover as one of the Test and Development Projects run by the Federal Agency for Nature Conservation of Germany (Klaffke et al. 2000). As is necessary for all modern landscapes following the hypothesis of Vos and Meekes (1999), the objective of the project is to protect open landscapes in suburban areas by developing new conservation strategies that provide more space for nature.

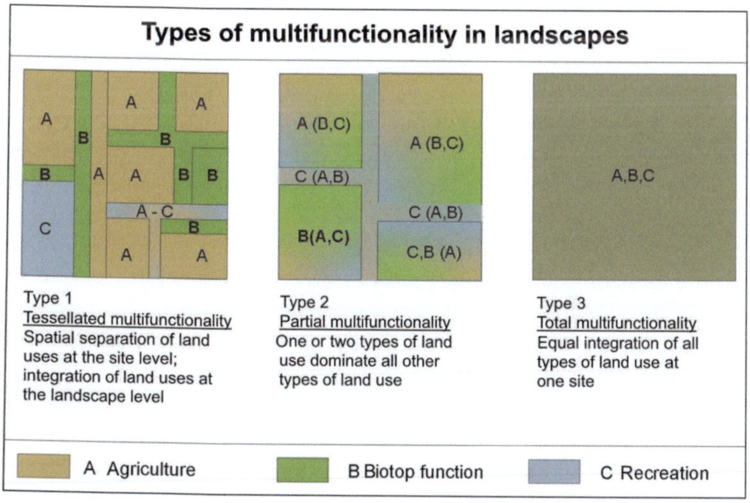

Fig. 19.1 Types of multifunctionality in landscapes (Haaren and Rode 2007; cf. Brenken et al. 2005; Haaren and Rode 2010)

The project was supported by extensive scientific studies undertaken by the Leibniz University of Hannover. This scientific investigation focuses on the possible synergistic effects of agriculture, recreation, and nature conservation, as well as the conflicts among these three types of land use at the site and landscape levels. In this context, the nature conservation research objectives were as follows: (1) to monitor the effectiveness of the measures implemented, (2) to determine whether the conceptual approaches are workable, and (3) to determine whether the project concept can be used as a model for the suburbs of other towns.

The last objective must also determine if the concept represents a viable alternative to conventional management and nature conservation strategies in suburban areas.

19.2.3 Developing the Kronsberg Landscape

Kronsberg is a low hill on the southeastern outskirts of Hannover. The shallow, lime- and loam-rich soils allow productive agricultural use. Hence, during the second half of the last century, agriculture at the Kronsberg intensified. Up until the early 1990s, intensive agricultural land use formed the Kronsberg landscape and was dominated by the cultivation of sugar beet and wheat. Large, open, and untextured arable land, intersected only by a few roads with narrow margins, dominated the landscape scenery (Fig. 19.2). However, since the turn of the last century, the open landscape of the Kronsberg area became popular with citizens seeking recreation. At this time, Kronsberg was the last great reserve of urban development in Hannover (Brenken et al. 2003).

At the end of the 20th century, the decision to carry out Expo 2000 in Hannover was followed by new pressures to expand residential areas to the Kronsberg countryside. A new suburban residential area in Hannover was constructed, with housing for nearly 6000 inhabitants. Nevertheless, according to the Expo's motto "Humankind, nature, technology", one of the main planning concerns in the redesign of Kronsberg was the balance between high-density housing schemes and open agricultural landscapes. A main target of the planners was also to define a new and permanent edge to the city, and concurrently, to protect the adjoining rural landscape against further settlement (Brenken et al. 2003).

Following these objectives, large parts of the countryside were reshaped with the aim of a multifunctional, ecological, and aesthetic development of Kronsberg. After the completion of the residential community on the Western slope and transformation of the remaining landscape area, 600 out of the former 1200 ha were retained for agriculture. According to the targets of multifunctional land use, the implemented measures on Kronsberg can be assigned in different ways to the objectives of species and habitat conservation, recreation, and agriculture. A few measures served exclusively one form of land use (Brenken et al. 2003). Most of the measures followed the concept of multifunctional land-use and resulted in two or even all three types of use simultaneously (see Fig. 19.1).

Fig. 19.2 Untextured landscape of Kronsberg (Images by Rode in 1998 and Förster in 2000)

The shallow, chalky soils of Kronsberg and the presence of rare segetal flora provide good prerequisites for developing a rich structured landscape with a high quality of nature conservation, recreation, and extensive agriculture and forestry. Within the formerly unstructured agricultural landscape, new types of landscape elements have been initiated:

- The central element of landscape design on Kronsberg is the so-called **Allmende**. The Allmende is a typically common type of land, characterized by chalky, dry grassland. Including a number of orchards, it forms a narrow, nearly 3 km long and 50–250 m wide ribbon that marks the transitional zone from compacted city to open countryside. As the area is owned by the City of Hannover and is established as a "public park" in the development plan of the adjacent Kronsberg residents, the area should be safeguarded as an open space for the long term. The maintenance of the Allmende should be made by a separate flock of sheep that is financed by the City of Hannover. It should simultaneously include the implementation of cost-efficient maintenance by agricultural use, conservation objectives, and recreational area use (total integration of land uses).
- Beginning in 1987, on the crest of Kronsberg, **small forests** were created over time until a total area of nearly 60 ha was achieved in 2003. In addition to the Allmende, these wood plantations should simultaneously support recreational use, extensive forestry, and nature conservation (total integration of land uses). The edges of these forests are designed as richly structured forest edges that makes them equally geared to the needs of conservation and recreation. From the view of nature conservation, the woods should provide new habitats for region-typical herbaceous fringe, as well as shrub and forest vegetation and fauna. The long-term goal is the development of a sweet woodruff-beech forest, which is also usable in forestry. In addition, part of the long-term goal is the development of a space with natural scenery and functional improvements for species using biotope complexes.
- At the top of Kronsberg, artificial elements, such as two **look-out hills,** were constructed. These were constructed out of the chalky soil material excavated from the new housing areas at the western edge of the Kronsberg area. These hills are used equally for nature conservation and recreation (partial integration of land

uses). The look-out hills on Kronsberg, Hannover's highest peak, offers a wide panoramic view of the city skyline and surrounding hilly landscape. The calcareous substrate, shallow soil, and steep slopes allow, particularly on the South Side, the creation of new habitats for flora and fauna of calcareous grassland.

- As part of the restructuring measures on Kronsberg, the **country lane network** was expanded to approximately 13 km. **Wide field margins** and **hedges** border the newly created country lanes. They connect within the meaning of the integrative overall approach (total integration of land uses) the different usage requirements in an optimal manner by taking over low maintenance biotope network and habitat functions, opening up the landscape for a variety of recreational activities, allowing more attractive sensory impressions, and facilitating the agricultural use of Kronsberg.
- The remaining intensively used fields and meadows (agriculture), special viewing platforms (recreation), and borders of the fields for the protection of special segetal flora (nature conservation) demonstrate examples of segregated land use.

19.2.4 Limits and Opportunities for Integrated Multifunctional Land Use from the Perspective of Nature Conservation

19.2.4.1 Development of Agricultural Landscapes

The development of Kronsberg to a landscape with a multifunctional use led to a decrease in the agricultural area from approximately 1200 to 600 ha. In many suburban landscapes, such reductions in arable land have resulted in a growing competition within agriculture and a significant intensification in the use of the remaining fields (Walker et al. 1997; Vos and Meekens 1999; Schrijnen 2000). Such intensification is negatively associated with direct and indirect effects on numerous ecosystem services (Rode and Kanning 2010). In this context, the following question arises: To what extent can the concept of integrated multifunctional land use contribute to a reduction of negative impacts on the various ecosystem services?

In many agricultural areas, the intensification of agricultural land use causes an acceleration of crop rotation and a loss of landscape structure (Ruschkowsky and Wiehe 2008; Rode and Kanning 2010) (Fig. 19.3). As diverse agricultural landscapes offer many environmental services, such as providing viable conditions for agricultural production, enhanced biodiversity, and local recreation, this intensification negatively impacts both the view of the landscape and most ecosystem services (Swift et al. 2004; Rode and Kanning 2010). Even in intensive agricultural landscapes, this impact is combined with a decrease in habitat quality and biodiversity (Altieri 1999; Tscharntke et al. 2005).

In suburban areas, however, arable land for producing food, fodder, and biomass is as limited as the area for the provision of ecosystem services. Consequently, agricultural areas must be multifunctional (Lovell 2010). In this case, the purpose of agricultural areas is not only production but also the provision of various ecosystem services, namely, the maintenance of soil fertility and groundwater quantity and quality, prevention of soil erosion, greenhouse gas sequestration, landscape aesthetics, and biodiversity (Termorshuizen and Opdam 2009). Thus, multifunctional approaches for the remaining suburban agricultural areas are needed to avoid direct competitions with other land uses. In addition, they are needed to minimize the negative impacts on the various ecosystem services, and thus, indirect competitions with other spatial uses. Key elements to minimize negative impacts on landscape structure and ecosystem services are first, a diverse crop rotation; second, the involvement of perennial crops in the agricultural cultivation practices; and third, the creation of new and unused landscape elements (Wiehe and Rode 2007; Ruschkowski and Wiehe 2008; Rode 2009; Wiehe et al. 2009; Boll et al. 2015).

I. **Enhancing crop diversity**

The number of crops on rotation is an important indicator of the effects of agricultural production on biodiversity and ecosystem services. When considering effects on both biodiversity and recreational value of the landscape as well as on other ecosystem services, it is clear that the fewer the number of crops on rotation, the greater the negative effects (Power 2010; Wiehe et al. 2010; Karpenstein-Machan 2011; Davis et al. 2012). For example, the large-scale cultivation of a single culture has strong negative effects on faunistic biodiversity and population densities, and thus, on the biodiversity of intensively used agricultural landscapes (Reich and Rüter 2011). The same applies to the effect on flood protection, groundwater resources, and aesthetic quality of the landscape (Wiehe et al. 2010).

Therefore, increasing crop rotation and diversity with a mix of biomass, fodder, and food crops leads to higher structure, habitat diversity, and aesthetic values in the agricultural landscape (Fig. 19.3) and can help reduce the use of fertilizer, pesticides, and machinery. Additionally, integrating more humus-forming crops in

Fig. 19.3 Rich structured landscape with high crop diversity and poor structured landscape with low crop diversity (Images by Rode in 2004 and 2007)

the crop rotation impacts the soil organic matter content, thereby increasing the CO_2 storage (Wiehe et al. 2010; Karpenstein-Machan 2013). Thus, diversifying crops improves the environmental services of arable land and promotes the possibility of a multifunctional use of intensively used suburban agricultural landscapes.

II. **Benefiting from the positive effects of perennial crops**

Compared with the production of annual crops, such as sugar beet, wheat, rye, or maize, the implementation of perennial crops in agricultural landscapes offers many ways to achieve positive effects on landscape structure and ecosystem services in the agrarian part of the suburban landscape (Don et al. 2012; Boll et al. 2015; Power 2010). Examples for perennial crops in Europe are Miscanthus, Silphium perfoliatum, wild herbs mixtures, or short rotation plantations (i.e., poplar or willows), and on wet soils, reed (Karpenstein-Machan 2013; Kratz and Pfadenhauer 2001; Shurpali et al. 2009) (Fig. 19.4).

After the second year of establishment, perennial crops cover the soil the entire year and protect it against erosion. Through the absence of tillage, the soils of permanent crops store CO_2 and reduce leaching problems (Don et al. 2012; Drewer et al. 2012). Many permanent crops, such as short-rotation coppice and reed banks, are sparsely or not at all fertilized, and pesticide use is very low. Hence, they minimize the output of pesticides and fertilizers and have positive effects on soil humus content, soil erosion, and water retention (Börjesson 1999; Power 2010; Don et al. 2012; Karpenstein-Machan 2013). Therefore, perennial crops should grow on ecologically sensitive soils, which are susceptible to nitrate leaching, humus loss (organic soils), and erosion, in areas with high importance for water retention, and along bodies of water, ditches, and nutrient-poor habitats. Additionally, they can give open landscapes more structure and new characters. Thus, in a multifunctional way, soil and groundwater can be protected, and the spread of pollutants in sensitive ecosystems can be prevented. Simultaneously, the land is used for the production of raw materials, and the new landscape elements structure the landscape in a positive way compared with untextured landscapes (Karpenstein-Machan 2013; Boll et al. 2015).

Fig. 19.4 Perennial crops: Silphium perfoliatum (*left side*) and poplar (Images by Rode in 2012 and 2014)

III. **Promotion of landscape diversity through new landscape elements**

Complementing the cultivation of crops used for food, fodder, and biomass production, the addition of non-harvested elements gives a landscape greater structure and increased habitat qualities (Tscharntke et al. 2005). Examples of this case are as follows:

- Woody plant habitats: hedgerows (see Sect. 19.2.4.2), shrubberies, field-groves
- Uncultivated strips: waysides, perennial borders (see Sect. 19.2.4.2)
- Non-cropped field margins: buffer strips along ways, ditches, waters
- Special sites: moist swales, spring areas, headwaters, stony grounds

In recent years in Germany, as a part of new landscape elements, an increasing number of annual and perennial flower strips has been integrated into biomass cultivation on arable land. In particular, non-harvested flower strips, which comprise a mixture of different herbs, improve the structure and habitat qualities in agricultural landscapes (Haenke et al. 2009). Flower strips simultaneously improve the aesthetics of the landscape and provide additional structure and colors to the agricultural landscape, which have positive effects on recreational value (Fig. 19.5). The integration of flower strips and other structural elements, such as hedgerows, buffer strips, and wide field margins (cf. Sect. 19.2.4.2), in the cultivation of suburban farmlands may then also contribute to enhanced biodiversity and improved ecosystem services in agricultural landscapes (Vought et al. 1995; Haenke et al. 2009; Wehling and Dickmann 2009; Borin et al. 2010; Groot et al. 2010), providing an example of partial multifunctionality.

19.2.4.2 Landscape Development at the Kronsberg Area

At the landscape level, the effects of the implemented measures on Kronsberg were recorded from the perspective of species and habitat protection, over a four-year

Fig. 19.5 Flowering strips (Images by Rode in 2011 and 2012)

period, using semi-quantitative methods. The vegetation and three faunistic species groups (grasshoppers, butterflies, and birds) were studied to determine the spatial distribution, evolution over time, and rarity of the species and communities. Additionally, pedological investigations and biotope mappings were carried out to identify the nature conservation potentials of the landscape and track the overall development of the landscape.

After only a few years, the Kronsberg area developed from a blank and unstructured area dominated by intensive agricultural use to a richly structured landscape with different biotopes. Wide borders and hedgerows along a new network of country lanes, young forests, meadows, and orchards between the fields provide new habitats (Fig. 19.6). Field investigations show that the ecological and aesthetic quality of the landscape, as well as the species richness of plants, birds, grasshoppers, and butterflies, greatly increased during the first five years. Overall, landscape interactions between different biotopes diminish the fragmentation of the landscape and isolation of populations (cf. Brenken et al. 2003; Rode 2005b).

For example, the species composition of both the Allmende and forest plantations was characterized by successional processes during the investigation period. However, for both types of landscape elements, ambitious development goals had to be withdrawn during the course of the project. In the long term, the planted trees will most likely evolve into groves than into the originally intended woodruff-beech forests. A forest microclimate cannot fully develop owing to the small area. A typical forest biocenosis is not likely to establish itself. In this case, the landscape design for recreation restricts nature conservation, whereas forestry use is indefinite.

Given the prevailing soil properties, the Allmende has evolved into mesophilic grassland and not into the originally conceived semi-dry grassland (Fig. 19.7).

Fig. 19.6 The new rich-structured Kronsberg landscape with grassland (Allmende), forest plantations, ways with wide margins, and agricultural areas on top of Kronsberg hill (Image by Rode in 2003)

Fig. 19.7 Allmende at the Kronsberg [Images by Förster in 2000 and Rode in 2000 (in Brenken et al. (2003: 44, 41)]

Meanwhile, the number of species in the studied species groups remains low, as the Allmende is too evenly and extensively managed. Management changes to include temporal and spatial shifts, such as temporarily allowing unkempt "islands of vegetation" to exist, could lead to a significant improvement of the situation. However, this move would lead to restrictions on the agricultural use of the commons and recreation. The special requirements of nature conservation that entails possible restrictions of usage times, including the protection of grassland birds, limit the implementation of concepts of equal grassland use by agriculture, recreation, and nature conservation, especially for the needs of agriculture and recreation when considering the nature conservation-adapted pasturing and mowing regime.

The south side of the look-out hills progressed positively. Initiated by the seeding of hayflower of local origins, vegetation with a semi-arid grassland character developed shortly after. As a result, the look-out hills serve equally for recreation and as nature conservation. The newly created path country lane network is used without hindrance from agriculture, by recreation seekers, and nature conservation. In particular, the broad path margins allow a conflict-free coexistence of the different usage requirements (Fig. 19.8). Within integrated multifunctional land use concepts, it is possible, from the perspective of species and habitat protection, to tolerate wide boundary ridge activities of agriculture, including the transport of large machines, and recreation, such as extensively used horse trails. If

Fig. 19.8 Wide margins beside the ways at the Kronsberg (Images by Förster and Rode in 2000 and 2002)

the path and field boundaries are of sufficient size, mobile species may migrate easier and adapted plant species can move to directly adjacent areas. Under the influence of recreational and agricultural use in such wide-boundary ridges, species-richness develops, along with typical vegetation and moderate disturbance-tolerant biocenoses, which include rare and endangered species.

No possibilities of common use by two or more different types of land use on one field are feasible on agricultural acreages. In the case of farming, the need for economically viable management leads to the fact that the room for compromises is particularly narrow. Agriculture, also in the sense of landscape conservation as an agricultural economic activity, must achieve in the short term a positive operating result (cf. Swift et al. 2004). Only in this way can the running expenses be covered and sufficient funds for private withdrawals and reserves be formed, all of which are necessary for economic survival. Restrictions arising from measures that serve nature conservation and/or recreation must be reimbursed (Rode and Haaren 2005; cf. Wossink et al. 1999; Haaren and Bathke 2008).

In summary, at the landscape level, integrated multifunctional land use is more or less free from conflicts between the different types of use assessed in this project. Field interviews and observations provided evidence of people visiting Kronsberg and accepting the concept of integrated multifunctional land use (Fig. 19.9). They do not prefer a "real" public park, even if in an integrated concept areas such as arable fields are not directly available for recreational purposes (Tessin 2005). Meanwhile, in view of agriculture and nature conservation, the development at Kronsberg is assessed positively. The success of the project is mostly achieved by a mosaic of mono-functional areas within the landscape (tessellated multifunctionality, see Fig. 19.1).

By contrast, the equal integration of different types of land use at one site is difficult to achieve (total multifunctionality). The integrated combination of nature conservation, recreation, and agriculture at one place is especially difficult. The necessity of an economical cultivation of agricultural land drastically restricts possibilities for compromises. Nevertheless, it is much easier to combine within one site nature conservation and recreation or nature conservation and agriculture under partial multifunctionality, than agriculture and recreation. An immediate use of fields by recreation is impossible (Fig. 19.9).

Fig. 19.9 Recreational use of the landscape [Images by Förster in 2000 (in Brenken et al. 2003: 52, 76)]

19.3 Strategies and Requirements of Integrated Multifunctional Land Use in Suburban Landscapes

In intensively used suburban agricultural landscapes, a decrease in the number of crops on rotation and a loss of structural landscape elements are the main causes of increased negative impacts on biodiversity, recreational value of the landscape, and other ecosystem services by agriculture (Altieri 1999; Haynes-Young 2009; Karpenstein-Machan 2011, 2013; Wiehe et al. 2010). The increasing crop rotation, cultivation of perennial crops on problematic soils, and the implementation of new structural elements, such as flower strips, offer great opportunities to mitigate the known negative impacts (cf. Karpenstein-Machan 2011, 2013; Davis et al. 2012). These measures are essential components of multifunctional land use for mitigating the negative impacts on ecosystem services both in rural and suburban areas. Therefore, one aim of multifunctional land use is to diversify the agricultural landscape, thereby making agriculture more sustainable (Ruschkowsky and Wiehe 2008; Rode and Kanning 2010; Zasada 2011).

The best opportunity to diversify the agricultural landscape and protect nature and landscapes in suburban areas through multifunctional land use is in landscapes with (1) existing high nature conservation quality and (2) high potential for nature conservation development.

The aim of the former focuses on protecting (parts of the) landscapes with high biotic (e.g., high biodiversity, rare habitats and species) and abiotic quality (water quality, undisturbed or rare soil structure, special geological formations, high climatic importance, high quality of landscape scenery, and high cultural-historical values) (cf. Kiemstedt et al. 1996). In this manner, two or more of these landscape functions have to be protected at the same time. The second point is illustrated at Kronsberg in Hannover. The occurrence of a rare segetal flora and shallow chalky soil in the upper part, proximity to an urban settlement, high importance as recreation area, and positive climatic effects of the topography for the city of Hannover all provide excellent reasons and preconditions for protecting and developing this untextured open agricultural landscape.

To protect landscapes that have a high existing quality of nature conservation as well as develop landscapes with high potential of nature conservation, both site-integrated and site-segregated land-use forms can be developed. In the model of total site-integrated multifunctional land use, no form of land use (recreation, agriculture and forestry, nature conservation) has priority. Rather, through compromises, an attempt is made to maximize the benefits of each type of land use, without restricting the benefits of the other land-use types. The results of the investigations on Kronsberg show that this form of multifunctional land use can only be rarely achieved. In the case of partial site-integrated multifunctional land use, one land-use type takes precedence over the others within different sites of the landscape. In this case, the need for compromises on a single site is less than when achieving total multifunctionality. The results of this approach are as follows: (1) predominantly extensive agriculture or forestry that follow both economic and ecological principles,

(2) recreation that promotes a nature experience and an appreciation of nature conservation, and (3) nature conservation, which develops innovative ideas and approaches by benefiting from the potentials of recreation and agriculture.

The smallest pressure to find compromises in a landscape will occur in a site-segregated use of each site with a simultaneous integrated use at the landscape level (tessellated multifunctionality). Regardless of the land-use type, however, the intensity of area-segregated land use must be limited when it affects the land use in neighboring sites.

At the landscape level, all three combined-use strategies greatly increase and enhance the potential for protecting and developing agricultural landscapes in a multifunctional way. However, optimum protection in suburban areas is best achieved through a combination of the three described principal types of integrated multifunctional land uses within one landscape. This case depends on the existing natural, economic, social, and political conditions.

In addition to existing physical requirements for nature and landscape protection, the choice of landscape areas worthy of protection depends on political, legal, and social circumstances as well as on the practicality of the concept in space and time (Swift et al. 2004; O'Farrell and Anderson 2010). Hence, protection efforts follow strict requirements on urban, landscape, and regional planning (cf. Schrijnen 2000; De Groot et al. 2010; Lovell 2010; Aubry et al. 2012; Koschke et al. 2012). For instance, the main prerequisites for realizing the multifunctionality concept in a selected landscape are the availability of land (**property factor**), planning certainty (**time factor**; sustainable planning), infrastructure conditions (e.g., within reach for recreation; **spatial factor**), guarantee of maintenance (costs; **economical factor**), political consent (**political factor**), and identification of citizens and land users with the concept (**identification factor**) (for principles cf. Ott 1999).

To achieve multifunctional land use, urban and landscape planning must integrate the various objectives of agriculture, recreation, nature conservation, and other ecosystem services-based uses within one planning concept (cf. Ling et al. 2007; De Groot et al. 2010; Koschke et al. 2012) while also considering economic efficiency (integrated overall planning). Therefore, the most important step is to find common objectives for each landscape site in the context of the entire suburban landscape and then to put these common objectives into concrete forms. It is then essential to discuss the objectives of a multifunctional land use with all persons and groups affected by or participating in a multifunctional land-use project (Gough et al. 1998; Klug 2007; Termorshuizen and Opdam 2009). When the objectives are formulated, they need to be organized in a systematic and understandable format. Based on the general objectives, the next step is to develop specific objectives with reference to development schedules for all sites. Next, the accuracy and conformity of the special objectives, with respect to the common objectives, have to be examined. Conflicts among the different objectives should be minimized using a feedback process. Time- and site-specific measures have to be arranged. During the planning and discussion process, different requirements of the various land-use types need adjustment. Otherwise, different interpretations of the mutually formulated objectives result in conflicts later in the project.

However, integrated multifunctional land use is a dynamic process that needs dynamic planning and management. Given the complexity of multifunctional land use, predicting the further alteration of the landscape in space and time is not easy (Haynes-Young 2009; De Groot et al. 2010; O'Farrell and Anderson 2010). As such, specific objectives, management, and measures, may no longer conform to the common objectives of integrated multifunctional land-use. At worst, one type of land-use will eventually dominate (parts of) the landscape as described for the case of biomass production (Ruschkowsky and Wiehe 2008; Wiehe and Rode 2007). In order to prevent this, a flexible reaction using appropriate measures and objectives is needed, which responds to changes in the landscape situations, functions, and user, on a site and time specific basis. Simultaneously, a continuing evaluation of the project must be carried out together with all persons and groups who are involved or affected. Growing conflicts between the different land-use types can therefore be avoided. More importantly however, flexible responses to changing land-use requirements and flexible protection of nature in agricultural and suburban landscapes become easier. In this way, result oriented and flexible urban and landscape planning facilitates an integrated multifunctional land-use in the suburban area, making this type of land-use possible. This in turn, has positive effects on the protection of open spaces in the suburb as well as on nature conservation in agricultural landscapes.

Acknowledgement Financial support of the Kronsberg-project received from the German Federal Agency for Nature Conservation (BfN) is gratefully acknowledged.

References

Antrop M (2004) Landscape change and the urbanization process in Europe. Landscape and Urban Plann 67:9–26

Altieri MA (1999) The ecological role of biodiversity in agroecosystems. Agric Ecosyst Env 74:19–31

ARL (Akademie für Raumforschung und Landesplanung) (ed) (1997) Open space in urban areas. Verlag der ARL, Hannover, 224 p

Aubry C, Ramamonjisoa J, Dabat M-H, Rakotoarisoa J, Rakotondraibe J, Rabeharisoa L (2012) Urban agriculture and land use in cities: an approach with the multi-functionality and sustainability concepts in the case of Antananarivo (Madagascar). Land Use Policy 29:429–439

Beckmann J (1997) Thesen zur Podiumsdiskussion. ILS 106:127–131

BfLR (Bundesanstalt für Landeskunde und Raumordnung) (1996) Raumordnungsprognose 2010: Teilbereiche private Haushalte, Wohnungen, Wohnbauland. Materialien zur Raumentwicklung 74:173

Boll T, Haaren CV, Rode M (2015) The effects of short rotation coppice on recreation and the visual landscape—results of a survey using 3D visualisations for scenarios in different landscape types. In: Bemmann A, Butler-Manning D, Bredemeier M, Lamersdorf N, Ammer C (eds) Bioenergy from dendromass for the sustainable development of rural areas. Wiley-VCH, Weinheim (in press)

Borin M, Passoni M, Thiene M, Tempesta T (2010) Multiple functions of buffer strips in farming areas. Eur J Agron 32:103–111

Börjesson P (1999) Environmental effects of energy crop cultivation in Sweden I: identification and quantification. Biomass Bioenergy 16:137–154

Brenken H, Rode M, Haaren CV (2005) Konflikte und Synergien zwischen unterschiedlichen Ansprüchen an die Landschaft und Landschaftsfunktionen. In: Rode M, Haaren, C. v. (Bearb.) Multifunktionale Landnutzung am Stadtrand. Naturschutz und Biologische Vielfalt 15:152–171

Brenken H, Brink A, Förster A, Haaren CV, Klaffke K, Rode M, Tessin W (2003) Naturschutz, Naherholung und Landwirtschaft am Stadtrand. Angewandte Landschaftsökologie 57:151

Buhr N, Rode MW, Kanning H (2013) Effectiveness of planning instruments for minimizing spatial conflicts of biogas production. Eur Plann Stud 24 p. doi:10.1080/09654313.2013.798266

Davis AS, Hill JD, Chase CA, Johanns AM, Liebman M (2012) Increasing cropping system—diversity balances productivity, profitability and environmental health. PLoS ONE 7(10): e47149, 8 p

Decker EH, Elliott S, Smith FA, Blake DR, Rowland FS (2000) Energy and material flow through the urban ecosystem. Annu Rev Energy Env 25:685–740

De Groot RS, Alkemade R, Braat L, Hein L, Willemen L (2010) Challenges in integrating the concept of ecosystem services and values in landscape planning, management and decision making. Ecol Complex 7:260–272

Don A, Osborne B, Hastings A, Skiba U, Carter MS, Drewer J, Flessa H, Freibauer A, Hyvönen N, Jones MB, Lanigan GJ, Mander Ü, Monti A, Djoma SN, Valentine J, Walter K, Zegada-Lizarazu W, Zenone T (2012) Land-use change to bioenergy production in Europe: implication for the greenhouse gas balance and soil carbon. Glob Change Biol Bioenergy 4:372–391

Drewer J, Finch JW, Lloyd CR, Baggs EM, Skiba U (2012) How do soil emissions of N_2O, CH_4 and CO_2 from perennial bioenergy crops differ from arable annual crops? Glob Change Biol Bioenergy 4:408–419

Findlay CS, Houlahan J (1997) Anthropogenic correlates of species richness in southeastern Ontario wetlands. Conserv Biol 11:1000–1009

Gough C, Castells N, Funtowicz S (1998) Integrated assessment: an emerging methodology for complex issues. Environ Model Assess 3:19–29

Groot JCJ, Jellema A, Rossing WAH (2010) Designing a hedgerow network in a multifunctional agricultural landscape: balancing trade-offs among ecological quality, landscape character and implementation costs. Eur J Agron 32:112–119

Haaren CV, Bathke M (2008) Integrated landscape planning and remuneration of agri-environmental services—results of a case study in the Fuhrberg region of Germany. J Environ Manage 89:209–221

Haaren CV, Rode MW (2007) Potentials and limits of multifunctional landscapes: a case study of the Kronsberg district of Hannover, Germany. In: Kenneweg H (ed) Planning the urban environment: 2nd international congress on environmental planning and management—visions, implementations, Results. Univ.-Verl. der TU Berlin; Landschaftsentwicklung und Umweltforschung – Sonderhefte, vol 20, pp 49–53

Haaren CV, Rode MW (2010) Potenziale und Grenzen multifunktionaler Landnutzung am Beispiel Hannover-Kronsberg. In: Harth A, Scheller G (Hrsg.) Soziologie in der Stadt- und Freiraumplanung - Analysen, Bedeutung und Perspektiven. VS Verlag für Sozialwissenschaften, Wiesbaden, pp 381–391

Haenke S, Scheid B, Schaefer M, Tscharntke T, Thies C (2009) Increasing syrphid fly diversity and density in sown flower strips within simple vs. complex landscapes. J Appl Ecol 46:1106–1114

Haynes-Young R (2009) Land use and biodiversity relationships. Land Use Policy 26S:178–186

Karpenstein-Machan M (2011) Implementation of integrative energy crop cultivation concepts on biogas farms. In: Savolainen M (ed) International nordic bioenergy 2011—book of proceedings. Finbio publication 51, Finland, pp 127–133

Karpenstein-Machan M (2013) Integrative energy crop cultivation as a way to a more nature-orientated agriculture. In: Ruppert H, Kappas M, Ibendorf J (eds) Sustainable bioenergy production—an integrated approach. Springer Verlag, Dordrecht, pp 143–180

Kiemstedt H, Mönnecke M, Ott S (1996) Methodik der Eingriffsregelung. Vorschläge zur bundeseinheitlichen Anwendung der Eingriffsregelung von §8 BNatSchG. Naturschutz und Landschaftsplanung 9(96):261–271

Klaffke K, Brink A, Beck S (eds) (2000) Kronsberg, Hannover—nature conservation, recreation and agriculture on the urban margins—a model project. Press and Information Office, City of Hannover, Druckerei Pinkvoss, Hannover, 28 p

Kratz R, Pfadenhauer J (Hrsg) (2001) Ökosystemmanagement für Niedermoore, Strategien und Verfahren zur Renaturierung, Verlag Eugen Ulmer, Stuttgart, 317 p

Klug H (2007) Participative landscape planning using a GIS approach for facilitation. In: Mander Ü, Wiggering H, Helming K (eds) Multifunctional land use meeting future demands for landscape goods and services. Springer, Berlin, pp 195–223

Koenigs T (1993) Zur Zukunft des Städtischen. In: Koenigs T (ed) Stadt-parks. Urbane Natur in Frankfurt am main. Campus-Verlag, Frankfurt, pp 50–59

Koschke L, Fürst C, Frank S, Makeschin F (2012) A multi-criteria approach for an integrated land-cover-based assessment of ecosystem services provision to support landscape planning. Ecol Ind 21:54–66

Kroll F, Müller F, Haase D, Fohrer N (2012) Rural–urban gradient analysis of ecosystem services supply and demand dynamics. Land Use Policy 29:521–535

Lambin EF, Turner BL, Geist HJ, Agbola SB, Angelsen A, Bruce JW, Coomes OT, Dirzo R, Fischer G, Folke C, George PS, Homewood K, Imbernon J, Leemans R, Li X, Moran EF, Mortimore M, Ramakrishnan PS, Richards JF, Skånes H, Steffen W, Stone GD, Svedin U, Veldkamp TA, Vogel C, Xu J (2001) The causes of land-use and land-cover change: moving beyond the myths. Glob Environ Change 11:261–269

Lambin EF, Geist HJ, Lepers E (2003) Dynamics of land-use and land-cover change in tropical regions. Ann Rev Environ Res 28:205–241

Lautenbach S, Kugel C, Lausch A, Seppelt R (2011) Analysis of historic changes in regional ecosystem service provisioning using land use data. Ecol Ind 11:676–687

Ling C, Handley J, Rodwell J (2007) Restructuring the post-industrial landscape: a multifunctional approach. Landscape Res 32(3):285–309

Lovell ST (2010) Multifunctional urban agriculture for sustainable land use planning in the United States. Sustainability 2:2499–2522. doi:10.3390/su2082499

Lovell ST, Johnston DM (2009) Creating multifunctional landscapes: how can the field of ecology inform the design of the landscape? Front Ecol Environ 7:212–220

Metzger MJ, Rounsevell MDA, Acosta-Michlik L, Leemans R, Schröter D (2006) The vulnerability of ecosystem, services to land use change. Agric Ecosyst Environ 114:69–85

O'Farrell PJ, Anderson PML (2010) Sustainable multifunctional landscapes: a review to implementation. Curr Opin Environ Sustain 2:59–65. doi:10.1016/j.cosust.2010.02.005

Ott S (1999) Bevorratung von Flächen und Maßnahmen zum Ausgleich im Rahmen der Eingriffsregelung. Ergebnisse eines Expertenworkshops am 9./10. Dezember 1998 in Hannover. BfN Scripten 14:39

Power AG (2010) Ecosystem services and agriculture: tradeoffs and synergies. Philos Trans R Soc Biol Sci 365:2959–2971

Reich M, Rüter S (Hrsg) (2011) Auswirkungen des großflächigen Anbaus von Energiepflanzen auf die Tierwelt der Agrarlandschaft. Umwelt und Raum, Band 2, Cuvillier Verlag, Göttingen, 244 p

Rode MW (2005a) Energetische. Nutzung von Biomasse und der Naturschutz. Natur und Landschaft 9/10:403–412

Rode MW (2005b) Die Entwicklung des Kronsberges für den Arten- und Biotopschutz. In: Rode M, Haaren CV (Bearb) Multifunktionale Landnutzung am Stadtrand. Naturschutz und Biologische Vielfalt 15:35–76

Rode MW (2009) Bioenergieproduktion – Auswirkungen einer neuen Raumnutzung auf den Naturschutz. In: EUROPARC Deutschland (Hrsg) Abschlussdokumentation "Bioenergie - Fluch oder Segen für Nationale Naturlandschaften". Eppler & Buntdruck GmbH, Berlin, pp 20–25

Rode M, Haaren CV (Bearb) (2005) Multifunktionale Landnutzung am Stadtrand. Naturschutz und Biologische Vielfalt 15:188 p
Rode MW, Kanning H (2010) (Hrsg) Natur- und raumverträglicher Ausbau energetischer Biomassepfade. Ibidem-Verlag, Stuttgart, 296 S
Ruschkowski EV, Wiehe J (2008) Balancing bioenergy production and nature conservation in Germany: potential synergies and challenges. In: Yearbook of socioeconomics in agriculture. Schweizerische Gesellschaft für Agrarwirtschaft und Agrarsoziologie, Zurich, pp 3–20
Saathoff W, Haaren CV, Rode MW (2013) Scale-relevant impacts of biogas crop production: a methodology to assess environmental impacts and farm management capacities. In: Ruppert H, Kappas M, Ibendorf J (eds) Sustainable bioenergy production—an integrated approach. Springer, Dordrecht, pp 181–216
Schmidt A (1997) Peripherie und Freiraum. Am Rand der Stadt. Ballungsraumperipherie als Planungsschwerpunkt kommunaler Stadtentwicklungspolitik. ILS 106:29–32
Schrijnen PM (2000) Infrastructure networks and red-green patterns in city regions. Landscape Urban Plann 48:191–204
Shurpali NJ, Hyvönen NP, Huttungen JP, Clement RJ, Reichstein M, Nykänen H, Biasi C, Martikainen PJ (2009) Cultivation of a perennial grass for bioenergy on a boreal organic soil—carbon sink or source. GCB Bioenergy 1:35–50. doi:10.1111/j.1757-1707.2009.01003.x
Simpson IA, Dugmore AJ, Thomson A, Vésteinsson O (2001) Crossing the thresholds: human ecology and historical patterns of landscape degradation. Catena 42:175–192
Strubelt W (1997) Am Rand der Stadt - Thesen und Ansichten aus wissenschaftlicher Sicht. ILS 106:111–118
Swift MJ, Izac A-MN, van Noordwijk M (2004) Biodiversity and ecosystem services in agricultural landscapes—are we asking the right questions? Agric Ecosyst Environ 104:113–134
Tan MH, Li XB, Xie H, Lu CH (2005) Urban land expansion and arable land loss in China—a case study of Beijing—Tianjin—Hebei region. Land Use Policy 22:187–196
Termorshuizen JW, Opdam P (2009) Landscape services as a bridge between landscape ecology and sustainable development. Landscape Ecol 24:1037–1052
Tessin W (2005) Die Entwicklung des Kronsberges für die Naherholung. In: Rode M, Haaren CV (Bearb) Multifunktionale Landnutzung am Stadtrand. Naturschutz und Biologische Vielfalt 15:77–106
Thomlinson JR, Rivera LY (2000) Suburban growth in Luquillo, Puerto Rico: some consequences of development on natural and semi-natural systems. Landscape Urban Plann 49:15–23
Thomlinson J, Serano M, López T, Aide M, Zimmermann J (1996) Land-use dynamics in a post-agricultural Puerto-Rican landscape (1936–1993). Biotropica 28:525–536
Thomson AM, Simpson IA (2006) A grazing model for simulating the impact of historical land management decisions in sensitive landscapes: model design and validation. Environ Model Softw 21:1096–1113
Tscharntke T, Klein AM, Kruess A, Steffan-Dewenter I, Thies C (2005) Landscape perspectives on agricultural intensification and biodiversity—ecosystem service management. Ecol Lett 2005(8):857–874
Vought LB-M, Pinay G, Fuglsang A, Ruffinoni C (1995) Structure and function of buffer strips from a water quality perspective in agricultural landscapes. Landscape Urban Plann 31:323–331
Vos W, Meekes H (1999) Trends in European cultural landscape development: perspectives for a sustainable future. Landscape Urban Plann 46:3–14
Walker RT, Solecki WD, Harwell C (1997) Land use dynamics and ecological transition: the case of South Florida. Urban Ecosyst 1:37–47
Wehling S, Diekmann M (2009) Importance of hedgerows as habitat corridors for forest plants in agricultural landscapes. Biol Conserv 142:2522–2530
Whited D, Galatowitsch S, Tester JR, Schik K, Lehtinen R, Husveth J (2000) The importance of local and regional factors in predicting effective conservation—planning strategies for wetland bird communities in agricultural and urban landscapes. Landscape Urban Plann 49:49–65

Wiehe J, Rode MW (2007) Auswirkungen des Anbaus von Pflanzen zur Energiegewinnung auf den Naturhaushalt und andere Raumnutzungen. Rundgespräche der Kommission für Ökologie 33: Energie aus Biomasse: Ökonomische und ökologische Bewertung, Verlag Dr. Friedrich Pfeil, München, pp 101–113

Wiehe J, Rode M, Kanning H (2010) Raumanalyse I - Auswirkungen auf Natur und Landschaft. In: Rode M, Kanning H (eds) Natur- und raumverträglicher Ausbau energetischer Biomassepfade. Ibidem-Verlag, Stuttgart, pp 21–90

Wiehe J, Ruschkowski EV, Rode M, Kanning H, Haaren CV (2009) Auswirkungen des Energiepflanzenanbaus auf die Landschaft am Beispiel des Maisanbaus für die Biogasproduktion in Niedersachsen. Naturschutz und Landschaftsplanung 41(4):107–113

Wossink A, Van Wenum J, Jurgens C, De Snoo G (1999) Co-ordinating economic, behavioural and spatial aspects of wildlife preservation in agriculture. Eur Rev Agric Econ 26:443–460

Zasada I (2011) Multifunctional peri-urban agriculture—a review of societal demands and the provision of goods and services by farming. Land Use Policy 28:639–648

Chapter 20
Multi-dimensional Experience of the Rural Landscape in Chinese Organic Farms

Jun Shao

20.1 Introduction

During the process of rapid urbanization in China, people living in urban areas have to face increasingly serious issues, such as food safety and pollution. Further, many urban residents in China yearn for the Chinese traditional rural landscape, which advocates an environment-friendly and self-contained lifestyle. Beginning in the 1990s, urban residents in major cities in China began visiting suburban areas in their leisure time to experience the rural landscape, participate in agricultural production, and enjoy a "slow" life (Shao et al. 2012). Correspondingly, organic farms emerged in suburban areas, providing an alternative rural landscape. In the No. 1 document issued in 2014, the China Central Government clearly put forward a long-term mechanism of agricultural sustainable development to promote the development of eco-friendly agriculture (Xinhua News Agency 2014). As an important part of ecological civilization, ecological agriculture would become the future of China's agricultural development direction. Although no statistical data have been published on the exact expanse of organic farms in China, it is safe to say that rural tourism via organic farms has not yet become a major source of local economic growth. In addition to the economic importance of rural tourism (Bramwell 1994; Greffe 1994; McIntosh and Campbell 2010; Oppermann 1996; Weaver and Fennell 1997), organic farm tourism is considered as alternative ecological tourism with respect to its environmental significance (Choo and Jamal 2009; Clarke 1999).

As tourism landscapes have meaning and could be shaped and interpreted by insiders (hosts) and outsiders (visitors) (Daugstad 2008; Knudsen et al. 2008), understanding the landscape experience in organic farms could provide decision support for the sustainable development of rural areas. Despite the abundance of

J. Shao (✉)
School of Landscape Architecture, Beijing Forestry University, Beijing, China
e-mail: ninashaojun@qq.com

F. Wang and M. Prominski (eds.), *Urbanization and Locality*,
DOI 10.1007/978-3-662-48494-4_20

literature on rural tourism in China, none have mentioned the organic farms in China from the perspective of urban dwellers' landscape experience. Therefore, this study conducted an exploratory research of urban residents' landscape experiences with respect to the rural landscape at organic farms in suburban areas nearby major cities. Specifically, this research aims at investigating the cases of organic farms in suburban Beijing.

20.2 Background

20.2.1 Landscape Experiences in Rural Areas

The concept of landscape combines the material surroundings of tourism sites and representations of culture contained in these sites (Daugstad and Kirchengast 2013; Knudsen et al. 2008). Landscape is a visual space that could be experienced by way of seeing, which has been described as "tourist gaze" and "place consumption" (Urry 1995, 2001, 2003a, b). In addition to the visuality, landscape is also perceived in a multi-sensory way, including taste, smell, audio, and touch (Cosgrove and Daniels 1988; Daugstad and Kirchengast 2013; Karjalainen and Tyrväinen 2002; Raivo 1996; Uusitalo 2010). As the rural areas become getaways from the noisy urban life, urban residents pursue rural landscapes, activities, peaceful recreation, and a wish for insightful knowledge from the people living in and from the landscape (Daugstad 2008).

Landscape studies have a consensus on "the role that culture plays in shaping landscape and vice versa" (Knudsen et al. 2008: 134). Therefore, applying landscape perspectives to tourism studies, especially within the increasingly popular "tourist landscape" literature (Aitchison et al. 2001), could lead to a better understanding of how meaning is conveyed by the cultural and social processes of tourism (Knudsen et al. 2008). However, there is a lack of focus on rural or natural landscape experiences in tourism research until fairly recently (e.g., Daugstad 2008; Daugstad and Kirchengast 2013; Kangas et al. 2008; Oliver and Jenkins 2003; Soini 2001; Tilt et al. 2007; Uusitalo 2010; Young 1999). Tourists experience multi-sensory traditional and genuine elements of rural landscapes at farms (Daugstad 2008; Daugstad and Kirchengast 2013; Uusitalo 2010). Among the various experiences of tourists, active farming is important as it is regarded as representing the authenticity of the local rural landscape (Daugstad and Kirchengast 2013).

20.2.2 Rural Tourism and Organic Farms in China

In China, the central government has been a vital player in guiding and encouraging the development of rural tourism (Gao et al. 2009). Since 1998, rural tourism in

China has developed rapidly and diversely, stimulated by many governmental policies and financial incentives to rural development and a series of promotion campaigns initiated by the China National Tourism Administration, including "China Rural Tourism Year 1998," "China Eco-tourism Year 1999," and "Chinese Life Tourism Year 2004" (Su 2011). However, there is limited research on Chinese rural tourism in international literature (Gao et al. 2009), among which the studies focus on the general overview and brief evaluation of the development process and patterns of rural tourism in China. According to the summary of Su (2011: 1440), Zheng and Zhong (2004), and He (2005), there are generally five inter-related models identified for rural tourism development in China: "individual farmstead" based on farmer autonomy (Wang and Fang 2008), "farmer family plus farmer family" characterized by the mode of "one family with one rural tourism-related specialization" (Zheng and Zhong 2004), "corporation plus farmers," "corporation plus community plus farmers" (Han 2009), and "government plus corporation plus farmer" (Ding 2009). The dominant form of rural tourism in China is the Happy Farmer's Home (Mandarin: *Nong jia le*) tourism, in place since the early 1990s (Gao et al. 2009; Hu 2008; Su 2011).

Unlike the general development of rural tourism in China, organic farm tourism development is market driven. As a pattern of sustainable agriculture, and motivated by concerns over food safety and quality as well as awareness about the problems of the global economy, organic farms have been developed rapidly since early 2000s (Shao et al. 2012). Before 2008, organic farms emerged in China under organic campaigns of non-government organizations, such as the Urban–Rural Mutual Support initiative created by scholars, and the small-scale ecological agricultural program initiated by Hong Kong Community Partners (Shi et al. 2011). There were many organic farms initiated by grassroots groups who follow the traditional Chuang-tzu philosophy of doing nothing or the modern Lifestyles of Wholly Harmonious, pursuing absolute harmony between human and nature (Shao et al. 2012). In 2008, Community Supported Agriculture (CSA) farms were introduced to China. The term CSA is mostly used in the US (Wikipedia 2011). Urban CSA farms refer to farms where community individuals, growers, and consumers provide mutual support and share the risks and benefits of food production (De Muth 1993; Miles and Brown 2005). These farms provide local and fresh products via a healthy, safe, and environment-friendly process. The idea of CSA was inspired by the small-scale agricultural economic ideas of Rudolf Steiner, an Austrian philosopher, and experiments using biodynamic agriculture. Terms used worldwide referring to this similar production and economic sub-systems include *Teikei* in Japan and Gruppi di Acquisto Solidale in Italy (Wikipedia 2011).

However, the exact number of organic farms throughout China is difficult to determine, as many small organic farms are not registered in the Administration for Industry and Commerce or local tourism bureaus owing to budget limitations; organic certification entails a high cost. Although the construction of a large number of recreational facilities is not allowed in agricultural land, there is a "gray zone"; as long as village committees do not oppose, individuals or organizations can carry out recreational activities in their farmland or deploy ancillary facilities, such as cottages, in the vicinity of their leased or owned land. Nonetheless, over 200 organic farms are registered on the Chinese Willing Workers on Organic Farms website (http://www.wwoofchina.org/main/index.php). They are widely distributed throughout approximately 20 provinces, located near large cities, such as Beijing and Shanghai, where they could be accessed by self-driving tourists. This trend is gradually taking hold in smaller cities as well. Of the 200 registered farms, 80 are CSA organic farms (Shi 2013).

Meanwhile, the exact volume of Chinese organic farm consumers is likewise undetermined. However, the majority of this segment seems to be well-educated people with upper-middle income who live in big cities, and this segment is growing rapidly, especially with the worsening food safety situation in China. In addition to organic farm members who have contracts with organic farms, as organic farms normally would attract more potential consumers and advocate their lifestyle, common urban dwellers can visit organic farms and join various programs to experience a close relationship with the land and the farmers. Therefore, in absolute terms, this phenomenon involves a large number of people.

Currently, there is limited research on organic farms within tourism studies (Choo and Jamal 2009; Holm et al. 2013; McIntosh and Campbell 2010; Yamamoto and Engelsted 2014). Among them, only the research on organic farms in South Korea (Choo and Jamal 2009) and Denmark (Holm et al. 2013) mentioned tourists' experience. Given the lack of literature on landscape experience in organic farms from the perspective of visitors, this research seeks to fill this gap by investigating the landscape experiences in the rural cultural landscape provided by organic farms.

20.3 Methods

To explore the multi-dimensional landscape experiences of urban residents involved in organic farms, qualitative studies were conducted from October 19, 2011 to October 12, 2014. Currently, there are 97 organic farms in the suburbs of Beijing, spread over 13 districts. Shunyi District has 23 organic farms, accounting for 23.71 % or the biggest share of the total. Among the organic farms in suburban Beijing, 17 claim to operate in the mode of CSA. Two famous organic farms, namely, Little Donkey Farm and Emerald Bay Farm, were selected as the cases for this research. Little Donkey Farm is a pioneer in the field of organic farming, whereas Emerald Bay Farm, located in Shunyi District, was chosen because of convenience sampling.

20.3.1 Organic Farms: Case Studies

Little Donkey Farm, founded in April 2008 by a team of scholars from Renmin University of China, was the first CSA farm in China. It covers an area of 250 acres in a northwestern suburb of Beijing. It has more than 500 members. Its founding team has initiated various programs, including Eco-agriculture Environment-friendly Rural Areas, Green Alliance of Cooperation, Urban–Rural Mutual Support, and Civic Farms since 2003. From 2009, Little Donkey Farm provided two types of memberships: labor share and delivery share. This farm also holds various events to attract urban residents. Little Donkey Farm has been reported by more than 200 domestic and foreign media outlets.

Emerald Bay Farm is a small organic farm of 7 ha, founded in March 2010 in Dabeiwu Village, Shunyi District. It has about 150 delivery share members and does not provide labor share membership. Its owner, Mr. Sun, is a controversial figure after his public disclosure of the fraudulent and dark practices of organic farms in China. He is active on Sina Weibo. Reportedly, the farm remains unprofitable even after operating for nearly five years.

20.3.2 Data Collection and Analysis

Onsite observation and in-depth interviews were conducted at Little Donkey Farm and Emerald Bay Farm.

In the case of Little Donkey Farm, general information was first collected via interviews with operators, volunteers, tourists, and farm members working there in October 2011. Follow-up interviews were then conducted in April 2012. As for Emerald Bay Farm, two rounds of interviews were done in April and May 2012. Social media posts related to both farms were gathered as supplemental information. Content analysis and netnographic study (Kozinets 2002) were conducted on Little Donkey Farm and Emerald Bay Farm separately.

As regards Little Donkey Farm, up to August 5, 2012, 281 postings and 17 newsletters from the farm's online official forum (http://www.littledonkeyfarm.com/forum.php), 1095 blogs on Sina Blog, and 1790 original micro-blog messages on Sina Weibo related to Little Donkey Farm were procured. In the case of Emerald Bay Farm, online chat records from the farms' QQ group were collected. Thematic analysis (Aronson 1994; Attride-Stirling 2001; Boyatzis 1998; Fereday and Muir-Cochrane 2006) was applied to process the data.

20.4 Results and Discussions

The thematic analysis on the data collected from onsite observation and in-depth interviews revealed two types of landscape experiences by urban residents at organic farms: experiencing organic farming landscape and engaging in multi-sensory recreational activities. Further, in either farming or recreational experiences, a multi-dimensional experience pattern emerged, including Education, Association, Relaxation, Trust, and Health (EARTH).

20.4.1 Educational Experience of the Rural Landscape

Interviewees at the two organic farms reported that the rural landscapes provided an educational experience, which refers to natural, cultural, social, or environmental education via farming or participating in rural recreational activities. Little Donkey Farm organized a series of educational programs, including summer camps for children, in which visitors were guided to participate in nature-based activities, such as recognizing insects, composting vermin, or picking vegetables. Emerald Bay Farm did not arrange any specified educational service, but visitors there could pick vegetables or grapes by themselves or by communicating with farm owners or employees. Taking the youth summer camp Heart Plan of Roots & Buds as an example, children growing up in cities experience the happiness of touching the soil and the rigor of physical labor by experiencing picking vegetables, collocating them, and preparing them for lunch. They learned where and how food is from. They learned to respect nature, traditional culture, producers of food, and the environment. One respondent expressed his environmental experience after attending a summer camp hosted by Little Donkey Farm as follows:

> Different from the previous events [I participated before], this camp was very interesting, and extremely educational. What impressed me most is the consciousness of environmental protection. Human waste here could be composted, not to mention the deciduous and kitchen garbage. People here use wheat bran to wash dishes instead of detergents, pour leftovers into swill buckets to feed pigs instead of just dumping them, irrigating the fields with the water used for washing hands, and so on…

In addition, Little Donkey Farm offered many seasonal cultural events during Chinese traditional festivals, such as Start Hoeing Festival, Dragon Boat Festival, Harvest Festival, and Mid-Autumn Festival. Emerald Bay Farm offered outdoor barbecue facilities and public kitchens for visitors to entertain themselves during festivals. All these events held at organic farms offered great opportunities for urban residents to be educated in traditional culture. For instance, urban residents lead their children to attend activities during Dragon Boat Festival Experience at Little Donkey Farm to experience traditional customs, including making rice dumplings, painting foreheads, painting eggs, making Chinese knots, appreciating paper-cut art, engaging in calligraphy and other traditional crafts, as well as preparing and tasting holiday food, such as Chinese medicinal liquor, rice dumplings, and salted eggs. One respondent shared the cultural experience from the performance on the threshing floor at the Start Hoeing Festival in 2012:

> On the threshing floor stage, a donkey race performance received loud applause. Modern dance music played by professional singers lingered throughout the rural fields. The harmony between human and nature, and the integration of urban and rural cultures, represented a distinctive flavor.

Therefore, an excellent way to experience natural, environmental, and social education of rural landscape is evolving in organic farms, not only for children but also for adults. Emerald Bay Farm, which did not organize many recreational activities, reported they would arrange festivals and provide outdoor educational opportunities when they have sufficient labor and funds.

20.4.2 Association Experience of the Rural Landscape

Both farms in this study showed that visitors also had association experience, which means being associated with family, relatives, and friends as well as with nature in the atmosphere of the rural landscape. Visitors to these organic farms often come with their family and friends, no matter if they have leased lands at farms. They interact while farming or relax together. One respondent who has a land share at Little Donkey Farm said he made new friends while working there:

> What makes me very happy is that I came to know plenty of people at the farm, including old aunts, old uncles, and many children. I also brought my family and friends here to work together. The land we own here is not only ploughed by my family but also by those delivery members who have no lands here. Many old aunts have farming experiences [during the Chinese Cultural Revolution period]. They are attached to the farms, and their sons helped me plough.

At the Little Donkey Farm, which provides a new type of neighborhood by lending lands to labor-share members, the relationship among plot owners is harmonious, as reported by one respondent:

> My neighbors are very kind. They work at their plots very carefully and manage everything in good order. I am very happy to see their love for nature and the rural life. We have endless talks about farming and housework. We exchange vegetables that are not planted by others.

In addition, considering the original social relationships of urban residents, the research found that the rural experience at organic farms strengthened the connections among the respondents' relatives and friends. They shared their harvest after working at farms:

> I performed well under the farmers' guidance. I harvested produce with my lands and shared these with my relatives who live in the city. I am very proud and feel fulfilled.

The traditional neighborhood relationship within a number of urban communities has also changed. Urban residents live in the same community but do not know one another until they meet at the same organic farm. They become close and spontaneously initiate a range of interest groups for their kids in their residential community. From the chat records of Emerald Bay Farm's online group, consumers participated in farm chores voluntarily, such as organizing group buying of farm goods, designing farm brochures, donating furniture and office supplies, and providing labor at the farm. They contributed generously as they felt strongly associated with the farm.

20.4.3 Relaxation Experience of the Rural Landscape

Both interviews and content analyses revealed that urban residents feel relaxed by planting or participating in recreation activities at organic farms as well as enjoying a getaway from urban life. In addition to feeling the fresh air, watching the pleasant visual rural landscape, tasting local food, and talking with family members, friends, and friendly local farmers, respondents claimed that they also appreciate the soundscape, enjoying the absence of urban noise. The multi-sensory experience of rural cultural landscapes makes for an idyllic getaway for them to escape the stressful urban life. Both planting vegetables and participating in leisure activities could make them feel relaxed. One respondent who has planted at his leased field for more than three years expressed his feelings towards organic farms:

> The Phoenix Mountain [nearby] is especially delicate and seems extremely quiet. The Jingmi Canal is also winding around our farm. There are so many employees here, with kids dabbling, young people farming in the field, and old people chatting. What a beautiful painting it is! Scenes of working and daily life are actually like pictures.

Another respondent described his multi-sensory relaxation experience when walking around the farm:

> I woke up early, then walked around the farm. Looking at the sky, I felt relaxed. I listened to the grass sounds, smelled the vegetables. What is blowing on my face is not only the soft flavor of things in our universe but also the quiet breath of the earth. It is such a dreamland, intoxicating to my heart and calming to my spirit.

One respondent expressed his spiritual pursuit of getting far away from the hubbub of common customs by posting a poem on the website of one organic farm:

> All people in the world are busy pursuing fame and wealth. Why not just visit here and plant green onions? All is not worth mentioning. Just as transient as a fleeting cloud.

20.4.4 Trust Experience of the Rural Landscape

Trust experience refers to the trust between urban residents and organic farmers, which is the essential difference from other types of recreational farms. Industrialization and urbanization in China since modern times have destroyed the traditional community social life. Therefore, the trust network based on it collapsed. A new trust system has not been established, and a trust problem widely exists in various fields. Trust even becomes a luxury, especially in the organic food industry. However, respondents in both farms indicated that farmers no longer use chemical fertilizers or pesticides hazardous to health and the environment by working together and participating in various farming and planting stages. Urban residents' participating in the production of local products at organic farms strengthened the trust between consumers and producers, among the community, on the safety and qualities of products, and on the authenticity of the rural cultural landscapes at the farm. A respondent who is a delivery-share member claimed the following:

> Look at the mud and holes made by worms on these vegetables. I feel reassured! Trust is my only concern when buying and selling. I hope [the organic farms] would not violate our trust [on them], and plant healthy green vegetables without any fertilizers forever!

Meanwhile, the farm manager of Emerald Bay Farm reported that their purpose for encouraging urban residents to experience directly agricultural activities at their farm is to establish trust on food producers. Producers could then gain their consumers' financial support and ultimately share the agricultural risks together. Thus, in this sense, as a way of communication and supervision, the city residents' involvement in the leisure activities organized by organic farms is inseparable from building and demonstrating trust.

It should be noted that a number of members of Little Donkey Farm transferred to Emerald Bay Farm after a cheating scandal at Little Donkey Farm was exposed. This case illustrates the critical role of trust in experiences at organic farms.

20.4.5 Health Experience of the Rural Landscape

Health experience was a common theme in both the interviews and content analyses. Respondents pursue physical and spiritual cultural rural landscape experiences at organic farms by engaging in exercise through working at farms and practicing a healthy harmonious lifestyle. They said that eating seasonal local food is both healthy for themselves and environment friendly. In terms of health and food safety, urban residents who planted at their leased lands generally agreed that ingredients produced from the farms are green and healthy, and giving labor at organic farms could also be considered as a welcome kind of physical exercise. One respondent who planted vegetables at her leased lot claimed that the produce comprises "truly healthy green food [that] is added to our table," adding that for "the two seasons of spring and summer, basically every day our family could eat fruits and vegetables grown by ourselves." She also thought that the feeling of working at the farm is like taking a rural leisure journey by doing exercises. Similarly, another retired urban citizen who also leased lot from one farm said the following:

> Your feet could touch the earth, and it is particularly wide there. Feeling fresh and relaxed, you could breathe fresh air there. Then you could eat fiber food planted by yourself, with the sun shining on you. The sun can produce vitamin D and make your physical health better and your bones stronger. Then your harvest is your health. This is what I experienced through my labor [at the farm].

This healthy experience via rural landscape was confirmed by another respondent:

> By practicing this lifestyle for three years, my heart feels nourished. I have thoroughly enjoyed various benefits. On weekends and holidays, my family would go to our small garden. We do everything we could do there, feeling our health improve by the day. I have experienced that this is a good place for exercise, wellness, and leisure.

In addition, respondents reported that, through the practice of leisure and labor at organic farms, they realized the environmental implications of eating local and fresh food, and reflected on their life attitude and lifestyle. A respondent who worked as a volunteer at an organic farm said as follows:

> This is not simply an issue of using wheat bran to wash dishes. Behind the practice is the attitude. The issues is whether we can solve problems in life with a sustainable and healthy attitude. If we adopt this attitude, then life would naturally become safe and healthy.

One respondent with years of experience summarized the change in his lifestyle:

> Greater benefits lie in my thoughts. The concept that human beings should coexist harmoniously with nature gradually became clear. The small garden [at the organic farm] is linked with a big target. Influenced by college students [working at the organic farm as volunteers], I have made a habit of reusing plastic boxes and nets for packaging eggs and small tomatoes. In addition, I have practiced separating different types of rubbish at home, and paying more attention to saving water and electricity.

Beyond perceiving the vegetables and animals in organic farms as a healthy signal of the cultural landscape at rural areas, the lifestyle in idyllic rural areas with Chinese traditional farming is a common dream for many respondents, especially those well-educated ones. A respondent described his happiness in farming and reading at organic farms:

> Could farming go with the joy of reading? Under the sun, immersed in the rural landscape, who would talk about complicated art concepts, entangled metaphors, recondite thoughts, or any concept people argued about endlessly? My sweat falling to the dirt; enjoying a cup of tea under the shade of a tree: this is all I need.

20.5 Conclusions

The landscape experiences of urban residents or visitors, whether farming or recreation oriented, represented an EARTH pattern. Trust and organic farming represented the most essential differences between organic farms and other recreational farms. Understanding the EARTH pattern in the experiences of urban residents in their pursuit of the rural landscape is important for decision making related to restoring and upgrading the rural landscape as well as developing both urban and rural areas in a sustainable way. Considering the fervent demand for outdoor activities, parent–child activities, and educational experience in environmental conservation and organic lifestyle, organic farms should be encouraged to maintain their rural landscapes by offering a variety of recreational and educational opportunities to let tourists become close with nature, enjoy healthy fresh local food in season, pursue an authentic farmer experience, and interact better with farmers. Stakeholders, especially local farmers, should be considered and involved in landscape planning and management processes, as meeting with the farmers is a basic association experience for tourists (Holm et al. 2013). In terms of relaxation experiences, organic farms need to learn from leisure-oriented farms and increase the added value of rural landscape experiences in their farms. As for the trust experience, the authenticity and locality should be enhanced while maintaining the trust between farmers and consumers, and with consideration for the importance of tourists' participatory experience. Organic farms in China should ensure the authentic tourist experience by strictly obeying the standards of organic farming and avoiding cheating; consumers pay great attention to the authenticity of the organic farming process, which is the foundation of their trust. The locality experience of the rural landscape in organic farms could be enhanced by such efforts as planting native plants, providing local food, organizing local cultural events, protecting traditional rural houses, and promoting interactions with local people. In the aspect of health experience, organic farms could make their own brands convey a theme of healthy lifestyle and extend their value chain.

Although the agricultural scale of organic farms is still relatively small, and the operation and development of organic farms face many challenges, the future of organic farms surrounding metropolises is bright. This observation takes into account the increasing desire of urban residents for experiencing the rural life and landscape. These residents are motivated by serious issues of food safety and environmental pollution amid the rapid industrialization and urbanization of China's cities.

References

Aitchison C, Macleod NE, Shaw SJ (2001) Leisure and tourism landscapes: social and cultural geographies. Routledge Publications, London

Aronson J (1994) A pragmatic view of thematic analysis. Qualitative report, vol 2, no 1. Retrieved July 5, 2010, from http://www.nova.edu/ssss/QR/BackIssues/QR2-12

Attride-Stirling J (2001) Thematic networks: an analytic tool for qualitative research. Qual Res 1 (3):385–405

Boyatzis R (1998) Transforming qualitative information: thematic analysis and code development. Sage, Thousand Oaks

Bramwell B (1994) Rural tourism and sustainable rural tourism. J Sustain Tourism 2(1, 2):1–6

Choo H, Jamal Z (2009) Tourism on organic farms in South Korea: a new form of ecotourism? J Sustain Tourism 17(4):431–454

Clarke J (1999) Marketing structure for farm tourism, beyond the individual provider of rural tourism. J Sustain Tourism 7(1):26–47

Cosgrove D, Daniels S (eds) (1988) The iconography of landscape. Essays on the symbolic representation, design and use of past environments. Cambridge University Press, Cambridge

Daugstad K (2008) Negotiating landscape in rural tourism. Ann Tourism Res 35(2):402–426

Daugstad K, Kirchengast C (2013) Authenticity and the Pseudo-Backstage of Agri-Tourism. Ann Tourism Res 43:170–191

De Muth S (1993). Defining community supported agriculture. Retrieved Nov 19, 2011, from http://www.nal.usda.gov/afsic/pubs/csa/csadef.shtml
Ding H (2009) Exploration and discussion on developing model of rural tourism in Jiangsu Province. Jiangsu's Agric Sci 5:14–16
Fereday J, Muir-Cochrane E (2006) Demonstrating rigor using thematic analysis: a hybrid approach of inductive and deductive coding and theme development. Int J Qual Methods 5 (1):80–92
Gao S, Huang S, Huang Y (2009) Rural tourism development in China. Int J Tourism Res 11:439–450
Greffe X (1994) Is rural tourism a lever for economic and social development? J Sustain Tourism 2 (1, 2):22–38
Han J (2009) The classification and comparison of China's rural tourism organization. Commer Cult 10:147 (in Chinese)
He JM (2005) On the development of rural tourism in China's urban suburbs: a case study on the evolution of Nongjiale in Chengdu. Tourism Tribune 20(6):71–74 (in Chinese)
Holm J, Pedersen L, Soerensen S (2013) Experiencing organic farms and food by regional tourism innovation. Acta Agriculturae Scand Sect B Soil Plant Sci 63:85–93
Hu YH (2008) A study on the participation of community in rural tourism. Bus Times 30:89–90 (in Chinese)
Kangas A, Haapakoski R, Tyrväinen L (2008) Integrating place-specific social values into forest planning—case of UPM-Kymmene forests in Hyrynsalmi, Finland. Silva Fennica 42(5):773–790
Karjalainen E, Tyrväinen L (2002) Visualization in forest landscape preference research: a finnish perspective. Landscape Urban Plann 59:13–28
Knudsen DC, Metro-Roland MM, Soper AK, Greer CE (2008) Landscape, tourism, and meaning. Ashgate, Aldershot
Kozinets RV (2002) The field behind the screen: using netnography for marketing research in online communities. J Mark Res 39(1):61–72
McIntosh A, Campbell T (2010) Willing workers on organic farms (WWOOF): a neglected aspect of farm tourism in New Zealand. J Sustain Tourism 9(2):111–127
Miles A, Brown M (2005) Teaching direct marketing and small farm viability: resources for instructors—part 4, community supported agriculture. Retrieved Nov 19, 2011, from http://escholarship.org/uc/item/69w2d0nv
Oliver T, Jenkins T (2003) Sustaining rural landscapes: the role of integrated tourism. Landscape Res 28(3):293–307
Oppermann M (1996) Rural tourism in southern Germany. Ann Tourism Res 23(1):86–102
Raivo PJ (1996) Maiseman kulttuurinen transformaatio. (Summary: the cultural transformation of landscapes). Nord Geogr Publ 25(1):15–46
Shao J, Zhang Y, Li X, Li Z (2012) Study on the recreational mode of community-supported agriculture-type urban farms, Tourism. Tourism Tribune 12(12):74–79 (in Chinese)
Shi Y, Cheng C, Lei P, Zhu Y, Jia Y, Wen T (2011) A correlation analysis of the development of ecological civic agriculture and the rising of urban moderate income group. Guizhou Soc Sci 254(2):55–60 (in Chinese)
Shi Y (2013) The list of community support agriculture in China. Retrieved Jan 28, 2015, from http://blog.sina.com.cn/s/blog_55a11f8e0102eluk.html (in Chinese)
Soini K (2001) Exploring human dimensions of multifunctional landscapes through mapping and mapmaking. Landscape and Urban Plann 57:225–239
Su B (2011) Rural tourism in China. Tourism Manag 32:1438–1441
Tilt JH, Kearney AR, Bradley G (2007) Understanding rural character: cognitive and visual perceptions. Landscape and Urban Plann 81:14–26
Urry J (1995) Consuming places. Routledge, London
Urry J (2001) The tourist gaze. Sage, Thousand Oaks
Urry J (2003) The 'consumption' of tourism. In: Clarke DB, Doel MA, Housiaux KML (eds) The consumption reader. Routledge, London, pp 117–123

Urry J (2003) The sociology of tourism. In: Cooper CP (ed) Classic reviews in tourism. Channel View Publications, Clevedon, pp 9–21
Uusitalo M (2010) Differences in tourists' and local residents' perceptions of tourism landscapes: a case study from Ylläs, Finnish lapland. Scand J Hospitality Tourism 10(3):310–333
Wang J, Fang XH (2008) Study on the operational model of rural tourism based on the farmer's autonomy. Modern Sci 1:123–124 (in Chinese)
Weaver DB, Fennell DA (1997) The vacation farm sector in Saskatchewan: a profile of operations. Tour Manag 18(6):357–365
Wikipedia (2011) Community-supported agriculture. Retrieved July 28, 2012, from http://en.wikipedia.org/wiki/Community-supported_agriculture
Xinhua News Agency (2014) Suggestions for deepen the rural reform comprehensively and speed up the modernization of agriculture. Retrieved Jan 28, 2015, from http://www.gov.cn/jrzg/2014-01/19/content_2570484.htm (in Chinese)
Yamamoto D, Engelsted A (2014) World wide opportunities on organic farms (WWOOF) in the United States: locations and motivations of volunteer tourism host farms. J Sustain Tourism 22 (6):964–982
Young M (1999) Cognitive maps of nature-based tourists. Ann Tourism Res 26(4):817–839
Zheng QM, Zhong LS (2004) A discussion of developing model of community-involved rural tourism. Tourism Tribune 19(4):33–37 (in Chinese)

Chapter 21
Generic Design Tools to Produce Site-Specific Solutions: Three Projects

Vanessa Miriam Carlow and Yeon Wha Hong

21.1 Introduction: Nature of Future Urbanization

In 2006, the earth was home to 6.6 billion people (UN DESA 2013). The United Nations estimated that beginning the same year, the majority of the world population would live in cities and urban areas (UN DESA 2013). Some estimate an increase in world population to as much as 10 billion in 2055 (Emmott 2013). At that point, 75 % of the world population is expected to live in cities and urban areas (UN DESA 2013). In arithmetic terms, cities for up to two billion people will emerge in the next decades, whether planned or unplanned.

The future and nature of urbanization remains open. While countries of the global north, such as Japan, Germany, and certain parts of the US, face demographic changes and decrease in population (UN DESA 2013), many regions of the global south are experiencing a massive increase in population (Burdett and Sudjic 2010), often in an unplanned way, manifested in the form of slums, favelas, ville spontanée, and informal camps (Davis 2006). In countries where economic development, urbanization, and population growth go hand in hand, such as Brazil, China, and those in West Africa, a large increase in urban population is expected (UN DESA 2014). Accordingly, newly built quarters, settlements, city districts, and even entire cities will emerge in such regions (Saunders 2011).

Sustainable urban planning is key to managing this explosive growth in population in an environmentally sound, economically robust, and socially responsible manner. Planning for (rapid) urbanization requires the integration of essential services, such as water and energy supply, consideration of low-emission forms of mobility, local climate conditions, and affordable and socially-appropriate housing, in order to orient these emerging settlements toward environmental sustainability

V.M. Carlow (✉) · Y.W. Hong
Department for Architecture, Institute for Sustainable Urbanism, Technische Universität Braunschweig, Braunschweig, Germany
e-mail: v.carlow@tu-braunschweig.de

F. Wang and M. Prominski (eds.), *Urbanization and Locality*,
DOI 10.1007/978-3-662-48494-4_21

and healthful lifestyles as early as possible. However, even with planned, well-intentioned projects, the nature of large-scale projects faces other challenges. For example, critics have problematized the decontextualized, faceless, and generic quality of such new districts (see Koolhaas 1995, 2002, 2010).

This article discusses how methodological design principles for sustainable design can be adapted in practice to produce site-specific solutions in different climatic and socio-cultural contexts. Specifically, this research focuses on three design principles, namely, the Five-Minute City, Blue and Green Network, and Preservation of Built Heritage, to demonstrate how they can be adapted to different contexts, with case studies in Asia, Europe, and Africa, to yield context-specific solutions. The article will also present a discussion of the challenges to sustainable urban development and planning unique to each context, and the creative ways each project responded to local limitations to meet the design principles goals.

21.2 Design Principles

In urban design, designers depend on certain design principles, or tools, to orient large-scale growth toward sustainability. These principles are guiding concepts, or methodologies, that can help determine the formal organization of a site, its density, distribution of institutions and services, and transportation network. While "generic" in the sense that these principles can be used as a starting point to guide the design of a site, they may and should also be adapted to specific local conditions of the site, in terms of the climate, culture, and logistic resources.

21.2.1 The Five-Minute City

The first of the three design principles under discussion is the Five-Minute City. The idea is relatively simple: everything that a person requires on a daily basis should be reachable within a five-minute walk from a public transport stop. This normally includes the home, educational facilities, a market or other shopping facilities, a public park or open area, and potentially also the workplace. With the average walking speed of a person calculated to be 5 km/h, the distance an average person will cover in five minutes is 420 m (Fig. 21.1).

The Five-Minute City is essentially a spatial module that contains the essential aspects of everyday life, scaled to be walkable, cyclable, and/or easily reachable by public transport, thus promoting at once healthy behavior and forms of mobility that are low emission and often also more socially equitable. The presupposition of the inclusion of a public transport system, existing or proposed, in the scope of the project indicates a clear reorientation of a city away from the private car toward public forms of transportation.

The Five-Minute City principle also promotes multi-functional zoning and transport-oriented development, one that features a mix of housing, commercial,

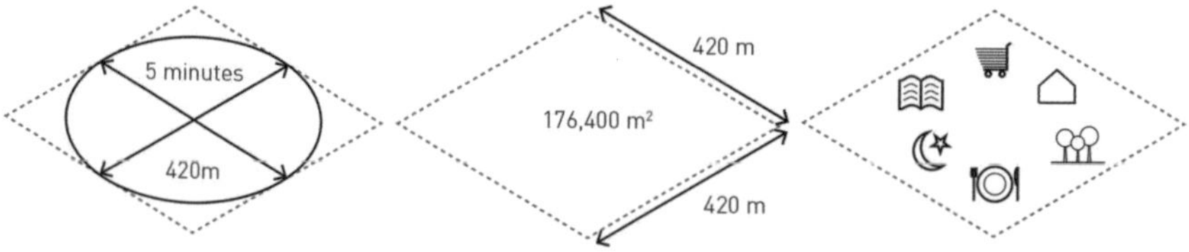

Fig. 21.1 Diagram of the Five-Minute City concept. Image by COBE Berlin

and educational facilities, as well as recreational areas around public transportation nodes, with the goal of fostering a more vibrant and diverse urban life. At the module scale, these elements can remain relatively modest. However, the principle remains that within a five-minute walking radius of any public transport stop, more than simply housing or commerce should be found.

Despite its simplicity, this design principle can yield a great variety of solutions. Programming of the daily needs alone varies depending on the society or culture. It can also yield highly distinct urban districts, depending on the parameters of density, plot ratio, lot coverage, and other urban design regulations.

21.2.2 The Blue and Green Network

The second design principle is the Blue and Green Network. The idea is that the design should preserve and enhance the networks of green (vegetation, e.g., trees, shrubs, woods), as well as the blue (water-related areas, e.g., lakes, ponds, wetlands) spaces existing in a site. By preserving such spaces, the project can protect habitats for the existing flora and fauna of the site, and also importantly, maintain whatever uses these spaces already host. By enhancing these spaces, or by providing improved connections and including design elements or additional programming, the project maintains the existing culture of the site and improves the daily life of its users. Thus, this tool is important for increasing ecological resilience as well as maintaining the history and identity of the site. Furthermore, these blue and green networks have the valuable possibility of additionally and more actively serving as ecosystem infrastructure, and can be incorporated into rainwater or wastewater management concepts; food or renewable energy production; concepts for improved natural lighting, cooling, heating, or ventilation; and recreational functions, among others. Naturally, the extent to which this tool can be applied to a project depends heavily on the existing conditions of the natural habitat of the site, local climate, and political will to value these aspects above economic growth or real estate potentials.

21.2.3 Preservation of Built Structures

Similar to the Blue and Green Network, this principle maintains and, if possible, improves upon the existing heritage of a site by preserving existing built structures.

Built structures include streets, street structures, individual buildings or districts (such as historic city centers), and other artifacts of significance for the local community. In a sense, existing structures can be considered as energy already embedded in the site, in terms of its building materials, design and planning efforts, time, public investments, and history and memory. Again, whether this tool can be implemented within a project or not depends greatly on the political will of the owners and community to value the heritage and maintained memory of a place or respective planning objectives.

21.3 Site-Specific Design: Case Studies

This section of the paper discusses how the design principles mentioned in the previous section have been implemented in designs in a locally specific manner, for three projects in three extremely different contexts, namely, three different cities in three different continents. One is in an intensely urbanizing region of China, Chongqing, where the rural-to-urban migration and economic industrialization are driving a massive boom in population and building. One is in the European context of Copenhagen, where immigration is driving a modest population growth (Danmarks Statistik 2014). One is in a growing area of greater Dakar, between two established urban centers. These projects vary in their phase of development, but the design intent is nonetheless comprehensible in all three.

21.3.1 Magic Mountains, Chongqing, China[1]

The project proposal to be discussed is entitled the Magic Mountains. It is in Chongqing, China, located at the confluence of the Yangtze and Jialing Rivers (Fig. 21.2). The site is located in the mountainous and densely built center of Chongqing, where "the pace and scale of urbanization is faster and bigger than anywhere in the world today" (Watts 2006). This site is also heavily affected by the controversial Three Gorges Project. Although the retaining wall of the dam is situated in the neighboring province of Hubei, 80 % of the impact area of the mega-project is in Chongqing (Hartmann 2004). The project comprises an 800 km long water reservoir with a 2300 m long and 200 m high retaining wall. It is the largest hydroelectric dam ever constructed. As a consequence of the rising water level, 2005 estimates indicated that 13 cities, 140 towns, and 1352 villages would be submerged, and an estimated 1.2 million people would have to be resettled, 85 % of them from Chongqing (Carlow and Stubberggard 2006).

[1]This project was a collaboration between the Danish Architecture Centre, COBE, and Chongqing University.

Fig. 21.2 The Magic Mountains. Image by COBE

This city faced an extreme degree of urbanization at the time of the proposal in 2006 (Fig. 21.3). According to projections, by 2015, an additional 10 million people would have moved from the fields to the new skyscrapers in downtown Chongqing (between 2005 and 2015). By then, 37 million people would be registered residents in Chongqing, which was already the biggest municipality worldwide in 2006, with 31.7 million inhabitants. In this high-speed urbanization, 50 million m^2 of residential and commercial floor space would be developed, equivalent to the completion of three Chrysler buildings every other day. In addition, another 500 km of highways, 3 airports, and 17 new bridges were or are being built, nearly equal to two wide-span bridges being added to the urban landscape every year (Carlow and Stubberggard 2006).

In the context of this urbanism at break-neck speed, the task of this project was to design Chongqing's new "Green" Central Business District (GCBD), to accommodate one year's additional population of roughly 1 million people, and the associated buildings, facilities, infrastructures, public, and open spaces. The project aimed to reduce the overall consumption of resources and energy by 22 % using architectural and planning solutions. This reduction rate equals the amount of the national energy demand that the Three Gorges Dam produced at the time. The larger project ambition was to eliminate water, air, and soil pollution by reducing energy consumption and reversing the rise of private car ownership. The guiding question for the design was: How can this boom be steered in a sustainable way so that the millions who dream of a good life by migrating to the city do not exhaust the very resources needed to provide it?

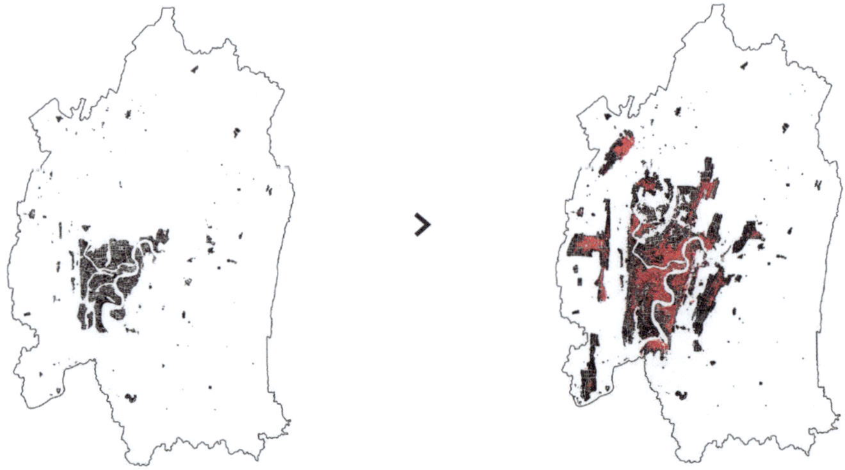

Fig. 21.3 Urban development in Chongqing from 2005 to 2015. Image by COBE

21.3.1.1 Connecting the GCBD

In this project, the Five-Minute City principle was implemented in the GCBD area: everything is reachable in this GCBD within a five-minute walk, namely, the next public transport stop, cultural, commercial, and social institutions, and a park. The urban layout radically promotes walking and the use of public transport, while deliberately excluding individual motorized transport. To justify this aspect, a state-of-the-art monorail spine is proposed, linking the site on a regional level to the "old" and the other planned business districts across the rivers, where such a monorail system is already in place. The 5.5 km long loop ensures fast and easy transit within the GCBD. Monorail stops are located in the densest centers of each neighborhood. Additional stations on the continuous green park take people to the social and cultural amenities or riverbanks quickly and efficiently. Every point within the site is within a five-minute walking distance from one of the monorail stops.

Discouraging the use of cars in favor of "green" transportation is no easy task in the contemporary Chinese cultural context, because car ownership is heavily associated with upward social mobility and economic prosperity. However, by making walking, cycling, and the use of public transport fast, efficient, attractive, and simply the most convenient way of getting around, it would be possible to make the GCBD a car free district.

21.3.1.2 New Green Network

This project dealt with the intense competing needs of urbanization and preservation of the natural landscape. With the much employed and much-criticized practice of land clearances prior to development, a tabula rasa situation already existed on site when the project was commissioned. All existing buildings, vegetation, and the local community had been removed. Already, as a mountainous region, land is especially scarce in metropolitan Chongqing. The fertile, arable land and human habitation are limited to the lower river valleys. These also constitute the prime locations for Chongqing's future growth. However, most of this land is already urbanized. Most of the area that is easily accessible is already under heavy use. Further, by 2008, large areas of this habitat were flooded as a consequence of the Three Gorges Project. The available land reserves have been dedicated as building sites to accommodate partially the growth up until 2015.

Thus, given the intense pressure of urbanization on the existing land, the main strategy for the design was to accommodate the population growth through an intensification of the existing land use, and an increase in urban density in metropolitan Chongqing, to limit sprawl. In the proposal, one-third of the site is dedicated to the "living machine," a productive green park landscape. The rest of the site is therefore more densely developed.

In the context of the especially intense degree of urbanization and the impacts of the Three Gorges Project, the Blue and Green Network principle was incorporated into the proposed architectural design itself. As the site is not sealed to motorized traffic, up to 95 % of the entire surface can be used to "bring back the trees." Even on the terraced roof spaces of each building, huge areas of greenery can be planted. This strategy not only creates high quality outdoor spaces but also helps to considerably reduce the carbon footprint and improve the micro-climate of the area, allowing for natural lightning and ventilation.

As another form of ecosystem infrastructure, an underground root zone system was proposed underneath the entire complex, for the purpose of cleaning wastewater from the area. This 0.75 km^2 ecological system is capable of cleaning almost all of the daily wastewater produced. By re-introducing clean water to the Yangtze and Jialing Rivers, the project could modestly contribute to their ecological restoration.

21.3.1.3 Reconstructing a Built Heritage

As a result of the densification, the current trend of construction of compounds or walls of high-rise buildings in the area not only blocks the visual connection with the surrounding mountains but also threatens to blur the city's image as a mountainous city. By 2015, only few buildings constructed before 1980 are left in Chongqing (Sucher 2005). The main impetus for the design was this question: Can the native landscape of Chongqing become a valuable element of identification, when much of its built heritage is already lost?

The proposed design, called Magic Mountains, sought to reinstate the mountainous feeling deep into the dense and urbanized areas of Chongqing. The proposed skyline consisted of a composition of inhabited mountains, with the peaks as the high-density centers mainly containing commercial functions, hotels, and places of business; the lower reaches of the mountains are areas with low density, mainly containing housing. The valleys are green open spaces.

The regulations allowed for an extremely dense floor area ratio (FAR) of 7, which meant the site had a capacity of 15.4 million m^2 of floor space. The design called for the reservation of a third of that area for the integration of an ecological chain, in which production, consumption, waste, and circulation are linked to produce less pollution, be more energy-efficient, and require low energy input. To realize the site's building potential of 15.4 million m^2 and to balance the loss of valuable square meters, density in the remaining area was increased to FAR = 10. The project sought to meet the demands for high-density settlement with low-density qualities of traditional Chinese neighborhoods: open green spaces, fresh air, lively street atmosphere. On an architectural scale, the living machine integrated low-tech solutions for the high-tech demands of high-speed urbanism (Figs. 21.4 and 21.5).

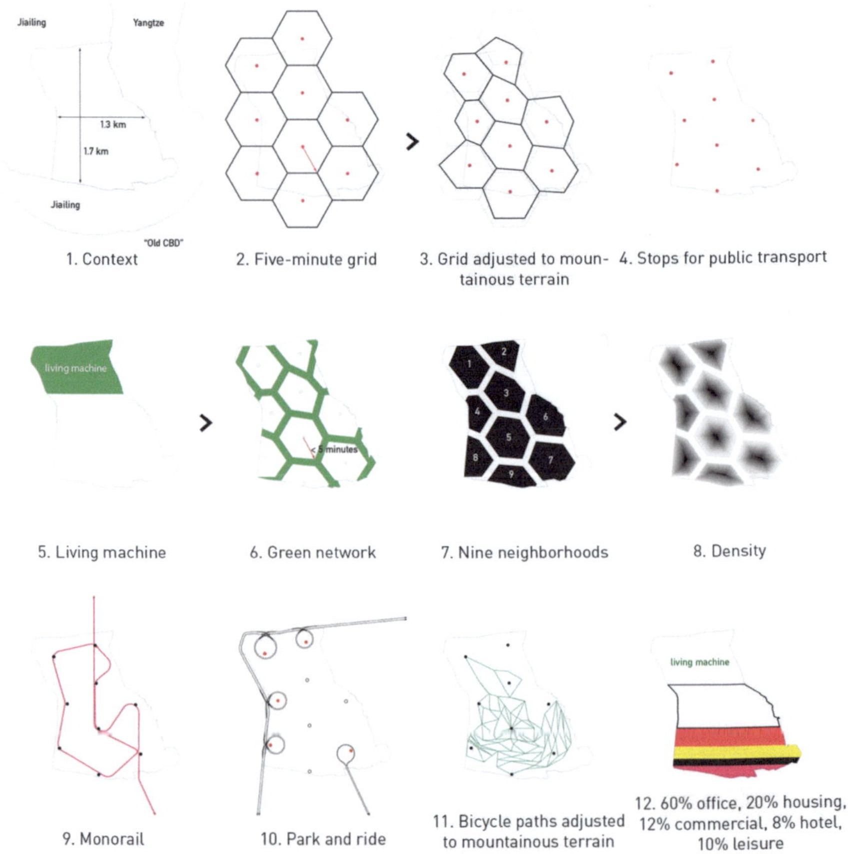

Fig. 21.4 Planning principles for the new district. Image by COBE

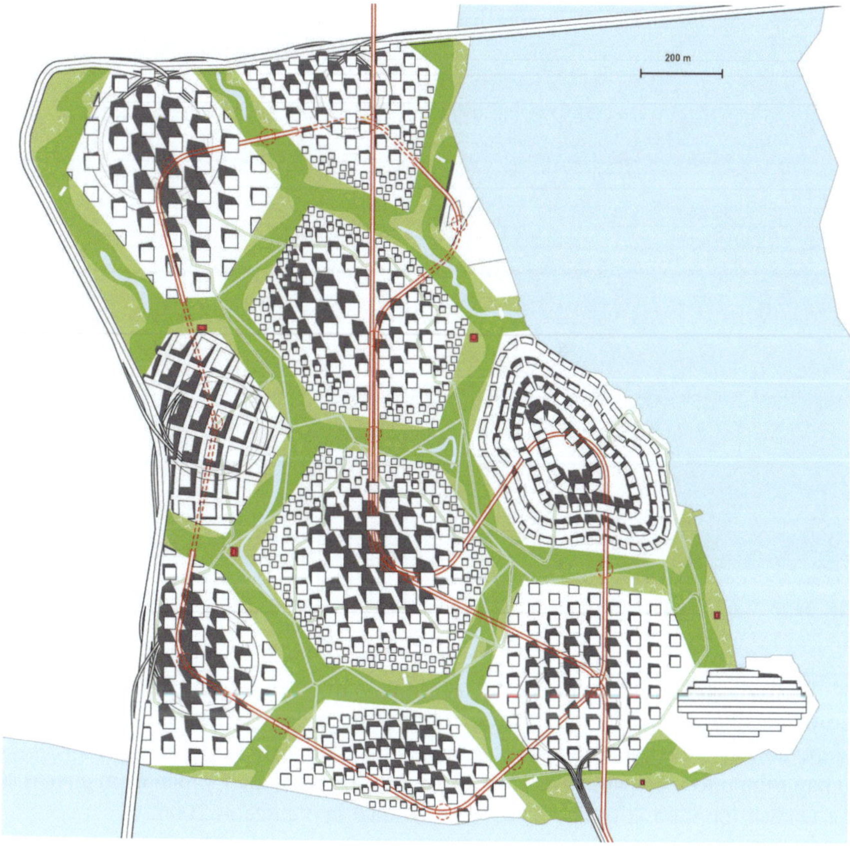

Fig. 21.5 Magic Mountains site plan. Image by COBE

21.3.1.4 Magic Mountains: Observations and Conclusions

Although never realized, this project offered valuable insights into the challenge of how to provide local connections within a very large-scale project built more or less from scratch. If this project had moved forward, it would have undoubtedly met some resistance to the measures to minimize the access of private automobiles for meeting the goals of the Five-Minute City principle, even with such provisions as a dedicated monorail service for the new development. With regard to the other two design principles of preserving and enhancing the natural networks (Blue and Green Network) and existing heritage (Existing Structures), a more inventive approach was needed, as the historic city was already razed. Much of the built heritage was already lost, and environmentally, the project had to deal with the consequences of the Three Gorges Project. Thus, the proposal took on a more inventive, daring approach, with a design that integrated the Green Network into architectural and infrastructural elements, and an infrastructure-oriented Blue Network, to manage the waste produced

Fig. 21.6 Magic Mountains at night. Image by COBE

by the development as well as help with the ecological health of the two rivers. However, this case study can be understood as an example where the design had to adapt radically to (re-)produce a localized context, by proposing a new built heritage to pay tribute to what was lost. The project was awarded the Golden Lion as part of the Danish Pavilion at the Architecture Biennale in Venice in 2006.

21.3.2 Nordhavnen Urban Delta, Copenhagen, Denmark[2]

The project Nordhavnen (English: North Harbor) is a master plan for the conversion of a former industrial harbor site into a new urban district, where up to 80,000 people will work and live (Figs. 21.6 and 21.7). Currently under construction, the planning began in 2009 with an open international competition. The project's first phase is scheduled to be completed by 2017. A number of the design principles developed within the study of Magic Mountains were employed in the design of this new urban district.

[2]This project was undertaken as a collaboration between the City and Port Development of Copenhagen and the firms COBE, SLETH, Polyform, and Rambøll.

Fig. 21.7 Nordhavnen, Copenhagen. Image by COBE

21.3.2.1 The Five-Minute Urban Delta

The concept of the Five-Minute City is not radical in the context of Copenhagen or compact European cities in general. For Copenhagen, promoting sustainable modes of transport is already a major part of the city's culture and political goals (City of Copenhagen 2012b). In recent years, the City of Copenhagen has emerged as a role model in promoting smart and sustainable mobility. In this project, the ambition is, as a minimum, to live up to the objective of the City of Copenhagen of obtaining the following distribution: at least one-third of all traffic in the area should be cyclists, at least one-third should be public transport, and car traffic should account for no more than one-third (City of Copenhagen 2009). To accomplish the above, the Nordhavnen project was designed such that inhabitants and visitors would find it simply much easier to walk, cycle, or use public transport than travel by car. In addition, the scale of the project opens the opportunity to make walking or biking even more attractive and enjoyable than in other parts of the city, which must be retrofitted for those uses.

The master plan is consistently laid out on the basis of the Five-Minute City principle, with short, walkable distances from housing and workplaces to public transport stops, public institutions, recreational spaces, the waterfront, and commercial facilities. Bicycle paths and green areas are distributed throughout the entire district to form a continuous network (Figs. 21.8 and 21.9). A green mobility loop is used as the unifying, identity-creating element in the district. The loop serves multiple purposes and works on several scales. As a figure, the loop connects the various neighborhoods in Nordhavnen with one another, as well as the rest of Copenhagen. The green loop contains the public transport systems at Nordhavnen: an elevated Metro line and a public Bus Rapid Transit (BRT) in the initial phases of the project. In addition, there will be a "super bicycle highway" that will enable cyclists to reach their destinations quickly, directly, and efficiently without having to share the road with automobiles. Up to two-thirds of all people going in or out of the district in the future will move along the green loop; the rest will cross the loop

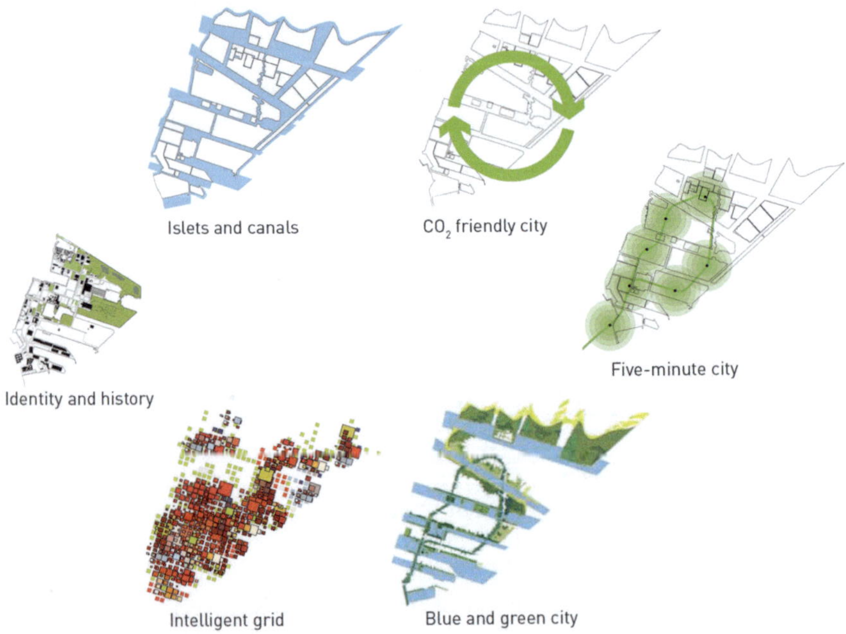

Fig. 21.8 Nordhavnen design principles. Image by COBE

Fig. 21.9 Nordhavnen, Five-Minute City principle. Image by COBE

on their way through Nordhavnen. Education, sports, trade, and cultural facilities are vital to the urban structure, and are located at places intersecting the loop. The green loop will thus be a lively urban space hosting multiple urban functions.

21.3.2.2 Blue Fingers, Green Links

The idea of developing the site's larger Blue and Green Network was also easy to integrate, as the site is formerly an industrial harbor (Fig. 21.10). The entire site area is on reclaimed land, and with its basins, canals, and coastlines, Nordhavnen is a water-oriented site. A central element of the proposal is to increase the water–land interface, by digging out new canals to form an archipelago of islands. Each island functions as a micro-neighborhood. By enlarging the waterfront, the hope was to provide a number of those qualities that people seek when settling outside the core city: proximity to nature. The island structure ensures that the water is never far away. Canals and basins create different spatial experiences and provide a setting for a variety of activities. All waterfronts are public. Direct contact with water is important, especially in south-facing, sun-lit areas. Blue spaces were developed as open coastal expanses, enclosed water squares that can be used for different sports, beaches, and large scenic areas. Access to these water-oriented spaces is provided by stairs, low promenades, and piers. The water spaces will be integrated to adjacent facilities on land, which will reveal the special qualities of a city along the waterside.

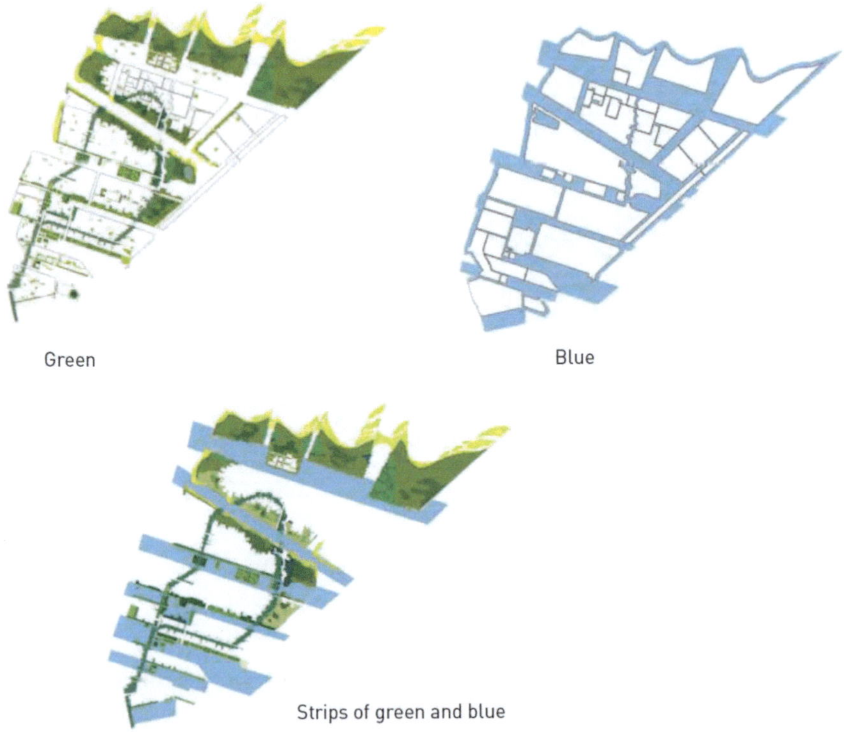

Fig. 21.10 Nordhavnen Blue and Green Network. Image by COBE

In the design, green features, such as pocket parks, playgrounds, planted promenades, and green urban spaces, were integrated with water features in each islet. Extensive grass plains, presently a nesting site for migrating birds, are preserved and integrated into the network. The green structure in Nordhavnen is laid out as an uninterrupted network that interweaves with the blue network. There are smooth transitions between the different types of natural and nature-like landscapes. As such, special places and new opportunities for special experiences are created. In all, a transition from more urban open spaces closer to the central city to more natural urban spaces toward the open sea can be felt in moving from the city to the harbor. The green loop is an integral part of this green structure, which ensures that Nordhavnen will feel like a green city district to the people moving about in it.

This structure delivers a series of different landscape experiences. The strips of green and blue running east to west draw the natural landscape and water across the district. People going through the area will therefore see the varied urban spaces. The closeness of natural landscapes is conducive to a rich and active outdoor life for Nordhavnen's and Copenhagen's residents and visitors. Canals and basins will be used for sailing and other water sports, whereas the green areas offer a wealth of opportunities for physical exercise.

21.3.2.3 Built and Unbuilt Heritage

In this project, the design principle of preserving existing structures was a part of the larger development strategy. The existing harbor lent itself to this principle. However, the challenge in this case was how to install the future in historic surroundings and design the site to be developed over a long time span, adapted for new functions. A dynamic structure to govern the physical organization of the site was proposed, as opposed to a classical master plan. The reasoning behind this approach was that this structure must be sufficiently strong to form a robust framework for urban development, yet sufficiently flexible to adapt to future trends without jeopardizing the main structure. In other words, there is a framework, but not a detailed plan.

Incentives were offered to encourage the preservation of existing industrial and maritime structures, such as silos or other harbor-related buildings. For example, a higher-than-average plot development allowance was offered for those projects that could preserve and renovate existing structures (City of Copenhagen 2012a). Under this strategy, the use and development of existing buildings on a temporary or permanent basis could serve as an anchor of sorts in an as-yet indeterminate plan. While the layout of the islets was determined on the structure plan level, the size and function of building zones will not be determined until buildings are ready to be erected. The ratio of housing to commercial facilities was defined for each individual islet on the basis of its position in the greater urban fabric, but there is greater flexibility inside the boundaries of the individual islets, in terms of the location of housing and commercial facilities (Fig. 21.11). Thus, the urban structure can be developed on the basis of market demand within a flexible buffer zone over a number of years, without deviating from the urban development principles of mixed functions and diversity (Fig. 21.12).

21.3.2.4 Foundation for Adaptive Development

The case study illustrates that the design principles of the Five-Minute City, Blue and Green Networks, and Preservation of Built Structures can provide a robust backbone for the development of a new urban district over time, while integrating and building on top of local cultural and historical qualities. In a planning culture like that of Denmark, high considerations are placed on participatory forms of planning and building a city. These design principles accommodate both the daily needs and wants of the city's population, for example by fostering a local urban culture of walking and cycling. In combination with additional design strategies, current requirements, such as the provision of affordable housing, can also be achieved. The first phase of the project shows that basing the development on the above mentioned design principles also allows different actors, both public and private, to participate in the development. Further, the methodological approach allows for a phased development that can be adjusted to the current demands of the city and its population, while safeguarding the overall quality of open space provisions and sustainable mobility.

Fig. 21.11 Preservation of Built (and unbuilt) Heritage in Nordhavnen. Image by COBE

21.3.3 *The City Between the Forest and the Ocean, Dakar, Senegal*[3]

The third project under discussion is set outside Dakar, in Senegal, Africa, currently in the preliminary design phase. In Africa, under the pressure of urbanization, entire cities are being built into deserts without proper infrastructure, such as water or electricity, and without any involvement of the local workforce. These ghost towns

[3]The project team consists of COBE Berlin, Mobility in Chain MIC, Transsolar, Gesswein Landschaftsarchitekten, Ingenieurbüro Kraft, and the Institute for Sustainable Urbanism TU Braunschweig. The project was commissioned by iQ Engineering.

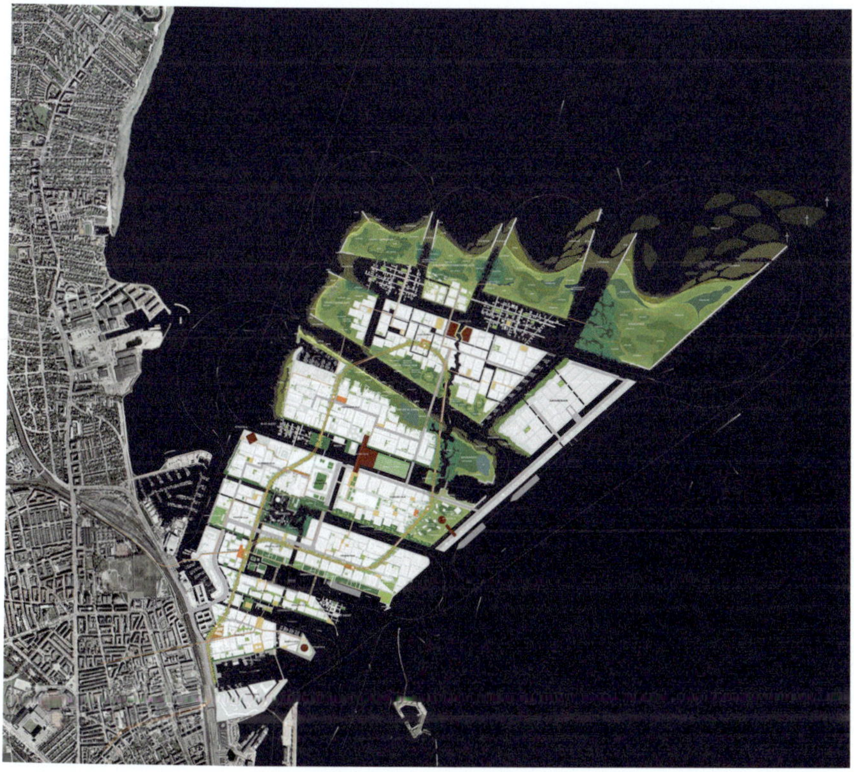

Fig. 21.12 Nordhavnen, structure plan. Image by COBE

are devoid of identity or benefit for the local communities. These developments, often built by foreign developers, can be considered as symptoms of an un-integrated, un-sustainable, and un-ethical approach to planning.

The project under discussion has as its basis the construction of 125,000 new houses to be built in and around Dakar in the near future (Fig. 21.13). With an average household size of six to eight people, a city with up to one million inhabitants will emerge in or around Dakar. This new city provides a huge potential to positively impact the wellbeing of its citizens, as well as push the development of the Dakar region as a whole toward sustainability.

This project takes an integrated approach, with an interdisciplinary team of architects, urban designers, landscape architects, water-, climate-, and transportation engineers, and in collaboration with a material technology firm that provides high-tech materials to be assembled in low-tech manner within a short timeframe and in a responsible way. The goal is to build a truly sustainable, resource-saving, livable, inclusive, and human-scale city, while meeting the challenges posed by the pressure to urbanize rapidly in Africa.

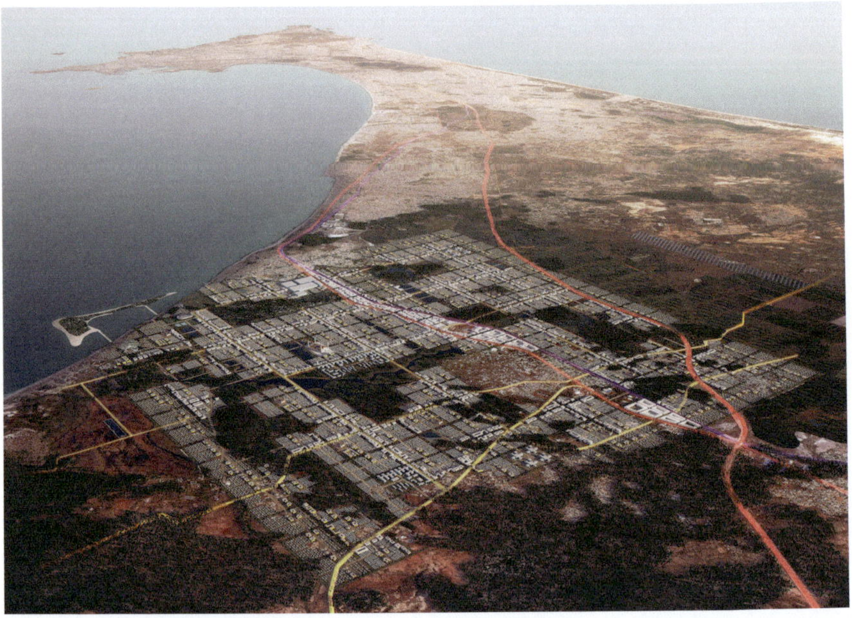

Fig. 21.13 The city between the forest and the ocean, Dakar. Image by COBE Berlin

21.3.3.1 The Five-Minute City as a Basic Building Block

The Five-Minute City principle is used in this project as the basic building block for urban design. The main impetus for this design decision is that this project requires a large amount of housing to be built quickly, but a main goal for the project is to "grow" the city, rather than build it from scratch, in order to successfully embed it in its local context. In Dakar's context, the daily requirements within this radius include the mosque, a kindergarten or schools, the market or other shopping facilities, sports fields and playgrounds, a park, and possibly the workplace. As a building module, the Five-Minute City module makes this massive project essentially phase-able, and thus able to flexibly address the shifting demands under different phases of development.

Each module of the Five-Minute City can be subdivided into micro-neighborhoods and then developed individually, with a variety of plot sizes and housing types. The maximum density of single-family homes is set at 50 % per Five-Minute City module, to encourage population mixing in terms of family size and lifestyle or housing preferences. The maximum amount of housing is set to 40 %, to encourage a mix of functions. Accordingly, within each Five-Minute City, functional and housing mix can be observed, which would increase social cohesion and facilitate everyday activities without dependency on private cars.

When six Five-Minute Cities are established, this cluster forms the larger unit called a Jumma City, derived from the name of a typical Friday mosque. Home to between 30,000 and 40,000 people, this district is large enough to host additional functions, such as a larger Friday mosque, fire and police stations, a post office, places for adult education, healthcare facilities, and larger sports fields. This district is also of a size large enough to make local management of rainwater economically and logistically sensible. To realize the total of 125,000 housing units, 25 such districts should be built. Together they form what can be called the New City between the Forest and the Ocean (Fig. 21.14).

To help achieve the functional goal of the Five-Minute City, a public BRT system is proposed to provide the backbone of the development. The BRT system allows for efficient and flexible connection within the area and to its surroundings, the core city of Dakar, and the newly built airport. By developing the new city around the existing old town of Diamniadio, located approximately 30 km from the existing urban poles of Thiès and Dakar, the large project can take advantage of existing infrastructure, namely, the existing national road, highways, and railways. A new bus and train station located in the heart of the proposed master plan will provide direct access into the center of the new city. With the functional mix of the city itself, this transport model considerably reduces the overall need for individual motorized transport.

Fig. 21.14 Modular masterplan. Image by COBE Berlin

21.3.3.2 Integrated Blue and Green Network as Soft Infrastructure

All existing green (trees, shrubs, etc.) and blue (lakes, ponds, ravines) networks in the area are preserved. These spaces give a sense of identity to the new city, help manage rain- and stormwater, and greatly improve the micro-climate of their immediate areas, improving livability for the inhabitants. An internal park system connects all the green and blue patches to enhance their overall performance and appeal. These spaces can also be used for recreational purposes.

A large Green Belt landscape is employed in the master plan as a means to prevent uncontrolled sprawl. This Green Belt is conceived as a productive landscape, containing tree nurseries, reforestation areas, agricultural fields, renewable energy production, water treatment and waste handling facilities, and larger-scale recreational and sports areas, including a public beach at the waterfront, which will attract visitors as well as enhance the quality of life for the residents. The Green Belt allows preservation and extension of existing agricultural areas. In this area, much of the trees and shrubbery in the design will be locally produced. Apart from the designated tree farms, the Green Belt provides additional spaces for local and ecological energy production, such as on-shore wind power or biogas plants. The Green Belt also hosts cemeteries.

Another key function of the Blue and Green Network in this project is its role in flood and water management. Dakar has a tropical climate, with a rainy reason lasting for three months followed by nine hot and dry months. The highest temperatures in southern Senegal are measured in April, when temperatures of 40 °C are not uncommon. The lowest temperatures are measured between December and February at around 17 °C.

For long-term sustainability, the management of water in this climatically challenging environment is key. To minimize the impact of the additional demand for water by the new city, the project plans the extensive capture and reuse of storm and wastewater (Fig. 21.15). To accomplish this, the provision of large storage capacity to distribute the harvested water evenly over a period of nine months is required.

Within each Five-Minute City block, storm water runoff is drained from the surface of the roads into a Stormwater Retention Basin (SRB). The flow direction of the runoff follows the slope of the area, which is orientated to the south, toward the sea. Therefore, the SRBs are located in the southern corner of each block. From here, the accumulated runoff can be drained onto the surface of two roads, which drain into to the SRB. The profile of these streets is designed to handle the required amount of storm water runoff. With this strategy, the construction of expensive piping can be avoided and the speed with which the city can be built in a resilient way can be drastically increased.

The inflow to the SRB must be treated mechanically and biologically. In order to accomplish this, new lakes are introduced in each Jumma City district. The lakes will be provided with a recirculation system that pumps the water from the bottom of the lake to the inflow of the treatment facilities along the lakeshore. This system provides a continuous flow and exchange of water in the lake. Keeping the water in circulation

Fig. 21.15 Local storm water management through green networks and road surface drainage in a Jumma City district for up to 40,000 inhabitants. Image by COBE Berlin

helps to avoid breeding mosquitoes. Additionally, fish will inhabit the lake system. The lake will be the main purification stage for harvested rainwater. For the production of potable water, the lake water will be pumped to a waterworks facility where the final purification will take place. All organic matter and remaining bacteria will be removed by membrane filtration before the water is supplied to the city.

This system of rainwater harvesting in the area of the new city and from the catchment area of the adjacent valleys can meet up to a third of the water demand in the new city. The remaining needs to be supplied from an external source, preferably groundwater from a nearby source.

Thus, the new Blue Network will contribute significantly to the overall sustainability of the region by providing an essential water management function. The spaces associated with this function, such as retention ponds and purification facilities, are expected to become highly significant landmarks for the area. These places ensure that the new settlement will not overwhelm the currently scarce and precious sources of water. Further, they can also serve recreational functions for the communities.

One last small additional function of the Blue and Green Network is its role in orientation within the new city. The entire city is rotated 22.6° from north to maximize shading and cooling winds in the hot season. In the new design, palms are used in streets oriented north to south, and deciduous trees are used in streets oriented east to west. This scheme will help orient visitors within the new districts.

21.3.3.3 Building upon Existing Settlements

Also important to this project is for this growing city to develop its own distinct identity, while fitting well into its existing context. The master plan is based on the growth of an existing town, Diamniadio; the new city can grow from existing landmarks and features, rather than being built from scratch. Set between Dakar and the new airport, Diamniadio has great location potential as the core of a new city. This new city can function as an overspill area and a complimentary town to Dakar. Diamniadio is connected to Dakar by the national road, toll road, and rail. Building on the town of Diamniadio as the core for a new city relieves Dakar of the high development pressure it currently faces, as well as utilizes the large economic potential the development of the airport entails. The site around Diamniadio is not a tabula rasa. A high-resolution satellite image helps identify existing settlements and valuable natural elements, such as agricultural land use, vegetation (such as Baobabs), ravines, and water networks. These elements should be preserved where possible and integrated into the new city to enhance its distinctive identity. Citizens already in the area should benefit from the new development, rather than being dislocated by it.

In exploring the rich building culture in and around Dakar, in particular in the historic site of Touba, a few design principles become apparent that can also be replicated in the new city (Fig. 21.16). These include the grid of streets, the human- and walking-scale of the existing streets, the central place the mosque occupies in each neighborhood (its spires are almost always the tallest point in an area), the mix of walled and solitary buildings, varied and usually small plot sizes, infiltration of the landscape into the settlements, and specific elements of architectural detailing to provide shading and passive cooling.

The architecture and urban design for the new district draws heavily from principles and design elements of traditional Senegalese town planning and architecture. Design-wise, the new city is conceived of as a re-combination of the achievements of contemporary infrastructure planning, water management, climate design, and building techniques with the old city, featuring a lively blend of African, Arab and European influences. This aspect is special, and visible on all scales: from the design of public spaces, architectural typologies, well into the detailing and coloring of the buildings. The hybridization of African, Arab and European influences is especially visible in public buildings, but also in everyday constructions, such as markets and residential buildings.

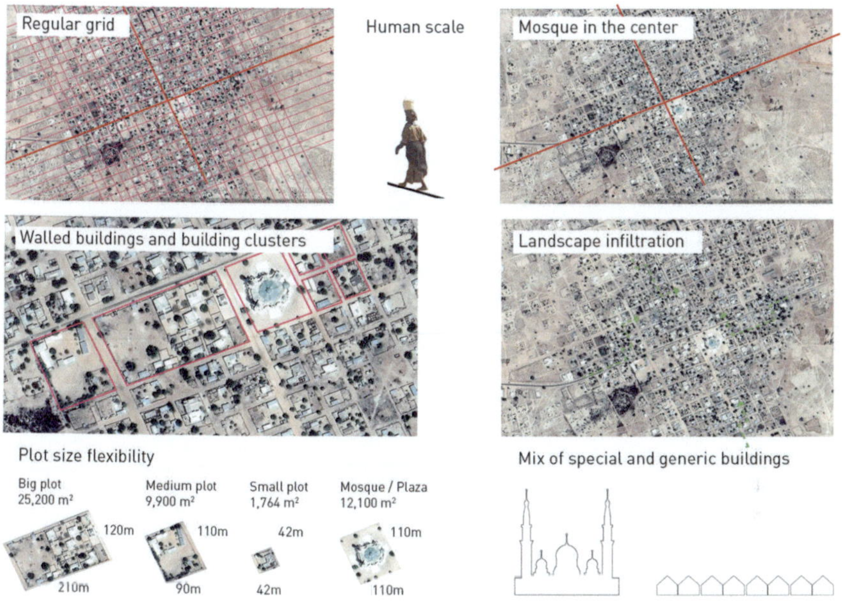

Fig. 21.16 Design principles for a new sustainable city. Image by COBE Berlin

Unlike many other metropolises in Africa, Dakar is more compact and less sprawling, a major advantage that should be preserved in the future. In particular, the well-proportioned, elegant and sleek, light-colored modernist apartment and commercial buildings often radiate a great sense of style. According to architect Adjaye and Allison (2011), most middle-class people live in well-organized apartment buildings that contribute to the urban character of the city, whereas the colonial villas along the waterfront are prime examples of elegant architecture. In the new city, elements found through analysis of typical examples of Dakar architecture will be used to continue the building culture and sense of place currently existing in Dakar.

21.3.3.4 Dakar: Vision for a New City

The vision for this New City between the Forest and the Ocean is that it be a radically sustainable city, for everyone. The current design is marked by its mix of housing, workplaces, and facilities attracting a large diversity of people from different social strata. Mixing types of housing and functions, and thus people, will reduce the overall need for transportation in the Dakar region, help overcome social disparities, and increase the overall quality of life in the area. With its parks, beach,

Fig. 21.17 Vision for a new sustainable city. Image by COBE Berlin

hospitals, university, and water treatment facilities, the city provides opportunities for already existing communities in the region and invites visitors from the outside (Fig. 21.17).

21.4 Conclusion

In this research, three cases of how the generic design principles of the Five-Minute City, Blue and Green Networks, and Preservation of Existing Structures can be adapted to local contexts were presented: The Magic Mountains, which was never realized but whose design principles have been successfully employed in other realized projects; Nordhavnen in Copenhagen, which is under construction; and The City between the Forest and the Ocean, in Dakar, Senegal, which is in its initial planning stage. The three generic tools were adapted to each context to reflect the local culture and habits of its communities, and to compensate for deficiencies of each site where required, thus to establish an urban structure that would be more conducive to environmentally and socially sustainable growth. Specific measures include ways to encourage walking, cycling, and using public transport to get around, as opposed to owning private automobiles; taking full advantage of the existing natural environments to increase liveability, to improve the micro-climate and resilience to disasters; reducing the use of resources and energy; and utilizing buildings and other existing artifacts in the site as a part of the site's unique heritage, as objects with embedded grey energy.

Often, generic design tools form the basis for the larger design strategy, for example, as a means to "grow" a city in a more integrated, more involved manner, as in the case of the Dakar project; as a means to provide other essential services, such as transport or water engineering, as in the Nordhavnen project; or as a means to improve local climate and environmental conditions, such as in the Chongqing project.

As shown in the three case studies, the foundation of a project can vary greatly in different contexts owing to climate and societal differences, or the specific requirements of the development. However, these tools can be adapted specifically to each of these contexts. Often, the tools cannot be fully applied because of financial, logistical, cultural, or socio-political limitations, as was discussed above. However, in such cases, the designer may find creative ways with which to achieve the goals behind the principles.

In the context of today's rapid urbanization in developing economies, as well as shifting development agendas in established urban centers, sustainability principles such as those described above are important tools to lay the groundwork for sustainable urban development. As demonstrated in this work, these generic tools do not produce generic results but are fully flexible to produce local, site-specific solutions. Responding to site-specific challenges and project requirements while steering the project toward greater sustainability requires ingenuity on the part of the designer. Adapting and implementing these principles to the widely varying cultural, political, socio-economic contexts (and limitations) are crucial to the design process. By navigating and negotiating the limitations and challenges of the local context, these generic design principles can be adapted and deployed to achieve the goals behind these principles, and thus establish a sound foundation for sustainable growth.

References

Adjaye D, Allison P (2011) Adjaye, Africa, architecture: a photographic survey of metropolitan architecture. Thames & Hudson, London

Burdett R, Sudjic D (eds) (2010) The endless city: the urban age project by the London school of economics and Deutsche Bank's Alfred Herrhausen society, Reprint edn. Phaidon Press, London

Carlow VM, Stubbergaard D (2006) Magic mountains—how to build a sustainable city. In: Valeur H, di Venezia B, Architettura S (eds) Co-evolution: Danish-Chinese collaboration on sustainable urban development in China. The Danish Architecture Centre, Strandgade, pp 96–121

City of Copenhagen, City and Port Development (2009) Nordhavnen strategy. Sustainable city the Copenhagen way. City of Copenhagen, City and Port Development in collaboration with COBE, SLETH, Polyform and Rambøll

City of Copenhagen, City and Port Development (2012a) Inner Nordhavn—from idea to project. City of Copenhagen, City and Port Development in collaboration with COBE, SLETH, Polyform and Rambøll

City of Copenhagen, Technical and Environmental Administration (2012b). CPH 2025 climate plan: a green, smart, and carbon neutral city. City of Copenhagen
Danmarks Statistik (2014) Befolkningsfremskrivninger 2014–2050
Davis M (2006) Planet of slums. Verso, London
Emmott S (2013) Ten billion. Penguin, London
Hartmann H, Becker S, King L (2004) The Three Gorges Project: its influence on the flood risk along the middle reaches of the Yangtze River and on the economy of the region surrounding the reservoir. In: Jiang T, King L, Gemmer M, Kundzewicz ZW (Hrsg.) Climate change and Yangtze floods. Science Press, Beijing
Koolhaas R (1995) Generic cities. In: OMA & Mau B (eds) S, M, L, XL. Monicelli Press
Koolhaas R (2002) Junkspace. In October, vol. 100, Obsolescence. MIT Press, pp 175–190
Koolhaas R (2010) In search of authenticity. In: Burdett R, Sudjic D (eds) The endless city: the urban age project by the London school of economics and Deutsche bank's Alfred Herrhausen society, Reprint edn. Phaidon Press, London
Saunders D (2011) Arrival city. Windmill Books, London
Sucher J (2005) Mega-Metropole Chongqing: Die umgekrempelte Stadt. Spiegel Online. Retrieved from http://www.spiegel.de/wirtschaft/mega-metropole-chongqing-die-umgekrempelte-stadt-a-389299.html
United Nations, Department of Economic and Social Affairs, Population Division (2013) World population prospects: the 2012 revision, highlights and advance tables. Working paper no. ESA/P/WP.228
United Nations, Department of Economic and Social Affairs, and Population Division (2014) World urbanization prospects: the 2014 revision
United Nations Human Settlements Programme (2012) The state of Arab cities 2012: challenges of urban transition. UN-Habitat, United Nations Human Settlements Programme, Nairobi, Kenya
Watts J (2006) The megalopolis you've never heard of. Retrieved February 28, 2015, from http://www.theguardian.com/world/2006/mar/15/china.china

Author Biographies

Prof. Dr. Vanessa Miriam Carlow is Professor at the Department for Architecture at Technische Universität Braunschweig, where she heads the Institute for Sustainable Urbanism (ISU). Dr. Carlow is a registered architect and urban planner.

Yeon Wha Hong is Assistant Professor and Ph.D. candidate at the Institute for Sustainable Urbanism at Technische Universität Braunschweig. Hong is a LEED accredited professional.

MIX
Papier aus verantwortungsvollen Quellen
Paper from responsible sources
FSC® C105338

If you have any concerns about our products,
you can contact us on
ProductSafety@springernature.com

In case Publisher is established outside the EU,
the EU authorized representative is:
Springer Nature Customer Service Center GmbH
Europaplatz 3, 69115 Heidelberg, Germany

Printed by Libri Plureos GmbH
in Hamburg, Germany